Democracy and Democratization

*Post-Communist Europe in
Comparative Perspective*

John D. Nagle and Alison Mahr

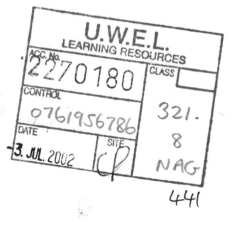

SAGE Publications
London • Thousand Oaks • New Delhi

First published 1999

SAGE Publications Ltd
6 Bonhill Street
London EC2A 4PU

SAGE Publications Inc.
2455 Teller Road
Thousand Oaks, California 91320

SAGE Publications India Pvt Ltd
32, M-Block Market
Greater Kailash – I
New Delhi 110 048

British Library Cataloguing in Publication data

A catalogue record for this book is available
from the British Library

ISBN 0 7619 5678 6
ISBN 0 7619 5679 4 (pb)

Library of Congress catalog record available

Typeset by Mayhew Typesetting, Rhayader, Powys
Printed in Great Britain by Redwood Books, Trowbridge, Wiltshire

Summary of Contents

Contents

List of Figures and Tables

Figures

Tables

Oslo

NORWAY

Helsinki

FINLAND

Stockholm

Tallinn

SWEDEN

ESTONIA

RUSSIA

North
Sea

Baltic Sea

LATVIA

Riga

DENMARK

LITHUANIA

Copenhagen

Vilnius

Minsk

NETH.

Berlin

Russia

BELARUS

GERMANY

Warsaw

Kiev

Elbe R.

POLAND

UKRAINE

Prague

Vistula R.

Danube R.

CZECH REP.

Dnestr R.

SLOVAKIA

Bern

Vienna

Bratislava

MOLDOVA

SWITZ.

AUSTRIA

Budapest

Kisinöv

Ljubljana

3

HUNGARY

ROMANIA

Zagreb

Po R.

ITALY

CROATIA

Bucharest

San
Marino

Adriatic
Sea

Sarajevo

Belgrade

Danube R.

Black
Sea

Tiber R.

2

YUGOSLAVIA

BULGARIA

Roma

Sofia

1 : MACEDONIA
2 : BOSNIA / HERZEGOVINA
3 : SLOVENIA

Tiranë

Skopje

Istanbul

1

ALBANIA

0   kilometres   600

GREECE

Aegean
Sea

TURKEY

PART ONE

THEORETICAL AND HISTORICAL BACKGROUNDS FOR DEMOCRATIZATION

1

The Democracy Project and the Development of Comparative Politics

---

CONTENTS

The democracy trend and a new task for comparative politics

With the historic collapse of European communism at the end of the 1980s, the literature on democratization has quickly expanded to embrace the most recent and perhaps most important experiments in the recent 'democracy trend' since the end of the Second World War. The spread of democratization to a post-communist Europe has for the first time given comparative politics a truly global task in its study of democratic political development. How different this is from the situation which presented itself at the end of the Second World War, and the origins of the Cold War in Europe and in the world.

This text provides a comparative analysis of one portion of the most recent wave of democratization, in the East-Central European region. For our purposes here, East-Central Europe comprises the nations of Poland, the Czech Republic, Hungary, Slovakia and Slovenia, the area of the former communist East bloc which was historically associated with Central Europe, either as independent nations or as components of the Holy Roman Empire of the German Nation, and later the Austrian and German Empires. Our main focus is on the three nations of Poland, the Czech Republic and Hungary. The Slovak Republic is included in specific chapters and comparisons (and of course as part of the Czecho-slovak experience before the Velvet Divorce of 1993), while the small Slovenian state is only treated in larger cross-national comparisons. The 'big three' cases (Poland, Czech Republic, Hungary) are the key to our analysis, since they are the first post-communist nations invited to join the NATO alliance, and they are also first-round nations (the so-called 5+1 nations including also Slovenia, Estonia and Cyprus) which began negotiations in early 1998 to join the European Union. Democracy and democratization in these three key states provides a major test, and possible models for other transitional nations, in post-communist Europe generally; they represent the core group for our comparisons with other regions (Southern Europe, Latin America, East and Southeast Asia).

Democracy and comparative studies in the Cold War era

At the dawning of the East–West confrontation, the experiment in resurrection of a democratic politics in Germany, Japan and Italy rep-resented a major strategic effort to present an attractive alternative to Soviet communism, and to overcome the legacy of fascism in advanced industrial society. Robert Dahl (1995), in a review of the 'Time of Triumph' for democracy, reminds us that even in the stable Western democracies, there were major shortcomings (Dahl names the denial of voting rights for women in Switzerland prior to 1971, and the sup-pression of Black voting rights in the American South before the civil rights legislation of the 1960s) which by today's standards would disqualify a nation from democratic standing. In the late 1940s and early 1950s, the Western effort to support post-fascist democratization in these nations was one of the pillars of the postwar era, and the success of democratization in these nations was of great importance not only in solidifying the anti-communist alliance for the Cold War, but was a signal reason for the West's eventual victory in the Cold War struggle with Soviet communism.

Now, we would argue, the stakes in post-communist Europe are comparably high for the shaping of a post-Cold War world. The chance for democracy to prove itself once again in new and difficult circum-stances would complete the historic victory in the second half of this century over the Leninist species of modern anti-democratic politics; the triumph of democracy in former communist countries would be comparable in value to the triumph of democracy in the former fascist nations. The new attention given by comparative politics to the fortunes of democratization in post-communist Europe has been deservedly great, in recognition, explicit or implicit, of the historic importance of the political developments now under way in that region. Within the post-Cold War global order, non-European regions may well play increasingly important roles, and it would be a mistake to rely solely on Western or European developments to characterize this new era. Democratization in post-communist Europe will be one of several major changes from the Cold War mapping of world politics, but it does represent in the clearest form the demise of the Leninist challenge, and the clearest commitment to adopt a democratic politics compatible with Western understandings.

Not since those early postwar years has so much been at stake in exiting from dictatorship and attempting to launch and consolidate a democratic politics. Democratization in post-communist Europe, it is safe to say, will be a focus of attention for policy makers and scholars for many years to come. The consequences of democratization in Europe after the Cold War, whether outstanding success, dismal failure, or limited achievements, will certainly be major elements in the reshaping of global politics in our times. To that end, this study applies the tools of comparative political analysis to the democratization process of post-communist Europe, with Poland, the Czech Republic and Hungary as the primary subjects. This study continues in the well-established tradition of comparative politics as it developed after the Second World War, the scholarship of liberal democracy as the system deemed most desirable for citizen freedom, economic prosperity and international peace.

The war had broken the tradition of American isolationism, and had involved American policy makers in Europe on a long-term and systematic basis. European fascism and communism had forced many talented scholars into exile in the United States, and they had introduced their own concepts of European political systems into American scholarly debate, enriching American scholarship and expanding its concerns in the fields of comparative politics and international affairs. These European émigré scholars had been scarred by European totalitarianism, and they turned their energies to study the causes of modern anti-democratic politics, in order 'to prevent any similar forms of fascism and totalitarianism from ever coming to power again' (Wiarda, 1985: 12).

Indeed, it was reaction to the failure of democratization in interwar Europe and the renewed communist challenge of the Cold War that gave an initial impulse (cf. Chilcote, 1994; Lipset, 1959a; Macridis, 1955; Wiarda, 1985) for the development of a new type of study of foreign government, one which was more consciously comparative, more realistic, and more like a science than the eclectic wisdom of individual

country specialists or 'old hands'. Howard Wiarda notes that among
the first generation of postwar comparativists, most were committed
to the Western Cold War agenda, which meant a clear commitment to
Western models of democracy as well as a commitment to a new and
radically different approach to studying different political systems. The
Social Science Research Council (SSRC) in the United States specifically
commissioned the path-breaking work of Gabriel Almond and James
Coleman on *The Politics of the Developing Nations* (1960), which extended
the West's Cold War perspective in Europe to the entire developing
world. 'Anyone seeking to understand this enormously influential
volume in the comparative politics field, and the work of the SSRC's
Committee on Comparative Politics, which sponsored the volume and
whose views dominated the field for the next decade, should first read
Almond's *The Appeals of Communism* (1954) or Lucian Pye's *Guerrilla
Communism in Malaya: Its Social and Political Meaning* (1956)' (cited in
Wiarda, 1985: 13).

This pattern of Cold War thinking, embedded deeply within the field
of comparative politics in the West (and especially in the United States),
provided the foundations for forty years of work, with its achievements
and shortcomings, for both the supporters of Western Cold War policies
and for their critics. Supporters of Cold War anti-communism were led
into collaboration with intelligence agencies committed to anti-
communism at any price, including support for the nastiest right-wing
dictators and for Western intervention abroad. The leading comparative
scholar Karl Deutsch, in his 1970 American Political Science Association
presidential address, raised the question of 'why political scientists had
failed to provide policy solutions during the US debacle in Vietnam'
(Chilcote, 1994: 32–33).

At the same time that comparative politics had achieved a new
mission and sponsorship in the Cold War, there were limits on mainstream thinking and criticism. What has been learned from the era of
Cold War comparative political analysis, and can these lessons be of use
in our study of the post-Cold War democratization in post-communist
Europe?

First, over the course of the Cold War, comparativists did come to
recognize their preoccupation with *the* Western model of political development in contrast to the communist model. This overconcentration
tended to blind researchers to other variations and other paths; always
the question was whether a particular regime was tending towards the
Western path of development, or was deviating towards the Soviet path.
Clearly, over the years, the charges of Eurocentrism from dissident
voices brought fuller realization of the poverty of the East–West schem-
atic approach. Other varieties of political development, including Latin
American corporatism, Third World dependency politics, indigenous
systems, and most recently East Asian developmentalism, have made
their way into the comparative politics literature. Mattei Dogan and

Dominique Pelassy have argued: 'Comparative studies point out and denounce ethnocentrism, and in this way they certainly contribute to its lessening. One must test one's own limits in order to transcend them. Like any discipline, international comparison will progress by correcting a series of errors progressively revealed' (1990: 13).

Mainstream comparative politics in the West once had visions of achieving higher status as a 'science'. In part because Marxism claimed to represent 'scientific socialism' and in part because of the high status accorded to the hard sciences at the end of the Second World War (and especially to physics), Western comparative politics also set out on a quest to achieve a new value-free and rigorously scientific paradigm (Holt and Richardson, 1970). Despite the seemingly obvious Western bias of modernization theory, this effort too was considered an important element for comparative politics in the Cold War combat. To the extent that a new scientific paradigm could be developed and widely recognized, the comparative researchers could then pursue normal science, with predictive capabilities that would lie beyond partisan emotions or unscientific moralizing (cf. critical commentary on this effort by Lapalombara, 1968; Sartori, 1970). This forced march towards a physics-type model for comparative political science, in dubious admiration of Thomas Kuhn's notion of the 'paradigm revolution' which physics had achieved, ended in a muddle by the mid-1970s. The futility of trying to duplicate any of the natural sciences gradually was recognized, as was the self-deception of any value-free position for the researcher (Chilcote, 1994). In general, the field of comparative analysis has become much more aware of its own limitations as an organized branch of social science, and has given up the illusion of being able to deliberately re-engineer itself along the lines of any natural science. Especially in regard to predictive capacity, comparative analysis has learned a great deal of humility (cf. Dogan and Pelassy, 1990: esp. ch. 24).

Comparative politics and regional studies of democratization

Comparative politics began as a clearly Eurocentric field of study, and even in the early postwar years this concentration on Europe and the conceptualization of politics from European perspectives was still very pronounced. It is still a matter of some contention as to how Eurocentric comparative politics remains today, and it is important to note that some leading East European scholars have warned that Western European ideals and democratic values are being inappropriately assumed for the post-communist East. Six years after the fall of communism, Vladimir Tismaneanu, dismayed at the rise of anti-democratic ethnic nationalism in post-communist Europe, asks: 'Whatever happened to the ethical, transnational project of "civil society" and "Central Europe"? Was the celebration of dissent more the result of the Western intelligentsia's narcissistic projection and search for political atonement than expression of homegrown intellectual and moral trends?' (1996: 533). This is the classic question for comparative analysis, of whether those political values and concepts which emerged first and most clearly in the West are in fact universal in potential application (Zakaria, 1997), so that there can be no generalized accusation of Western bias or cultural imperialism when it comes to values of human rights and personal liberties (Goldfarb, 1992).

The field of comparative politics grew in geographical scope in the postwar years in stride with decolonization, with the birth of new nations in Africa, South Asia, East Asia, the Middle East and the Caribbean. To this one must add the increased attention to Latin America within the context of the Cold War. Comparative scholarship began a long process of struggling with questions of Eurocentrism and Eurocentric bias as the field of comparison widened to encompass a global community of nation-states.

With the expansion in the number of independent nations, fewer than fifty at the end of the Second World War and nearly 200 today, the field developed regional concentrations of research and analysis, which grouped regional trends and exceptional or counter-trend cases together, in the belief that broad regional similarities (sociocultural background, political history and economic level of development) would allow researchers to focus more clearly on political system variables which could explain differences in outcome. At the same time, comparisons within a given region would permit some overall generalizations about the politics of Latin America, or the politics of Africa, or of East Asia. While it was recognized that there were considerable variations within each region, the regional concept has remained a strong conceptual organizing tool for comparative analysis. In fact, one might argue that after the nation-state level of analysis, it has been the regional level of grouped nation-states that has achieved most attention. This has also led to growing comparisons between regions, with regional trends and patterns providing the basis for generalization and theorizing about regional differences.

This regional focus has often been combined with a research concern for political democracy, its success or failure, as part of the overall research agenda since the end of the Second World War and the emergence of the Cold War. After the breakdown of so many new democracies in Europe in the interwar period, the subjects of democratic transition and democratic consolidation (cf. Linz et al., 1995) became grand themes of comparative research and theorizing. The initial concern was the redemocratization in irreversible form in postwar Germany, Italy and Japan, the building of a democratic capitalist bloc of industrial nations to oppose the emergent Soviet bloc in Eastern Europe and China (before the Sino-Soviet split in the 1960s). In West Germany especially, tremendous attention was given to every sign of democratic stability, and tremendous anxiety was raised by any signs of democratic weakness (the 'Weimar syndrome') or the revival of any neo-fascist politics, for example through the right-radical NPD in the latter 1960s (Nagle, 1970). From this starting point, comparative scholars in the West have been drawn to each new 'wave' or 'wavelet' of democratization, as well as to reverse 'waves' and 'wavelets'.

With the consolidation of the East–West Cold War logic as a global conceptual framework both for Western policy making and for mainstream Western scholarship, political leaders hoped that the developing nations in each region would emulate the Western pattern of economic modernization and political development (or at least not challenge it openly), and feared that political instability in this area would give opportunities for the competing Soviet communist model. Each nation in the developing world became a test case, with an elevated importance; even small nations (Cuba, Nicaragua, Grenada) which clearly challenged the Western pattern became objects of severe discipline (especially from the United States), and efforts to bolster pro-Western forces. After the Cuban Revolution had clearly veered toward communism, for example, the Kennedy Administration in Washington undertook offensive overt and covert actions to overthrow the Castro regime, and a major new effort to boost democratic forces (as long as they were also pro-American) in Latin America through the Alliance for Progress. This effort, while extremely flawed, demonstrated the ideological importance placed on avoiding any wider (regional) political trend which might bolster communist claims as an alternative for modernization. In principle, the West was committed to the proposition that, in the long run, democratization was the appropriate political correlate for economic development; in actual practice, Western governments often supported anti-democratic regimes in various regions as a better defence against presumed communist threats, domestic and international. The severe internal contradictions of Western policies were revealed after every failure of democratization, especially when these failures were clustered by time and region.

A wave of democratic breakdowns in Latin America in the 1960s and 1970s, coming after the illusory early optimism of President Kennedy's Alliance for Progress, gave rise to military juntas throughout that region, and a whole new literature was devoted to analysing that general phenomenon. This breakdown literature (cf. esp. Linz and Stepan, 1978) voiced concerns about the 'inevitability' of democratic expansion, about the whole prospect for Western-style political development to accompany economic modernization in other regions, and about Western relations with non-democratic authoritarian regimes in the Cold War environment. The field of comparative political analysis during the Cold War developed much of its research and theorizing on democratization by reacting to apparent clusters of success cases or failure cases, most often in the form of regional groupings of nations.

With the birth of the so-called Third Wave (Huntington, 1991) of democratization in the late 1970s (primarily focusing on Southern Europe and then Latin America), again new interest was generated in making broad comparisons between democratization processes in different regions. Attention would later be extended to democratic trends in East Asia and South Asia, some anti-dictatorial movements in Africa, and finally to the stunning democratic breakthroughs in communist Europe. Only the Islamic societies of the Middle East region have been largely left out of this growing literature; the failures of democratization in Islamic societies generally have left them out of the democratic trend of recent decades.

Studying democracy and democratization: conflicting views

The new task for comparative politics in studying democratization after the Cold War has been made more complex because of two longer-term developments: (1) the study of democracy in the Western nations during the Cold War era, which generated debate about the proper extent of citizen participation in modern democracy; and (2) studies of the increasing pressure on the Keynesian welfare state democracies in the West since the 1970s, which have raised questions about the capacities of nation-state politics in a global economy.

In the midst of the struggle with European fascism and Soviet communism in the 1930s, the Austrian political economist Joseph Schumpeter (1942), pessimistic about the chances for fulfilling the ideals of a citizen-based and grassroots democratic polity, borrowed from the insights of classic elite theorists (especially from Michels, Pareto and Mosca) to produce a new major conception which came to be known as an elite theory of democracy (Nagle, 1992). Schumpeter stressed in his formulation a minimalist role for the citizen, and a much more prominent role for political elites, as the key to building and maintaining a stable democracy. Schumpeter viewed this elite-oriented democratic theory as a mark of political realism, the best that could be hoped for if the dangers of fascism and communism were to be avoided. Schumpeter's critique of classic democratic idealism as dangerous utopianism was clearly a product of his times, in which many interwar democracies in Europe had collapsed and been replaced by right-wing authoritarian or fascist regimes. His theory of a realistic democratic politics sought to recognize what he regarded as weaknesses of these interwar democracies, and to reconstruct a short and more practical list of requisites for democratic politics.

According to the view we have taken, democracy does not mean and cannot mean that the people actually rule in any obvious sense of the term 'people' and 'rule'. Democracy means only that the people have the opportunity of accepting or refusing the men who are to rule them. But since they might decide this also in entirely undemocratic ways, we have had to narrow our definition by adding a further criterion identifying the democratic method, viz., free competition among would-be leaders for the vote of the electorate . . . (Schumpeter, 1942, cited in Etzioni-Halevy, 1997: 81)

For a successful (that is, stable) democracy, Schumpeter stressed the need for a political leadership of 'high quality,' for which it would be important to 'increase their fitness by endowing them with traditions that embody experience, with a professional code and with a common fund of ideas' (1997: 82). These elites would require a high measure of autonomy, that there be a capable and independent bureaucracy, and that the public and the opposition exercise self-restraint. Citizens should not put undue pressure on their elected representatives. Schumpeter suggested that such practices should be avoided both formally and informally – 'also less formal attempts at restricting the freedom of action of members of parliament – the practice of bombarding them with letters and telegrams for instance – ought to come under the same ban' (p. 84). For Schumpeter, the English system came closest to his realist theory, since it rested upon a wide and traditional elite consensus on rules of the political game.

For many years after the end of the Second World War, Schumpeter's realist or elite-oriented theory of democracy gained in acceptance as the standard by which democratic politics should be judged. Given the still-vivid challenges of anti-democratic alternatives, proponents of democracy were generally more willing to accept a watered-down and elite-oriented version of democratic theory. Democratic leaders were regaining their confidence, and were still attempting to avoid the worst, rather than seeking to maximize citizen participation. Some scholars took Schumpeter's ambiguity about the citizen's democratic potential even further, expressing an inherent distrust of popular participation in the era of modern mass society (Kornhauser, 1959).

Isaiah Berlin (1958), in his famous lectures at Oxford in 1958, stressed a related point, in urging first and foremost the defence of negative liberty (the freedom from tyranny) as opposed to positive liberty (direct citizen participation in governance). Berlin urged his listeners to take a modest view of liberal democracy's possibilities, and not to get overly confident about its abilities to solve all problems and master all social ills. Too much reliance on government, and too much responsibility placed on government, were not welcome. Berlin's defence of an anti-totalitarian definition of liberty fitted well with the ideas of a realistic and stable Schumpeterian democracy for the Cold War era.

Yet by the 1960s, the liberal democracies of the West, including the reconstructed democracies in West Germany and Italy, had proved their stability and their ability to govern effectively across a wide and growing range of policy issues. The rise of a Keynesian consensus across the political spectrum had reduced extremist parties to manageable proportions, political class warfare had declined markedly, and widespread economic prosperity had exerted a moderating force on political life generally. With rising standards of living and education, many citizens, especially among the younger generation, began to raise their expectations about political participation, and to question the legal or practised limits on citizen involvement in political life. A new cohort of scholars of democratic theory began to criticize the Schumpeterian model as too elitist, too compromised by its acceptance of the insights of Mosca and Pareto, who were at best ambiguous towards democracy and who had collaborated with Italian fascism (Nye, 1977). Building on the earlier criticism of the new and unaccountable 'power elite' growing within American democracy by C. Wright Mills (1956), left-liberal theorists like Peter Bachrach (1967), Jack Walker (1966) and Henry Kariel (1970) sought to retrieve more of the classic vision of a democratic politics, in which the citizen had more access to political information, more access to political leaders, and more direct input into political processes, both in choices of candidates and in shaping policy making. Their radical or participatory theories of democracy were more optimistic about citizens, and less willing to concede such large roles to political elites, whether elected or unelected (Bottomore, 1966; Jaeggi, 1969). The challenge from this new participatory democratic theory coincided with the student and youth rebellions of 1968 throughout the West, and continued on with the emergence of new social movements in the 1970s around issues of war/peace, environment, women's rights, gay rights and anti-imperialist solidarity. The most apparent vehicle for a more participatory politics in Europe was the environmentalist movement and then the Green parties. Die Grünen became in the 1980s a new German political party, able to force new ideas into national politics through its electoral challenge, and through the example of its own ideas (Markovits and Gorsky, 1993). By the end of the 1980s and the collapse of the Berlin Wall, the Greens had become part of the normal political landscape, but had also helped to change ideas about how citizens could participate in political life beyond simply voting in elections.

The participatory democracy challenge to Schumpeterian elite democracy did not go unanswered of course; conservative thinkers like Edward Shils (1982), Sam Huntington and Michael Crozier warned of the threatened 'ungovernability' of democracy if citizen demands on the system continued to grow (Crozier et al., 1975); they argued that the new social movements were weakening the legitimacy of the established party system, without which leaders could not exercise their authority

(Eulau and Czudnowski, 1976). In their dark scenario, the liberal demo-cracies of the West were becoming ungovernable. This response coincided with the early decline of the Keynesian consensus, which since the 1970s has come under ever greater pressure, as growing budget deficits, slow growth, and rising unemployment in an ever more globalized financial and trade-oriented economy have sapped public confidence in their national government and in the major political parties. One result has been a gradual downsizing of government responsibilities, privatization of public enterprises and roles, and deregulation of private market forces. The Thatcher and Reagan politics were a first response to the perceived oversizing of government, an attempt to reduce the burdens of responsibility, especially for social problems, on democratic governance.

Yet once the new social movements had taken hold, there was little possibility for a return to the type of party politics which had been built up in the first phase (up to the early 1960s) of the Cold War. The new social movements and their participatory democracy orientation did not in any case completely displace the established party system and established elites, but they did carve out some significant political space for themselves in their long march through the institutions; moreover they had enough impact to force the established party elites to refor-mulate the political agenda to include the main issues of these move-ments. The liberal democracies did not become ungovernable, but they did move away from the more narrow-gauge Schumpeterian model of the immediate postwar years.

It is fitting to note that the great liberal thinker Isaiah Berlin (1907–1997), in the development of his later writings, moved gradually to a position which included more elements of 'positive freedom' and stressed the need for a balance between negative and positive freedoms in a healthy democratic society (Joas, 1997). Berlin recognized that his concept of negative liberty was only one competing version, and he avoided any dogmatic view that this was the last word on the subject. In his last interview, Isaiah Berlin, while standing by his life-long defence of negative freedom, expressed some regret that he had not given more credit to the ideals of positive freedom and to the darker potentials of negative freedom (for example the exploitation of child labour under *laissez-faire*). 'I still stand by that today. But I should have stressed the horrors of negative freedom and where they have led more strongly' (1997: 14, authors' translation from the German).

Long-time theorist of democracy Robert Dahl, who started out very close to the Schumpeterian model, has moved somewhat forward in his definitions of democracy, at least in terms of minimal standards. Dahl still defines democratic regimes as those which provide 'selection of top officials in free and fair elections, extensive freedom of expression, wide access to alternative and independent sources of information, rights to form relatively independent associations and organizations, including political parties entitled to compete in elections, and an inclusive electorate' (1995: 4). But Dahl acknowledges that standards have risen even within the West, so that 'modern democracy, at least if it is defined by the full set of political institutions I just described, is distinctly a creation of the twentieth century, a fact that suggests the following arresting thought: even in the oldest existing democracies . . . democracy in the full-fledged modern sense is younger than its oldest living citizens' (p. 5). We will be studying the democratization process in East-Central Europe as a part of this ongoing struggle between competing conceptions of democracy.

Varieties of democracy and democratization

In the current era, the spread of democracy and democratization to most regions has shifted the attention of comparative analysis from concentration on democracy versus anti-democracy, which was so central in the struggle against fascism and communism, to a growing interest in the possible varieties of democracy. Our contention is that comparative politics as a field is now better prepared to take up this issue, having exercised considerable self-criticism over its early Eurocentric bias, and having overcome its earlier illusions about developing a scientific paradigm with strong predictive powers. While these issues were never entirely resolved, comparative political analysis now is much more likely to recognize important differences among nations and between cultures in terms of the nature of its political life, without trying to squeeze each nation (or culture) into just one-size-fits-all democratic model or else into the anti-democratic category. The end of the East–West struggle and the painful transformation of Keynesian welfare state democracy in the West have both facilitated a greater openness to greater variation within the camp of democracy.

Fareed Zakaria has worried that as democracy has spread around the world, there is a new danger in what he terms the rise of illiberal democracy, that is, elected regimes lacking constitutional liberal foundations. 'There are no longer respectable alternatives to democracy; it is part of the fashionable attire of modernity. Thus the problems of governance in the 21st century will likely be problems within democracy. This makes them more difficult to handle, wrapped as they are in the mantle of legitimacy' (1997: 42). Zakaria, an unabashed proponent of Western liberal democracy, fears that in the rush to embrace the current wave of democratizations, important qualitative differences will be glossed over. By his count, at the end of the 1980s, 22 per cent of democratizing nations could be termed illiberal democracies, but by 1997 this figure had risen to 50 per cent. We need a clear recognition of the conceptual distinction between democracy and liberalism, which have generally gone hand-in-hand in Western experience, and the greater disconnection between the two which now seems to be emerging in many regions. Zakaria argues that Western policy should try consciously to 'encourage the gradual development of constitutional liberalism across the globe. Democracy without constitutional liberalism is not simply inadequate, but dangerous, bringing with it the erosion of liberty, the abuse of power, ethnic divisions, and even war' (1997: 42–43). Zakaria's point is that the new terrain for political struggle is among competing visions that characterize the quality of the democratic order.

The experience of post-communism has already given rise to new issues of how far previously developed concepts of democratization can be stretched. Philippe Schmitter and Terri Lynn Karl (1994) have argued, for example, that post-communist transitions are quite comparable to other regions of the world. They support the general comparability of post-communism with post-authoritarianism generally. Valerie Bunce (1995), on the other side, argues the uniqueness of the post-communist experience, and is suspicious of stretching the notions of democratic transition to Russia and much of post-communist Europe, because a too general comparison will neglect the unique circumstances of post-communism and miss the chance to understand it on its own terms (cf. Koff and Koff, 1997). The general issue may not be settled through deductive reasoning, but only through empirical research. The results of this research will then provide the evidence as to whether the differences between post-communism and other post-authoritarian experiences are qualitative in nature. Democratization in East-Central Europe offers a good test of this argument, and we will be attentive to the issue of how these new democracies are related to democracies in the West and in other democratizing regions.

2

Historical Legacies of Regional Democratization

From empire to nation-state: impact on the 'lands between'

Historian Alan Palmer has characterized the societies of East-Central Europe as 'the lands between', the lands between Germany and Italy on the West, and Russia on the East, lacking natural frontiers. 'Open to wandering races from the east and attracting colonial settlement from the west, this region became the home of at least fifteen distinctive nationalities even though it covers, in area, less than two thirds the size of Western Europe' (1970: 1). This region was, in medieval times of western expansionism, the easternmost part of Western Catholic culture, and in times of Russian or Slavic strength, the westernmost reaches of Slavic civilizations. With the rise of the modern nation-state in the West, and the successes of Russian imperialism in the East in the seventeenth and eighteenth centuries, the peoples of this region were challenged to maintain their national identities even when they had lost, for extended periods, their independence. By the end of the Napoleonic Wars and the Congress of Vienna in 1815, Poland had been divided up among Russia, Prussia and Austria, and Hungary and the Czech and Slovak lands existed as constituent parts of the Austrian Empire. This region therefore had a rich history of various coexisting and often conflicting cultures, each adding its weight to the politics, economic development and social identities of each nation, whether that nation was independent or whether it was incorporated within the boundaries of a powerful neighbour.

The political economy of empire (Germanic, Ottoman or Russian), the provision of tribute in return for security, allowed for many peoples and cultures to be brought into or exit from imperial control on a constantly shifting basis. The decline of empire and medieval institutions in Europe reflected the long-term basic shift from one form of institutionalized political economy (pre-industrial empire) to a more successful and more powerful one (the modern nation-state). Beginning with the challenge of the French Revolution to the *ancien régime*, political intellectuals and their followers within these societies began the long search for a modern and independent nation-state of their own. This search was not just limited to Poland, Hungary, and the Czech and Slovak lands. It also affected the Germanic peoples of Central Europe, and increased the complexity of the issue for 'the lands between'. Napoleon's final disbanding of the Holy Roman Empire of the German Nation in 1806 gave birth to the 'German Question' in Central Europe, the question of how Germany could be revitalized as a modern nation-state, under whose leadership, and with what consequences for Europe? The German Question, with its associated search for a modern German nation-state, proved to be both an example for East-Central Europe, and a threat; from the mid-nineteenth to the mid-twentieth century, the unification of Germany was associated with territorial expansionism to the East at the expense of its neighbours. Further to the East, during the same period, the prolonged decay of tsarist rule in Russia, and the search by the Russian intelligentsia (Westernizers, Slavophiles, Marxists) to find their own new success formula, would also pose alternative visions and new dangers for national aspirations within East-Central Europe.

Decline of empire in Europe would elevate the hopes of the peoples of Poland, Hungary, and the Czech and Slovak lands; the chances for independence, for national liberation, were increased in times of weakness of Austrian, German and Russian power. But at the same time, revitalizations of Germany to the West or Russia to the East would restore their considerable influence in the region, and perhaps impose a modernized German or Russian concept of political economy. For the political intelligentsia of East-Central Europe, this was a period of great searching for an appropriate path to modernity and national success, within a general atmosphere of the end of an era in Europe. Is this historical legacy now continued after the end of communism? Does the concept of the 'lands between' still apply in the current period?

The Concert of Europe and the idea of national liberation

The Congress of Vienna and Metternich's Concert of Europe were designed primarily to prevent any recurrence of French revolutionary fervour in the west, but this also meant a continuous imperial watchfulness against nationalist rebellions in East-Central Europe. The last century of monarchic great power rule in Europe was marked by reaction and repression for the peoples of 'the lands between'. In this environment, the idea of freedom for the peoples of this region was nationalist to the core; other political ideologies were to be measured by their service to the goal of national independence. With the defeat of the great Polish uprisings of 1830–31 against Russian rule, thousands of political exiles made their way to Paris, London, the United States, or even Latin America, and came to startlingly different conclusions as to what kind of politics could free their peoples and offer a happier future. Some remained strong supporters of an enlightened aristocratic rule (Czartoryski) for a sovereign Poland, others (Lelevel for example) came into contact with the new socialist revolutionaries in Brussels and London. Welcomed and financially supported by the liberal regimes of Paris and London, the emigré community had a strong cultural influence through their literature (Mickiewicz, Krasiński, Slowacki) of romantic nationalism (Palmer, 1970: 44–5).

In the Austrian Empire, as the Hungarian nobility became junior partners (and finally in the Ausgleich of 1867 formal co-rulers of the Dual Monarchy of Austria–Hungary), they enforced a Magyarization in the Eastern provinces which they governed. The educated Hungarian upper class, almost all aristocratic landowners, assumed that the political emancipation of Hungary would require reinforcement of the Magyar language throughout the Middle Danube region. The notion of Hungarian liberation and its cultural renaissance was therefore effectively combined with disregard for other (Slovak, Croatian, Ruthenian) minorities. Even within the broad definition of Hungarian liberal nationalism, the debate over Magyarization between the moderate Count Istvan Szèchenyi and the radical Lajos Kossuth was won by Kossuth in the court of popular opinion.

> But, by 1848, the Magyar people – especially the lesser nobility – were far too proudly headstrong for political restraint: Szèchenyi's protests at Magyarization had destroyed his following; and it was the brilliant orator and journalist, Lajos Kossuth, who voiced such of the national will as was allowed to be articulate. . . . It was a tragedy for all Central Europe, and not least for Hungary, that his love of country should by its intensity have aroused a lasting hatred among those who were its victims. (Palmer, 1970: 50–51)

Hungary's treatment as a vanquished enemy nation at Versailles, rather than one of the liberated nationalities, impaired Hungary's democratization and cooperation with its neighbours for most of this century. Hungary's extensive political contact with the West and with the beginnings of democratization in the Austrian realms became entangled with territorial revisionism after the Treaty of Trianon, which to this day remains a rallying point for conservative parties.

The nationalism of Central and Eastern Europe was intensely ethnic and patriotic, tied to the idea of blood belonging, and therefore defined in opposition to others of different lineage (Ignatieff, 1993; Kohn, 1945; Pfaff, 1993). Ignatieff in particular argues that German romanticism was responsible for the rise of ethnic nationalist concepts in East-Central Europe generally.

> All the peoples of nineteenth century Europe under imperial subjection – the Poles and Baltic peoples under the Russian yoke, the Serbs under Turkish rule, the Croats under the Habsburgs – looked to the German ideal of ethnic nationalism when articulating their right to self-determination. When Germany achieved unification in 1871 and rose to world-power status, Germany's achievement was a demonstration of the success of ethnic nationalism to all the 'captive nations' of imperial Europe. (Ignatieff, 1993: 7)

This romantic nationalism of the region, born of serial defeats in the eighteenth century and the oppressive rule of the great monarchical empires of the nineteenth century, coincided with the (delayed) industrial and commercial revolutions of capitalism; in this sense too the societies of East-Central Europe were 'the lands between'. The foundations of the modern nation-state in Western Europe had been laid before the social turmoil (as Schumpeter called it, the 'creative destruction') of a modernizing capitalism, and the basic national identities had formed around issues of territorial citizenship; the 'Eastern nationalism' as Kohn describes it, revolved around ethnic identity (usually associated with language and religion), regardless of territory or of formal citizenship. Although the definition of just what constitutes a nation is still very much in dispute (Pfaff, 1993: ch. 2), there is widespread consensus on the impact that German romanticism (Herder) had in East-Central Europe among nationally conscious intelligentsia, and their efforts to inspire national liberation for Poles, Hungarians, Czechs and Slovaks. The new intelligentsia of East-Central Europe often connected this romantic nationalism with the classic Western political values of conservatism, liberalism and socialism, producing *hybrid* political movements and parties, including anti-Semitic populism and fascism, liberal nationalism and socialist nationalism.

While the Germans achieved unification and the means to press for great-power, even super-power status under Bismarck in 1871, it was not until the end of the First World War that independent Poland, Hungary and Czechoslovakia appeared on the maps of Europe. These nations-in-waiting were definitely a part of Europe (and did not face the

Westernizer-Slavophile tension of the Russian intelligentsia), but at the same time they had missed the essential nation-building experiences of Western Europe. In this sense they stand apart from the Western experience, as borderlands. Krzysztof Pomian makes the key point that this 'zone' of Western civilization had for several centuries been subjected to Mongol or Russian or Ottoman domination, and thus was 'literally cut out of European history' (cited by Pfaff, 1993: 86). As these lands now seek to 'join the West' to which they really belong, they do so with little experience of national self-government and a very different perspective on the political values, in particular the values associated with liberal democracy, which have gradually and with no small difficulty evolved in the Western European nation-states over the past several centuries. The legacy of suppression of nationhood for the peoples of East-Central Europe was a strong factor in the weakness of liberal political thought, even among the middle classes. Samuel Huntington (1996), in his essay on the 'clash of civilizations,' thus treats these East-Central European lands as potentially assimilable borderlands, largely on the basis of their Western Christian heritage, but requiring a major effort on the part of both elites and masses.

But there was another perspective on the struggle for national liberation of the nations of this region, which was to grow in influence from the nineteenth into the twentieth century: the American liberal idea of international cooperation among free states. From the perspective of top American leaders, even in the first years of the Concert of Europe, the liberal formula on which the United States was founded had always seemed to be the answer to the wars and ethnic conflicts of the Old World. In an era of continual European warfare and failed peacemaking from the outbreak of the French Revolution in 1789 through the final military defeat of the Napoleonic armies in 1814, a core of American thinkers looked to their own experience as a radically new success formula.

This specifically American intellectual tradition would nurture, in another era of European warmaking (the First World War), the ideas of President Woodrow Wilson and others concerned with international peace and conflict resolution among nations. The First World War occasioned a new round of American Plans, each with its own distinctive features, but all grounded in peculiarly American (and thus liberal) understandings of the basic concepts of 'nation' and 'state', which were to be the components in a new 'United States of Europe' (Samuel Eliot Morrison of Harvard) or a 'new State, or new Power' (Darwin Kingsley of the League to Enforce the Peace) which would use the Constitution of the United States as its model (Kuehl, 1969: 250–259). These ideas, through their American intellectual history with which Wilson, the most intellectual President since Jefferson, was well acquainted, and through direct contact by their proponents with Colonel Edward House, Wilson's closest adviser, fed into Wilson's own Fourteen Points and his League proposals. Wilson's advisory group (the so-called Inquiry) set out to redraw the borders of Eastern and Central Europe in accordance with the notion of self-determination of nations, understood as ethnic nationalities, with the intention of fostering liberal democratic governments throughout the region; it was the first attempt to super-impose an American Plan for a peaceful and democratic Europe on the realities of the Old World (Pfaff, 1992).

In general, the American backers for the new nations of the region were blind to the motives of the independence leaders, and conflated their drive for national self-determination with the establishment of liberal democracy. Ethnic tensions and ethnic self-aggrandizement were ignored or downplayed, whereas the postwar opening for democracy was seen as the inevitable victory of the 'modern' present and future over the 'reactionary' past. When the Czech leaders Masaryk and Beneš argued their case with American officials during the war years, they naturally presented an image of a Czech people brutally repressed by the Austrian authorities in Bohemia and Moravia, whereas the reality was much more complex.

Washington thus decided to back exiled leaders' claims for the new Czechoslovakia to the historic borders of Bohemia and Moravia despite the attempts by the German ethnic minority to have the German-populated Sudetenland in Bohemia recognized as a province of Austria after the 1918 armistice, while in Slovakia Washington agreed to Slovak claims to expand on historic borders in Slovakia and Ruthenia on ethnic nationalist grounds (cf. esp. Rothschild, 1974: 77–79). The Czechs also used their leverage with the Western Allies to gain control of the small but economically important area of Tesin from Poland in 1920. The true state of ethnic tensions in the new Czechoslovakia, between Germans and Czechs, but also between Czechs and Slovaks, began to emerge at the Paris Peace Conference of 1919, but by then the die was cast, and the Allied leaders simply pressed on with their original commitments.

In the very aftermath of the collapse of empire, the conflict between nationalism and democracy was already emerging, and it was this singular tension between *ethnos* and *demos* that would bring an unhappy end to the interwar democratic experiment. The first birth of democracy in these new nations coincided with sharp ethnic conflicts and nation-alist irredentism, which would bedevil attempts to build social plural-ism, compromise and tolerance within a democratic politics.

The legacy of the interwar period: the triumph of ethnic nationalism over democracy

In the wake of the collapse of the Russian empire, the military defeat of Germany and the breakup of Austria–Hungary, the audacious Wilsonian programme would promote and legitimize the successor states of East-Central Europe, seen as the new foundation for building a democratic and peaceful Europe. Although each was initially committed to a democratic politics, these new nations also contained many minorities and new antagonisms with dominant majorities, as well as new border grievances against neighbouring states. The young George Kennan judged that this exercise illustrated the 'colossal conceit of thinking that you could suddenly make international life over into what you believed to be your own image, when you dismissed the past with contempt, rejected the relevance of the past to the future, and refused to occupy yourself with the real problems that a study of the past would suggest' (quoted in Pfaff, 1992: 68). Alan Palmer argues that, in retrospect, the Peace Settlement at Versailles has been subjected to more criticism than was warranted, as a first attempt at self-determination of nations in East-Central Europe.

> Even at the most generous estimate, national minorities constituted nearly a third of the population of Poland and Czechoslovakia . . . Six-and-a-half million Germans were neither citizens of the German Republic nor of Austria, more than five million Ukrainians were outside of the Soviet empire, and three million Magyars were beyond the frontiers of Hungary. . . . Over the whole area of East-Central Europe it is probable that one person in five was a member of a national minority; some accepted their position; some voiced their hostility from the earliest days; and many grew to resent it through years of frustrating inequality. (1970: 171)

Yet the peacemakers were aware of some of these problems, and there were procedures and special treaties to protect minority religious, linguistic and cultural rights. The League Covenant contained grievance procedures to head off border and minority conflicts. And efforts were made to offset economic losses and economic access problems caused by the Peace Settlement. Palmer argues that 'the number of nationalities which benefited from the various treaties was greater than those which suffered, and it is probable that, given the temper of the times and the excessively confused ethnic pattern in the major areas of dispute, no fairer or more equitable system could have been devised by any gathering of victors from a long and bitter war' (pp. 172–173). Joseph Rothschild estimates that three times as many people were freed from alien nationality rule as were newly subjected. What was lacking, finally, was a change in mentality, which would have allowed grievance procedures and minority protections to function effectively. The redrawn borders did not reshape the climate of intolerance and historic animosity which predated the war. 'What was reshaped in 1919–20 was the map of Europe, not the habits of its peoples' (1974: 4).

Still, the disappearance of Austria as a major power, and the simultaneous weakening of both Germany and Russia provided a historic opportunity for the nations of the region to exercise real self-government;

and at the outset, the Western-style parliamentary democracy (mostly on the French proportional representation system) was the model to be emulated. Even during the suppression of leftist revolutionary uprisings in several areas at the end of the war, political leaders from the broad middle of the political spectrum moved to establish their credentials as new democracies, in an earlier 'joining the West' phase of optimism. Western constitutionalism, multi-party politics with a wide-ranging choice of parties, elected parliaments on the basis of broad franchise (except Hungary, which had a quite narrow electorate), a relatively free press and respect for personal liberty seemed to be the new defining characteristics of the politics of national independence.

Would the institutions of liberal democracy, instituted in 1919–20, find sufficient support among elites and masses to succeed, and produce an authentically Polish, Hungarian or Czechoslovakian democratic politics? Unfortunately, the answer was not long in coming, and it was negative, with the important exception of Czechoslovakia. In the first decade of post-First World War independence, most institutions of parliamentary democracy were largely corrupted or strangled in their infancy, giving way to more authoritarian practices under the cover of formally democratic institutional arrangements. In the second decade of independence, with the onset of the Great Depression, the last vestiges of democracy were swept aside in favour of anti-democratic right-wing regimes, in some ways drawing on the new 'success model' of European fascism in Italy and especially Germany. The bitter experience of this era, the failure of liberal democratic forces, was epitomized by the betrayal in 1938 at Munich of Czechoslovakia, the one viable democracy of the region, by the British and French governments, presumably the defenders of democratic freedoms in Europe. The interwar period belongs to what Huntington (1991) has called a 'reverse wave' of democratization, which destroyed liberal democratic politics and strengthened anti-democratic elites and mass movements of the left and right.

Even before the Great Depression, democracy in Eastern and Central Europe was in decline, with powerful elites determined to progressively undermine its key institution, a freely elected and politically powerful parliament. With so many enemies and so narrow a base of support, it is a testimony to the idea of democracy that it should have lasted as long as it did. Perhaps, given healthy economic growth and an extended period of peace, a democratic politics might have held on, and gradually regained the initiative, but this was not to be.

With the onset of economic crisis in 1930–31 throughout the region, there was a general trend towards a more explicitly anti-democratic politics, with fascism as the new model of modern successful politics, as exemplified by Italy and Germany. The new semi-fascist leaders and movements attempted to ape the features of fascism, first in order to gain power and then to bolster the power of the central government over independent and oppositional political and social organizations. The

Nazi-inspired Hungarian National Socialist Party of Ferenc Szálasi played to the most radical anti-Semitic sentiments, while in Poland the National Radical Camp (a splinter from the National Democratic Party in 1934) employed a similar ideology to attract young people into the Union of Young Poland. In Czechoslovakia Heinlein's Sudeten German Party was the only unabashedly anti-Semitic party. In Romania, the Iron Guard and the National Christian Party, and in Bulgaria, the less important Nazi-oriented Radnitsa, were further examples of this trend. While these extremist movements did not generally take power themselves, they reinforced the anti-democratic rightward movement of politics in the region generally. 'In most cases existing governments merely sought to refurbish conservatively-minded regimes with the trappings of fascism in order to give an appearance of modernity' (Palmer, 1970: 123). Parliaments were reduced to puppets, the military elites entered political life in a more direct and bluntly anti-democratic fashion, and conservative elites in politics, business and industry collaborated comfortably with the final destruction of democratic institutions. As Joseph Rothschild (1974) points out, in many cases conservative regimes staged pre-emptive shifts to the right, often with explicit military backing and leadership, to forestall a direct takeover by radical-right movements. Clearly conservative leaders did not want the demagogic mini-fuhrers of the radical right to come to power, not because they were anti-democratic but because they were socially unacceptable, not from the proper class background. Yet conservative leaders in Poland, Austria and Hungary were quite willing to use the rightward shift of political sentiment for their own anti-democratic politics. This was also true in Germany, where Hugenburg and von Papen schemed to utilize Hitler's Nazi Party to destroy Weimar democracy (cf. Hörster-Philipps, 1983; Schweitzer, 1964). This logic allowed conservatives to support the far right in its anti-communist and anti-socialist crusade, and yet pretend that they were not really responsible for the brutalities of the semi-fascist regimes in which they participated.

The demise of democracy in the interwar period showed that, at the elite and mass levels, there were powerful interests and powerful cultural legacies which could, in the right circumstances, be mobilized for an anti-democratic project. Most clearly, on the right, mainstream conservative politics, reinforced by the Catholic Church, the military officer corps, the top levels of the civil service and judiciary, and the aristocracy, were hostile to liberal democracy, which was seen as a threat to their social and institutional interests. Liberal politics, based on a weak business and professional middle class in the cities, was indecisive, fearful of socialism, and terrified by the spectre of Stalin's communism. The weakness of liberal political values symbolized the failure of a democratic centre to take hold in this first democratization effort. Socialists were split by an internecine warfare between democratic socialism and Leninist revolutionism. The left was inevitably tarred as 'internationalist,' and with fears of Russian domination of the region. Democracy had too few loyalists, especially in times of crisis, and many powerful enemies; with the rise of European fascism as a modern political alternative, enemies on the right came together in mixed and often muddled coalitions to end the democratic prospect and construct explicitly anti-democratic regimes.

Only in Czechoslovakia were the social and economic preconditions for democracy favourable, providing the necessary but not sufficient underpinnings for stable democracy (Lipset, 1959b; Palmer, 1970: 174ff). In the Czech lands of Bohemia and Moravia, modern industry had developed, a modern middle class had grown up in the cities, and the economy was closer to the more developed Western nations than anywhere else in East-Central Europe. Agriculture employed only one-third of the population (less than half the percentage in Poland and Hungary), even though the great gap in development between the Czech lands and Slovakia and Ruthenia did create tensions, which were exploited by Hitler in his destruction of Czechoslovakia. The clerical fascism of Father Jozef Tiso in Slovakia is a chilling reminder that a brutal anti-democratic politics was acceptable to the Catholic hierarchy; the interwar Church was no defender of liberal democracy.

The birth of nations in 1918–19 was seen idealistically as a victory for both democracy and nationalism. The course of events proved that nationalism was not only the stronger force in the region, but incompatible with democracy. In the exceptional Czechoslovak democracy, the aggression of German nationalism under the Nazis provoked not international defence, but appeasement by the Western democracies. It is symptomatic of the unequal contest between ethnic nationalism and liberal democracy that after the Munich betrayal of Czechoslovakia, neighbouring Poland took the opportunity to exact its own revenge by seizing Tesin on 30 September 1938, redressing the Czech takeover of 1920 (cf. Rothschild, 1974: 132). This was a sad era for democratization, one which led to a temporary loss of confidence in the strength of liberal democratic values, and a postwar search in the West for new institutional and socioeconomic requisites necessary for 'stable democracy'.

The evolution of communism in the Cold War

One might expect that the period of communism in East-Central Europe could be simply written off as an interlude of anti-democratic one-party rule, a negative legacy in all respects for democratization. Indeed, some (cf. for example Chirot, 1996; Mason et al., 1991; Tismaneanu, 1996) have argued that the communist regimes of the region destroyed whatever elements of democracy and civic culture had survived fascism and the Second World War, and left in its wake a psychologically uninvolved, uncivil, cynical culture (for an extreme example cf. Zubek, 1994). Yet this view neglects that very real evolution of communist politics which led to the final and peaceful collapse of communism in 1989–90 throughout East-Central Europe (the counter-examples of bloodletting in Romania in December 1989 and the brutal crackdown on the Tiananmen democracy movement in China in June 1989, offer striking evidence that a peaceful regime change from communism to democracy was by no means predetermined, and gives testimony to the changed nature of the political dialogue in Poland, Hungary, East Germany and Czechoslovakia in the last years of communist rule). Even in Czechoslovakia and East Germany, where anti-reform hardliners were in control, their commitment to use all possible means to retain power had faded. A totalitarian regime would be expected to use whatever means necessary to retain political power, and would never agree to free and fair elections to decide the political future of the country. The concept of totalitarianism was inspired by the classic features of the Stalinist and Nazi regimes of the 1930s and 1940s, but this original model of totalitarianism (Arendt, 1960; Fainsod, 1953; Friedrich and Brzezinski, 1956) contained no place or possibility for political evolution.

Clearly, something had changed in the course of forty years of communist rule, at least in Poland, Hungary, East Germany and Czechoslovakia, so that by 1989 a democratic change of regimes was not only thinkable, but quickly became the overwhelming consensus, even including much of the communist party and state apparatus (the so-called nomenklatura or professional staff and functionaries), once Soviet power withdrew from the region.

In the first period of communist takeovers and consolidation of power, totalitarianism was a plausible description for the new regimes and their political practices. Indeed, a Moscow-regimented Soviet model was pushed on the East-Central European regimes, as Stalin's response to the emergence of the Cold War conflict in Europe and to the dangers of Titoism. At the end of the Second World War, the old regimes in the region had been destroyed, and the peoples of East-Central Europe desired some sort of change, a break from the calamitous past. Initially, except in Yugoslavia and Albania, communist parties rose to power within coalition governments, and it was not immediately clear just how much influence their coalition partners, socialists, peasant parties, and even liberals, might have within these new regimes. Yet within a few years, the new communist ruling parties destroyed much of their initial support through brutal purges of enemies, real and imagined, as ordered by Moscow. Joseph Rothschild views this first phase of communist consolidation as Stalin's attempt to eliminate unwanted political diversity and intra-regional wrangling so as to ensure Moscow's tight control over this region in the Cold War environment.

Within two or three years of the end of the Second World War, each Communist party in East Central Europe was well on the way toward capturing and/or consolidating political power in its country. Nevertheless, from Moscow's perspective, the overall picture was still one of excessive diversity. Not only did the pace of establishing Communist rule, and its comprehensiveness, differ from state to state, but several of the Communist-dominated regimes were at loggerheads as a result of having succumbed to 'national domestic' perspectives. (1989: 125)

Polish and East German communists differed on the status of the Oder–Neisse border, Polish and Czechoslovak leaders raised competing claims to the Teschen (Tesin) district, Czechoslovak and Hungarian communists clashed over the treatment of the Hungarian minority in Slovakia, and Hungarian and Romanian communists debated the treatment of the Hungarian minority in Transylvania, to name only a few points of intra-regional contention. More threatening still was the diversity of early responses to the American Marshall Plan put forward in 1947, which some regime spokesmen seemed willing to accept. This worrisome syndrome of indiscipline and regional attention to local national concerns was summed up in the emergence of the first real challenge to Soviet dominance and control by Marshall Tito and his Yugoslav communist regime. Although Tito initially seemed a most orthodox Stalinist, his boldness and self-assurance over the Trieste conflict with Italy gave indications of his willingness to act independently of Moscow's wishes. Since Tito's partisans had conquered political power in Yugoslavia on their own, they could indeed present a bad example for other communist regimes as an alternative form of communist politics. The birth of Titoism as a statement of local sovereignty and independence from Moscow unleashed a series of Stalinist blood purges throughout the region, to stamp out any deviationism within the newly established communist regimes.

Stalin's method for imposing political and structural order on the East Central European Communists was characteristic and reminiscent of the tactics by which he had consolidated his personal mastery of the Soviet Union in the decade after Lenin's death. First, he created the Cominform in September 1947, using the Yugoslavs as his hatchet men to discipline and bully the more laggard Communist parties. Then he turned around and used this same instrument, the Cominform, in his effort to liquidate the excessively independent and rambunctious Titoists. (1989: 126)

Over the next four years, anti-Titoist purges swept through the ranks of communist parties of the region; classic 'show trials' were staged to denounce and then condemn to death the supposed ringleaders of various anti-Moscow deviations. Top communist leaders, whose loyalty and past sacrifices for the communist cause were legendary, were now denounced and purged as traitors. Gomułka in Poland, Slánský in

Czechoslovakia, and Rajk in Hungary were all sacrificed to prove their parties' absolute loyalty to Stalin. The most famous of the anti-Titoist show trials was that of Rudolf Slánský and thirteen others in Czechoslovakia from 20 to 27 November 1952. The Slánský group, all of them long-time party members, was charged with all manner of deviation – Trotskyism, Zionism, Titoism, bourgeois nationalism, and serving as spies for the West. In the Slánský trial, anti-Semitism also played a leading role, since many of the defendants were of Jewish origin. In Hungary, however, it was the leading Jewish group of Mátyás Rákosi, Ernő Gerő, Mihály Farkas, and József Révai, who had been trained in Moscow and had solid Stalinist credentials, who were able to carry out the anti-Titoist purges, including most prominently the purge of László Rajk, who had been a key figure in the climb to power of the Hungarian communists from 1945 to 1947. The victory of the Jewish Stalinists and their purge of the ethnic Hungarian Rajk consolidated for many ethnic Hungarians popular anti-communist sentiment with anti-Semitism. Rajk, he too a ruthless political operator, now found himself accused of Titoism, and after a spectacular show trial in September 1949, was hanged on 15 October 1949. In Hungary, 2,000 communist party members were executed, 150,000 imprisoned and 350,000 expelled from the party (Rothschild, 1989: 137).

The whole anti-Titoist purge era served to solidify Stalin's personal domination in the region, but at tremendous cost to the legitimacy and popular support for local ruling parties (cf. Ulam, 1952). Even here, however, the drive to create totalitarian controls over society were not completely successful. In Poland, the independence of the Catholic Church, the missing ingredient of a collectivized agriculture, and the troika of leadership rather than one top leader, led Juan Linz and Alfred Stepan to label the communist regime there as more authoritarian than totalitarian, even in the 1949–53 period (1996: 255–261). With the death of Stalin in March of 1953, a gradual thawing of Stalinist terror in the Soviet Union began immediately, and a new dynamic gradually began to replace the homogenizing force of Stalinism in East-Central Europe.

Post-Stalinist trends – development of statist pluralism, and the return of the past

The period of high Stalinism (1945–52) brought indeed a revolutionary rupture with the past, and the forced imposition of a foreign model on all of the nations of East-Central Europe. However, with Stalin's death and the beginnings of destalinization in the Soviet Union, the region's politics began an evolution which over the next thirty-six years (from 1953 until

1989) was marked by two major trends: the gradual emergence of a statist interest-group politics, and the revival of pre-communist cultural, traditional and national characteristics of each society. Both trends are important for understanding the legacy of this period for post-communist democratization.

Once the Stalinist terror of the early postwar years was over, political discourse within the party, and then increasingly outside the party, evolved towards abandonment of the classic Leninist system, and towards more significant openings of political life. This dynamic was limited by Moscow's political will to maintain its dominance in East-Central Europe, and the Soviet leadership intervened many times to prevent the political discourse within Poland, Czechoslovakia and Hungary from formally abandoning the Leninist model, the party-state monopoly, in favour of a democratic pluralism.

After the death of Stalin, Soviet politics signalled the first political 'thaw' with the ending of the new purges (the so-called Doctors' Plot) and the arrest and execution of Lavrenti Beria, Stalin's last secret police chief. In fact, as Khrushchev recalled in his memoirs, the Communist Party of the Soviet Union essentially carried out a military-backed coup against the NKVD (renamed KGB) terror apparatus, and put safeguards in place to assure that a blood purge would never again be unleashed against the party. This partial thaw of 1953–4 expanded over the next three years of intra-party succession struggle into Nikita Khrushchev's famous 'Secret Speech' to the 20th Party Congress in 1956, a broad though still selective denunciation of Stalin's misdeeds and failures, and a launching of the first wave of 'destalinization'.

In 1953–54, the new Moscow collective leadership moved quickly to restore normal diplomatic relations with Tito's regime in Belgrade; in 1955 a Soviet delegation led by Khrushchev and Bulganin visited Belgrade to normalize relations. Tito in turn visited Moscow in 1956 after Khrushchev had denounced Stalin's crimes at the 20th Party Congress of the CPSU; the Cominform, designed by Stalin to enforce rigid bloc unity, was dissolved in April of 1956. Ideological differences could not be fully eliminated, but the partial reconciliation meant a grudging Soviet acceptance of an independent communist regime in Yugoslavia, beyond Moscow's control. In Soviet ideological terms, the road of 'national communism' was no longer the object of vilification.

In Eastern Europe, destalinization campaigns of various intensities now blossomed, with varying outcomes. In Hungary, destalinization led quickly to the ouster of the hardline Rákosi regime and the installation of a reform communist government under Imre Nagy. Nagy went so far as to include non-communists in his cabinet, but when he proposed taking Hungary out of the Warsaw Pact, and adopting the status of a neutral state between East and West (similar to Austria under the 1955 State Treaty), this became intolerable for Khrushchev, and Moscow cracked down, provoking the October 1956 Hungarian uprising. In

Poland, destalinization led to the ouster of hardline Stalinists (who were often of Jewish origins like Ochab and Berman) from the Polish communist leadership, and the return of Władisław Gomułka, an ethnic Pole with some presumed nationalist credentials. Gomułka had been purged by Stalin in the latter 1940s as a suspected nationalist. Gomułka and his leadership faction kept the destalinization of the 'Polish October' within bounds which were acceptable to the Soviets, although just barely; there was a face-off between Gomułka and Khrushchev at the Warsaw airport, in which Gomułka threatened to oppose with military force any attempt by Moscow to intervene in Poland as it did in Hungary. One result of the Polish destalinization campaign was the decision to abandon forced collectivization of Polish agriculture, and to instead allow small private family farms to continue their operations, a clear deviation from the Soviet model and from totalitarianism. In Czechoslovakia on the other hand, the hardline leadership under Antonín Novotný was able, for more than a decade, to forestall more than superficial destalinization (which made the Prague Spring of 1968 all the more dramatic as a repudiation of past policies and practices).

Destalinization was the first stage in the gradual decompression of political life after Stalin's death; it revived, at least for party leaders, some political space for discussion and debate, without the threat of secret police terror being unleashed against the losers in any policy conflict. At first this easing of political terror was limited to the party itself, but gradually it carried over into the larger society. After destalinization, it became easier to identify policy and interest 'groups', and to talk about hardline and reform 'wings' or 'factions' within the communist parties of the region. Although formal intra-party faction-alism was, in Leninist practice, still politically taboo, destalinization was an opening wedge for a kind of institutionalized but not democratic pluralism of interests within these societies (cf. esp. Skilling and Griffiths, 1971). In the aftermath of the failed Hungarian Revolution, the regime of János Kádár proclaimed a new policy of reconciliation ('who-ever is not against us, is for us'), which did not require explicit loyalty to the communist party or government, but only restraint from open political opposition. Especially within the ruling Hungarian and Polish parties, reform and orthodox factions became more visible over time, representing varying policies and social interests (but always within the basic constraints imposed by Moscow, which included the maintenance of the Leninist party in power, suppression of direct political challenges, and loyalty to Moscow and to the Warsaw Pact).

A second wave of political reform arose in the late 1960s and 1970s, under the general banner of 'liberalization'. This phase of political evolution encompassed the Polish regime under Edward Gierek, the New Economic Mechanism of the Kádár regime, and most prominently the Czechoslovakian 'Communism with a Human Face', the Prague Spring of 1968. Liberalization in Poland and Hungary was mainly a response to growing desires of citizens for better consumer goods, and more of the middle class lifestyles that now were broadly available in the Western democracies. With the ending of mass terror as a result of destalinization, ruling parties sought a new kind of social compromise with their people; a more satisfying consumerism in exchange for political acceptance, or at least passivity. The Polish regime under Gierek practised what Jeff Goldfarb has called 'repressive tolerance'. Goldfarb recalls his experience in 1974 in Lublin:

> On the day of the theater festival, a special delegation from the Soviet Union was commemorating Soviet-Polish friendship. And so the Polish authorities, who usually demonstrated little tolerance for unsupervised public activity, were especially touchy. Ordinarily, their attitude to youth theater involved a typically socialist sort of repressive tolerance. Youth theater was viewed by those at the top as a carefully controlled safety valve for critical students. It kept them off the streets, out of politics. The students could create a fictive world of critical judgment, but through censorship and controlled publicity, that world was contained, and at the same time its mere existence gave an appearance of liberalism. (1992: 4)

This limited and seemingly stunted liberalization of the 1970s played an important role at that moment when the Soviet Union no longer applied its hegemonic control.

> In Poland and the other countries of Eastern and Central Europe, there was some real tolerance contained within the socialist repressive tolerance, and it led to the development of dynamic movements of political transformation initiated by citizens as autonomous agents. In the Soviet Union, when the repression was lifted, first the change came from above and then there was confusion and disorder below. (1992: 4)

In his recalling of these events after the fall of communism, Goldfarb re-evaluates just how important this limited liberalization had been:

> For the authorities, youth theater was a safety valve. For those involved in these events, well understanding their situation, it was a base of resistance, to be expanded whenever possible. They were not dissenters, they were oppositionists. They were the precursors of Solidarity, glasnost, and the fall of communism. (1992: 7)

The Hungarian Kádár regime, with the official launching of the New Economic Mechanism (NEM) in 1968, liberalized its agricultural policies, its trade with the West (especially Austria), and its policies toward small enterprise, especially in the service sector. Peasant families were able to rent land from collective farms for their own use, small family-run businesses sprang up in the cities associated with the growing service economy and tourist trade, and a thriving commerce developed with

Western markets, especially along the Budapest–Vienna nexus dating from the times of the Austro-Hungarian Empire. New consumer goods trade with the West also expanded, especially after the normalization of relations with West Germany under the Brandt/Schmidt governments in the 1970s, which allowed for a modest boom in East–West trade and finance. Along with this came greater regime tolerance in culture and the arts, and in the social sciences. A long process of economic commercialization was set in motion, so that at the point of regime change in 1989–90, Hungary had advanced farther down the road of marketization and privatization than other former communist societies. It is, as they used to say in communist political jargon, no accident that the 'gradualist approach' to marketization and privatization was associated mainly with Hungary, since this slow evolution from central planning to market-type economics had been developing for over twenty years in that nation. In the realm of economic reform, Hungary travelled quite far from the classic GOSPLAN Soviet model, with the tacit approval of Moscow. In both Poland and Hungary, new middle class lifestyles and a consumer culture (very imitative of Western styles) made their appearance in these communist societies; communist regimes now tried to co-opt popular materialist desires rather than suppress them. One price for these economic liberalizations was, for Poland and Hungary, a growing indebtedness to Western banks and governments, a debt trap which by the 1980s had made Poland and Hungary dependent on further Western credits for supporting the new consumer-oriented culture.

The Prague Spring was a more far-reaching liberalization, sponsored by the ruling communist party in Czechoslovakia, especially the constituent Czech Communist Party (the reform impulse was significantly weaker in the Slovak Communist Party). Party secretary Antonín Novotný had prevented the first-round destalinization from running its course in Czechoslovakia, but by late 1967 the reformists within the Czech Communist Party were ready to revolt against this hardline course. Beginning with a revolt in the Writers' Union, reform communists quickly and decisively defeated the conservative old guard and took over the Czech Communist Party. A reform leadership team, headed by Alexander Dubček (a Slovak), Oldrich Cernik, Josef Smrkovsky, Jiří Hajek, Frančisek Kriegel and Ludvík Svoboda, launched a series of reforms designed to humanize communism in Czechoslovakia, to build a communism with a human face. In a matter of months, press censorship was suspended, freedom of speech flourished, independent voices from outside the communist party joined in public debate, new voluntary citizen organizations were formed, and in short, a new civil society began to emerge, pressing forward towards a free and open society. A new relationship was worked out between the Czech lands and Slovakia, which gave equal status to the Slovak republic within the new federal Czechoslovakia. Economic reform was also envisaged, involving significant decentralization of economic decision making and greater worker participation in industrial enterprises. Most troubling for the Soviet leadership, however, was the decision of the Prague reformers to permit genuine electoral competition, to allow voters to decide whether the communist parties should remain in power. Independent public opinion polls (which were allowed during the Prague Spring) showed strong popular support for the Dubček reform team; this political liberalization did in fact amount to real democratization, and it included virtually all of the freedoms of press, speech and assembly required for free and fair elections.

'The many organizations, new and old, began to go through an internal process of democratization, replacing conservative with more progressive leaders through genuine elections, and proclaiming their intention of acting as interest groups in the proper sense, representing concerns of their members' (Skilling, 1970: 287–288). Even though the Prague Spring was relatively short-lived, its long-term impact was tremendous: Josef Blahoz suggests that 'the events of 1968–69 did serve to revive democratic values and left a lasting trace in the political consciousness of the population. This brief democratic renaissance also left an enduring hatred for the Soviet Union, a political value now imprinted indelibly on the thinking and feelings of a majority of the population, however concealed by extraneous manifestations of friendship' (1994: 232).

This liberalization was a reform project of a different Marxism, a Marxist humanism, which inspired Eastern European intellectuals in the 1960s (Avineri, 1968; Kolakowski, 1968; McLellan, 1970; Ollman, 1972) from the popularization of the works of the young Marx, giving rise to a Marxist vision of human emancipation which could be used against the entrenched communist party-state and its bureaucratic controls over the individual citizen. The '2000 Words' proclamation written during the Prague Spring, and the writers in the Zagreb journal *Praxis* (Mihailov, Stojanovic) throughout the 1960s were close to the spirit of the young Marx.

For the Brezhnev leadership in Moscow, this 'communist humanism' was an ideological challenge against which, in the course of 1968, they warned the Prague Spring leaders repeatedly. Having accepted the new Dubček regime initially, the Soviet leadership became convinced that this experiment in communist humanism presented an alternative to the Soviet model which could spread throughout the region (Rothschild, 1989: 170–171).

Yet despite Soviet pressures, Prague's liberalization politics continued to gather momentum; a new Extraordinary Party Congress was scheduled for 9 September, a party congress to elect new leaders by secret ballot after open discussion of issues. This Extraordinary Party Congress was apparently the trip-wire for the Soviet leadership, who then scheduled the military intervention of 20–21 August, to put a halt to the

Prague Spring and 'normalize' the Czechoslovak regime. Even after the intervention had begun, and the reform leaders had been arrested and taken to Moscow, the Czechoslovak Communist Party held an emergency congress which ousted the minority hardliners (Husák, Bilak, Indra, Strougal) who had supported the Soviet invasion, and reaffirmed its support for the reform communist leaders being held captive in Moscow. Czech passive resistance to the Soviet occupation was impressive, and the Soviets did allow the reformers to formally return to office, but only temporarily. Over the next several years, the reform leaders were first demoted and then forced from political life, press controls were gradually reimposed, and independent organizations banished. This 'normalization' process finally removed from the party ranks anyone who still supported reforms, and imposed instead an orthodox and completely non-innovative leadership team to run the country. For all intents and purposes, the Czechoslovak Communist Party over the next twenty years ceased to have any political discourse of any interest, and after the democratic changeover of 1989 the political legacy of this 'normalization' (especially in the Czech lands) was that of an ex-ruling party with virtually no learning capacity for the post-communist era, a situation quite different from the Polish and Hungarian parties (Mahr and Nagle, 1995).

Suppression of the Prague Spring, the Soviet assassination of 'socialism with a human face', turned many young Czech, Polish and Hungarian intellectuals away from Marxism or socialism of any sort, with many later embracing the opposite ideological pole of *laissez-faire* capitalism, as embodied in British Thatcherism (Goldfarb, 1992: 29–31). Among dissident intellectuals, the end of the Prague Spring signalled the end of the dissident Marxist project for a humanist class politics in a democratic socialism; now many leading dissidents (Václav Havel, Adam Michnik, George Konrád), turned to what Ivan Szelenyi has called 'antipolitics,' the oppositional 'struggle of *civil society* against *those in power*' (Szelenyi et al., 1997: 206). Thus, 'a politics of a new ethics was counterposed to politics based on class divisions, to the politics based on manipulating particularistic interests.' (p. 207) This accounts for the later ability of the opposition movements in the 1980s to include liberals, reform socialists, nationalists and religious leaders under an umbrella movement to challenge the communist state; it also helps to account for the difficulties that former oppositional groups experienced in representing emerging social interest groups in the early years of post-communism.

Communist-era liberalization was a second step away from Stalinist politics; it carried with it a recognition, in both economic and social policy, of the basic autonomy of citizen desires, and tried to accommodate these interests while still maintaining a general acceptance of the existing regime and its institutions. Scholar Sidney Ploss (1965) advocated an interest group approach to the study of policy making in the 'system-management phase' of communism. Zygmunt Bauman, echoing Ploss a decade later, argued that: 'The theoretical model of totalitarianism – i.e. this methodological refutation of the applicability of analytic categories made to the measure of Western political experience – has been gradually abandoned, replaced by a plethora of concepts which, their apparent diversity notwithstanding, bring into the open models employed by Western scholars in describing their own societies' (1976: 82). The Canadian scholar Gordon Skilling in particular viewed communist evolution as progressively moving toward a system of interest group representation, in which 'the single party must fill many roles performed in other systems by various institutions and, above all, must serve as a broker of competing interest groups' (1966: 435). One group of Western scholars viewed this liberalization process already in the latter 1960s as the inevitable emergence and halting political recognition of a more pluralist society with increasingly differentiated and autonomous interest groups, which political elites would try to accommodate in some sort of political bargaining (cf. Bertsch and Ganschow, 1976; Farrell, 1970; Fleron, 1969). In this view, these communist societies could no longer be usefully analysed from the totalitarianism model, and their overall evolution should be compared with other non-communist societies using similar methods and data where available. Even many scholars who believed that 'liberalization' and 'democratization' had run their course by the mid-1970s, and had been reversed in some cases (most notably Czechoslovakia), now wanted communist studies to utilize the general approaches of the social sciences, and break through its self-imposed isolation. This convergence of communist studies and social science generally in the West was connected to the clear understanding that these regimes had now exited from their earlier 'mobilization system' phase into a more institutionalized 'system-management phase' (Janos, 1976: v).

Michael Waller has argued that there were in fact four different strands of interest group formation within the communist system, not all of them supportive of a later democratization. There were the recognized groups within the system itself, which over time became one basis for interest group politics: 'The role of what Griffiths termed "tendencies of articulation" was to grow with time, as technical and administrative competence became less rare and more vocal, constantly pressing against the limitations imposed by the communist power monopoly (Skilling and Griffiths, 1971). The debate over change in the Soviet Union and in Eastern Europe was conducted, not on the floor of a parliament, but within the administrative, technical and academic elite' (1994: 136). But in addition to this important source of group formation, there were the 'cliques and mafias' which formed as a part of the pathology of the power monopoly at the centre: 'But these cliques and mafias contributed nothing to the development of democracy within the womb of communism . . .' (1994: 136). Thirdly, there were the mass organizations, theoretically intended as loyal 'transmission belts' for the party and state, but which, by the 1980s, began to develop autonomous roles, especially the youth leagues and peace councils. Finally, there were the churches, especially in Poland and in East Germany, which managed to lead a semi-autonomous existence throughout the communist era, developing a dynamic coexistence with the regime. These were what Waller terms 'growth points' for autonomous or semi-autonomous interest group formation, from which democratization would start after the formal end of communist power in 1989–90.

As this interest group formation proceeded, the original regime ideal of constructing, from state propaganda and mass agitation, a new Soviet man, or a new type of communist personality, who would behave in an altruistic fashion from inner conviction, disappeared from the political agenda. Liberalization politics assumed a greater autonomy of society apart from the state, and a practical need of the communist state to respond to social pressures. It seems clear in retrospect that the liberalization reforms would have gone further in Hungary if Soviet controls had been reduced or eliminated; it is virtually certain that the Prague Spring, if the Soviet Union had allowed it to proceed, would in a short time have produced a relatively democratic politics for Czechoslovakia, under the leadership of the reform communists. The evolutionary drift of domestic politics in East-Central Europe was in the direction of liberalization, though not without internal conflict, but it was the reactionary weight of Soviet power that slowed that process and, as a last resort, forcibly ousted reform communists.

Democratization was the final stage in the political discourse under communism before its demise. Liberalization had advanced the discourse of reform beyond destalinization, by widening the scope of reform to include the interests of the general public in economic and political matters; the Prague Spring had in fact bordered on a reform communist democratization project, while the Hungarian NEM had quietly and gradually introduced marketization and commercialization on a broad enough scale to change the face of Hungarian economics. With the challenge of Solidarity in 1980–81, however, the political debate turned to democracy, the illegitimacy of communist party rule over society, and the demands by society for democratic participation. Although Solidarity was nominally a trade union, and began with trade union demands and tactics, its great appeal in 1980 was as a vehicle for Polish opposition to the monopoly of power by the Polish communist party. In its early years, the intellectuals who advised Lech Wałęsa and who spoke for Solidarity envisioned a self-governing society, a democratic society apart from government power and the professional bureaucracy (Singer, 1981). Both in its short legal existence during the regime of Stanislaw Kania and in the first years after its suppression under the martial law regime of General Jaruzelski, Polish Solidarity built an impressive network of social, educational and economic operations which were an integral part of that vision of a self-governing, radically democratic, society. Although Solidarity would evolve into something quite different by 1989, and shortly after gaining power would splinter into numerous conflicting cliques and parties, for most of the 1980s it stood for the ideal of democracy, and its aims were nothing less than a democratization of Polish society.

The key to a qualitative breakthrough in the politics of democratization rested with a basic political change in Moscow. The politics of democratization was revived and accelerated with the ascension to power in the Soviet Union of Mikhail Gorbachev in March of 1985. Gorbachev's reform agenda of glasnost, perestroika and *demokratisatsia* signalled the end of an era of stagnation in political thinking (the Brezhnev–Andropov–Chernenko years), and serious reform initiatives in virtually all areas of Soviet life. Over the next several years, Gorbachev opened the gates for free and wide-ranging discussion and debate; press censorship was largely abandoned, dissidents (Sakharov among them) were released from detention or internal exile, and previously taboo subjects (Katyn massacre, Molotov–Ribbentrop protocols, corruption in high places) publicly aired. The whole idea of glasnost was a public discussion of the many failings of the Soviet system, as a prerequisite for reform of the economy, government and foreign policy.

With respect to democratization, Gorbachev and his reform team scheduled and carried out the first competitive elections for the new Congress of Peoples Deputies in February–March of 1989. For many citizens, this was the point at which they felt free from the fear that the authorities could restore the old order, and confident that the momentum for democratization could not be stopped. Gorbachev's *demokratisatsia* also clearly legitimized efforts by both dissidents and reform communists in Hungary to end the communist party's monopoly on political power in that nation; by spring 1989 Hungarian opposition political parties were coming into open public debate on the scheduling and structuring of multi-party elections for a new president and a new parliament. Then Gorbachev announced that the Soviet Union was scrapping the Brezhnev doctrine, admonished the anti-reformist leadership in East Germany and predicted that those who resisted change would be punished by history.

Change in the direction of real democratization was now on the agenda for the Soviet Union, and the accomplishments under Gorbachev by early 1989 gave hope and support to those in all of Eastern Europe who in one way or another wanted to break with communism. With its Soviet orthodox support gone (or at least severely weakened), hardliners in Eastern Europe now faced the situation of dealing with citizen demands for democratization on their own. The old men (Honecker, Husák, Jaruzelski, Zhivkov, Ceauşescu) of the old regime were now unable to play the Moscow card against democratic reform both within their own parties and within the society at large. Only in Romania did one entrenched leader, the maverick communist Nicolae Ceauşescu, attempt a bloody Beijing-style 'Tiananmen solution' to cling to power by brute force, and this attempt was quickly reversed by his own army commanders. More importantly, however, a good portion of the ruling party organization also accepted democratization, and did not put up organized or militant resistance to the collapse of the old institutional order.

The other overarching trend, the return of the pre-communist past, represents the gradual decompression of cultural life in each of these societies, and the search for historical, traditional roots and identities. It includes also the surprising continuities in behaviour from the pre-communist era that emerge (or re-emerge) both within opposition groups and within the ruling nomenklatura. It accounts for the growing diversity among communist regimes, the development of specifically Hungarian, Czechoslovakian and Polish characteristics and traits in politics, economics and cultural life.

Joseph Rothschild, writing just before the 1989 collapse of communism, had argued that by the 1980s, East-Central Europe had moved to re-embrace its own past practices, though in the context of a socially and economically transformed environment – historical continuity had reasserted itself within the evolution of the communist regimes.

> To our predecessors and teachers, the Stalinist imposition of monopolistic Communist rule appeared – quite understandably – to be a profound revolutionary rupture with earlier patterns, traditions, and histories. Today, we are more impressed with the survival and resurgence of political continuities from the interwar period in such dimensions as the styles and degrees of political participation, the operational codes and cultures of political elites, the processes of recruiting these political elites, their definitions of economic priorities, and so forth. This emphatic difference between the perspectives of the 1950s and those of the 1980s need not be surprising. The tension between the principles of continuity and of change is the motor of history, and great revolutions . . . embody the tension in a particularly acute form. And the longer the time elapsed since the zenith of the revolutionary paroxysm, the more palpable become the threads of continuity, which not only survive but resiliently reassert themselves even after the seemingly most disruptive of revolutionary upheavals. (1989: 222–223)

For Rothschild, the return of the past also meant that, by the 1980s, the communist regimes represented a form of statist or *dirigiste* politics of development which looked in historical perspective surprisingly familiar. Speaking about the style of governing among the communist elite, he notes:

> As regards a major functional responsibility of this elite – the setting of economic priorities in order to achieve rapid modernization – its choice of strategy, though imitated from the Soviet model, also happens to be an

unacknowledged continuation of the policy of bureaucratic-politicians of the 1930s in most of the area's states: to give top priority to industry, spearheaded by heavy metallurgy, while squeezing the necessary capital investments out of agriculture, consumption, and foreign credits. Nor is this particularly surprising, since the repertoire of possible paths to belated yet rapid modernization is, after all, limited, and the decision makers of the 1930s were no more free-market capitalistic entrepreneurs than are the contemporary ones; rather, both sets are state-capitalistic bureaucrats. State capitalism and state direction of the economy were quite extensively developed in interwar East Central Europe, and in this dimension, the policies of the postwar Communist regimes have expressed a high degree of strategic continuity within a setting of ideological change . . . (1989: 224)

Within the realm of culture as well, the past had revived and reasserted itself in each nation. Far from having succeeded in imposing a uniform socialist culture or carrying through a proletarian cultural revolution,

the persistence and resilience of distinct and diverse political cultures within the matrix of common Communist institutions is quite striking and lends support to the often maligned, much abused, and admittedly imprecise notion of national character. . . . Without going into depth or detail, one can assert that, at a minimum, the citizens of each East Central European nation perceive their particular state as having a moral and historical significance far beyond being a mere unit in a supposed 'socialist fraternity' of states and peoples. An old Leninist–Stalinist adage has been reversed: culture in contemporary East Central Europe may (or may not) be 'socialist in form' but it is very much 'nationalist in content'. (p. 225)

These are important and contentious points, since Rothschild is arguing that the future after communism would, for both communists and oppositionists, contain much continuity with the past, including the unhappy interwar period of rampant nationalism and failed democratization. His sense of historical swings from a period of great change, followed by a period of tradition-oriented restoration, is of course a commonplace notion among historians; it can be extremely impressionistic and imprecise. What elements of the past will survive to reassert themselves – certainly not all, and not necessarily in their precise earlier form. Societies can also learn from past calamities, so that not everything is simply repeated over and over. In East and Central Europe, the decimation of the Jewish community and the expulsion of the German minority have changed the ethnic landscape in several countries so that a resurgent ethnic nationalism could not simply repeat past practices.

One might argue that, having already experienced some nostalgic return to tradition even in the last stages of communist rule, the pendulum might again swing toward innovation and change with the sudden collapse of the old order. The revivalist argument cuts both ways: while many historical patterns of the prewar era survived Stalinism to reappear once again, this argument also foreshadows potential return or survival of communist-era practices and socialist value culture after some initial period of upheaval and great change (democratization and marketization).

What is the historical legacy? What is its impact for democratization?

What can we learn from this historical legacy? In one sense, the experiences of these nations with democracy, with freely elected and popularly responsible government, have been limited, even for the Czechoslovakian case. The regional experiences of social and political pluralism, and aspects of democratization from earlier eras, up until 1989, had failed to consolidate political democracy as the 'norm' for political discourse among elites and citizens. Even the interwar Czechoslovakian democracy did not carry a wholly positive legacy, and it could not survive both Nazi aggression and Western betrayal.

On the other hand, these nations have made progress in developing as nation-states; they are now, through the most unfortunate of reasons, more homogeneous than ever before in their histories, and have a much longer history of national sovereignty than after the First or Second World Wars. They enter the era of post-communism with greater territorial security than in prewar years (although there are lingering elements of Polish irredentism with regard to Vilnius and of Hungarian irredentism with regard to several neighbours). The inter-regional border conflicts and territorial anxieties which permeated the interwar period seem now unlikely to return.

During the Cold War period, the communist regimes in practice evolved a sort of statist interest group representation which was not nearly so monolithic as the concept of totalitarianism would indicate. In the post-communist transition, some forms of state-oriented interest group politics might well be expected as a carryover from this evolution, especially in those areas of the economy and in those social institutions which are most closely state-connected. The continuation of statist interest group politics for some sectors might not meet ideals for building a civic culture, but it represents one organizational basis for democratic politics of competing and organized social interests, rather different from the often-presented image of the atomized and passive society which communism supposedly produced.

At the same time, the return to diversity in the region had begun long before 1989, and the shaping of political, cultural and economic life in Poland, Hungary and Czechoslovakia had increasingly deviated from the Soviet model, which during the Brezhnev era of political stagnation had ceased either to inspire or to convince. East-Central European societies had in this view already begun the process of distancing from Moscow which would be accelerated during the Gorbachev reform years, and which would finally end the fiction of system uniformity. A considerable diversity had been achieved by the 1980s, so that Hungary's 'goulash communism' (the NEM) under Kádár looked very different from the 'normalized' orthodox Czechoslovak regime of Husák and Strougal, or from the prolonged social struggle between the Polish martial law regime of General Jaruzelski and the outlawed but resilient Solidarity. Intra-regional diversity in East-Central Europe was already increasing from different local struggles and local political choices.

British historian Timothy Garton Ash has recently announced that 'Eastern Europe no longer exists' (1997). In fact, he has now also dropped his support for the term 'Central Europe' which he helped to popularize in the 1980s. Garton Ash instead argues that this is a period of disorder and reformation, affecting all regions of Europe, including Western Europe. In this sense, the concept of the 'lands between' would seem to be of little use, since there is no sense of what models or threats will appear to the East or to the West. This is a good point, since it allows for the possibility that the nations of this region (if we may still call it East-Central Europe for convenience) will find their own special path for political and economic development. And yet, despite the changes now under way in Western Europe, which are steadily under-mining the Keynesian welfare state, there is still a strong Western discipline and a Western model being applied or overlaid on the earlier Soviet discipline and model. In this sense, these lands are still 'lands between' in terms of external influences.

But these 'lands between' are not territorially threatened by an expansionist Russia or Germany as before. With greater security, their politics can seemingly afford greater tolerance of domestic difference and dissent without fears of undermining national sovereignty and integrity. These societies are also much more urbanized and indus-trialized (overly industrialized unfortunately), and they have a fairly well-educated population and a more differentiated social structure. This legacy too may lend itself to support for a democratic pluralism.

Most hopeful however for these 'lands between' is that the inter-national environment of the current era is strongly supportive of political democracy, of the forms of citizen liberties and freely elected and responsible governments which have since the Second World War become well established in Western Europe, in the nations of the European Union and NATO. The nations of East-Central Europe have been strongly influenced by the success models of their stronger neigh-bours: in the interwar period by the fascist models of Italy and Germany, and after the Second World War by the Soviet model, although not through free choice. In the interwar period, democracy seemed to be a failure in Europe, and in the early years after the Second World War, the Soviet Union seemed to offer a successful model for industrialization and military strength. After 1989, however, there can be no doubt as to the success model to emulate, and there seems to be no visible alternative. This great historical difference bodes well for democratic prospects now as never before.

PART TWO

THE EMERGING POLITICS OF THE NEW DEMOCRACIES

3

Conceptualizations of Transition: Early Dichotomies and Evolving Complexities

CONTENTS

The sudden and spectacular events of the autumn of 1989 gave the impression that the defeat of communism represented clear rational choices for a democratic politics, a capitalist market economy, and a pluralist civil society. Perhaps in those heady days it was predictable that overly simplified visions of the post-communist order would predominate among analysts in the East as well as the West. The Cold War dichotomy had become an institutional framework for analysis, and gave credence to the thought that post-communism must reshape Europe along the lines of the clearly victorious Western model. Without past models for the rapid demise of an ideology, or time for careful scholarship on the accelerating changes, early conceptualizations of these events and their future consequences were quite naturally broadly speculative. With some hindsight from the late 1990s, we can now view post-communism in more complex terms as befits the experience of each country. This chapter deals with the evolution of conceptualizations during the 1990s, emphasizing the reasons for rethinking the nature of the transitions, the meanings of 'joining the West', and the variety of potential longer-term outcomes from post-communism.

After the autumn of 1989, the mainstream concept was an optimistic vision, expressed succinctly by President George Bush, of a Europe free and whole. Scholars and intellectuals were more careful in their pronouncements but the overarching vision was similarly optimistic (Dawisha and Parrot, 1994; Garton Ash, 1990; Goldfarb, 1992; Stokes, 1993). While details of democratic institutions (Anglo-Saxon or Continental, parliamentary or presidential, proportional representation or single-district plurality electoral systems) needed to be worked out, this almost seemed secondary. Likewise, the development of functioning market economies would be achieved one way or another (gradualism or shock therapy, privatization by coupon schemes, auction, or buyouts). The term 'normality' was often used (normal politics and normal economics) to identify what would now be achieved and its time frame was thought to be quite modest, perhaps only a few years. Helmut Kohl's promise that eastern Germany would achieve Western standards of living in three to five years contained all the ingredients of the optimistic scenario: parity with the West within a few years, only winners and no 'losers', and no need for significant Western sacrifice or Marshall Plan-type aid. This early formulation of the post-communist era encouraged overblown illusions which would soon lead to bitterness and a new alienation.

To be sure there was a pessimistic minority view that the collapse of communism created a dangerous vacuum which potentially could be filled by ethnic nationalism and intolerance rather than by liberal democracy and pluralism (Hockenos, 1993; Ignatieff, 1993; Jowitt, 1992; Pfaff, 1993). These worries were given substance by the ethnic bloodletting in ex-Yugoslavia. The pessimists tended to see the future of post-communism as a return to the destructive practices of the pre-communist past more than any quick 'joining the West'.

Disillusion quickly set in when the social, economic and psychological costs started to sink into popular consciousness in the first years of transition. After only a few years, ex-communists won elections in Lithuania, Poland and Hungary. Was this the beginning of a return to communism? Were the new democracies so weak that they would fail within just a few years (the Weimar Republic syndrome reincarnated)?

The disappointments of the early optimists have been matched by the unrealized doomsday scenarios of the early pessimists. Ethnic warfare, while terrible in its consequences in ex-Yugoslavia, Chechnya and Nagorno Karabakh, has not spread like a virus across the region, but rather was contained, albeit without courageous peacemaking by either local elites or foreign powers. By the middle of the decade, the countries of East-Central Europe all managed to post positive economic growth. The return to government of ex-communists through democratic elections did not signal any return to communism, but rather indicated a strengthening of democratic competition and democratic change of government (Linz and Stepan, 1996: 454). A few years later, parties without communist roots were again victorious in Poland (1997) and Hungary (1998), and for the first time in Romania (1996) and Bulgaria (1997). Observers who took a longer-term view of the transition have been rewarded for their patience. For example, when ex-communists seemed able to hold onto power indefinitely in Bulgaria, Larry Garber correctly suggested 'the need to view a first election as part of a continuing process and to avoid premature characterization of a transition as complete or as failed' (Garber, 1992: 136–137). More realistic scenarios now vary widely in the vast middle ground between prosperity and stability ('joining the West') and chronic underdevelopment and instability ('joining the Third World').

With some greater time perspective and practical experience, the original picture has become more complex, and the time frame for analysis has been lengthened. Whereas polar dichotomies dominated early conceptualizations, now many hybrid conditions are being recognized. However, the original goals of transition, anchored in the political discourse since 1989, have not disappeared but have been reworked in accordance with ongoing trends. We now examine several key components of the transition discourse to illustrate the evolving framework for understanding post-communist democratization, including the issues of European unification, joining the Western institutions, and bringing East-Central Europe into compatibility with the Western model.

Unifying Europe

After 1989, West and East Europeans envisioned a united, prosperous Europe, free of the Cold War tension between the Soviet and Western blocs. The post-communist countries were free to pursue their own international political and economic agendas, admittedly with some constraints. A voluntary alliance with Moscow was almost universally rejected as an undesirable remnant of the communist era. Instead, these countries chose a 'return to Europe', a return to their asserted historical roots. But the early euphoria of joining the West began to evaporate for several reasons. Large-scale economic assistance or free and fair trade were not the top priorities of the West European countries; rather, they focused on the double digit unemployment at home and coming to terms with the financial pressures to retreat from the Keynesian welfare state. The EC/EU became consumed by 'introspection and self-doubt' (Hyde-Price, 1996: 4) caused not only by the economic malaise but also by the inability of the West Europeans to develop a viable strategy to end the ethnic turmoil in the former Yugoslavia. While Eastern Europe continued to look westward, Western Europe looked inward.

Across the Atlantic, Presidents Bush and Clinton likewise failed to develop cohesive strategies to address the political, economic and security needs of the transitional countries. Discussions over the best use of the 'peace dividend' virtually ignored the needs of the transitional countries in favour of domestic concerns. With the Cold War over, the United States preferred to leave European issues to the Europeans. American foreign policy was focused on areas of greater strategic importance – the Middle East and the oil-rich Persian Gulf region.

The war in ex-Yugoslavia created further disillusionment about the prospects for a united, peaceful Europe from the Atlantic to the Urals. People began to look critically at the other multi-ethnic states for signs of turmoil. The spectre of large waves of refugees pouring into the West to escape ethnic cleansing or economic catastrophe further dimmed hopes for unity. Although remarkably peaceful, the demise of the Czechoslovak state also raised questions about a wider European democratic order, particularly because this clearly went against the will of the majority in both parts of the federation, and was never put to popular vote. In hindsight, the collapse of the three federated communist states (the Soviet Union, Czechoslovakia and Yugoslavia) was not surprising, since in each case 'the very identity of the state had been questioned' (Eyal, 1997: 3). Forced federations of disparate socioeconomic and ethnic groups proved untenable when the political elites were released from Moscow's grip.

By the mid-1990s, Easterners remained greatly disillusioned about the prospects for successful integration into the prosperous, stable Western institutions, and for good reason. The economic downturn in the East was far more severe than anticipated. Even as the post-communist countries began to post positive economic growth, unemployment and inflation remained high, average standards of living remained low and social inequalities began to rise. East-Central Europe was far from ready to join the West in an economic union. In addition to the economic problems, political problems surfaced between Hungary and Slovakia and Hungary and Romania over the protection of minority rights. Russia, demoralized by the loss of its status as a world superpower, again became a worrisome political player as it sought to reassert its role in the international relations of the region. Finally, the European Union and NATO were not as welcoming as the initial post-Cold War rhetoric had led East-Central Europeans to believe.

It is impossible to generalize about the transition process due to the considerable economic, political and cultural diversity which existed in the region in 1989. The communist countries never formed a homogeneous bloc despite popular stereotypes and the habit of grouping all countries into one category, the 'Soviet' or 'Eastern bloc', nor would they progress along the same trajectory toward democracy and a market economy. 'Eastern Europe' was a convenient geostrategic description coined by NATO states for the Cold War era. Czechs proudly point to the fact that Prague lies some one hundred miles farther to the west than Vienna, and the citizens of the Baltics generally feel a closer affiliation with the Nordic countries than with Russia. As Soviet dominance waned, and the differentiation of cultures became apparent, the West was forced to start looking at these individual states as they perceived themselves (Sheehan, 1997: 19) and respond accordingly.

Joining the West European institutions

A number of early scenarios were proposed for the former communist countries in the post-Cold War economic, political and security orders. The three prominent strategies, according to Michael Sheehan, were the nationalist model, pan-Europeanism and joining/rejoining the West. The nationalist strategy of which Sheehan speaks is not one of ethnic-nationalist competition but instead emphasizes maintaining the national sovereignty achieved after nearly fifty years of subordination to Moscow. Having fought long to achieve their own identity in the inter-national arena, it was not expected that these states readily would join the European security order dominated by the only remaining super-power. These countries feared once again losing their identity and having to subordinate their international interests to those of the United States and the West European powers.

In the initial post-transition phase, the emphasis in international relations was on developing cooperative military, economic and political relations with one's immediate neighbours, both East and West. Diplomatic efforts focused on dismantling the old Soviet order: a negotiated removal of Soviet troops, the breakup of the Warsaw Pact and the Council for Mutual Economic Assistance, and settling the various bilateral debts which had to be recalculated in convertible currency. Diplomatic negotiation rather than military undertakings were the chosen means to resolve border disputes between Eastern states. The ethnic conflict in ex-Yugoslavia did not spill over into other Balkan countries (the region feared to be most vulnerable), though by mid-1998 it was continuing to spread in Yugoslavia, with ethnic Albanians in Kosovo being violently repressed.

These countries were constrained in their economic development due to limited access to Western markets, the non-competitiveness of their products and the economic slowdown in the West. Despite these problems, trade relations with other socialist countries often were quickly abandoned in pursuit of trade with the more profitable West. The rush to purchase Western goods only deepened the recession in the

East but a pendulum effect began to occur as these countries realized the need for greater economic self-reliance. A number of bilateral and multilateral trade agreements were reached, the most notable being the Central European Free Trade Agreement (CEFTA). This originally involved only Poland, Hungary and Czechoslovakia (and later its successor states) but Slovenia and Romania later joined, Bulgaria is slated to become a member in 1999, and the Baltic states and Ukraine have also expressed interest.

The characteristic feature of pan-Europeanism 'was the belief that the end of the Cold War had made it possible to fundamentally reshape the European security order' (Sheehan, 1997: 20). The new security order might be founded on a vastly strengthened Conference on Security and Cooperation in Europe, backed perhaps by the force of a European military unit, without the dominance of the United States. It was believed that the end of the competition between the two Cold War camps would also open up the space for the development of a more mixed economic system between Anglo-American market capitalism and state socialism. However, pan-Europeanism proved to be overly idealistic and disappeared from the agenda in 1992 (Sheehan, 1997: 20). The fear of military dominance by Russia, fears of the development of rogue Soviet successor states, and the inability of the European Union to develop a meaningful response to the Yugoslav crisis led to the realization that the United States would continue to play a critical role in the European security order. The brief search for alternative security arrangements was replaced by the active pursuit of full NATO membership at the earliest possible juncture. In economic terms, constraints placed by the IMF and World Bank, as well as the dependence on West European markets, put a quick end to idealistic searches for alternative economic systems.

The third international relations strategy, 'joining the West', quickly became the norm. The dual collapse of the CMEA and the Warsaw Pact left the Eastern states outside of multilateral economic and security arrangements at a time when their political and economic stability were most threatened. Attention quickly turned to Western institutions in hopes of regaining stability. While economic, military and political integration with Western associations was the goal, bilateral and multilateral ties within the East would remain important components, especially as peaceful relations with one's neighbours is a prerequisite to membership in Western alliances. The collapse of the communist bloc came at a time when the European Community was in the throes of a debate over the relative merits of deepening (West) European integration versus widening the Community. This debate intensified with knocks at the door by East European aspirants. Already facing an identity crisis, the EC was unprepared to handle many of the issues which expansion to the East would entail.

Integration of post-communist countries into Western alliances has been uneven, and often a factor of how much the West must sacrifice.

The earliest integration into a West European multilateral institution was with the Council of Europe. Established in May 1949 with a mandate to foster pluralistic democracy, human rights and the rule of law, it was the first integrative European organization founded after the Second World War. The Council began to reach out to the communist countries during the era of glasnost, with visits by its Secretary General to Hungary in 1987 and Poland in 1988. In June 1989, the Council offered guest status to Hungary, Poland, Yugoslavia and the Soviet Union, and to Czechoslovakia the following May, but full membership depended on holding fully democratic parliamentary elections. Thus, Hungary became a member in November 1990, Czechoslovakia in February 1991 and Poland in November 1991. The Czech Republic and Slovakia were admitted as separate states in June 1993 (Hyde-Price, 1996: 191). The Council offers expertise in the areas of law, human rights and minority questions and fosters cooperation in the fields of culture, education and scientific research. Perhaps most importantly, it has served as a venue for informal dialogue between countries. Romanian Foreign Minister Adrian Severin, a former guest parliamentarian, has stated that contacts with his Hungarian counterparts in the Assembly proved useful in achieving better cooperation between the two countries (Blocker, 1997a).

The Council of Europe is viewed by many Eastern states not only as a moral voice but also as the gateway into the EU since Council membership is considered the rubber stamp of approval that a country has satisfied the EU's democracy criteria. However, in recent years, considerable criticism has been leveled at the Council for what appears to be a dilution of its admission standards, first in 1993 with the admission of Romania and later of Albania, Ukraine, Russia and Croatia. It is widely believed that political pressure from France, Germany and other EU members led to the acceptance of otherwise unqualified countries. 'The reason is said to be EU's reluctance itself to grant early admission to Eastern states and its desire to throw a sop to them with Council membership' (Blocker, 1997a). The special guest status could have been used more judiciously to encourage those states which had not yet passed the Council's democracy litmus test but who appeared committed to democratization. Such countries would have benefited from the Council's consultative structures but only could have earned voting privileges after a proven commitment to pluralistic democracy.

The Conference on Security and Cooperation in Europe (CSCE), begun in 1972, was the only multilateral organization during the Cold War which brought together East and West European states (as well as Canada and the United States) in an effort to ease tension. The process culminated in the Helsinki Conference of 1975 and accords on security matters, human rights and cooperation in the realm of cultural, scientific and environmental concerns. The CSCE suffered from institutional limitations: it was a process, rather than an institution with formal structures and mandates, and its agreements had to be adopted unanimously but were merely political statements 'of intent and commitment' rather than legally binding treaties. Nevertheless, the CSCE kept human rights on the international agenda and served as a critical East–West forum on security matters (Hyde-Price, 1996: 240–241). Because of this facilitative role and its inclusion of the United States, many East European leaders hoped that the CSCE could take the leading role in the post-Cold War European security order. Small member states in particular hoped that its pluralistic nature could be used as a counterweight to the dominant powers (Mason, 1996: 159).

In late 1990, the member states signed the 'Charter for a New Europe' spelling out their commitment to a liberal economic and political order. The Conference was insitutionalized with the establishment of a permanent secretariat in Prague, the Conflict Prevention Centre in Vienna and an institution in Warsaw to monitor elections (Mason, 1996: 158). Since December 1994, the CSCE has been known as the Organization for Security and Cooperation in Europe to reflect its more institutional nature, and it currently consists of fifty-four members: all the European states, the United States, Canada, and some Central Asian Republics. The OSCE focuses on developing a new, comprehensive security arrangement; fostering greater economic cooperation, especially regarding the free movement of capital, goods and services; and improvements in the 'human dimension' (including protection of human and minority rights, securing free and fair elections, a free press and the rule of law) (Eggleton, 1997).

Early proposals for the CSCE to form the basis of an organization to replace both NATO and the Warsaw Pact proved to be overly idealistic due to its institutional limitations and the United States' commitment to preserving NATO's role in Europe. The clearest example of the CSCE/ OSCE's limitations as a guarantor of international security was its inability to act effectively in response to the war in ex-Yugoslavia, largely due to its lack of enforcement mechanisms.

The dissolution of the Warsaw Pact in 1991 led some to believe that NATO was another Cold War remnant which could be dissolved. However, the spectre of ethnic warfare in other countries and the potential security threat posed by Russia led even the most idealistic pan-Europeanists to conclude that formal security arrangements were still necessary. In 1991, Václav Havel warned that 'our countries are dangerously sliding into an uncertain political, economic and security vacuum. . . . it is becoming increasingly evident that without appropriate external relations the very being of our young democracies is in jeopardy' (quoted in Hyde-Price, 1996: 230). NATO, for its part, did not immediately embrace the countries which had thrown off communism, in part to mollify Moscow. A key component of NATO's security arrangement is the organization's commitment to aid any member state under attack, and NATO feared becoming entangled in dirty ethnic wars. Debates arose regarding sharing the costs for inclusion of the Eastern countries. The United States felt that it had carried the financial burden of the alliance too long and let it be known that the Europeans would have to assume greater responsibility; Europeans proved to be just as reluctant. Finally, neither NATO members nor East Europeans have been able to articulate the appropriate role of the alliance in a post-Cold War Europe. With the Yugoslav conflict, NATO has begun to transform its identity from one of a transatlantic security alliance committed to the defence of Western Europe to that of an organization committed to the security of the entire European continent.

NATO formalized institutional relations with some Eastern countries by establishing the Partnership for Peace programme in 1994. This promotes military cooperation between NATO and the former Warsaw Pact countries and provides training through joint military exercises in order to help Eastern troops prepare for membership. In July 1997, NATO announced that the Czech Republic, Hungary and Poland would be the first eastern members. Formal membership is expected in early 1999. The Baltic states were disappointed at not being included in the first round (largely so as not to provoke Russia). Romania's membership was championed primarily by France, but overridden by the United States due to the relatively short period of healthy democracy in Romania. Slovakia was not included in the first round either, due to the domestic political conflict between President Kovac and Prime Minister Mečiar, the treatment of ethnic Hungarian minorities, and irregularities in the democratic order. Both NATO and the first prospective new members made it clear that this expansion was only the first wave in a process which would be open to any European country demonstrating a commitment to democracy and peaceful neighbourly relations.

The post-communist governments often had unrealistic expectations of what NATO membership would mean for their state security. 'Many even tended to view NATO membership as a panacea for all their problems. If they got in, they would be taken care of and their security would be assured. But if they did not, then they would be left without hope of a secure future' (Goble, 1997a). In the intervening years, these countries have come to better understand NATO's limitations. It exists to defend its members from outside aggressors and was never intended to deal with internal strife or to confront forces which can undermine already weak states, such as illegal migration, organized crime, subversion of the banking system, drug trafficking and widespread social disorder caused by uneven economic growth. Increasingly cognizant of the limitations of NATO, the ex-communist countries nevertheless continue to pursue membership as they strive to become 'normal' members of the European family.

The most prized membership is that of the European Union, as this is widely regarded as the crucial factor for long-term economic prosperity. However, 'of all Western Europe's multilateral groups, the

European Union has promised the most and delivered the least . . .
since the fall of the Berlin Wall' (Blocker, 1997b). In the initial years of
the transition, German Chancellor Helmut Kohl and French President
Jacques Chirac repeatedly promised EU membership to the first Eastern
states by the year 2000 but this has proved unrealistic for reasons both
internal to the EU and specific to the ongoing economic transitions. As
the full extent of economic dislocation in the East became apparent and
the economy slowed across Western Europe in the early 1990s, hopes
for relatively smooth and quick integration of the former CMEA
countries began to dim. The European Community, plagued by internal
problems, chose to turn inward rather than outward at the Maastricht
Summit of 1991. In fact, the Maastricht plan for deepening the Community may be viewed as a defensive reaction to the collapse of the
communist bloc (Blocker, 1997b).

In late 1991, the European Community signed Associate Agreements
with Czechoslovakia, Hungary and Poland which outlined the steps for
the establishment of free trade areas over a period of ten years, called
for the alignment of the associate members' laws with EC laws, and
established institutional links to coordinate this alignment. No membership guarantees or time frames were included but the intent of
membership was clear from both sides. In June 1993 the EC detailed the
prerequisites for membership: the establishment and stability of democratic institutions including the rule of law, respect for human rights
and the protection of minority rights; a functioning market economy
capable of withstanding the competitive pressure and market forces of
the EC/EU; and the ability to meet the political, economic and fiscal
obligations of membership (Sheehan, 1997: 21). For the first time,
expansion to the East became the EC's official policy (Blocker, 1997b). In
July 1997 the European Union announced that the Czech Republic,
Hungary, Poland, Slovenia and Estonia (and also Cyprus) would be
invited for talks in the first wave of eastward expansion. It is not
expected that membership will be granted before 2002, more likely 2004.
By the end of 1997, the EU had announced that membership talks with
Bulgaria, Latvia, Lithuania, Romania and Slovakia could begin later.
The outreach to these countries was in response to heavy lobbying by
those left off the initial invitation list, often with the public support of
the new invitees.

The commencement of membership talks with Eastern countries
by no means signifies that they are in the final stages of achieving
membership. It took seven years for Spain and Portugal to attain
membership after the commencement of entry talks, and it is expected
that the process for the former communist countries also will be
lengthy. At a 1997 EU summit, Helmut Kohl blocked attempts at the
institutional and decision-making reforms necessary for expansion
(Blocker, 1997b), backsliding somewhat on his earlier commitment. The
EU is divided between those who believe that such reforms must

precede the next expansion and those who wish to put off the reforms until after expansion begins. It appears that significant institutional reform will be forced upon the EU sooner rather than later, as the Union already has deemed such reform necessary if enlargement would lead to a Union composed of more than twenty states.

The EU cannot afford to maintain the current level of financial assistance to its members, much less extend that to new members. Presently, about 80 per cent of the EU budget goes to the Common Agricultural Policy (CAP) and the structural funds (the European Regional Development Fund and the Social Fund) (Hyde-Price, 1996: 204). The CAP already has proven to be a politically divisive issue in Western Europe. Attempts to curtail generous subsidies to farmers have resulted in angry, highly visible public demonstrations by French farmers. The inclusion of Poland and other Eastern states could double the amount of money paid out under the CAP, according to some studies. Germany is opposed to increasing the structural funds, while Spain is demanding that the level of assistance to current members not be cut. Without an increase in funds, the addition of new members, all of which are poorer than the existing member countries, would result in a politically unsustainable redistribution of existing moneys (Mihalka, 1997).

The process of integration into the different Western organizations is forcing these institutions to rethink their *raison d'être*. All run the risk of becoming unmanageably large and face significant restructuring both of their institutions and their policy making processes. Despite such complications, they would find it difficult to refuse membership to qualified candidates.

Why the variegated development in East-Central Europe?

Timothy Garton Ash's commentary that in Poland it took ten years to defeat communism, in Hungary ten months, in East Germany ten weeks and in Czechoslovakia ten days, overlooks pre-1989 trends through which some countries positioned themselves more favourably for inclusion in Western multilateral institutions. By placing human rights on the international agenda, the 1975 Helsinki accords empowered many dissidents (Albright, 1992: 15–18) and gave rise to organized opposition movements in Poland and Czechoslovakia. While some societies could point to a healthy opposition (Poland, Czechoslovakia and Hungary) or a proud heritage of revolution against the government (Hungary and Poland), other communist countries were without strong democratic tendencies in their political culture. While the declaration of martial law in December 1981 and the subsequent crackdown on Solidarity ended the dialogue of democracy between the Polish ruling party and the opposition for the time being, discussions of democracy continued in the underground press, laying important groundwork for the later 'revolution'. Martial law was a response to signals from Moscow that the Polish opposition movement had got out of hand, for it risked spreading to other countries. Had a more reformist leadership been present in Moscow, Poland's transition to democracy might well have begun in 1980–81. When the signals from Moscow changed under Gorbachev, General Jaruzelski experimented with greater openness and reform. In 1986–87, during visits to Warsaw Pact countries, Gorbachev indicated that he wanted the pace of reforms to quicken, to which Poland and Hungary acceded. While Gorbachev did not interfere directly in the internal policies of Eastern bloc countries, communist leaders who resisted the reformist path found their authority undermined as Gorbachev took his appeal directly to the people during his travels in the region. The failure of some communist parties to embrace reforms in the 1980s made the transitions more difficult, though not impossible, as evidenced by Czechoslovakia. Though lacking a reform wing within the communist party after the crushing of the Prague Spring, Czechoslovakia had a small but strong democratic elite who, together with non-ideological technocrats, formed the core of the post-communist governments.

Free and fair elections often serve to consolidate regime changes which have taken place, and not necessarily as the progenitor of democracy. In the period from June 1989 to June 1990, all the independent countries of Eastern Europe, except Albania, held elections which served as referenda on communism. While Czechoslovaks, Hungarians and Poles clearly rejected the bankrupt communist systems, Bulgarians voted for a somewhat reformed communist party (the Bulgarian Socialist Party) and Romanians retained in power members of the old guard who had taken over after the palace coup which eliminated Ceauşescu.

With democratic systems in place, there was still no clear picture how these societies would develop. J.F. Brown commented that broadly speaking, two paths awaited the former communist states: civil society 'based on law, constitutionality, and liberal values' or 'the retrograde path toward traditional ethnic divisiveness' (1991: 248). At the time of Brown's writing, there was very grave concern about the possible eruption of ethnic wars beyond Yugoslavia, particularly in the Baltics (with their Russian minorities), Romania (Transylvania) and much of the former Soviet Union. Fears of a return to a period of sustained ethnic conflict proved to be exaggerated, for they overlooked the fact that history did not end in 1945 for the countries of the Eastern bloc. The communist era marked a period of irreversible social and economic development in comparison to the previous era, with high rates of literacy, urbanization and social mobility being achieved by many ethnic groups.

Even more than the progress toward democracy, there is significant differentiation in the level of economic development. While Poland and Hungary got a head start during the late communist era, this alone does not account for their positions as leading countries in the transition. The Czech Republic also has been at the forefront for most of the transitional phase, although it had not experimented with market-type reforms prior to 1990. The Czech Republic had the advantage that, unlike Hungary and Poland, it was not saddled by heavy foreign debt at the time of transition, nor did it have a large, outmoded agricultural sector. Furthermore, upon the split with Slovakia, the Czech Republic shed most of the unprofitable defence industry, the decline of which contributed to the initial recession in Slovakia.

Post-communist Europe is characterized by different levels of joining the West. In the early years of the transition, regional specialists already began grouping the countries according to their progress. The 'northern tier' (J.F. Brown, 1991), or 'first tier', countries contrasts with the 'southern tier' (Tismaneanu, 1992: 93) or 'second tier'. Charles Gati (1996, 1997) speaks of leaders, laggards and losers and Paul G. Lewis (1997) differentiates between 'Group 1' and 'Group 2' countries. Though the terminology differs, there is general consensus as to which countries belong among the top performers: Poland, Hungary, the Czech Republic and often Slovenia and Estonia. For Brown, writing shortly after the demise of communism, the Baltic states form the leading edge of the second tier, while Gati includes the Baltic states plus Slovenia in his category of leaders. Lewis includes Slovenia as a 'probable' Group 1 country but since his categorization does not include any states of the former Soviet Union, it is not clear where the Baltics would stand in his framework. Slovakia is categorized as a 'laggard' or 'Group 2' country although it, along with Bulgaria, is at the leading edge of this category. Rounding out Lewis' Group 2 countries are Romania, Croatia, Albania and Serbia. Completing Gati's list of laggards are Romania, Albania, Croatia, Serbia, Macedonia, Bosnia-Herzogovina, Russia, Ukraine, Belarus and Moldova. The losers are all in the former Soviet Union: the dictatorships of the Caucasus and Central Asia, which remain largely unreformed and oppressive (Gati, 1996, 1997: 351–352).

A number of cultural and historical factors contribute to the differentiated development. One factor often cited as advantageous is the Western Christian orientation of the northern states versus the Eastern Orthodox tradition (which is viewed as morally passive) of the southern ones. Gale Stokes points out that the three revolutionary movements of the post-Stalinist period occurred in the traditionally Western (Catholic or Protestant) countries while none occurred in the Orthodox countries. The key element of the religious tradition, according to Lewis, is the greater emphasis on collectivity in Eastern Orthodoxy, versus the emphasis on the individual in Western Christianity (1997: 6). This might help explain why few opposition elites emerged in Southeastern

Europe but one must recall that the communist regimes in Bulgaria, Romania and Albania were very orthodox and tolerated neither popular nor internal party dissent (Lewis, 1997: 7). While the religious/cultural tradition may have some validity, Stokes cautions that, because it is so widely accepted, it stands in the way of other explanations (1993: 50) and it also reflects a Western ethnocentrism. Furthermore, if the Catholic culture, once thought inimical to democracy, was able to change, why not the Orthodox culture (Miller et al., 1998: 10)?

For the 'southern tier countries', notably Romania, Bulgaria and Albania, 'the challenge of creating a lawful state based on accountability of the government and separation of powers is further aggravated by the relative weakness of political traditions of independent activism during the phase of the civil society' (Tismaneanu, 1992: 174). These countries had few revisionist Marxist thinkers who, in Hungary and Poland, provided much of the opposition before 1968 and helped open the intellectual space for party reform. The Hungarian opposition can be traced to the 'Budapest school' of humanistic Marxist philosophers which developed in the 1960s and centred around György Lukács, the minister of culture in Imre Nagy's 1956 cabinet (Stokes, 1993: 87).

The degree of political instability under communism is another factor differentiating first from second tier countries. The political instability in first tier countries was not just the threat from below but also the threat from within the communist party as reform elements battled the orthodox leadership. As a result, different patterns of elite–mass relations developed than in the countries to the southeast. The impact of these alternative patterns can be seen in the post-communist era in terms of earlier political party consolidation and more constructive political debate between government and opposition. Those countries without political turmoil during the communist regime retained the communists in power longer than those with reform movements, leading to a later start of political pluralism.

The development of civil society in Poland, Hungary and Czechoslovakia is cited by many analysts as a critical factor in the strength of their post-communist systems. Broadly speaking, civil society comprises the organizations and mediating institutions between the individual and the state (Chapter 4 offers a more complete treatment of this topic). While the communist regimes retained control of society in general, certain spheres were open to the development of civil society, namely religion in Poland but also a limited freedom of expression through the samizdat press. Gradual party reform in Hungary and Poland in the 1980s was complemented by steady pressure from below. The relatively tolerant attitude on the part of Hungary's communist party opened the space for the development of political parties prior to the collapse of communism and by the mid-1990s, Hungary had arguably the most stable, solidified party system in the post-communist countries. Reform elements within the communist parties in Hungary and Poland broke

TABLE 3.1 *Comparison of the standard of living of East-Central European states with the European Union, 1995/6 (GDP per person as a % of EU average)*

Slovenia	59%
Czech Republic	57%
Hungary	37%
Slovakia	34%
Poland	31%

Figures for Slovenia and the Czech Republic from 1996; others from 1995.

Source: Adapted from *Economist*, 28 February 1998, p. 55 and Sheehan, (1997: 22)

from the more orthodox wings in the waning days of communism and, as the successor parties, formed some of the closest approximations to social democratic parties in the region. The mode of exit from communism is also a strong factor differentiating Group 1 from Group 2 countries. Whereas Group 1 countries made a clean break with the communist past in 1989 due to the influences of social movements and counter-elites, Group 2 transitions resulted from 'the rearrangement of elite forces' which led to a slower process of democratization (Lewis, 1997: 8).

Finally, higher levels of socioeconomic development tend to favour Group 1 countries, though this advantage should not be overstated. Modernization theory holds that higher levels of socioeconomic development are more conducive to the development of democratic pluralism, but overall, Lewis rejects modernization theory as an explanation for *why* democracy is likely to occur, for it never has been able to demonstrate a clear cause and effect relationship (1997: 13). He does cite the level of socioeconomic development as useful in explaining the *sustainability* of democratic practices, though. Widespread poverty, income gaps and maldevelopment within a country could lead disadvantaged groups to seek redress through non-democratic means, or to support anti-democratic (nationalist, populist, communist) parties in the electoral process. At the start of the transition, Group 1 countries had higher GDP per capita than the Balkans, with Hungary and Czechoslovakia having a much smaller percentage of the workforce employed in agriculture than did Bulgaria, Romania and Albania. (The size of the agricultural sector in Poland is fairly close to that of Bulgaria, but still below that of Albania and Romania.) Slovenia, a strong contender for Group 1 status, has the highest GDP per capita of the former communist countries (see Table 3.1).

Charles Gati, while recognizing clear differentiations within the region, remains far more pessimistic about the overall prospects for all the countries. According to Gati, the transition to market democracy

TABLE 3.2   *Public satisfaction with development of democracy, 1991 v. 1994[a]*

	1991	1994	Trend
Czech Republic	−25	−9	+16
Hungary	−19	−43	−24
Poland	−21	−40	−19
Slovakia	−55	−62	−7
Estonia	−21	−26	−5
Latvia	−9	−42	−33
Lithuania	+23	−31	−54
Albania	−17	−33	−16
Bulgaria	−6	−87	−81
Romania	−11	−36	−25
Average	−16	−40	−24
European Russia	−51	−75	−24

+ = satisfaction, − = dissatisfaction

[a] Results are expressed as the percentage of positive responses minus the percentage of negative responses.

Source: Gati, 1996, 1997: 345. Reprinted by permission from M.E. Sharpe, Inc., Armonk, NY.

had neither failed nor succeeded in any country by the mid-1990s. While there are clearly leaders and laggards, Gati doubts whether these countries remained committed to the Western ideals of pluralist democracy and market economics after the first half-decade of the transitions. Comparing the results of the Eurobarometer surveys from 1991 and 1994, he sees a clear pattern of retrenchment across the region, including in the leading countries. Taken together, the results show 'a systematic challenge to the essential characteristics of Western-style democracy'. While most people appreciate the features of liberal democracy, 'they reject the way democracy is working and long for a strong, paternalistic leader who would presumably look after their welfare' (Gati, 1996, 1997: 344). The people of East-Central Europe may reject the way that democracy and capitalism are functioning but we would argue that this has not caused most to seek paternalistic leadership, but rather competent leaders untainted by corruption.

Table 3.2, which illustrates the responses to the question, 'On the whole, are you very satisfied, fairly satisfied, not very satisfied or not at all satisfied with the way democracy is developing in your country?' shows a measurable drop in popular satisfaction with democracy from 1991 to 1994. The figures given are the percentage of positive responses to the above question minus the percentage of negative responses. The results show that in 1991, the number of respondents expressing satisfaction with the development of democracy exceeded the number expressing dissatisfaction only in Lithuania, but by 1994 in no country did the number of satisfied respondents exceed the number of dissatisfied respondents. Even more discouraging is the fact that the level of dissatisfaction increased over the level of satisfaction in all countries except the Czech Republic. While in the Czech Republic the satisfaction deficit decreased by 16 points, it increased in all other European countries by an average of 24 points. But while the satisfaction deficit in the Czech Republic greatly narrowed between 1991 and 1994, the overall level of satisfaction still remained negative in 1994. This is significant, since the Czech Republic to that point had experienced very stable party politics and a remarkably peaceful, smooth divorce from Slovakia (which nevertheless was unpopular with the majority of the citizenry).

Given these results, Gati asks why Western governments continue to see progress in the region and is very critical of what he sees as the West's hasty dismissal of the numerous setbacks in the democratization process.

> Election results revealing the appeal of reformed or unreformed ex-communists and demagogue nationalist parties are explained away as a 'protest vote', preference for 'familiar faces', or simply the return to 'experienced administrators'. As poll after poll shows immense and increasing dissatisfaction with the region's democratic parties, the significance of such attitudes is minimized as an 'understandable reaction' to the initial dislocations that accompany the introduction of democracy. The disparity between the few who are rich and the many who are poor – a major source of social strife – is seen as an inherent problem of 'early capitalism'. The power wielded by criminals and the atrocities committed by them are being compared to the Chicago of the 1920s and thus excused. (1996, 1997: 341)

According to Gati, the main reason for the disparate views is that the East and the West have different criteria for evaluating the transitions. In the transitional countries, people ask themselves, 'What have I gained from the changes that have taken place since 1989 or 1991?' while in the West, the dominant themes are the institutions and structures of democracy: 'Compared with the communist era, do the governments respect political rights and civil liberties? Are the elections more competitive, and is the press freer? Is there a more impartial legal system?' (Gati, 1996, 1997: 345). Because the democratic *processes* are functioning reasonably well, the answers to these questions from Western analysts are largely affirmative, at least for the first tier countries. There are now few election irregularities and the press is independent of the government. However, the elections have not always resulted in the election of the 'best and the brightest', nor always in the formation of workable coalition governments. Repeated attempts by politicians to influence the media, while not ignored by the West, are not seen as real threats to the democratic process. A more nuanced interpretation would show that such actions undermine the development of civil society necessary for the consolidation of liberal

TABLE 3.3   Public belief in a market economy, 1991 v. 1994[a]

	1991	1994	Trend
Czech Republic	+39	+11	−28
Hungary	+52	+20	−32
Poland	+47	+26	−21
Slovakia	+29	0	−29
Estonia	+32	+14	−18
Latvia	+43	−5	−48
Lithuania	+55	+9	−46
Albania	+45	+41	−4
Bulgaria	+45	−2	−47
Romania	−5	+50	+55
Average	+38	+16	−22
European Russia	+8	−44	−52

+ = right, − = wrong

[a] Results are expressed as the percentage of positive responses minus the percentage of negative responses.

Source: Gati, 1996, 1997: 348. Reprinted by permission of M.E. Sharpe, Inc., Armonk, NY.

democracy. The people of the transitional countries are far more interested in the *substantive* achievements of the new political system and, most importantly, whether it has increased their individual prosperity. By the mid-1990s, a deep cynicism had set in, directed at Eastern politicians for their unrealistic electoral promises and at Western leaders for their unfulfilled promises of economic assistance.

The level of satisfaction with the market economy, while more promising, still offers cause for concern. Table 3.3 illustrates responses to the question 'Do you personally feel that the creation of a market economy that is largely free of state control is right or wrong for your country's future?' In contrast with the perceptions of the performance of the democratic system, these results show that, in general, people in 1994 were more accepting of the liberal economic system than the liberal political system. However, in all the countries except Romania, a growth in the percentage of people rejecting the market system as the right one for their country exceeded the growth in the percentage accepting it as the right system. Again, the Czech case is worth noting, since the satisfaction deficit grew by 28 points, more than the regional average. This is surprising given the relative ease of the economic transition in the Czech Republic. Not only had economic growth returned by 1994, but the dislocation associated with the transition was far less severe than in other countries, with unemployment remaining very low. However, the decline in real income was comparable to other countries and could account for the growing dissatisfaction. Gati warns of retrenchment in the economic sphere, of the desire for 'neo-egalitarianism' (1996, 1997:

TABLE 3.4 *Public agreement with the direction of the country, 1991 v. 1994*[a]

	1991	**1994**	**Trend**
Czech Republic	+37	+25	−12
Hungary	−19	−34	−15
Poland	+13	−29	−42
Slovakia	+13	−39	−52
Estonia	+30	+17	−13
Latvia	+47	−9	−56
Lithuania	+28	−49	−77
Albania	+45	+41	−4
Bulgaria	+38	−39	−77
Romania	+26	−6	−32
Average	+26	−12	−38
European Russia	−12	−51	−39

+ = right, − = wrong
[a] Results are expressed as the percentage of positive responses minus the percentage of negative responses.

Source: Gati, 1996, 1997: 351. Reprinted by permission of M.E. Sharpe, Inc., Armonk, NY.

349). As with support for democracy, this downward trend can be attributed to the lack of substantive results for the average person, or at least the gap between what was expected and what actually did result.

Overall, people are quite dissatisfied with the progress in the transitional countries. Table 3.4 illustrates responses to the question, 'In general, do you feel things in your country are going in the right or wrong direction?' In 1991, greater numbers of respondents expressed satisfaction with the direction their country was going than dissatisfaction in all European transitional countries except Hungary (Hungarians have a reputation for their pessimism). In 1994, only Albanians, Czechs and Estonians still expressed greater satisfaction than dissatisfaction and the trend was negative for all European transitional countries. According to Gati, 'What these polls show is discontent so acute and so pervasive as to invite comparison with public sentiments that prevailed under communism' (Gati, 1996, 1997: 350). He warns of a fundamental correction ahead which will likely take a semi-authoritarian form. 'The countries of the former Soviet Union can be expected to develop somewhat milder and less centralized political practices than those that once characterized totalitarian states, while the countries of Central and Eastern Europe may embrace somewhat harsher and more centralized political practices than can be found in Western democracies' (Gati, 1996, 1997: 352).

Gati sees these semi-authoritarian regimes dominating public affairs and circumscribing citizens' rights to practise civil liberties through such means as limitations on strike activities, intimidation of the media resulting in self-censorship, and the imposition of banking, tax and other regulations to limit private entrepreneurship. The characterization of semi-authoritarian regimes is appropriate for Russia, Belarus and to a lesser extent Slovakia and Romania under Iliescu but Gati does not sufficiently differentiate between states, only between broad regions, in his decidedly pessimistic prognosis. Manipulation of the press is evident even in states more committed to political pluralism, such as Poland and Hungary, but these could hardly be seen as threatening a return to semi-authoritarian rule.

Gati sees the West as increasingly willing to allow the development of semi-authoritarian regimes because nationalist regimes may be viewed as being willing to resist Russia, thus contributing to Western security (1996, 1997: 353). What Gati overlooks in his analysis is the democracy test that each NATO and EU candidate must pass before achieving membership. While the timetable for membership in these multinational organizations has been slowed as the West's commitment to the East waned, the eventual goal (for both sides) of membership and the prerequisites for that membership have not slackened.

Juan Linz and Alfred Stepan are more optimistic than Gati when viewing similar survey data. They acknowledge the simultaneity problem (the difficulty of transforming both the economic and political systems at the same time), but argue that economic difficulties do not threaten to derail the democratization process. Linz and Stepan believe 'that for imploded command economies, democratic polities can and must be installed and legitimized by a variety of appeals *before* the possible benefits of a market economy actually materialize fully' (1996: 439). While many analysts reject the need for prior state restructuring, and believe that people's pent-up demands for material well-being have to be satisfied at the same time as changes in the political system, Linz and Stepan believe that 'if assessments about politics are positive, they can provide a valuable cushion against painful economic reforms' (1996: 439). In the New Democracies Barometer surveys conducted between November 1993 and March 1994, respondents were asked to compare the functioning of the communist political and economic systems with those at the time of the poll. For six Eastern European countries, the mean percentage of those rating the communist economic system positive was 60.2 while the mean positive rating for the post-communist economic system was only 37.3. The mean percentage of those rating the communist political system as positive was 45.7 while the mean positive rating for the post-communist political system was 61.5. Such polls demonstrate that people 'are capable of making separate and correct judgments about a basket of economic goods (which may be deteriorating) and a basket of political goods (which may be improving)' (Linz and Stepan, 1996: 442).

Is there still a danger that the economic shortcomings of post-communism could derail the political reforms? In sharp contrast to Gati's

TABLE 3.5 Change in condition over the period 1989-1994

Social measure	CE	SEE	Baltics	WFSU	Caucasus
Real wages (%)	−21.6	−51.8	−57.3	−53.3	−58.7
Poverty rate (%)	+18.6	+40.7	+55.3	+50.2	+50.0
Male life expectancy (years)	+0.6[a]	−0.7	−4.3	−3.4	−1.2
Morbidity rate (%)[b]	+4.3	+6.1	+62.6	+38.5	+80
Homicide rate (%)	+23.9	+51.2	+127.7	+69.7	+687.1

[a] In Central Europe, only Hungary showed a decline in life expectancy in this period. The Czech
Republic, Poland, Slovakia and Slovenia posted net gains.

[b] Morbidity rates of 20–39-year-olds increased due to homicides, war, suicide, alcoholism and stress-
related illnesses.

Source: UNICEF, International Child Development Center (1995) 'Poverty, Children and Policy.
Responses for a Brighter Future' Regional Monitoring Report #3. Florence: UNICEF (cited in Deacon,
1997: 77).

pessimism, Linz and Stepan express optimism. Not only do the results of
the New Democracies Barometer poll demonstrate that people dis-
tinguish between the performance of the economic and political systems,
they also indicated an optimism that by 1998 (some five years after the
survey) both the economic and political systems would be rated positively in contrast with the past (Rose and Haerpfer, 1994, cited in Linz
and Stepan, 1996: 444). Linz and Stepan conclude that 'In East Central
Europe the evidence is thus strongly in favour of the argument that
deferred gratification and confidence in the future is possible even when
there is an acknowledged lag in economic improvements' (1996: 444).

The differentiation between regions of the post-communist world
goes beyond the economic and political restructuring and is perhaps
more evident when viewing changes in social conditions between 1989
and 1994. UNICEF, in a 1995 report on children and poverty, divides
the transitional countries into five different groups (see Table 3.5):
Central Europe (CE: Poland, Hungary, the Czech Republic, Slovakia and
Slovenia); Southeastern Europe (SEE: Albania, Bulgaria and Romania);
the Baltics (Estonia, Latvia and Lithuania); Western former Soviet Union
(WFSU: Belarus, Moldova, Russia and Ukraine) and the Caucasus
(Armenia, Azerbaijan and Georgia). Former Yugoslavia and Central Asia
were omitted due to the difficulty in obtaining meaningful data.

UNICEF monitored between twenty and thirty indices of social well-
being over the period 1989–94. For each of the countries, the number of
social conditions which improved is listed first and the number of
conditions which declined is listed second: Slovenia (17, 8); Poland (15,
14); Slovakia (13, 16); Hungary (12, 17); Albania (4, 6); the Czech
Republic (11, 17); Romania (9, 19); Latvia (8, 20); Georgia (5, 15); Estonia
(6, 21); Armenia (6, 23); Lithuania (6, 22); Moldova (6, 22); Bulgaria (6,
23); Azerbaijan (5, 21); Belarus (4, 21); Ukraine (4, 21) and Russia (2, 22)

(Deacon, 1997: 77). Albania, with the small sampling of statistics, should be removed from comparison here, especially in light of the turmoil in 1997 which could lead to a drastic change in conditions in the second half of the decade over the first half. The Central European states show decline across the smallest number of social welfare indices. Thus, whether economic, political or social criteria are used, a clear regional differentiation and ranking is evident.

Some reflections on changing concepts

The outline given here illustrates the evolution of understandings of what is going on under the general heading of post-communist transition. The initial understandings, and the powerful expectations that they nurtured, are still alive, but have been battered by events and rising realizations that things still are not going in a positive direction for many people. Western government pronouncements steadfastly adhere to the invitation to 'join the West' through membership in NATO and the European Union, and most of the new democratic governments of post-communist Europe, from centre-left to centre-right, press enthusiastic claims for these goals. Yet at the level of popular opinion, the disappointment with the real results of democratization and marketization is strong and has risen considerably in most countries. Even the 'success model' Czech Republic evidenced rising popular dissatisfaction during the 1997 demise of the Klaus government and bitter recognition of financial mismanagement and economic slowdown.

Time frames set by the Western powers for the realization of Eastern membership aspirations have been stretched out, and will perhaps suffer further delays, although the West cannot afford to formally abandon its initial invitation. Post-communist democratic leaders will actively press their cases but there is a danger that the broad-based public disillusion (currently expressed mainly by abstention and alienation from all politics) may be mobilized into an anti-Western, anti-elitist, nationalist populism (which has not yet materialized).

The conceptual framework has now come to grips with several new realities. The major transitions in economics, politics and especially individual psychologies, will take longer and involve more conflict. There is no assurance that countries will reach the original goal, and there will probably be many nations that fail in the attempt. The 'return to history' theme does not mean a replay of any earlier period, but signifies a recognition of the underlying strength of tradition and culture (Rothschild, 1989). Attention to differentiation of outcomes and paths, even within an integrating Europe and a globalizing economy, now plays an increasingly strong role in new conceptualizations of transitions in post-communism. The terminology of a 'multi-speed' Europe, of 'tiers' of association, or of ranked circles around a core Europe has become a new and probably long-term focus of scholarly analysis and political contention.

At the outset of democratization in post-communist Europe, a deductive conceptual model, derived from Cold War dichotomies, predominated in the discourse about the new era. With more time for reflection, the inductive process of generalization and concept-building has made its mark. Ongoing events and trends (providing new fuel for inductive analysis and bottom-up generalization) as well as the expression of principles and ideals (giving deductive direction to hypothesis formulation and testing) will continue to refine, challenge, and reform our understandings of these processes; complexity and long-term change are now part of the new landscape for thinking about democratization in this region.

4

Civil Society: Using the New Freedoms

The development of a post-communist liberal democracy requires that
societies be transformed along with the political and economic systems.
Central to the discussion is the role of civil society in creating sustainable market-based democracies but the absence of a widely accepted
definition of civil society complicates the discussion. The term is often
used loosely by Western political pundits to describe the new democracies, with little critical analysis regarding whether civil society has
been achieved and which elements might be lacking.

Broadly speaking, civil society is the space between the individual
and the state. More important is the nature of the organizations and
institutions, both independent and parastatal, which occupy that space
and issues of utilization and control of these mechanisms in the policy
process. Moshe Lewin's definition of civil society provides a useful basis:
'the aggregate of networks and institutions that either exist and act
independently of the state or are official organizations capable of developing their own spontaneous views on national or local issues and then
impressing these views on their members, on small groups and, finally,
on the authorities' (Lewin, 1988: 80). Lewin's definition allows for the
critical links to civil society development of reform communists in
Hungary and Poland, without whom the initial breakthroughs would
not have occurred. Because of civil society's role in the collapse of

communism in Poland and, to a lesser extent in other countries, the term has come to be identified primarily with opposition to an authoritarian regime. Some analysts even argue that civil society is now little more than an outmoded historical concept (cf. Krygier, 1997; Kumar, 1993).

The concept of civil society, which can be traced to Aristotle and includes the contributions of such diverse political philosophers as Paine, Hegel, Ferguson, Marx, de Tocqueville and Gramsci, was revitalized by Polish dissidents in the 1970s as a strategy for reform from below. This strategy emphasized the establishment or re-establishment of connections between members of society to act as a brake on the state (Krygier, 1997: 60). The civil society movement was intentionally self-limiting: its ultimate goal was not the overthrow of the communist state, for the events of 1956 and 1968 clearly demonstrated the limits of such an effort as long as Moscow enforced its Leninist discipline. Rather, the conscious objective was gradual social, political and economic change within the communist system in order to address the needs of society unmet by the state. The strategy proved highly successful, culminating in the establishment of the first legal, independent trade union in the communist world. The reforms set in motion by Mikhail Gorbachev encouraged dissidents elsewhere to push the limits of civil society. Its subsequent blossoming has been designated by Vladimir Tismaneanu as the 'reinvention of politics' (Tismaneanu, 1992), though not yet in the sense of freely competing interests for even up to Poland's roundtable talks in early 1989, the goal of civil society remained reform and not overthrow of the communist system.

The early gains in freedom – particularly of press and religious activity – gave the new liberalization its earliest concrete meanings for people and serve as critical underpinnings of a post-communist civil society. Furthermore, these freedoms allowed for the development of complementary intermediary institutions between state and individual interests. The range of resources available for making use of these new freedoms is enormous and for many citizens confusing, given both the socialist value culture and the culture of dependency on the state held over from the communist era. There is good evidence of popular support for the new liberties but also of disillusionment over the concentration of beneficiaries, particularly the nomenklatura. As the new political economy of individual liberty takes shape, it is helping to define the democratization trend and its deficiencies.

Civil society in transition: from a parallel force under communism to a base for liberal democracy

The destalinization campaigns of the Krushchev era loosened state controls, allowing for the establishment of limited structures of independent thought and action parallel to those of the official state organs. Grass-roots organizations were formed primarily by a small circle of intellectual dissidents who sought to moderate the policies of the state. Civil society development was highly differentiated from one country to the next depending on the degree to which the communist party withdrew from control of everyday life.

Throughout the communist era, Poland enjoyed greater economic and political freedom than other Soviet bloc countries. The abandonment of collectivization of agriculture after the events of October 1956 left a critical sector of the economy in private hands. The Catholic Church, the historical defender of the Polish nation, acquired and consolidated an autonomy that religious institutions in other communist countries never were allowed. Economic and political developments in the 1970s led to a joining of the powerful forces of intellectuals, workers and the Catholic Church in the strongest incarnation of civil society in the region. Strikes in 1976 protesting price increases followed on the heels of a petition by intellectuals calling on the party to harmonize Poland's human rights statutes with the Helsinki accords, to which Poland was a signatory (Rupnik, 1979: 78). Intellectuals formed the Committee for the Defence of Workers (KOR) later that year to mobilize public opinion and provide legal and other assistance to workers. The Catholic Church collected money for the families of workers arrested or fired after the strikes. In no other communist country was there such a coordinated effort to effect change in state policies.

The moderation of the Polish communist party created the space for the development of civil society and repeated economic crises provided the stimulus. An attempt by the government to raise consumer prices in the summer of 1980 led to a series of strikes, which the government attempted to quiet with promises of higher wages. Though this tactic had succeeded previously, workers now demanded and won the creation of an independent trade union, Solidarity. The worker/intellectual link solidified as Solidarity expanded from a labour movement to a mass social movement. The imposition of martial law on 13 December 1981 and the ban on Solidarity the following year did not put an end to civil society. Through the 1980s, the samizdat press operated as a strong parallel to the official media, enabling a relatively free civil discourse despite martial law. Constant pressure from below began to effect a fundamental change in the relationship between society and state.

Civil society in communist Hungary and Czechoslovakia was far less integrative than in Poland. Due to the gradual reforms of Kádárism, Hungary lacked the stimulus of economic crisis which was fundamental to the widening of Polish civil society. The reforms permitted limited private entrepreneurship, which resulted in the development of informal networks linking private initiatives. However, because the majority of these enterprises were conducted as side businesses in addition to one's state job, the newly developing middle class quickly became overburdened by work and concerns of getting ahead. These entrepreneurs lacked the time and energy to expand from the economic realm of civil society into the social and political realms.

The early civil society movement in Hungary had an active membership of probably fewer than one hundred intellectuals with supporters in the low thousands at most. But by the mid-1980s the democratic opposition was able to mobilize the public around the proposed construction of a dam on the Danube River. An emboldened opposition organized limited demonstrations around anniversary dates important to Hungarian nationalism (Stokes, 1993: 90–95), giving the movement further public exposure.

On 1 January 1977, some 250 Czech (and a handful of Slovak) intellectuals signed a charter calling for the respect of internationally accepted civil and human rights. Charter 77, as this group came to be known, largely refrained from attempts to widen its appeal to the masses because of the repressive nature of the Czechoslovak Communist Party. Additionally, the more severe persecution of intellectuals and the clergy prevented the type of civil society development seen in Poland (Garton Ash, 1990: 64–65).

One mechanism common to civil society in all three countries was the 'flying universities', which began around 1978 to present a more balanced picture of history and politics. Lectures were held in private homes on topics not discussed in the state media and educational institutions. In Poland and Hungary, the state essentially turned a blind eye to these activities – although participants' comings and goings were monitored, serious crackdowns were uncommon. Participants came primarily from the dissident ranks and would go on to form the early post-communist political elite.

Even with the joining of forces of intellectuals, the Church and workers in Poland, nowhere was civil society able to put down strong roots. The mass membership in Solidarity and the images from the demonstrations in Leipzig, Prague and Bucharest in the autumn of 1989 gave the impression that the transitions to democracy were engineered by the masses, when in fact they often resulted from carefully negotiated settlements between regime and opposition elites. Intellectuals in post-communist East-Central Europe failed to sustain popular participation and apply it to the new politics. The former 'movement' type political associations – primarily labour and the environment – were transformed into more formal, elite-centred political parties (Lomax, 1997).

Despite the analytical ambiguities of the term 'civil society' and the poor development of citizen participation in post-communist politics, civil society is still relevant to the development of a liberal democracy responsive to the needs of the citizenry. In order for this to happen, the institutions and norms that develop must be authentic to a country's political culture; otherwise, they will be embraced by neither polity nor leaders. Many Western analysts bring their cultural biases to the analysis of civil society. American analysts, in particular, often take a libertarian approach, emphasizing such concepts as unrestricted freedom of speech and the press while West Europeans generally take a more temperate view. Germans stress the primacy of the rule of law (*Rechtsstaat*) and accept certain limitations on freedom of speech, the press and political assembly in order to protect the state from anti-democratic excesses. Despite such restrictions, the space between individual and the state still allows for the expression of a wide range of political values, demonstrating that variations in accordance with a country's political culture do not necessarily preclude the establishment of a strong civil society.

Pluralistic civil society: collective versus individual rights

The process of building a pluralistic civil society requires resolution of the debate over group versus individual rights. After a long history of discrimination, anxious minority groups have sought protection of their collective rights within the new democracies and political leaders of the majority populations often feel besieged by such demands and struggle to strike a tenable balance between the political interests of all populations. Article 27 of the International Covenant on Civil and Political Rights from 1966 established the norm 'that the rights of individual members of a minority are protected, but not those of the group qua group' (Karkoszka, 1993: 215). Yet, equality under the law and respect for the integrity of each individual implies the right to express one's unique identity (cf. Gyurcsik, 1993) and that identity is derived from membership in a larger ethnic, religious or linguistic group. Thus, the development of a pluralistic civil society requires legal prescriptions for a balance between group and individual rights.

The recognition of minority language rights (a group right) has been a contentious issue, particularly in Slovakia and Romania, with their Hungarian minorities, and in the Baltic states, with their Russian minorities, and is linked to the concern on the part of the state over the political loyalty of ethnic minorities. Herein lies one of the implications of the recognition of group rights, for with those rights comes the responsibility not to undermine the political and geographical integrity of the majority state. A state will be unwilling to grant collective rights without a certain degree of international trust. When domestic politics of neighbouring states include calls for greater protection of 'populations living abroad', the majority leadership may retreat from policies to protect minority rights, individual or collective.

Essential characteristics of a liberal democratic civil society

Zbigniew Rau, legal adviser to Solidarity in Łódź in 1980–1, suggests that individualism, pluralism and the market constitute the essential elements for a liberal democratic civil society. Associations derive their values and receive legitimacy from the values of their individual members. Liberal democratic civil societies are pluralistic by nature because relatively autonomous associations compete for the distribution of political power, wealth and social prestige. Finally, civil society is inherently market oriented, for voluntary transactions determine the allocation of goods, services and resources. Market forces apply not only to economic exchanges, but also to political and cultural transactions. Since individualism, the market and pluralism are historical and not organic phenomena, their relative strength depends on political, cultural and economic traditions (Rau, 1991b: 5).

Rau's key components appear to have a libertarian bias, but he does not deny the cruciality of the state which facilitates civil society in all its operational spheres: the economy, politics, communication, education/ culture and religious life. Each sphere includes institutions directly established, funded or at least regulated by the state. Economically, civil society functions through banks, corporations, stock exchanges and laws governing labour relations and ownership. Politically, civil society operates through such institutions as political parties and lobby groups through which citizens seek to influence policy. The realm of communications involves the media, publishing houses and public opinion institutes which seek to shape public opinion either from above or below. Intellectual life is developed in the educational/cultural sphere through such instruments as schools and foundations. Finally, civil society operates through religious institutions, sometimes with state funding, which shape the spiritual lives of their members (Rau, 1991b: 5).

Rau's emphasis on the rights of the individual disregards the fact that collective minority rights do not automatically preclude the development of a healthy civil society. Switzerland offers a successful mode of a multi-ethnic state which guarantees certain collective minority rights, particularly in the linguistic and cultural realms. Post-communist Hungary has taken a collective rights approach with constitutional guarantees of political representation; self-administration at the local and national levels; the right to collective participation in public matters and of education in one's native language (Ígyártó, 1993: 277–278). In late 1997, the left-liberal Hungarian government proposed collective political representation at the national level through the addition of special minority seats to parliament and reducing the number of votes necessary for parliamentary representation of ethnic minorities but a vote in March 1998 postponed such representation until the 2002 elections, provided that requisite constitutional amendments first be passed (RFE/RL, 17 March 1998).

The concept of consociational democracy, developed by Arend Lijphart, offers a possible system for societies with deep ethnic cleavages. Such democracies are characterized by 'overarching cooperation at the elite level with the deliberate aim of counteracting the disintegrative tendencies' in multicultural societies (Lijphart, 1969: 211). Lijphart (1979) suggests that peaceful democratic change in a plural society requires consociational decision making including grand coalitions, segmental authority, mutual veto and proportionality. A grand coalition provides joint governance by leaders of all segments of the plural society, as contrasted with majority rule. With segmental autonomy, decision making is delegated to the individual component groups on issues exclusively relevant to them, with joint governance on all other issues. Formal or informal mutual veto would prevent tyranny by the majority. Civil service appointments and public resources would be distributed proportionally to the different groups. Within the former communist bloc, Czechoslovakia held the best promise of being transformed into a consociational democracy but its political elites destroyed any such chance.

Given the widespread disinclination to grant political rights to sizable minority populations, a legalistic approach to minority rights is more realistic. This would include a system of checks and balances; observance of the rule of law, including the independence of the judiciary; legal and institutional safeguards for freedom of expression; democratic local self-governance; and legal guarantees for a free market economy (cf. Gyurcsik, 1993). But since free market guarantees in and of themselves do not guarantee opportunity for minority business professionals, governments could offer targeted measures for minority business development.

The key elements for civil society according to Australian political scientist Martyn Krygier are a commercial economy, civility (relations between individuals should be based on trust and restraint) and tolerant pluralism. These in turn are dependent upon the state, the law and the nature of politics. An anti-state bias is apparent in most liberal but also some post-communist conceptualizations of civil society, the latter a holdover from the camp mentality of civil society against the communist state. But in post-communism, these have to develop as partner entities. 'In modern settings, the interplay between strong public institutions, such as those provided by an effective state acting within the rule of law, and strong social relations, such as those of civil society, is central to the ways in which power is exercised – by the state and in the society' (Krygier, 1997: 88).

The transition to liberal democracy requires not an end to strong state rule, but rather the change in its mandate to that of creating the conditions in which all citizens can exercise their political and economic freedoms. 'Authority must be . . . strong and unified enough to impose a single set of rules on all citizens' (Holmes, 1993: 202) but that authority must be exercised according to the rule of law, within a system of checks and balances, and with the genuine consent of the governed.

Early gains in freedom

Religion: an important force in civil society but a declining post-communist social force

During the communist era periods of intense religious persecution were interspersed with periods of a *modus vivendi* between Church and state. Immediately after the Second World War, the Polish Communist Party sought to weaken the Catholic Church by establishing and supporting pro-government Catholic organizations, but starting in 1948 the state attempted to gain complete control over the Church. Primate Wyszynski responded by alternately asserting the rights of the Church and retreating from its strong stance as the political climate required. The state responded to Church protests by arresting priests who sided with Wyszynski and creating groups of loyal priests and laymen who accused the Church of being reactionary and feudal (Mojzes, 1992: 284–285). In 1950, an accord was signed between the Church and the state, with the consent of the Vatican, under which the Church recognized the existing social order and agreed not to support activities hostile to it and the government recognized the Pope as the Church's supreme head. Despite the accord, the state continued to arrest disloyal clergymen, including Wyszynski himself. Catholic publications and religious schools were closed and a state office was established to monitor religious activities.

Following the 1956 unrest, the Party needed the Church's support to achieve legitimacy with the public (Goldfarb, 1992: 142). Wyszynski and other clergy were released from prison and restrictions on the Catholic press lifted, but the repression resumed once the state regained control over society. The millennium of Polish Catholicism in 1966 proved to be pivotal. The Church organized an extensive mix of pilgrimages, lectures, youth activities and other public events to mark the anniversary. With this increased visibility, people started pressuring the Church to take a more active oppositional role (Mojzes, 1992: 193).

The elevation of Karol Wotyła to the papacy in 1978 gave Poland a world spokesman in its struggle against communism. After Pope John Paul's visit to Poland in 1979, Poles developed a premature view that communism would soon be on its way out, a sentiment which helped energize the Solidarity movement. With its strong religious overtones, Solidarity was openly supported by most of the Church hierarchy, though some were hostile to its secular/intellectual wing. After the crackdown on Solidarity some prominent union leaders were sheltered by the Church and parish houses throughout Poland hosted meetings and speeches by regime opponents.

During the 1980s, the Polish episcopate tried to 'keep in check' the more radical members of the clergy, while the state sought not to completely alienate the Church, as it counted on it to help mediate the social crisis (Mojzes, 1992: 299). The regime even openly courted the Church, issuing about a thousand building permits for houses of worship (Nagorski, 1993: 238). But in 1984, the young Warsaw pastor Jerzy Popiełuszko, an outspoken critic of the communist regime and a strong supporter of Solidarity, was kidnapped and murdered by secret police. His murderers were put on trial and sentenced to lengthy prison terms. Popiełuszko was not the only priest to die under mysterious circumstances in this period (Nagorski, 1993: 238) but investigations into the other deaths were not forthcoming.

Full religious freedom was legally established in Poland in May 1989. With the Church no longer needed as an oppositional force, Poles increasingly express dissatisfaction with its role in society. The Church struggles to remain the pre-eminent social institution as it has plummeted in popularity, consistently drawing lower approval ratings than the military or the police (see Table 4.1). Many Poles are particularly dissatisfied with the Church's political activism and its firm stance against abortion. A concordat signed between Poland and the Vatican in 1993 was finally ratified in early 1998 after years of bitter debate. It recognizes that the Church and state are independent and commits the state to allow religious education in public schools.

Despite its large Catholic majority, Hungarian society is far more secular than Polish society and exhibits greater religious diversity. Consequently, the Hungarian Catholic Church did not play a comparable unifying role in the battle against communism. The ultimate goal of the Hungarian Communist Party from the start was the abolition of all religions. In the 1940s, Catholic clergy were arrested, Catholic schools nationalized and religious orders dissolved. The state forced the Protestant churches to sign concordats promising fairly broad religious and charitable activities, by which the state never intended to abide. Cardinal József Mindszenty defended the Catholic Church's independence and refused to sign a similar concordat. After his arrest and conviction on charges of treason in 1948, a weakened Church was forced to acknowledge its subservience to the state by signing the concordat.

Liberated from prison during the 1956 revolution, Mindszenty was forced to take refuge in the US embassy after the crushing of the revolution and the execution of oppositional clergy. Without his leadership, Church hierarchy buckled under the pressure and became more compliant. A moderation of state policies toward the Church began in the 1960s within the context of a broader liberalization programme and continued after Mindszenty's departure for Austria in 1971. Restrictions on religious education were eased, police surveillance of religious services ended, and official denunciation of the Church declined. During the communist era, Catholic activists challenged the regime on such issues as conscientious objection to military service but the Church never served as a strong moral counterweight to the party.

In early 1990 the Law on Religion granted church status to any religious group composed of at least 100 members, with written by-laws and a governing body, and whose activities did not violate the constitution or laws of the state. In 1993, an amendment was proposed to limit official recognition to churches with at least 10,000 members, which had been operating in Hungary for at least 100 years, and whose activities did not 'damage common morals' (Commission on Security and Cooperation in Europe, 1993: 9). The amendment, ostensibly designed to limit the number of religious institutions qualifying for state funding, failed. The post-communist Hungarian Catholic Church is experiencing the same problems of the modern Church in the West – declining active membership and decreased influence in people's lives (Nagorski, 1993: 248) – although religious involvement among young Hungarians is still noticeably stronger than in the communist era.

The Czechoslovak Catholic Church, the country's largest religious institution, was heavily persecuted from the 1950s and into the 1980s. The Novotný regime, unhappy with the Church's ties to the Vatican, attempted to create a church subservient to the state with measures far more repressive than in Hungary or Poland. A state office to oversee and control the activities of all churches was established and many ecclesiastic appointments came under state jurisdiction. Monastic orders were closed; clergymen were deported to forced labour and concentration camps; Church property was seized and legal restrictions were placed on religious activities (Mojzes, 1992: 163). The state fomented strife within the Church leadership and limited contact between the Church and the Vatican. Other churches were persecuted to a lesser degree. During the Prague Spring, imprisoned clergymen were released and legal restrictions on church activities suspended, but the persecution resumed after the crushing of the Prague Spring. Due to the effective persecution of the Church and the more secular nature of Czechoslovak society, churches did not play a collective role in the struggle for human rights, although individual clergymen did sign Charter 77.

Fearing the spread of social/religious activism from Poland and wary of the Pope's challenge to communism, the Czechoslovak state increased pressure on the Catholic Church in the early 1980s. The Church's previously cautious stance now gave way to a more defiant one. Clergy and laymen contributed to the samizdat press and were arrested for their activities. In 1985, Cardinal František Tomáček invited the Pope to participate in a celebration of Saint Methodius (who helped

Christianize the Slavs). Permission for the visit was denied but more than 100,000 people attended the ceremony in Velehrad (Stokes, 1993: 152). Pilgrimages to religious sites in the second half of the 1980s regularly drew large crowds, despite roadblocks and the absence of adequate facilities or public transportation (Mojzes, 1992: 182–183; Stokes, 1993: 152). Slovaks participated in far greater numbers than their more secular Czech compatriots. In 1987, a group of Moravian Catholics circulated a petition calling for separation of Church and state and for religious freedom. Responding to Tomáček's call, hundreds of thousands of people, the majority Slovaks, signed the petition. This petition drive, as well as organization of the annual Velehrad pilgrimages, was among the few large-scale activities of Czechoslovak civil society. Thus, while civil society in the Czech lands was led by a small group of mostly secular intellectuals, Slovakia's civil society centred around the Catholic Church (Stokes, 1993: 152). The pilgrimages and petition notwithstanding, the Catholic Church in Slovakia did not play a steady leadership role as did the Polish Catholic Church.

After the Velvet Revolution, the state removed all restrictions on religious activities and training. Imprisoned clergy were released and priests who had been ordained clandestinely received official assignments. The upsurge in religious activities in the 1980s quickly subsided in the free society as people no longer needed the pretext of religious activities to oppose the state.

Post-communist societies now struggle with questions of the proper role of religion in society and the degree of religious tolerance. For most of East-Central Europe, the role of organized religion in civil society is beginning to parallel that of churches in Western Europe: as a charitable organization and an alternative to public education. But in Poland (as well as Croatia, Serbia and Russia) the Church retains a high political profile.

Liberal democracy precludes an official political role for religion but does not necessarily require complete separation of Church and state. Such a separation is generally not favoured in post-communist Europe because it would end state funding (cf. Mojzes, 1992) upon which religious institutions depend. The experience of West European countries where churches are funded through universal taxes demonstrates that complete separation of Church and state is not a general prerequisite for religious liberty.

Freedom of the press: overcoming the conditioning of communist era practices

When the communists took power after the Second World War, they seized control of the media as part of the monopolization of political life. Private newspapers were nationalized and the media transformed into tools of ideological education to help create the 'new socialist man' (cf. Jurrjens, 1978). Independent groups generally were denied the right to publish. Freedom of the press was a constitutional guarantee in many communist countries but with the contradictory corollary that the press had to serve the interests of the workers or the socialist state. Through the control and manipulation of information, both internal and external, the communist regimes sought to keep a lid on dissent.

Vertical integration of the media and rigid control over financing enabled the state to use the media as 'transmission belts' to society. Directives, workplans and propaganda were transmitted from above, while affirmation of the leadership was expected from below (Goban-Klas, 1994: 13–14). Newspapers were subject to censorship with severe penalties for editors who violated regulations on content. Pieces critical of the communist system or reports of economic downturns, dissent within the party, human rights violations, or environmental and industrial accidents were prohibited. As journalists and editors internalized the state's dictates, self-censorship became normal professional behaviour. Party organs such as trade unions and women's organizations had their own publications but these served the party's interests, not the authentic interests of the organizations' members. The Polish Catholic Church was allowed its own publications as part of the policy of accommodation intended to gain greater public support for the communist party but when the Catholic media became too critical of communism, the authorities did clamp down.

International coverage glorified the achievements of the Soviet Union and denounced the imperialist tendencies and social deficiencies of the West. Interviews with émigrés from the Eastern bloc showed that people were influenced by the state's propaganda against the West, particularly regarding the portrayal of American imperialism during the Vietnam War. However, attempts by the state to convince people of the benevolence of the Soviet Union generally were unsuccessful (Volgyes, 1975a: 126).

The effectiveness of political socialization through the media was limited by infiltration by foreign broadcast systems. Radio Free Europe, the Voice of America and the British Broadcasting Corporation offered regular programming in local languages to counter the official information. Jamming of these broadcasts was used extensively in the Soviet Union but such tactics were not completely effective. Hungary and Poland were relatively free of jamming after 1956, while Czechoslovakia continued to utilize it during times of crisis (Volgyes, 1975c: 21).

The Polish media were the most active and subversive in the communist world, due in part to the historical legacy of patriotic underground journalism during the Second World War and in the years of Prussian, Russian and Austrian rule (Goban-Klas, 1994: 5, 41). The first wave of 'journalistic professionalism' in communist Poland occurred after Stalin's death when journalists began to demand greater truth in reporting. The easing of restrictions on editorial boards in 1955 further emboldened journalists. A relatively obscure youth journal *Po Prostu* ('Quite Simply') was transformed into a vehicle for exposing corruption and shortcomings of life under communism. *Po Prostu*'s impact was such that Krushchev specifically mentioned its anti-Soviet stance in his confrontation with Gomułka at the Eighth Party Plenum in October 1956 (Goban-Klas, 1994: 107). A cautious liberalization of the Polish press followed the Plenum. Western publications were more readily available and ethnic groups were allowed to publish. Even after the normalization that began in 1957, the media in Poland remained far less restricted than in other communist countries.

In the 1970s, Poland's dissidents, supported by the Catholic Church and the Committee for the Defence of Workers, established an extensive network of samizdat publications parallel to the official newspapers. After higher wages, a call for truth, openness and freedom of the press was the second of Solidarity's demands to the government in 1980. Prior to the imposition of martial law, Solidarity was able to publish with virtual carte blanche despite the continued presence of censorship laws. Afterwards, the communist regime revamped the media laws, firmly placing control in the hands of the state but at the same time offering new opportunities for journalistic professionalism. The obligations of journalists to 'serve society and the state' were coupled with the right to 'professional secrets' (journalists could not be forced to reveal their source) and access to state information (with the exclusion of state and economic secrets) (Goban-Klas, 1994: 194–195).

Attempts at journalistic independence accompanied the Prague Spring, but after it was crushed, suppression of the press was far more severe than in Poland under the post-1956 normalization. Eight hundred members of professional journalist associations were expelled and replaced by party loyalists, leading to a decrease in journalistic standards (Giorgi, 1995: 109). In Hungary, Kádárism not only allowed for a greater degree of openness by the media but also eliminated some of the systemic problems which journalists in other countries tried to bring to light. Restrictions on the content of the official media in Poland and Hungary began to ease in the late 1980s. Previously taboo subjects were explored, such as environmental degradation, drug abuse, the Katyn massacre, the deteriorating economic conditions, and the historical legacy of the Second World War. The presentation of international news became more balanced, even to the point of criticizing communist leaders who refused to embrace glasnost and perestroika.

The collapse of the communist regimes brought an immediate end to censorship. The role of the media now has shifted from being an organ of the state (or in the case of the underground media, from serving the opposition) to being the intermediary between state and citizenry, facilitating public discourse on policy issues. The end of media control also brought an end to state financing of much of the media. Because domestic capital was inadequate, privatization was often effected through joint ventures with Western media concerns. In Hungary, 80 per cent of the investment in the print media has been of foreign origin and in the Czech Republic, half the newspapers are controlled by foreign companies (Giorgi, 1995: 5). With this came the fear that newspapers would become subject to the control and influence of their Western owners. Despite extensive foreign ownership, a healthy independent print medium has developed, with a broad spectrum of political views. Major communist party papers such as Poland's *Rzeczpospolita*, Hungary's *Magyar Hirlap* and *Mlada Fronta Dnes* in the Czech Republic were able to transform themselves into balanced, viable publications.

Few samizdat publications survived, as the demise of communism brought an end to funding from political supporters, both domestic and foreign. Those that survived, such as *Lidove Noviny* in the Czech Republic and *Gazeta Wyborcza* in Poland, learned quickly that the methods they had employed during the communist era did not necessarily serve them well in an era of political pluralism. *Lidove Noviny* earned the nickname 'Castle News' for its close affiliation with President Havel. It was slow to move away from the highbrow writing which suited its intellectual dissident readership but hindered efforts to achieve broader circulation. In the 1990 presidential elections, *Gazeta Wyborcza* became a forum for attacks on Lech Wałęsa by its editor, former dissident Adam Michnik. Michnik later acknowledged that the newspaper's reputation was damaged by such tactics, as did Konstanty Gebert, a founding staff member, who commented, 'The underground press does not prepare you for today's journalism. We were excellent, honest propagandists. We wrote honestly, checking our facts. But we never wrote as critically about our own side as we did the other side' (quoted in Nagorski, 1993: 211). Heeding criticism about the paper's partisanship, the editorial staff began to practise a more balanced style of reporting and today's *Gazeta Wyborcza* is highly regarded in the region for its non-partisanship.

The transformation of the region's press into non-partisan instruments of civil society is far from complete. Without a strong tradition of free press and civil society, journalists cannot overnight become interlocutors of the democratic process. While some have called for the widespread dismissal of journalists who had worked for the state-controlled media, journalism is being transformed through other means. Sponsored by the US government, many journalists received training in the United States on such topics as investigative journalism, the need for balanced reporting and the role of editorializing. Journalists who had served as foreign correspondents in the West under the old regime have helped transform their publications back home. Andras Kereszty, the managing editor of the Hungarian post-communist daily *Nepszabadsag*, and Zdenek Porybny, editor of Czechoslovakia's *Rude Pravo*, had both been correspondents in Washington. Seeing the importance of a non-partisan media, they ensured that the connection to the communist party was severed immediately after the transition. Porybny even took the step of removing about 40 per cent of the old staff (Nagorski, 1993: 215–216).

Privatization of the broadcast media moved more slowly than privatization of the print media. In all states of East-Central Europe, some of the television channels eventually were privatized, with others remaining in state control. Such hybrid ownership is common throughout Western Europe and does not necessarily augur poorly for the development of a liberal civil society. The process of broadcast media reform reflects the ongoing struggle to define the political culture in the region. Poland's 1993 broadcast law stipulates that both public and private programming has to respect the 'Christian system of values'. That year, 78 per cent of Poles said that public radio and television should respect their audiences' religious views (Herrmann, 1993: 59). Broadcasters who violate the provision may be fined, though no body was established to arbitrate in such cases (CSCE, 1994a: 12). Although this provision violates constitutional guarantees of freedom of religion and freedom of the press, it was upheld by the Constitutional Tribunal in 1994 which ruled that Christian values are to be interpreted as universal values, not those of a specific religion (Karpinski, 1996a). In practice it has served more as a guiding force than as a mechanism of censorship.

The debate over privatization of broadcast media in Hungary proved to be highly politicized. After initial media reform, nationalist opponents of media reform complained about a decline in religious broadcasting and broadcasts to Hungarian minorities abroad (Johnson, 1993: 18). The first post-communist government of József Antall viewed the broadcast media 'as a public service that should support the government and its guiding philosophy', while the opposition declared that the media's independence was vital to the country's interests (Szilagyi, 1996e). Antall's unyielding position, as well as political manipulation of the broadcast media, contributed to the Hungarian Democratic Forum's defeat in the 1994 elections. Prior to the elections, 129 state radio employees with social democratic leanings were purged under the pretence of budgetary constraints (Szilagyi, 1996d). Many of those reporters found jobs with state television after the Socialists' electoral victory. A law ensuring broadcast media independence was finally passed in December 1995, three years after a deadline set by the Constitutional Court. Oversight of broadcast media and licensing of new channels and frequencies has been depoliticized considerably with the establishment of the National Radio and Television Board (ORTT), whose eight members are elected by parliament.

In contrast, the initial appointment process for Poland's National Radio and Television Council (KRRT) left it more susceptible to political manipulation. KRRT's nine members were appointed by the Sejm and the Senate (three each), the president's office (two) and the president (the chair). In March 1994, President Wałęsa fired its chair, arguing that the presidential right of appointment also gave him the right of dismissal. Three months later, the Sejm passed a new law removing this right of appointment and sustained Wałęsa's subsequent veto (Karpinski, 1996b: 29). In August 1997, just prior to the parliamentary elections, KRRT appointed to public television's new supervisory board seven people with ties to the PSL and SLD. Similarly, people with ties to the SLD–PSL coalition were appointed to the supervisory board for public radio.

Politicians have sought to direct media content, especially of television broadcasting, the public's main source of news and information. President Wałęsa openly criticized the broadcast media for what he deemed inadequate coverage of presidential activities. During the SLD–PSL government, the head of the Office of the Council of Ministers proposed that a large time slot be set aside for government broadcasting during prime time. The SLD–PSL coalition and the left-wing press openly attacked broadcasts which they felt painted the communist system in a negative light (Karpinski, 1996b: 28). Public opinion surveys in 1994 revealed that 50 per cent of Poles considered television still to be dependent on the government and the state, compared with 36 per cent each for radio and the press (*Rzeczpospolita*, 1994).

In general, television coverage of politics in East-Central Europe retains a pro-government bias. An analysis of television reporting in the Czech Republic in 1994 concluded that most television news concentrated on official government statements and diplomatic visits (Carey, 1996: 20). However, this pro-government bias does not result from government manipulation of the media, which is virtually non-existent in the Czech Republic compared with Hungary and Poland (Giorgi, 1995: 9–10). Rather, journalists remain conditioned by their duties to the state under communism. A comparative survey of Hungarian Television's political and public service coverage by the Kod Institute of Market, Opinion and Media Research also showed a bias toward government parties. In the two periods surveyed (May 1993 and May 1996), the opposition in parliament was given the opportunity to voice its position in only one-fifth of the broadcasts in which politicians were presented. The share of opposition parties in news of economic issues was only 14 per cent in 1996, down from 33 per cent in 1993, although their overall share in news coverage had increased measurably (*Magyar Nemzet*, 1996).

In a civil society conducive to liberal democracy, the media serve as political watchdogs. East-Central European journalists often lack the critical scepticism needed to challenge the official version of events, a legacy of the 'transmission belt' role of the media. Certain topics, such as the military, intelligence and suspicions of political wrongdoings largely remain taboo because reporters tend to place what they see as their civic duty before their duty to inform (cf. Kayal, 1993). Much criticism was levied at Czech media in 1997 for its reluctance to pursue questionable financial dealings of Klaus' Civic Democratic Party. Adam Michnik has said that people are still too heavily conditioned to accept the word of authority and could benefit from a certain degree of irreverence for authority (Nagorski, 1993: 218–219).

An ongoing debate over the relative values of freedom of speech and freedom of the media is playing out in the parliaments and court systems of East-Central Europe. Laws designed to prevent disclosure of the identity of suspected secret police collaborators are thinly disguised as laws against the revelation of state secrets. Poland, Hungary and the Czech Republic all have passed laws against the defamation of state organs. Ostensibly to protect the new democratic state, these laws are reminiscent of communist laws designed to quell dissent and hinder journalists in their legitimate work to uncover wrongdoings of the political elite. Without legal protection for publishing unproven allegations, journalists will continue to practise self-censorship. Legislation governing defamation lawsuits should include provisions whereby the plaintiff is responsible for proving malicious intent or material damages, as is the case in American and West European law (Sadurski, 1996: 444). The continued maturation of civil society requires the codification of regulations on journalists' duties to reveal their sources in aid of criminal investigations, protection of media property from police searches, reporting of government and national security secrets, and the transmittal or reporting of hate speech. Such regulations would best be designed jointly by the state and independent journalist associations.

The criminal consequences of personal liberty

A critical component of a civil society supportive of market democracy is the respect for the rule of law by officials and the citizenry. A negative correlate to the new liberties is the rising crime throughout East-Central Europe. Traditional theories about the relationship between crime and economics hold that economic modernization leads to a decrease in the rate of violent crime but an increase in the level of property crimes (Tara McKelvey, quoted in Spolar, 1998a). However, with the elimination of state controls over society, the transitional countries experienced a tremendous rise in both property and violent crimes. According to official statistics from Hungary, crimes per capita increased by 22 per cent from 1988 to 1989 and another 54 per cent from 1989 to 1990 alone. Crimes against persons increased 19 per cent from 1989 to 1990. In Poland, crimes against socialist property more than doubled from 1989 to 1990 according to official statistics (Lotspeich, 1995: 558) and assaults with firearms increased more than tenfold in Poland from 1990 to 1994 (Krupa, 1995). Both countries experienced a rise in highly visible violent crimes in 1998, with a series of political bombings in Budapest, the assassination of a prominent publisher there and the murder of the former head of the Polish police. In response to increased crime, Polish troops began to patrol the streets of Warsaw in the summer of 1998 for the first time since martial law.

Despite the upsurge in crime, the countries of East-Central Europe still have much lower crime rates than West European countries. For example, crimes per capita in Hungary and the Czech Republic are about half the rate in Germany and about one-third the rate in Holland (cf. McClune, 1994; *Prognosis*, 1994). The rise in violent crime has spurred calls for renewal of the death penalty, which was abolished in most countries after the collapse of communism, but its restitution would violate the Council of Europe's membership terms. There is a strong correlation in people's minds between the abolition of the death penalty and the sharp increase in crime (*Prognosis*, 1994), even though studies of criminal behaviour in the West have failed to establish a correlation. Ninety-eight per cent of Czechs considered crime and citizens' safety to be the most pressing societal problem at the end of 1994 (*Prognosis*, 1994) and 60 per cent of Hungarians perceived that public safety was 'in a bad state' (Gaal, 1996).

There is no singular cause for the increase in criminal activity. Deficiencies in law enforcement coupled with inadequate regulation of economic activities play a major role. Increased impoverishment has led to an increase in the number of subsistence crimes (cf. Mason et al., 1997; *Nepszava*, 1996). As a result of the upsurge in crime, many people have become disillusioned with the new system and fearful that continued economic dislocation will cause further loss of personal security. Property crimes increasingly are directed at private property because of the higher ratio of private to state property, but also as frustrated individuals target those who have profited through questionable means. Kidnappings and murders serve as revenge for the perceived injustice over the way the nomenklatura grew wealthy and as blackmail by mafia, particularly in ex-Soviet states.

In the early post-communist period, police forces were not altogether clear on their proper role in a free society. The overly bureaucratized agencies lacked a sense of accountability for their work and did not necessarily view their role as that of public servants (cf. Legutko, 1994). In some countries, the police have managed to overcome the taint of enforcing party dictates. In Poland the police consistently receive higher public approval ratings (in the range of 60–70 per cent) than government institutions or prominent social organizations such as the Catholic Church and trade unions, despite their inability to combat the dramatic increases in violent crime (see Table 4.1). In contrast, 61 per cent of Czechs expressed distrust in the police and only 35 per cent expressed trust (*Lidove Noviny*, 1996), even though the crime rate in the Czech Republic is considerably lower than in Poland.

TABLE 4.1   *Approval ratings of public institutions in Poland, 1993–1997 (percentages)*

Institution/organization	December 1993	November 1994	September 1995	November 1996	February 1998
Polish Radio	N/A	N/A	80	78	87
Army	77	73	70	73	71
Public Television	66	67	69	65	77
Police	68	63	61	N/A	N/A
Local self-government	52	56	58	60	N/A
Roman Catholic Church	54	53	49	51	63
State banks	36	45	42	N/A	67[a]
Solidarity	25	37	40	N/A	N/A
Judiciary	45	52	40	N/A	N/A
Sejm	47	49	36	46	45
Senate	35	45	32	48	46
OPZZ trade union	35	34	28	N/A	N/A
President	30	22	23	59	70
Private banks	19	24	21	N/A	N/A

[a]   National Bank of Poland only.

Source: Adapted from Karpinski, 1995: 41; Nowa Europa, 1996; Gazeta Wyborcza, 1998

Organized crime groups in East-Central Europe have grown at a faster rate than in Italy (cf. Janecki and Ornacka, 1998). Criminal elements have the upper hand, with the legal system unable to respond adequately to new types of crime. Juridical definitions of organized crime fail to encompass the entire scope of activities or to anticipate the next area of mafia activity. But the growth in organized crime is also a consequence of the inadequately developed economic system. In the early transition period, the financial sector was unable to provide capital to many entrepreneurs. Those who had made money on the black market filled the credit gap, providing capital at exorbitant interest rates. Money lenders established small armies to enforce the terms of the loan on those who fell behind in payments. From there, organized crime expanded into other types of racketeering and is expected to enter new areas, such as drug trafficking and prostitution. Dr Janos Fabian, Hungary's deputy chief public prosecutor, contends that organized crime is not yet a grave problem and remains confined mostly to auto theft. In 1995, of the 305,000 crimes prosecuted (out of 500,000 reported), only 1,830 displayed characteristics of organized crimes. While Fabian admits that the actual volume of organized crime is likely to be much higher, he rejects calls to restrict constitutional rights in order to combat organized crime, as has been done in some Western countries (*Nepszava*, 1996). However, the Horn government decided in 1998 to allow wiretapping of mobile phones in the battle against organized crime. The control of organized crime will be an important issue for EU entry, with Eastern police, prosecutors and judges to receive training in Western Europe in preparation.

Adding to the sense of an increasingly criminalized society is the widespread corruption of bureaucrats who extract bribes for performing their duties and of the common people who evade taxes and economic regulations. According to the European Bank for Reconstruction and Development, corruption is more pervasive in the economies of post-communist Europe, especially in the former Soviet Union, than in any other region of the world (Done, 1997). Bribery and grey market activities are viewed by some as merely the continuation of behavioural patterns which developed under state socialism. Richard Lotspeich refers to 'the extensive human capital specific to law breaking' acquired in the years when consumer goods and state services were very difficult to obtain through legal means. He argues that social attitudes in the region are generally accepting of certain types of criminal activity (1995: 566). The remnant bureaucratic culture further invites the use of illegal means. According to Cezary Jozefiak, Chair of the Committee for Economic Sciences of the Polish Academy of Sciences, the 'pathological proliferation of government agencies' and the broadening of licensing domains for 'protégés' of the SLD–PSL government nourished corruption (Baczynski et al., 1997). Bribery is commonly used to influence the awarding of government contracts and the transfer of state assets to enterprise managers in the pre-privatization stage, or to obtain waivers from environmental and other regulations.

Managerial weaknesses of law enforcement agencies are compounded by a lack of resources and poor training of personnel. Beyond that, stronger legal protection of witnesses is critical in prosecuting crimes but 'the willingness of witnesses to cooperate with the police, the public prosecutor's office, or State Treasury agencies is also dependent to a large extent on the degree of trust society has in these institutions' (Legutko, 1994). In Poland, while the police receive high levels of support, the judiciary received a 46 per cent approval rating and the state prosecutor 44 per cent in September 1997 (PAP, 1997a). In the Czech Republic, only 34 per cent of the public trusted the court system in late 1996 (*Lidove Noviny*, 1996)

With the elimination of most border restrictions, drug traffickers and criminal gangs quickly established ties with organized crime groups in other countries. Police and border agents are poorly organized and lack the sophisticated equipment and training necessary to monitor cross-border criminal operations. Coordination with agencies in other countries remains inadequate, though such issues are regularly on the agenda at CEFTA and bilateral summits. The great influx of Western goods provides corrupt customs officials with ample opportunities for profiteering not only through the theft of goods and component parts but also by extracting bribes before issuing customs clearance. Polish police sources report that, after transportation department personnel and physicians, the position of customs official is the third most corrupt profession (Lesniewski and Szczesny, 1997).

Though the informal international trade of consumer goods presents a sizable law enforcement problem, it may actually provide a social benefit. Western consumer products have virtually pushed more affordable eastern goods off the official markets but inexpensive products from the former Soviet Union continue to be sold to the economically marginalized at open air markets. Illegal trade sustains the economies of many border towns in Poland, with large segments of the population either living directly off smuggling or profiting from the resale of contraband goods. 'Smuggling has reached such a scale that stopping it would cause huge losses, gaps in supply . . . and a rise of about 20 per cent in market prices' for some essential items (Lesniewski and Szczesny, 1997). Nevertheless, in response to EU pressure, Polish authorities began in 1998 to crack down on these informal markets through tighter border control and tax collection.

The free media have heightened people's awareness of crime but also facilitate criminal activity. It is commonly believed that coverage of ethnic violence breeds copycat crimes (cf. Hockenos, 1993), a phenomenon not restricted to racist crimes. Negative stereotypes of minorities propagated by the media also serve to incite violence. The impudence with which criminal groups, smugglers and experts on money laundering and tax evasion advertise regularly in newspapers (*Polish News Bulletin*, 1997) demonstrates the inability of these societies to strike a suitable balance between freedom of the press and its responsibility to serve society.

Criminality in the transitional countries has extensive economic and political repercussions. Bribes, protection money and the costs of private security forces reduce the financial resources available for the creation of productive jobs. Some prospective entrepreneurs are unwilling to risk doing business in this unstable environment. Foreign investment is directed toward countries with more stable economic conditions, clearly codified contract and copyrights laws and reliable legal and administrative systems. Crime can also have a political impact. In Hungary in early 1998, the Socialist-led government received only a 38 per cent satisfaction index on issues of public order and security, while 57 per cent of respondents rated this as an important area for government action. Only issues of economic management and the alleviation of welfare problems were more important to the general public (Zavecz, 1998). Concerns about widened crime and corruption contributed to the Socialists' defeat in the 1998 elections.

Lustration: pursuit of justice or political combat?

One of the more unsettling aspects of the societal transformations is the attempt to deal with the legacy of communism. Efforts at lustration

(cleansing the state apparatus and government of secret police informants and former communist officials) and trials of those responsible for
repression have raised important issues related to the establishment of
a civil society based on the rule of law. Can members of a previous
regime be prosecuted for actions which were not crimes at the time they
were committed? Given the widespread complicity with communist
authorities, is it fair to take retribution against individuals who collaborated with the secret police? Václav Havel has argued '. . . all of us
are responsible, each to a different degree, for keeping the totalitarian
machine running. None of us is merely a victim of it because all of us
helped to create it together' (quoted in Nagorski, 1993: 89). Coming
from a victim of that totalitarian machine, Havel's words serve as a
strong warning against vengeance under the guise of justice. Similar
sentiments have been expressed by former Polish dissident Jacek Kurón,
who spent a total of nine years in prison for his activities.

Czechoslovakia was the first East-Central European country to begin
lustration. In early 1991, the Federal Assembly established a committee
to screen its members for secret police (StB) connections. Members
of parliament identified as 'StB positive' were offered the option of
resigning, in which case their secret police connection would not be
revealed publicly but if they failed to resign, they would be identified.
One of the most controversial cases was that of Jan Kavan, a parliamentary deputy for the Civic Forum. Kavan had been a student in
London in 1968, where he chose to remain after the crushing of the
Prague Spring. For two decades he supported dissident activities from
London, returning to Czechoslovakia only during the Velvet Revolution.
Kavan was named as a collaborator on the basis of contacts with a
Czechoslovak embassy official in London who had claimed to be an
education counselor. When first denounced, Kavan was denied access to
his complete StB file, making it impossible to mount an adequate
defence. Furthermore, since the lustration commission was not a court of
law, he could not present witnesses to testify on his behalf. Despite the
apparent absence of proof of collaboration or even knowledge on
Kavan's part that he had been targeted by the StB, he lost an appeal to
have his name cleared. Kavan declared, 'I believed that, once this
country made the change, we would be more democratic than our
neighbors, simply because we had a long democratic tradition. I believed
this would prevent us from embarking on a McCarthy-type witch-hunt.
But it worked out the other way around: we seem to be at the top of the
league of witch-hunts' (quoted in Nagorski, 1993: 81). In 1998, Kavan
became Foreign Minister in the Zeman government, despite objections
from the president's office over continued suspicion of his alleged
contacts with the secret police.

Despite mounting controversies, or perhaps in response to them, the
Federal Assembly passed a lustration law in October 1991. It barred
secret police agents and collaborators, former senior communist party

officials and members of the People's Militia from state jobs for a period of five years. A number of disturbing issues quickly arose from the lustration process. Firstly, there was no presumption of innocence under this law. A draft submitted by Havel would have required the state to prove that a collaborator had caused actual harm to another person before he/she could be dismissed, but this version was rejected (Rosenberg, 1995: 97). Secondly, commissions blindly relied on the StB files, with little initial discussion as to their veracity. Under heavy pressure to recruit informants, it was plausible that StB agents who failed to meet quotas falsified their records, and in fact some alleged collaborators later demonstrated in court that their agreements to collaborate had been falsified (Nagorski: 1993, 84). The StB files did not provide a clear picture of 'collaboration'. Many people unknowingly encountered StB agents in the course of their normal work, yet did not necessarily inform on their fellow citizens. Such encounters were recorded but were not always distinguishable from acts of informing. Some people who signed on as collaborators had done so under threats of blackmail or torture, yet lustration allowed for no mitigating circumstances. Since large numbers of StB files were destroyed during the Velvet Revolution, lustration would forever be incomplete. The process was further discredited by leaks of informants' names to the press, even though the work of the lustration commission was supposed to be secret. A significant number of people on the published lists who later underwent full screening were judged to be StB negative. Finally, the law carried no statute of limitations on collaboration with the secret police, something that existed for more serious crimes such as murder.

Shortcomings in the lustration process have tarnished the Czech Republic's image at the forefront of the transition to liberal democracy and have brought upon it the disapprobation of international organizations and human rights groups. Moreover, the process failed to fulfill its promise of cleansing the public sector, for it probably only resulted in the dismissal of a few hundred people (Brown, 1997: 31). Nevertheless, in 1996 the lustration law was extended until the year 2000, but this time over President Havel's veto. [The lustration law was not enforced in Slovakia after the 1992 elections and ceased to be in effect on 31 December 1996.]

Poland's first attempt at lustration turned out to be a political weapon cloaked as an attempt at justice. In 1992, under a Sejm mandate, Interior Minister Antoni Macierewicz presented to parliament a list of elected officials who were former secret police collaborators or had been targeted for recruitment. The names, which included a number of political opponents of Prime Minister Jan Olszewski (among them President Wałęsa), were leaked to the media. J.F. Brown called it the 'high point of a squalid campaign against Wałęsa' (1997). Assembled by apparently inexperienced investigators, the list also contained many inaccuracies.

The already weak Olszewski government was forced to resign for mis-handling the process.

After repeated failures to draft acceptable legislation, a screening law was finally passed in early 1997, applying *inter alia* to the president, cabinet ministers, province governors and executive directors, members of parliament, judges, prosecutors and heads of public television, public radio and press agencies. Individuals holding these posts (and candidates for the elected posts) must declare service as agents or collaborators of the secret police during the period 1944–90. Those who admit to having such ties are not required to step down but anyone proved to have lied about past connections will be barred from public office for a period of 10 years. The law calls for the establishment of a special judicial commission to review the accuracy of all claims, but in June 1998, judges were still refusing to sit on the commission and the government and opposition were deadlocked over implementation of the law. Furthermore, in November 1998, the Constitutional Court declared two provisions of the law unconstitutional, leaving the lustration issue in Poland still unresolved nearly a decade after the fall of communism.

Prior to the 1997 parliamentary elections, eleven candidates admitted to having worked for the secret police. Only one, Jerzy Szteliga, was elected to the Sejm. The SLD deputy had signed a non-binding statement in 1993 claiming never to have collaborated with the secret police. Explaining the contradiction, Szteliga commented, 'Well, I wouldn't call that a lie. I would call that a lie-oriented statement' (Spolar, 1997a).

Hungary's coming to terms with the past focused first on the 1956 revolution. In 1991, parliament passed a law abrogating the twenty-year statute of limitations for murder, aggravated assault leading to death, and treason committed between December 1944 and May 1990. It was crafted primarily to allow prosecution of crimes committed against the people during the 1956 revolution. However, it was declared unconstitutional in March 1992 because of its vague wording and the retroactive waiving of the statute of limitations. In proposing a new package to parliament, the government argued that Hungarian laws from 1945, as well as the Geneva Conventions on the treatment of civilians during war, could be used to prosecute those responsible for crushing the revolution. This formulation withstood a 1993 court ruling (Commission on Security and Cooperation in Europe, 1993: 7).

During the 1994 election campaign, a lustration law was passed by the centre-right government, motivated perhaps by the strong showing of the Socialists in pre-election polls. The law established a committee to identify key government officials who had worked as secret police agents. This law was declared unconstitutional the same year because it failed to define the scope of applicability. In July 1996, an amended law was passed applying to the president, members of parliament, the government, the Constitutional and Supreme Courts, and executives of

Hungarian Radio and Hungarian Television. A panel of judges was set up to screen the officials. Those who are found to have collaborated have the option of resigning without being exposed. However, if the person identified does not resign within thirty days, he/she will be identified publicly, though not dismissed from office. The law encompasses only about 600 people, compared with perhaps 15,000 who are affected by the Polish law. With such a limited number subject to screening, the law cannot serve the purpose of thoroughly cleansing public life of former secret police collaborators (Szilagyi, 1997).

A comprehensive coming to terms with the past includes criminal proceedings against former communist authorities. In Poland, Wojciech Jaruzelski was put on trial for the declaration of martial law, the murders of striking miners and the deaths during the Gdańsk riots in 1970, when he was defence minister. He was cleared because the charges in the deaths were not proven and the martial law declaration was deemed not to have been a crime (Brown, 1997: 32). In June 1998, the Polish government began proceedings against seven communist party officials for the deaths in 1970 and made plans to try five more, including Jaruzelski again. In May 1997, treason charges were brought against former Czechoslovak communist leaders Milos Jakes and Jozef Lenart stemming from their attendance at a meeting at the Soviet Embassy a day after the Soviet-led invasion of Czechoslovakia. The two Politburo members allegedly discussed plans with Soviet officials to set up a new government (RFE/RL, 5 May 1997). In September 1997, a court halted the prosecution of Jakes and Lenart, arguing that the statute of limitations had expired and that the two had not acted unlawfully. In January 1998, that ruling was overturned by the Supreme Court which argued that only after a thorough investigation can the Prosecutor General's Office move to try the two (RFE/RL, 22 January 1998). Some have questioned whether the prosecution of former leaders is even legal, as the communist states were recognized internationally as sovereign political states. It is also disputable whether they can be charged with crimes if the actions were not crimes in the states over which they ruled. To avoid this dilemma, prosecutors have searched carefully for violations of communist era laws under which former leaders can be prosecuted.

The pursuit of justice for the sins of the past regimes was considered important for building a society based on the rule of law. Some Western observers even proclaimed that lustration would be the central political issue for the post-communist societies in the medium term (Brown, 1994; Rosenberg, 1995) but this proved to be shortsighted. Why have attempts at de-communization been incomplete? Concerns over the procedural shortcomings as outlined above offer only a partial explanation. More importantly, the process never gained momentum. 'Decommunization was mainly a game among elites, power elites and intellectual elites' (Brown, 1997: 34). The public showed a lack of commitment to a zealous cleansing of the political system in part because of the distance from the Stalinist terror and the realization that many of the chief perpetrators were long dead. The average citizen was 'more interested in to what extent the former nomenklatura has taken advantage of the economy (nomenklatura privatization), and in the abolition of privileges given to the former communist elite than in purges' (Welsh, 1996: 423). Also, given the primacy of the political and economic transitions, it was considered necessary to retain in place experienced civil service personnel. Many people judge state functionaries on their current performance rather than on previous party affiliation and recognize that, as functionaries, they were not in key decision-making positions (Welsh, 1996: 424).

Post-communist civil society: winning citizen support for democracy

While some have questioned the application of the concept of civil society to post-communist societies, we are witnessing not the demise of the concept, but rather its transformation from 'the uses of adversity' (Timothy Garton Ash) to the 'uses of freedom' (Bronislaw Misztal). Civil society under communism was constrained by state control of intermediary institutions, the absence of many civil liberties, and a system of justice often meted out not according to the rule of law but rather party dictates. In post-communism, uneven access to intermediary institutions and uneven distribution of power continue to constrict civil society. '[T]he establishment of democracy and freedoms did not produce, or coincide with, broader frames of citizenship rights for society's members; instead it produced the redefinition, or restructuring of privileges' (Misztal, 1995: 268). An equitable distribution of citizens' rights is essential to the development of a civil society broadly supportive of liberal democracy.

In some countries, the mechanics of the transition created imbalances which diminished trust in the democratic process. The negotiated transitions, while allowing for peaceful regime change, ensured the political survival of former communist elites. So-called 'gentlemen's agreements' reportedly prevent many former communist leaders from being brought to justice in Hungary and Poland. The 'people' have not emerged victorious, but rather it is the intellectual elites, educated classes, and technocrats who dominate political life. Today the elite often prove more interested in their own political careers than in strengthening civil society. 'In many respects, the failure to develop and strengthen civil initiatives and popular participation . . . represents a new, post-communist "betrayal of the intellectuals"' (Lomax, 1997: 41–42). Lomax argues that the intellectuals have come to oppose civil society, particularly in the form of mass social movements, because they pose a threat to elite democracy and economic liberalism. Intellectuals 'have sought to legitimize their opposition to all such forms of social self-organization in terms of an ideology of liberal constitutionalism that defines democracy in purely formal terms of elections, parliamentary government and the rule of law, and rejects any substantive element of direct, popular participation in the political process'. The potential for an elite-etatist model, with the political leadership presuming to know what is best for the country, is precisely why a broad-based civil society is needed (Lomax, 1997: 56).

The realization that the new political elites were perhaps only marginally more inclined than communists to address the interests of citizens has led to the formation of numerous interest groups (cf. Fábián). With the freedom to organize and express one's ideas, and with the availability of improved communications technology, tens of thousands of non-governmental organizations were created. Many which started as self-help groups have not been able to transform themselves into true interest advocacy groups. Nearly all suffer from inadequate funding or a dependence on state or external funding. The continued daily struggle for existence limits one's time, energy and disposable income available for interest group activities. The new middle and upper classes tend to concentrate their spending on consumer goods and lavish lifestyles and less on charitable work and policy advocacy than do their Western counterparts. But given the fiscal constraints of all post-communist states, a Western-style system of philanthropy may have to be developed by the new rich.

The roles and responsibilities of both citizen and state are still uncertain in East-Central Europe. While the state's role in the communist era was clearly delineated (though not legitimized), its role in the different spheres of civil society (economy, politics, communication, education/culture and religious life) has not been well defined in post-communism. In addition, the communist social pact (the state satisfied basic needs in exchange for loyalty) conditioned people to accept and even demand a greater state role in society, creating the danger of a state-dominated civil society. Consequently, there is an overwhelming sense of citizen powerlessness, resulting in weak and unstable citizen participation in political activities. 'While the repressive aspects of systemic limits have been lifted . . . and no longer render most disaffected citizens unable to engage in dissent, the memory lingers and the sense of personal helplessness to affect anything in politics *pushes* the disaffected firmly towards apathy' (Mason et al., 1991: 227; italics original). Political participation, including voter turnout, tends to be lowest among unemployed, the poor and the less well educated (whose economic prospects are bleak), and highest among those with higher education and incomes, the intelligentsia and managerial personnel

(Kwasniewska, 1994). Apathy also stems from the sense that civil society is powerless against the international financial institutions, for there exist no interest articulation mechanisms in the World Bank or IMF.

Since civil society is unique to the historical and cultural traditions of each country, it is difficult to rank its development in any country. One can, however, assess the strength of its components. The new democracies of East-Central Europe receive generally high marks for the protection of political and civil liberties in Freedom House's annual survey. The Czech Republic, Poland and Hungary each rated 1 in political rights and 2 in civil liberties on a scale of 1 to 7 (Slovakia rated 2 on political rights and 3 on civil liberties). Problem areas cited for the 2 ranking included lustration (Czech Republic); minority rights (Czech Republic and Hungary); issues of attempted political interference by the presidential office and the government; and inadequate funding for the judiciary (Poland) (Freedom House, 1996).

Perhaps more important than such a rating system is the level of public trust in the various institutions of civil society and liberal democracy. Without confidence in the ability of these institutions to meet the needs of the citizenry, civil liberties will remain underutilized and civil society stunted. People may turn to undemocratic means to further their interests if they perceive a deficiency in these formal institutions.

Freedom of the press is considered a paramount underpinning of a democratic civil society, yet East-Central Europeans do not necessarily place a high value on it. In a poll of Hungarians in late 1997, only 6 per cent believed it important that the government provide the conditions for freedom of the press. Related to that, only 19 per cent believed it important that the government pay attention to public opinion (see Table 4.2). In the midst of a heated debate over the government's role in the Polish media in 1994, public opinion polls demonstrated considerable ambivalence on the issue. Thirty-four per cent of respondents felt that state authorities should not have privileged access to the media; 28 per cent were willing to cede government such access, though only in exceptional situations; 31 per cent thought such a privilege was 'obnoxious' and 7 per cent expressed no opinion (*Rzeczpospolita*, 1994).

Public opinion polls from Poland over the years reveal varying degrees of support for the institutions of civil society and democratic government (see Table 4.1). Some of the lowest approval ratings are for economic institutions – trade unions and state and private banks. Highest support goes to broadcast media and the military. Local government, with which citizens have greater direct contact, receives higher levels of support than the Sejm and the Senate. The approval ratings for the presidency generally are more a reflection of the officeholder at the time, as it is difficult for people to separate the person from the institution in this case. The presidency received approval ratings in

TABLE 4.2   *Opinion of government's performance in Hungary, 1997*

Government function	Views on government[a]	Importance
Economic management	32	75
Social sensitivity	23	65
Ensuring public order and lawfulness	30	52
Combating corruption	22	44
Credibility	25	38
Attention to public opinion	30	19
Country's foreign reputation	50	10
Relations with neighbouring countries	58	10
Freedom of the press	60	6

[a] Average values, 0 = worst opinion; 100 = best opinion.

Source: Nepszava, 1997a

the low twenties in the last two years of the Wałęsa presidency but those ratings jumped to 59 per cent in the first year of the Kwaśniewski presidency.

Table 4.3 reveals varied support for institutions across transitional countries. The low levels of confidence in the Czech parliament, judiciary and military are surprising when compared to the levels in Hungary and Poland, and there are no obvious explanations. A poll in 1996 revealed that trust in the Czech parliament was only 35 per cent (*Denni Telegraf*, 1996b), which would place it more in the category of some former Soviet countries than with first tier countries. Trust in the Czech parliament (and other institutions) was strongest among young people, students and those in 'satisfied households' (*Denni Telegraf*, 1996a). The high level of confidence in the Church in Poland in 1994 when compared with support for the Church in Table 4.1 is probably due to the fact that many people expressed 'some' confidence, though not necessarily 'great' confidence in this institution.

While the democratic system may not be functioning to the satisfaction of the polity, perhaps due to the incompetence or corruption of leaders, the overall democratic processes (e.g. elections, party pluralism) retain high degrees of legitimacy (Linz and Stepan, 1996: 438). Early fears that economic crisis could reverse the transition to democracy have not materialized, but maintaining citizen support for liberal democracy through the difficult times is critical to its consolidation. The citizenry did not expect complete transformation overnight. Two-thirds of people surveyed in East-Central Europe and Southeast Europe in 1996 acknowledged that it would take many years for the governments to deal with all the problems of the communist era (Rose, 1996: 42).

Richard Rose claims that despite widespread dissatisfaction with the new system, the 'Churchill hypothesis' ('it has been said that democracy is the worst form of government, except all those other forms that have

TABLE 4.3   Percentage of respondents expressing some or great confidence in Church/state institutions, 1994/5

	Church	Presidency	Parliament	Judiciary	Military
Czech Republic	30	78	43	44	43
Hungary	57	74	57	71	75
Poland	70	43	55	61	85
Slovakia	59	58	49	53	64
Estonia	64	72	51	47	50
Latvia	68	69	38	48	32
Lithuania	80	34	27	29	38
Bulgaria	39	48	30	28	67
Romania	88	52	29	51	85
Russia	72	27	26	38	66
Ukraine	69	47	29	32	61
Belarus	67	50	27	38	59

Sources: OMRI AOR (Open Media Research Institute Audience and Opinion Research) Surveys, March–April 1995; RFE/RL MOR Survey in Hungary, April 1994. Adapted from Gibson, 1996 and produced here with permission from the publisher.

been tried from time to time') has been internalized by the people of East-Central Europe. In a 1996 survey by the Paul Lazarsfeld Society, 76 per cent of Czechs rated democracy and 27 per cent communism positively; 76 per cent of Poles rated democracy and 25 per cent communism positively. But the results in the first tier countries are uneven, since only 50 per cent of Hungarians rated democracy but 56 per cent communism positively (Rose, 1996: 40).

Still, while the ideal may be rated positively, the reality of how the system is functioning may cause dissatisfaction. As late as May of 1998, just 45 per cent of Poles thought present day Poland was a better country to live in than communist Poland, even though 55 per cent had begun to experience the positive effects of the transition (PAP, 1998a). Hungarians are particularly critical of the new system. The Eurobarometer poll of November 1996 revealed that 75 per cent were dissatisfied with market economic developments and 72 per cent dissatisfied with political democracy (MTI, 1997). More so than other populations of East-Central Europe, Hungarians are quite nostalgic about the communist era, in large part because they enjoyed greater economic and political freedom than their counterparts in other countries. In a January 1997 poll, 54 per cent said that living standards were better before the change of regimes, though freedom of the press and/or democracy has been greater since. Only 10 per cent considered the period after the regime change to be best in every aspect, including the economy. Almost 25 per cent believed that there was more democracy in the Kádár era than at any time since. Nostalgia for the old regime is highest among the rural population, the poorly educated, the elderly and those with below average income (Marian, 1997). A comparison of people's dissatisfaction with their living standards and self-perceived social standing at the time of the transition (1989–90) with their recollection of these levels when surveyed again in 1996 shows that people recalled their situation at the time of the transition as being far better than they assessed it at the time (Mason et al., 1997: 16).

The strong performance of the Czech economy and the absence of severe economic problems had led to a high level of support for market democracy. Repeated polls showed that Czechs tended to be more pleased with the direction their country was going than were citizens of other countries (cf. *Rzeczpospolita*, 1995). However, as the economic picture soured, support for the new system began to wane. In early 1998, a public opinion poll showed an increase in the number of Czechs saying they would prefer to live under communism, from 18.1 per cent in 1997 to 28.7 per cent. The majority of 'communist nostalgics' were pensioners and manual workers (RFE/RL, 25 February 1998).

Since such opinions are contingent upon the functioning of the new systems at the time of the survey, results from any given year cannot be used to predict longer-term trends. In the case of Poland, though, the trend is clearly a steady growth in confidence in democracy. The percentage of Poles saying that democracy has an advantage over any other form of government grew from 52 per cent in October 1992 to 62 per cent in June 1993 and 67 per cent in May 1995 (Public Opinion Research Center [CBOS], no. 99/95 June 1995, cited in Karpinski, 1995: 40). This upward trend in democratic support has accompanied steady, strong economic growth. If that growth continues, and the Aws–UW coalition manages to avoid ideological battles over policy, this trend should continue.

Still, there is reason for caution regarding the longer-term prospects for democracy in East-Central Europe. Citizen support for democracy will remain dependent on economic performance, much as tolerance for the communist system depended on the state's ability to maintain its social pact. If the new economies fail to benefit the majority, or are unable to reverse the fortunes of many losers of the transition, citizen affection for the elite-centred mode of democracy which has evolved will remain deficient.

5

Concepts of Economic Restructuring

Changing conceptualizations of economic restructuring

One of the most critical issues of the post-communist transition has been the strategy for economic restructuring and its impact on the democratization process. The early analysis centred on the debate between 'shock therapy' and 'gradualism', but this proved to be overly simplistic and short-sighted. Experience now reveals that economic restructuring is a lengthy and extremely complex process. The idealized system was a prosperous, market-based economy which would also address the needs of the most disadvantaged citizens, but the laws, institutions and forms of behaviour necessary for such a system could not be put in place overnight. Furthermore, the financial crisis in Southeast Asia at the end of 1997 pointed to the danger that policy makers in transitional countries may become complacent with the apparent success of macroeconomic reforms, failing to carry through with some of the more difficult institutional reforms.

The transitions in post-communist Europe present a new set of dilemmas for both analysts and policy makers due to the simultaneity of the political and economic reforms. Is it preferable for an authoritarian economic reform to come first, with political liberalization only coming later (the so-called Pinochet option?). Does shock therapy destroy the social consensus for liberal democracy? What has been learned from the reform process to date? How have the new governments responded to resultant economic crises and the new social demands arising from economic restructuring? Is the creation of a middle class the key to a solid and self-interested base for democratization, or does the working class have to be included in a broader consensus for a democratic class politics?

As with the political liberalization in East-Central Europe, the economic liberalization is greatly differentiated from one state to another, and one region to another. Nevertheless, there have been some common experiences. No country has been able to embark on the path to a market economy without considerable dislocation. Whether a country initially chose a radical break with the past (shock therapy), or a more gradual approach, policy adjustments have been necessary in response to economic realities, the demands of the international financial institutions or the domestic populace. Those countries which chose the shock therapy approach (notably Poland and Russia), have slowed the pace of large-scale privatization in order to conciliate workers. On the other hand, countries which chose the more gradualist approach (notably Hungary and Romania) have had to institute painful austerity measures after a number of years in order to combat macroeconomic problems and to stay in favour with the multilateral financial institutions. Due to the different conditions in each country, it is impossible to choose a 'best practices' model which can be applied across the board.

The new normative framework: the Washington consensus

The complete transition from a command to a market economy was unprecedented when the countries of East-Central Europe embarked on their economic reform processes, starting with the Balcerowicz plan in Poland, launched on 1 January 1990. There was great optimism that this radical macroeconomic reform package would achieve economic stability and pave the way for later prosperity but these policies came without guarantees. The successful Western market economies (many still fraught with market failures) are the result of decades, even centuries of evolution, trial and error, and policy experimentation. Many Western states are themselves retreating from some of the social market policies out of fiscal necessity in a time of changing demographics and economic globalization. The countries of Latin America and Southern Europe already were established capitalist systems when they initiated economic reforms. They were concerned primarily with economic stabilization and liberalization and not with the creation of an entirely new economic system. The newly industrialized countries of East and Southeast Asia, often regarded as models of successful transformation (at least up until 1997), followed carefully crafted economic programmes. The state played the leading role in macro- and micro-economic decision making and decided the pace and extent of both economic and political reforms. Asian governments largely controlled capital flows in a well-coordinated industrial policy and exercised extensive trade protectionism, allowing their industries to develop and mature before exposure to the rigours of international competition. These countries also enjoyed long periods of political stability (albeit accomplished through authoritarianism), enabling them to hold off political liberalization until the fruits of economic development were being enjoyed by sufficiently large segments of society.

The post-communist countries were unable to develop under the cloak of trade protection due to the influence of the international financial institutions, which held some of the new governments to strict liberalization guidelines in order to qualify for debt restructuring agreements, and the need to open their borders to trade to demonstrate a commitment to policies required for acceptance into the European Union. Even for those countries not faced with default on their debts, the role of the IMF was significant as it provided stabilization funds to back currency convertibility plans, while the World Bank offered loans to assist with budgetary arrears and economic restructuring.

The command economies were characterized by state ownership of the means of production (with some variation, notably in Poland and Yugoslavia, where the agricultural sectors largely remained in private hands, and in Hungary, with some small-scale private entrepreneurship in the late communist period); the bureaucratic establishment of prices and production levels rather than a reliance on the forces of supply and demand; heavy subsidies of energy, housing, foodstuffs, transportation and social benefits; state control of foreign trade and an over-dependence on the Soviet Union both as a market and a source of cheap raw materials. Centralized decision making, characterized by political power plays and bureaucratic inefficiencies, was incompatible with the new global economic order, with the emphasis on innovation and the rapid dissemination of information to assist in the efficient allocation of resources. The sectoral divisions found in the command economies were inconsistent with those of a modern, post-industrial society. Another factor in which the eastern economies were out of step with the demands of the global market place was the gross neglect of the service sector. Basic services such as retail and food-related services were inadequate to meet demand, while the mid-level services, such as financial intermediation, insurance, accounting, marketing and advertising were virtually absent. Finally, some of the former communist countries have disproportionately large agricultural sectors for modern economies. For example, more than 25 per cent of Poland's labour force is employed in agriculture (though a significant percentage of them obtain income from other sectors, as well), compared with the 5–7 per cent average for the European Union and 3 per cent for the United States (OECD, 1996). Poland's agricultural sector accounts for only 6–7 per cent of its GDP.

Regardless of the sequencing of reforms, all transitional countries faced the combination of reforms known as the Washington Consensus, because it comprises the elements required by the international financial institutions of countries seeking their assistance with debt relief in the 1980s and because it is tied to the *laissez-faire* ideology of the Reagan administration which prevailed at the time (Amsden et al., 1994: viii). It refers to the combination of

- *Fiscal discipline*: The benchmark for a budget deficit is around 2 per cent of gross domestic product.
- *Public expenditure prioritization*: State spending should take the form of investment in both physical and human capital in order to stimulate economic growth but should be reduced to essential levels for the provision of public goods, with the market allowed to operate where it can more efficiently allocate resources.
- *Tax reform*: The tax base must be broadened (or first established), and tax collection improved.
- *Financial liberalization*: Interest rates must be market-driven.
- *Trade liberalization*: Quotas protecting domestic industries should be eliminated. In their stead, selective tariffs may be applied but should be reduced over time to a minimal level, with the goal being complete elimination.
- *Exchange rates*: There should be a uniform, competitive exchange rate, driven by the currency markets, to encourage exports.
- *Foreign direct investment*: Barriers to foreign direct investment should be eliminated in order to increase competition and provide vital capital since domestic savings are insufficient.
- *Privatization of state-owned enterprises*: The privatization process will generate revenue and increase competition.
- *Deregulation*: Barriers to market entry for domestic and foreign firms should be eliminated.
- *Property rights*: Sound property rights must be incorporated into the body of law and supported by a legal infrastructure (Williamson, 1994a: 26–28).

The key elements of the Washington Consensus are those of a mature, integrated market economy. With the pervasive state sector in the socialist countries (and its associated interest groups), it has by no means been easy to undertake the required reforms, nor was it even known at the outset whether such a radical transformation in a condensed period of time was feasible. Such an overhauling of the economic framework requires state coordination of the myriad reforms, so that problems in one area do not derail successful movement in another sector. This runs contrary to the initial post-communist mindset which discounted the role of the state in the economic sphere, but the justifiable rejection of state *control* of the economy should not be taken for a rejection of the role of the state as *facilitator* of the economic transformation.

Arguments against the Washington Consensus stem both from the power imbalances between international institutions and the supplicant countries, and its dogmatism. A close look at the Western economies will show that many fail to follow the guidelines on fiscal discipline and trade liberalization themselves. Economic liberalization was untested on the scale needed for the ex-communist countries. The Western financial institutions took a firm position, threatening to break off debt reduction agreements or delay loan instalments if the post-communist governments deviated too much from prescribed norms. With little choice, policy makers in the transitional countries embraced the neo-liberal policies, even going beyond the demands of the IMF and the World Bank in the case of Poland (Nonneman, 1996c: 35).

Initially, the citizenry of East-Central Europe expressed a strong preference for the type of social market economy of Sweden or Germany, or the social corporatist model of Austria. Early on there was also much talk of a vaguely defined 'third way', a system between market capitalism and socialist planning which would combine the values of equity and economic security with the desire for prosperity. The results of a 1989 survey measuring Poles' level of acceptance of various methods of the Western economies illustrates considerable ambivalence. While 85.6 per cent agreed that 'incomes should be strongly differentiated depending on qualification and efficiency', 68.3 per cent agreed that the state should be concerned with 'reducing the differences in incomes between rich and poor'. Seventy-three per cent accepted that 'full freedom for the private sector should be ensured', yet 72.3 per cent were of the opinion that the state should be concerned with 'controlling profits of private enterprises'. There was also high support for a state role in 'compensating for price increases' (81.7 per cent) and in 'ensuring work for all who wanted to work' (90.2 per cent), with relatively low levels of acceptance of the risk of unemployment (46.6 per cent) (Morawski, 1992: 105).

This striving for 'capitalism with a human face' quickly gave way to the realities of the new international economic order. Even the wealthy models of Sweden and Germany have not been able to maintain high levels of social protection concomitant with strong economic growth. While German unification has posed a unique fiscal burden, this is by no means the only reason for the decline in the welfare state; changing demographics mean that there are too few workers paying into the state health insurance and pension funds. With the ease of international capital movement, investors can take their money where labour costs have a lesser impact on overall profits. With the social market economy beyond the reach of the former communist countries, there appeared to be no viable alternative to the neo-liberal model, at least in the medium term.

Sequencing of economic and political reforms

When the former communist countries embarked on simultaneous, radical political and economic reform, there was neither a proven blueprint to employ, nor assurances that the political and economic systems could be transformed together. In a number of the countries which are considered to have graduated from the status of 'developing' countries, notably South Korea, Taiwan and Singapore, economic liberalization preceded political liberalization. This generally was considered to be the necessary sequence of transition (cf. Köves and Marer, 1991). Economic modernization increased the average educational level of the people, which in turn exposed them to new ideas, engendering civil society. Increased trade liberalization exposed citizens to other systems and governments to international pressure for political openness (Nonneman, 1996b: 308–311). As the state decreased its role in the economy, it lost some of the control it had over the people, opening up space for the development of a civil society. The sequencing of reforms in Southern Europe in the 1970s and 1980s differed from the pattern in Asia by first shedding dictatorships and then tackling critical economic reforms. Spain and Portugal had the luxury of being able to delay the implementation of the more difficult economic reforms which would lead to greater unemployment until after democracy had been consolidated (Bermeo, 1994: 203). In contrast, the post-communist countries were not able to first consolidate the new democracies before having to implement radical economic reforms.

Fledgling democratic governments may have too little credibility to obtain from the people the degree of sacrifice required to implement stabilization policies. The economic restructuring in post-communist Europe brought immediate, negative results such as increased insecurity, greater and more open inequality, and the increased influence of foreigners at a time when the population was politically empowered for the first time (Nelson, 1994: 475). Low voter participation rates and general political apathy indicate that the *perception* of political empowerment remains low among East-Central Europeans but the election reversals in Poland in 1993 and Hungary in 1994 indicate that when the public is sufficiently dissatisfied with the government's performance on the economic front, they can and will seek to alter the course.

Initial fears that extensive economic reforms could not be implemented concomitant with political liberalization have been disproved by the success of Poland, Hungary, the Czech and Slovak Republics, Slovenia and the Baltics. The voters of these countries have exercised their political freedoms by turning out of power parties (on both sides of the spectrum) that were considered not to have responded adequately to the social costs of the transitions or to have kept a lid on corruption. Reversals of parliamentary majorities have not destabilized the economic reform process but have merely altered the pace of reforms in response to the political will of the electorate.

Gradualist versus shock therapy

At the beginning of the transition to a market economy the debate focused on the merits of shock therapy, propagated by most Western advisers and institutions, versus the gradualist approach, favoured by many, though not all, in the East. Shock therapy aimed at simultaneously establishing macroeconomic stabilization (reining in the inflationary forces through a tight monetary policy of positive real interest rates, a restrictive incomes policy and fiscal restraint) and liberalizing prices and foreign trade in order to bring on the disciplinary tool of competition. Large-scale privatization of state owned enterprises (SOEs) was to accompany or follow closely the other policies. Because of the complex linkages between market mechanisms, their simultaneous introduction was deemed superior to the gradualist approach by many economic theorists. The gradualist approach sought to implement these policies over a period of time in order to minimize their negative impact, with the question of the proper sequencing playing a key role. With the gradualist approach, policy makers sought to implement first those market procedures believed to be vital prerequisites of other reforms.

In actuality, the choice is not black and white, and elements of the two approaches have been combined in all transitional countries. While Poland successfully implemented the macroeconomic stabilization measures in rapid succession, it faltered in privatizing large state enterprises. Hungary, which took a more gradualist approach, was forced in 1995 to respond to stagnating economic growth and the prospects of not being able to meet its foreign debt servicing obligations. A radical structural adjustment programme, the Bokros Package, was instituted by the Socialist-led government to combat current account instability. As late as April 1997, two years after Václav Klaus had deemed the economic transition complete, the Czech Republic had to adopt austerity measures when the current account deficit became untenable and worker productivity declined, making that country less competitive.

While all the transitional countries faced a common set of constraints associated with state socialism, economic transitions are inherently path dependent, with the combination of past economic policies and the conditions at the start of the transition largely determining the type of reform programme implemented. Poland enjoyed the advantages of a partially privatized economy at the outset of the transition but economic policies of the late communist era had also created constraints on the manoeuvrability of the reformers. With annualized inflation rates reaching greater than 600 per cent at one point in 1989 and unable to make payments on its substantial foreign debt (which amounted to half of its GDP), Poland could not take the gradualist approach; macro-economic stabilization had to be restored in short order. Aiding the effort was the fact that Poles were willing to embark on a radical programme of economic restructuring after decades of piecemeal reforms which had failed to improve the overall standard of living as promised. Poland had entered a period of what Leszek Balcerowicz called 'extraordinary politics': 'a period of very clear discontinuity with a country's history' characterized by a 'stronger than normal tendency for politicians to act on behalf of the common good' (Balcerowicz, 1994: 176, 168). In contrast, Hungary was not in danger of defaulting on its loans, though it bore one of the highest per capita debt ratios in the world.

It is difficult to judge the overall merits of each approach until sufficient time has elapsed, since the costs of shock therapy are very much front loaded (Rodrik, 1993: 191). A longer-term perspective reveals advantages and disadvantages to each approach. While the gradual approach is less painful in the short term, it appears that this may simply spread out the pain over time, leading to a similar and perhaps greater overall drop in output. A comparison between Poland and Hungary demonstrates that Hungary experienced a greater total decline in GDP (18.8 per cent) before bottoming out in 1993 than did Poland (18.2 per cent), which bottomed out two years earlier (Crane, 1995: 31), and has posted significantly lower levels of economic growth. In fact, Poland fared better than any other country except Slovenia in terms of the maximum drop in GDP and was also the first transitional country to achieve the pre-transition level of GDP and industrial output. From a political standpoint, gradualism may be more susceptible to 'adjustment fatigue' (Rodrik, 1993: 191) with the electorate less willing to accept an economic downturn drawn out over several years.

A possible benefit of the gradualist approach can be derived from an analysis of the economic reforms in Portugal and Spain after the end of the dictatorships. Portugal, with a higher number of state owned enterprises than Spain at the start of reforms, chose the gradualist path. Jobs were preserved at the expense of faster wage growth while Spain moved more quickly to restructure state enterprises and shed excess labour. As a result, Portugal showed a lower level of strike activity than did Spain. Coupled with the slower wage growth, this has made Portugal more attractive to foreign investors (Bermeo, 1994: 200–202). The high level of strike activity in Poland in the initial years of economic reform was a key factor in making Poland an undesirable location for foreign investment, *vis-à-vis* the more stable Czech Republic and Hungary, both of which experienced little early worker unrest.

If the economic dislocation of shock therapy is too severe, political opposition can restrict the government's manoeuvrability. The metamorphosis of social costs into political costs (Kádár, 1993: 183) was most clearly illustrated in Poland where the economic downturn following the Balcerowicz plan was more severe and protracted than promised. In 1993, the electorate expressed its dissatisfaction by giving a plurality to the Democratic Left Alliance (SLD), successor to the Communist Party. The economic downturn caused by the austerity measures was compounded by several external shocks, including decreased demand for Polish goods as a result of both the collapse of the Council for Mutual Economic Assistance and the economic slowdown in Western Europe in 1991–2, and the increase in oil prices when Russia shifted from the barter system to international market prices for its fuel exports. Though these factors could not be anticipated or controlled by policy makers, the voters nevertheless felt that the government had failed to respond adequately to these circumstances, and had failed to explain fully the consequences of the economic reforms. The economic costs under gradualism can also turn into political costs if the government in power is deemed to be unresponsive to the economic predicament of the people, as happened in 1994 when the conservative Hungarian Democratic Forum (MDF) was voted out of power and replaced with the reformed communists.

One of the more sensitive issues of economic restructuring is that of privatization, not only out of fear of unemployment but also because of the way in which state resources would be reallocated. In the first wave, small SOEs were privatized through a combination of auctions, direct sales to the public and sell-offs to enterprise managers and workers. This privatization is generally considered to have been very unfair, with many of the small enterprises going to former black marketeers or party members who found themselves in advantageous positions, the so-called nomenklatura privatization. 'A grotesque situation developed when the government parties launched verbal attacks against the past and yet dealt a relatively adequate number of good cards to its representatives' (Leko, 1997). The resentment that arose after the privatization of small enterprises, coupled with the unacceptability of still higher unemployment, stalled further privatization. In Poland, although a mass privatization plan was in place in 1991, the process did not begin for another five years. Another factor in the privatization of large enterprises was the unwillingness by many to see the family silver sold to foreigners. Foreign firms were generally the only ones who could afford to buy large state enterprises outright or by entering into joint ventures with home companies. After four decades of domination by the Soviet Union, people opposed having their economic futures again determined by foreigners. The pace of privatization was also conditioned by the need for extensive enterprise restructuring since most were highly inefficient and unattractive to investors. The pattern employed in Britain during the Thatcher years entailed careful restructuring of an enterprise before putting it up for sale in order to make it more attractive to potential buyers. Transitional countries could not afford this pattern, both in terms of the cost and the time required to properly restructure thousands of enterprises. Another dilemma stems from the dual purpose of privatization: to raise much needed state revenue and to give the populace a stake in ownership of the enterprises in order to maintain political support for further restructuring. Since the communist system had demanded great sacrifices of the citizenry, it was felt that state assets should be divided among the people in as equitable a manner as possible. Since workers stood to lose the most in the downsizing of state industry, it was important to give them a stake in the privatization process and the overall economic development, lest they turn to anti-reform populist parties.

How was the state to reconcile these competing demands? Poland and the Czech Republic chose to subordinate revenue collection to the development of broad-based support for privatization. Both countries employed coupon privatization schemes to sell off large state enterprises, though these schemes were part of an overall programme which included direct sales and other transfer mechanisms. The idea was to create an extensive ownership class who would act as self-interested enterprise owners, supporting the necessary enterprise restructuring. Both programmes achieved high levels of citizen participation, but not without partial dependence on Westerners. In the Czech Republic, the initial subscription rates were disappointingly low until some Western investors created investment funds and offered guaranteed returns on investments if people transferred their shares to the funds. The Polish programme incorporated fifteen national investment funds, co-managed by Western fund managers, into which the citizens had to invest their vouchers (in the Czech Republic, such funds developed separate of the official scheme).

The effectively free distribution of state resources is in seeming contradiction to Klaus' neo-liberal thinking (which would dictate that the most efficient means of privatization would be auction to the highest bidder) but demonstrates that the priority was the 'immediate political economic impact in helping to consolidate the dominant position of Václav Klaus' Civic Democratic Party' (Myant and Waller, 1993: 168). While the Czech privatization programme boosted political support for Klaus' government for a time, the economic results have been disappointing. Badly needed enterprise restructuring has not followed the privatization wave because ownership is divided among individual investors, employees and investment fund holders, often with no one entity willing or able to impose discipline. Many investment funds are linked to as-yet-unprivatized banks, leaving an 'incestuous relationship' (Robinson, 1997) among the banks, funds and enterprises, with enterprise restructuring and financial responsibility remaining low priorities. Since many banks are both owners and creditors of the former state enterprises, unprofitable companies are rarely forced into bankruptcy.

Large-scale privatization in Hungary did not take the form of voucher programmes, but rather direct sales as a key revenue-generating component of the Bokros Package. This method, with clearly established new ownership structures, makes it easier to effect enterprise restructuring. Revenue from privatization tripled from 1994 to 1995 (EIU, 1997b: 15) and the money was used to decrease Hungary's international debt. Hungary has been able to make such rapid progress in part because there is less opposition to foreign ownership in key sectors, such as energy, than in Poland and the Czech Republic (though it should be noted that there is considerable opposition to foreign ownership of agricultural land in Hungary).

The differentiation among the countries by 1989–90 meant that each country had to develop a policy package appropriate not only to its economic conditions but also its political conditions. More importantly, the interplay of politics/economics and domestic/international economic conditions has required that each country revise its policy strategies after one strategy has played itself out. The apparent macroeconomic success of some countries (steady GDP growth, falling unemployment and inflation over the years) masks the more difficult tasks which still need to be addressed, such as full enterprise privatization and restructuring, bank privatization, capital market regulation and effective reform of social services. It is these factors which will enable the economies of East-Central Europe to qualify for eventual EU membership and make them more competitive in the global economy (see Tables 5.1 and 5.2).

The early economic reforms generally paid scant attention to the need to replace the communist era cradle-to-grave social security systems with a fiscally viable social safety net that would ensure a minimum level of protection. Pension reform in Poland remains one of the most politically charged and significant economic issues. Old age and disability pensioners number 9.2 million out of a total population of 39 million, or one for every non-farm worker. In 1995, subsidies to the pension fund consumed 13.1 per cent of the state budget because the pension fund itself was inadequate (EIU, 1997c: 17; McKinsey, 1997). Although pension reform had long been on the drawing board, no serious efforts began before 1997, when a three pillar programme was proposed. A bill approved by the Sejm in late 1998 would guarantee state pensions for those over age 50. Workers between the ages of 30

TABLE 5.1 Key economic indicators, 1989–1998

	1989	1990	1991	1992	1993	1994	1995	1996	1997	1998[b]
Czech Republic										
Real GDP growth (%)	3.5[a]	-1.2	-14.2	-6.4	0.5	3.4	6.4	3.9	1.0	-1.0
Unemployment (%)	–	4.0	3.0	5.1	3.5	3.2	2.9	3.1	3.9	7.0
Consumer price inflation (%)	1.4[a]	10[a]	56.6	11.1	7.0	10.1	9.1	8.8	8.5	11.9
Hungary										
Real GDP growth (%)	1.1	-3.5	-11.9	-3.1	-0.6	2.9	1.5	1.3	4.4	5
Unemployment (%)	–	1.7	8.5	12.7	12.6	10.4	10.2	10.4	10.4	–
Consumer price inflation (%)	17.0	28.9	35.0	23.0	22.5	18.8	28.2	23.6	18.3	15.7
Poland										
Real GDP growth (%)	0.2	-11.6	-7.6	2.6	3.8	5.3	7.0	6.1	6.9	5.3
Unemployment (%)	–	6.1	11.8	14.3	16.4	16	14.9	13.2	10.5	–
Consumer price inflation (%)	251	585.8	70.3	43	36.9	33.3	26.8	20.1	15.9	12.9

[a] Czechoslovakia.
[b] Forecast.

Note: Statistical information for the countries of East-Central Europe is subject to discrepancies due to different measurement techniques (especially when counting unemployment) and periodic corrections in data. Most of the figures were taken from the Economist Intelligence Unit Country Profiles and Country Quarterly Reports. As many of these figures were revised in later years, the most updated statistics were used. The only exceptions were the unemployment figures for the Czech Republic in 1990 and 1991 and for Hungary in 1991. Those were taken from the IBRD publication Foreign Direct Investment and Environment: A Survey.

Sources: EIU, IBRD

TABLE 5.2   *Comparative economic indicators, 1996*

	Czech Republic	Hungary	Poland	Slovakia
GDP per head	$5,063	$4,308	$3,501	$3,531
GDP per capita purchasing power parity	$10,136	$6,906	$6,025	$7,130

Source: Economist Intelligence Unit (1997c) *Country Profile: Poland,* p. 14

and 50 would be able to divide their pension contributions between state and private pension funds, while workers under the age of 30 could choose among state, private or mixed funds. Legislation governing reform of the health care system was finally passed in July 1998 requiring employee contribution to insurance funds. According to some critics, though, the level of contribution mandated would be insufficient to ensure solvency of the funds.

For Hungary, reform of the social sector was stalled in 1996 because of the unpalatable effects of the Bokros Package. Current health care delivery is a hybrid of the state system and an informal private system, with doctors seeing patients privately on their off time and collecting fees directly from the patients. An attempt to reform the health care system in 1997 was deemed unconstitutional because it required a minimum contribution on the part of the self-employed. A new pension system became effective on 1 January 1998, with a private plan to accompany the state-funded pay-as-you-go system. New entrants into the labour force will be required to participate in the private system, and workers under 47 years of age have the option of joining. By the middle of 1998, workers covered by the private pension plan will pay 1 per cent of their salary into the National Pension Fund and 6 per cent into private pension plans. In 1999 and 2000, an additional 1 per cent contribution to the private funds will be required each year (EIU, 1997b: 16).

The Czech Republic's reform of health and pension systems advanced more rapidly, but not without controversy. The initial reform of the health insurance system took place before the demise of the Federation. A 1992 law ended the monopoly of the General Health Insurance Fund by allowing private companies to enter the insurance market. With little regulation, a system emerged whereby private insurance funds took on the lowest risk patients, leaving the state fund with a growing burden of older, sicker patients. Financial oversight of the private funds was inadequate and the government was left with costly bailouts of insolvent funds. Reform of the pension system was legislated in 1995 over the objections of trade unions. It includes supplementary individual savings accounts, gradual increases in the retirement age and a reduction in the level of the basic state pension. Controversy arose when the requirement for employer contributions was eliminated (Orenstein, 1996: 18). Furthermore, the Czech National Bank has argued that the regulation of capital markets will need to be strengthened before the supplemental pension funds can be established (EIU, 1997d: 12).

Unrealized expectations

Perhaps the biggest obstacle to overcome in the rapid marketization was the gap between people's expectations and the realities of the new economy. The economic transitions have transformed social divisions, creating considerable inequalities of wealth and opportunity. While inequality did exist under communism, it was both more hidden and less severe than that which has resulted after just a short period of market capitalism. World Bank studies for Poland indicate that poverty during the communist era was primarily 'linked to dysfunction of the family, dependency, severe illness, old age, and the milieu of social pathology', as well as to political poverty, whereby regime opponents were denied access to employment (*Zycie Gospodarcze*, 1996). It was only with economic liberalization that poverty began to affect the occupationally active population. Hungary has seen a considerable decline in the middle class that had developed under Kádárism, with people pulled both downward and upward, creating a saddle effect in the social structure (Mason et al., 1997: 15).

Why were the people of East-Central Europe so unprepared for the realities? In part, the level of economic literacy was very low in the transitional countries, with people equating the market economy with prosperity (Schöpflin, 1993: 26). With the market system having helped defeat the discredited command system, people were unprepared for market failures. 'A fascination with the successes of the Western economy certainly does not go hand-in-hand with awareness of its rules' (Morawski, 1992: 105). People at first could not understand the complexities of a market economy and the demands it placed on workers, producers, consumers and yes, the state. The image propagated by Western governments and media was of limitless opportunity and financial reward. Many workers suspected that the transformation would be inherently pro-bourgeois, not pro-worker, but they thought that they would still be accorded the basic necessities and reasonable opportunity.

The initial results of marketization were positive. Shortages were eliminated overnight with the freeing of the trade regime. After decades of pent-up consumer demand in the shortage economy, consumerism was unleashed somewhat irrationally. Satellite dishes could be seen in even the smallest villages in the early years of the transition and increased automobile traffic caused problems for a road system designed around an extensive public transportation network. These countries experienced the near wholesale rejection of Eastern products in favour of the presumably superior Western goods, leading to severely diminished demand for Eastern goods. A pendulum effect began after a couple of years, with consumers returning to domestic goods, especially as Eastern producers improved their packaging and marketing. In 1997, a survey showed that 38 per cent of Poles trusted home products above all else while consumer patriotism was lower among Hungarians (20 per cent), Czechs (17 per cent), and Slovaks (18 per cent) (CEER, 1997). However, as prosperity has increased, so has the ability to purchase more expensive Western products, resulting in increased trade imbalances between West and East. It is estimated, for example, that much of the profit from the sale of individual shares in Czech investment funds during the privatization programme has been used to purchase imported consumer goods (EIU, 1997a: 12).

Unemployment, at least official unemployment, was virtually unknown under communism. Yugoslavia, a market socialist economy, was the main exception, experiencing open unemployment already in the 1960s which was resolved in part by exporting excess labour to West Germany during its economic miracle. Immediately after the launch of economic reforms, unemployment skyrocketed in most countries, and has remained in double digits through the 1990s, except in the Czech Republic (see Table 5.1). Economic growth, though steady in Poland since 1992 and more uneven in the other countries, has not been sufficient to absorb labour shed from the public sector. Most troubling about the unemployment picture is that many are long-term unemployed, lacking the skills demanded in the new economy. It is these people who make up a significant portion of the new poor. Institutions of higher learning have expanded to include evening and weekend programmes, as well as distance learning, but these programmes must be funded by the students themselves. State financed job retraining programmes have been started but they are of little value if economic growth is insufficient to reabsorb the unemployed. Older workers are marginalized in employment policies that focus retraining efforts on those for whom an investment in training will likely have a long-term payoff.

Economic theory holds that excess labour will migrate to areas of labour shortages. However, in East-Central Europe, the free migration of labour is inhibited by a chronic housing shortage, especially in large cities where growth rates have been the highest. In Hungary and Poland, the rate of new housing construction is still below that of 1989 (EIU, 1997b, 1997c). Even in the United States, where people are far more mobile than in Europe, pockets of chronic high unemployment remain. Theory aside, no degree of worker mobility can make up for the absence of skills.

The generally high levels of unemployment in East-Central Europe are beginning to converge with the levels in Western Europe in the late 1990s. In Western Europe, the high cost of social benefits packages means that firms are reluctant to take on additional employees and production increasingly is moved to lower cost countries. European Union countries are trying to adopt less restrictive labour policies and reduce generous benefits in order to bring down double digit unemployment figures, but this has met with considerable opposition from workers. Eastern countries likewise will have to adopt a flexible approach to labour markets, as the state budgets simply cannot provide the level of social support afforded by the West, nor will foreign companies be willing to invest heavily if other countries offer lower labour costs. Eastern labour unions have insufficient political clout (and the unemployed none) to prevent the adoption of a relatively unfettered labour market with less social protection.

Another source of disillusionment has been with the levels of assistance from the West. In the heady days after the collapse of communism, there was talk of a Marshall-style plan for the East which would enable the rapid restructuring of the economies and ensure the viability of the fledgling democracies, as the Marshall Plan had done for Germany. Why should the East not expect such extensive assistance? The West had long enticed the Eastern bloc with economic rewards in order to help break the bonds of communism. Economic assistance was considered a rightful reward for having achieved this.

Why were the levels of foreign assistance so low? With the end of the Cold War duality, there was no longer the need to keep countries in the Western camp with economic assistance. When Mikhail Gorbachev made it clear that the Soviet Union would not stand in the way of reforms in the Eastern bloc, the threat which had spurred the Marshall Plan was removed. Even the collapse of the Soviet Union at the end of 1991 did not pose a compelling enough security danger to induce the West to deliver substantial aid. Early in the transitions, the Western donor countries were faced with issues more critical to their domestic polities: the 1991–2 economic slowdown; the Gulf War; and the deepening of European integration. Germany, the largest contributor of foreign assistance, had unique reasons for its aid. With its liberal asylum laws and close proximity to Eastern Europe, Germany would be the destination of choice for many economic refugees. Bonn felt compelled to help with the recovery of Poland due to the historical burden of Polish-German relations. While the circumstances and extent of Germany's assistance were unequalled by other countries, they still were driven by self-interest.

A particularly troubling issue in East–West relations is the pace of opening Western markets to Eastern goods. While the transitional countries were required to eliminate many trade barriers as a condition to receiving World Bank and IMF assistance, Western countries did not practice what they preached because many of the goods in which Eastern producers have a comparative advantage, such as textiles, steel and agricultural products, are politically sensitive sectors in the West.

TABLE 5.3   *Percentage of countries' exports to the*
EU subject to non-tariff barriers, 1995

World	16.5
Industrialized countries	10.4
Developing countries	21.9
Poland	32.4
Hungary	37.5
Czech Republic	10.4
Former Soviet Union	19.1

Source: UNCTAD, adapted from Central European Economic
Review, November 1997: 9

Polish and Hungarian exports to the EU are subject to a higher degree
of trade protectionism than countries in other regions of the world (see
Table 5.3). Agricultural exports amounted to 25 per cent of Poland's
exports to the European Community in 1989; today they stand at 11 per
cent (Kaminski, 1997). Subsidies amount to half the retail price of
foodstuffs in the EU but only 15 per cent in Poland (Koza, 1997). The
export of Western goods is subsidized with government export credits
and other mechanisms. The tension between East and West over equitable market access will not fade until the Eastern states are granted full
membership in the European Union, but more likely than not, the
transition will be gradual for certain sectors, namely agriculture.

Labour, business and the state: emerging cleavages

As the former socialist worker states enter the globalized market
economy, a new cleavage between labour and capital is emerging. With
the newly gained freedoms of organization, collective bargaining and
the right to strike, it was hoped that trade unions would become an
integral part of the decision making process on economic affairs. As in
other regions, the interests of labour increasingly are at odds with the
interests of capital (both domestic entrepreneurs and foreign investors),
as well as the demands of the international financial institutions. East-
Central Europeans are still conditioned by the communist value system,
which rewarded workers with higher wages and privileges not
accorded other social groups. Now many workers, primarily the semi-
skilled and unskilled, find themselves losing ground or pushed out of
the labour market altogether. The cleavage between labour and capital
will become more pronounced in the private sector, where labour
unions are virtually non-existent. Many of the newly established
domestic companies are small enterprises, where attempts at unionization even in the West usually end in failure. There are even reports

that workers have been fired for attempts to organize new unions (cf. Ellingstad, 1997; Freeman, 1993).

The trade unions which existed under communism were established by the party and served workers' interests only in so far as those interests served party ideology and induced workers to meet state production targets. They were 'transmission belts' of the communist system, linking the masses with the party engine while restraining worker demand (cf. Myant and Waller, 1993; Tóth, 1993). The unions played an important role in the daily lives of workers, providing welfare benefits, holiday facilities, cultural opportunities and political education. This social role continued after 1989 and was critical in helping the old trade unions retain high membership levels in the early post-communist period.

The successor unions retained their dominant role in Hungary and the Czech Republic due to the financial and institutional resources held over from the communist era, the presence of experienced union representatives in state enterprises, and the weakness of new, independent unions. Governments have been slow to tackle the issue of rightful distribution of the communist era largesse of the successor unions, leaving start-up unions at a comparative financial disadvantage. The successor unions have also benefited from 'the ambivalence of the new governments toward reforming labour relations' (Freeman, 1993: 100) as labour relations have been subordinated to the need to institute macro-economic reform. Mechanisms for involving unions in policy formulation are underdeveloped. Today, successor unions compete for influence and resources with the independent unions which have been established, rather than joining together in defence of common interests.

In Poland, the All-Polish Federation of Trade Unions (OPZZ), the successor union, enjoys numerical superiority to Solidarity but is less influential. Solidarity remains unable to resolve its schizophrenic identity between labour union and reform political party. Having acted as a social movement rallying opposition to the communist state, Solidarity by 1989 found itself simultaneously pushing for radical economic reforms and defending the interests of those who faced the greatest dislocation as a consequence of the reforms – the workers. When the shock therapy plan was developed, the Solidarity Union was not consulted but its leaders nevertheless extended a protective umbrella over society in the early months of the transition, not agitating against decreases in the standard of living, which they believed would be relatively short-lived (Gortat, 1993: 118). As the pain of the reforms set in, Solidarity's inherently contradictory role sharpened (Cook, 1995: 15), causing some members to claim that the leadership had betrayed its core constituency. Union protests against the pain of the shock therapy developed by the summer of 1990 but were generally unfocused and the union was unable to present a viable alternative policy.

For Solidarity, the concept of a 'reformist' union which takes co-responsibility for the country prevailed over that of a labour interest group (cf. Vinton, 1991). At its third platform conference, held in 1996, Professor Jadwiga Staniszkis declared in the main address that Solidarity should be the country's 'sole force for reform' regarding both the 'economic efficiency and the functioning of democratic institutions' (*Tygodnik Solidarnosc*, 1996). Politically, Solidarity stands on the right with its anti-communist rhetoric and its support of continued market reforms but on such key economic issues as job protection and agriculture, the party remains left-of-centre. The union's protest tactics represent a populist backlash against painful reform, demanding additional subsidies to moribund state industries and inciting against the dominance of the international financial organizations, often with strong nationalistic and even anti-Semitic overtones. The schizophrenic identity is proving to be problematic in the Solidarity Electoral Action–Freedom Union (AWS–UW) government, particularly as the privatization process deepens and extends into the politically significant mining sector.

Although the OPZZ agitated in the early years of transition in an effort to disrupt the Balcerowicz plan (Vinton, 1991: 36), it generally had maintained a low profile in part because of its lower concentration of blue collar workers, the biggest losers of the transition. While it served in the government as a member of the Democratic Left Alliance from 1993 to 1997, it had little apparent influence on the economic reform process (Cook, 1995: 15). In fact, the SLD greatly distanced itself from a leftist agenda once in power, continuing the reforms of its predecessor as it recognized its lack of manoeuvrability within the constraints placed by the international financial institutions. Part of the opposition once again, the OPZZ has accused the government of favouring Solidarity in its contacts with labour unions and has become more publicly visible, with large public protests demanding to be included in the decision making on issues of health care reform, education and pensions.

The political role of trade unions in Hungary is less prominent than in Poland due to the earlier emergence of true political parties as oppositional forces (Myant and Waller, 1993: 175) and the greater plurality of unions. The successor union, the National Association of Hungarian Trade Unions (MSZOSZ), split into four confederations and has been joined on the scene by numerous occupational unions and workplace-level organizations. Enterprise unionism is a remnant of the New Economic Mechanism, which outlawed multi-employer collective bargaining but at the same time expanded the rights of workers who became part of the decision making process in the individual enterprises (Tóth, 1993). During the communist era managers of state enterprises were also union members. These close ties with management favoured the successor unions when other unions tried to establish themselves in enterprises.

Social protest against the initial economic reforms was dampened in part because of the absence of one or two dominant unions in Hungary and also the enterprise-level organizational structure which lessens unions' impact, allowing industry leaders to divide and conquer. In contrast, when a strong Western industrial union threatens action, the chances are greater for a favourable industry-wide agreement. MSZOSZ did propose to the government a system of sector collective agreements but the Labour Affairs Ministry rejected the proposal (*Magyar Nemzet*, 1995a). Such an agreement, with professional trade union representatives independent of specific enterprises, could have been extended to small private ventures in Hungary where unionization is virtually non-existent.

After the 1994 elections, the centre-left government announced as a primary goal the formation of a social-economic pact between the government and the public. Although the government pledged to strengthen the Interests Coordination Council (government, business and labour unions), the trade unions were hardly consulted prior to the announcement of the Bokros Package. 'Only the Finance Ministry's pragmatic fiscal advice, and the conditions set down by the International Monetary Fund for a standby loan, were given real attention' (Szilagyi, 1996c: 41). At the time, Endre Szabo, the chair of the trade union representing public employees, commented, '. . . it is to be feared that the government looks upon the trade unions as a danger rather than a chance to implement its policies' (*Magyar Nemzet*, 1995b).

The government lost credibility for allegedly putting IMF interests ahead of domestic interests. After the first year of positive GDP growth and measurable declines in both the unemployment and inflation rates in 1994, the sense of crisis had passed for most Hungarians and there was an obvious unwillingness to make further sacrifices. There was also a lack of consensus within the Socialist Party on the need for austerity measures. This was similar to the problem faced by the early Solidarity governments in Poland: how to remain faithful to its constituent base (left, labour) while at the same time proceeding with painful economic restructuring.

Civil service employees, who had essentially brought the Socialists back to power (Szilagyi, 1996c: 42), were especially threatened, as the package called for the first significant downsizing of the civil service. By the autumn of 1995, dissatisfaction over the pain of the Bokros Package led to the most significant strike activity in Hungary's transition, with strikes in education, public transport and energy, and demonstrations by students, health care workers and university lecturers. The government responded with negotiations on wage increases, which led to an eventual agreement in January 1996 raising the minimum wage and reducing the decline in real wages for 1996 (Szilagyi, 1996c: 43).

Laszlo Sandor, chair of the MSZOSZ, admitted that both the government and the trade unions had been at fault in handling the Bokros

Package. 'We had wanted to force too much into the social and economic agreement. On the other hand, the government had an exaggerated expectation that we would surrender certain trade union rights in the agreement. When it became clear that the government had to bring in restrictive measures, it should have compensated us in other areas, for example, in labour law and given more guarantees for the freedom to form organizations' (*Nepszava*, 1997b).

In the final years of communism in Czechoslovakia, no alternative unions were able to develop in a political environment controlled by hardliners. In Poland the Solidarity movement led the transition, while in Czechoslovakia, it was the Civic Forum (in the absence of a labour element) which held the confidence of the people in the initial transition period (Myant, 1993: 62). The dominance of centre–right forces in post-communist Czech politics forced the unions to pursue a conciliatory strategy with the government from the start. Former Vice President of the Czech and Slovak Confederation of Trade Unions (ČSKOS) Stanislaw Hošek concluded that the declared non-political approach of the unions was a mistake, for it yielded too much power to Klaus' party. While Hošek rejected an alliance with any one party, he believes that the ČSKOS should have sought to influence politics by working more closely with left-of-centre parties (Myant, 1993: 77). Having failed to assert itself strongly in the early transition, the ČSKOS continued to have little influence on national politics after the division of the Federation but it should be noted that with the extremely low unemployment rate in the Czech Republic, defence of jobs has not been as great a concern as elsewhere.

Tripartism has been utilized with varied success to bring labour and business interests into the political process but mainly it has been used in an effort to prevent widespread labour unrest. It does not necessarily offer labour or business an influential role in policy formation, for the elected elite tend to discount the importance of interest groups in the decision making process. The models for tripartism are the social contracts of Germany and Austria (*Mitbestimmung*, or co-determination) but the eastern tripartite institutions cannot yet be compared with them since the government retains primary decision making authority. Furthermore, with state enterprises dominating the employers federations, tripartite arrangements essentially shut out the private sector (Freeman, 1993: 104), adding to the tension between the still large public sector and the fledgling private sector.

Czechoslovakia was the first in East-Central Europe to develop tripartite structures, with the establishment of the Council for Economic and Social Accord in 1990 in response to demands by the trade unions for a say in economic and social policy (cf. Oberman, 1991). The Council brings together government, labour and business associations on a regular basis to discuss labour and social policy initiatives and to bargain jointly over wage and taxation issues in order to help prevent labour unrest. Angered by a series of strikes in 1994, Václav Klaus attempted to weaken the tripartite council but backed off when labour unrest heightened.

In forming the Council for Economic and Social Accord, the government forged an otherwise unlikely alliance among various business groups, the main players being the Union of Industry and Transport and the Association of Entrepreneurs. The Union is now the largest business association in the Czech Republic, organizing workshops and conferences and serving as an information clearing-house. It is considered a re-creation of the communist-era industrial organs and represents primarily the medium and large former state enterprises who collectively employ approximately one-fifth of the labour force. The Association of Entrepreneurs, representing small entrepreneurs, opposes what it considers the cosy relationship between the banking industry and large former SOEs which discriminates against small enterprises in their ability to obtain capital (Orenstein and Desai, 1997: 45–49). The Union of Industry and Transport later pulled out of the umbrella organization for business interests due to the divergent interests between the members. Although both the Union and the Association have achieved a virtual monopoly in their sectors because of their positions on the Council, they have not been very successful in pursuing their own agendas because the government's agenda remains the dominant force of the tripartite council (Orenstein and Desai, 1997: 49).

In Poland, tripartism played a sporadic role in policy formulation during the first period of centre–right rule, in part because of the conflict between the OPZZ and Solidarity. Consequently, Poland experienced 'a remarkable failure of social dialogue, with Polish governments consulting with employees only when forced to do so by major protests' (Myant and Waller, 1993: 179). This contributed to the high level of social unrest, particularly in the early 1990s. Tripartism was revived under the SLD-PSL government. According to Marek Borowski, Vice Speaker of the Sejm and SLD member, this was a major factor in the decline of strike activity, from 7,000 strikes in 1993 to just 42 in 1996 (Baczynski et al., 1997). In 1995 after the expiration of wage controls, the government consulted with the unions and employers to hold down excess wage growth in the public sector. Solidarity was successful in calling for a provision to renegotiate the arrangement if inflation exceeded the anticipated levels. At its third platform conference, Solidarity called for the development of a substantive tripartite council along the lines of the Swedish, Dutch or Austrian models (*Tygodnik Solidarnosc*, 1996), but such pacts will become increasingly difficult with the inevitable decline in labour's strength as the private sector becomes more dominant.

Entrepreneurs represent a newly emergent interest group but one which is not able fully to articulate its interests within the political system for several reasons. First, with the complexity and duration of the economic transition, institutions and the rules of the game for influencing economic policy making are not yet firm. Second, with frequent policy adjustments in response to changing macroeconomic conditions, or resulting from a change of government, business interests have not been able to focus on particular policy concerns for any extended period of time. Finally, the interests of small entrepreneurs and those of the heads of industry generally are not in accord with one another nor respected by the other side.

In East-Central Europe, the economic policies of the government are often seen as favouring the interests of the state sector over those of private entrepreneurs. Governments frequently reschedule payments of state enterprises' back taxes and social security dues. Without such extensions, enterprises unable to meet their payment schedules would be forced into bankruptcy. In the medium term, the governments may manage to stave off labour unrest which would accompany liquidation of state enterprises but in the long run, these delinquent enterprises will continue to drain state resources. The entrepreneurial class sees itself subsidizing industrial dinosaurs, preventing tax reductions which they say would enable them to expand. More acceptable to business interests would be proactive restructuring to make state enterprises profitable where possible, and policies to ease the unemployment pain through targeted assistance, job retraining, and job creation. Protective labour policies which are a remnant of the communist system are considered by entrepreneurs as a further hindrance to expansion. The Institute for Study of Democracy and Private Enterprises conducted a survey of company directors, managers and owners in Poland in response to the new labour code adopted by the Sejm in 1996. The respondents favoured liberalizing the labour code to allow unlimited numbers of temporary job contracts and increases in the amount of overtime that could be worked. They also wanted more effective tools against striking workers, including the right to declare lockouts (Luczak, 1997). Such extreme discipline of labour on capital's terms is unlikely but the trend clearly will be toward a less restrictive labour market.

With the absence of an effective tripartite mechanism in Poland, business groups have migrated along the political spectrum in search of parties supportive of their interests. In the 1993 parliamentary elections, the SLD was widely supported by businessmen, and Public Opinion Research Center (CBOS) surveys reveal that until 1994, left-wing views were generally very prevalent among entrepreneurs and businessmen. Even in the 1995 presidential election, SLD chair Aleksander Kwaśniewski, received 55 per cent of the business vote (Filas and Knap, 1997). Although his policies were not of the free market strain desired by businessmen, he was viewed as more stable and predictable than Wałęsa. Right-of-centre views now dominate, particularly among small and medium-sized businessmen who oppose excessive state intervention in the economy. A CBOS poll in April 1997 revealed that among Polish entrepreneurs, one-third had declared their support for the Solidarity Electoral Action, 24 per cent for the Freedom Union, and 14 per cent for the Democratic Left Alliance.

The liberal Freedom Union is the party most representative of Polish business interests. Its platform is more committed to continued market reforms than those of the SLD and AWS. As a member of the current governing coalition, it exerts greater influence than its electoral numbers would otherwise grant it. Once staunchly opposed to serving in a coalition government with the former communists, the UW was not as adamantly opposed to such a formulation during the 1997 parliamentary campaign. In the future, it could play a role similar to the FDP in Germany, acting as kingmaker for the other two parties (assuming that Solidarity, in some incarnation, continues to be a major player), thereby providing one of the few clear party links for an interest group in East-Central Europe.

Foreign investment plays a critical role in the development of the private sector and will alter labour–capital relations. With low wage, highly skilled workers, the proximity to West European markets and reasonably sound infrastructure, it was expected that the transitional countries would benefit considerably from foreign direct investment. The Economist Intelligence Unit calculates that, between 1990 and 1995, $24.78 billion had been invested in the Visegrad Four. However, this pales in comparison with the $698 billion which the German federal government transferred to its new eastern states over the same period. In a two-year time span, France alone received more foreign investment than the entire former Eastern bloc between 1989 and 1995 (Ellingstad, 1997: 7). Political instability, labour unrest, arcane regulations governing land ownership by foreigners, and uncertainty about the commitment to market economics caused many investors to hesitate. However, as the markets in the East mature, the rate of foreign investment has picked up.

Poland and Hungary have established special economic zones to attract foreign companies. The Polish Agency for Regional Development, with funding from the European Union, had established nine such zones by the end of 1997 with tax breaks and reduced customs duties in order to attract foreign investment and create jobs in the laggard regions. The Czech Republic, with its stronger commitment to market principles, has underutilized such methods and consequently has lagged behind Hungary and Poland in attracting foreign investment. The rewards of these zones have been uneven. While Poland has established zones in the hardest hit regions, many of the Western industrial parks in Hungary are near Budapest, leaving the under-developed eastern region out of the foreign investment picture. As regions (between and within countries) compete for foreign investors, they can end up in a bidding war whereby concessions offered to Western investors increase at the expense of rewards to their own citizens. Foreign companies can often negotiate very advantageous packages in which they contribute relatively little to the tax base or the development of local industry.

Foreign investment has had negative consequences for both local capital and labour. Much of it has turned out to be market seeking rather than production seeking (OECD, 1994: 5), with Eastern firms being bought out or driven out of business by wealthier, more savvy Western companies. In the automobile industry, when a foreign producer opens an assembly plant, other foreign firms move into the area, shutting out local suppliers. With high unemployment rates, the countries of East-Central Europe are in a weak bargaining position to pass domestic content laws to protect local industry. Laws to attract foreign investors allow for the easy importation of semi-finished products. The assembly jobs created through such schemes offer less remuneration than value added manufacturing. A major unknown factor is the role of local firms in research and development. The educational system of East-Central Europe produced many well trained scientists and engineers for whom labour costs are a fraction of those in Western Europe. Research and development activities may start to be located closer to the new Western plants, drawing on this talent pool, but as yet, much of the R&D for these industries is still conducted in the West.

There was fear that Easterners would be exploited as a source of cheap labour but wages in foreign owned enterprises tend to exceed those in domestic firms so far. The higher wages serve not just to attract the best employees from the local labour pool but also to reduce foreign firms' risk of attempted unionization at their plants. A comparison of wages from Hungary reveals that salaries for Eastern executives working in foreign firms are 44 per cent higher than in Eastern firms; for white collar employees, the lead is 25 per cent and for manual labourers it is 18 per cent (Abraham, 1996).

Foreign companies moving into East-Central Europe are finding that the labour market is still a buyer's market due to high unemployment and weakened trade unions. A study in 1996 sponsored by Hokkaido University showed that top managers in the East considered trade unions to be largely irrelevant. 'On questions about improvement in working conditions, dismissal of workers and privatization, over 50 per cent of all respondents replied that trade unions at their companies had absolutely no influence whatsoever' (Ellingstad, 1997: 15). Organization of unions in greenfield sites is more difficult than in former SOEs where unions already existed.

At this stage in the transformation, the establishment of 'normal' interest politics is still a distant goal and it is not yet possible to define precisely what issues constitute the 'legitimate' areas for labour and capital intervention in the political process. Even in well-established market democracies, coordination of government, capital and labour interests is a contentious process. The experience with tripartite councils has been disappointing across East-Central Europe. In some cases, they have diffused social unrest and postponed layoffs or limited the impact of inflation on wages and pensions. In other cases unions or employer associations have withdrawn from tripartite structures, citing alleged violations of the agreements or inherent incompatibilities between member organizations.

If not tripartism, what is the solution to the labour/capital cleavage? When viewed from the Western perspective, the formation of electoral alliances and the fielding of parliamentary candidates by labour unions is considered beyond the realm of their 'normal' activities – the enterprise level or, by extension, the sector level. It is unlikely that either labour or capital will directly form viable political parties in the long run (with Solidarity still a question mark), for their interests are generally too narrow to generate the necessary support. They might better focus their efforts on becoming well-organized interest groups, pressing political parties for defence of their members' material interests in exchange for their electoral support (cf. Myant and Waller, 1993).

With macroeconomic stability and positive growth having been achieved, are trade unions able to pull back from policy formulation efforts and concentrate on the traditional realm of union activities, namely issues relating to workplace conditions, compensation and job security? The middle ground between enterprise and the state, namely sector-wide trade unions and employer associations, is still only partially formed. As a result, conflicts which begin at the enterprise level are often pushed up to the national level in contrast with more developed market economies, where such conflicts often can be negotiated between industry associations and labour unions and rarely reach the level of national politics. Unions in all countries face decreasing membership, loss of influence in privatized enterprises, the absence of collective bargaining agreements in the vast majority of enterprises and difficulty organizing in the private sector. Therefore, even as the locus of conflict begins to shift to the level of employer–employee relations, the government still will be called upon to ensure that rules of collective bargaining be established and respected in order to create a more level playing field for labour.

Does the potential exist for labour to become an influential political force in post-communist East-Central Europe? Because of the current surplus of labour, the inevitability of industry downsizing following restructuring, and the growing role of the mostly non-unionized private sector, trade unions will continue to wield little influence on economic decision making. In Western Europe, unions have been most successful where they have formed national confederations with clear agendas, when both governments and employers saw the value in including labour in the economic policy process, and where left-of-centre political parties are strong. However, even these conditions provide less guarantee of success in the increasingly globalized economy. No amount of continued economic growth and political stability in East-Central

Europe will allow unions to achieve the level of influence enjoyed until recently by West European unions, though unions in particular state sectors such as health care, or even in heavy industry after privatization might retain measurable strength. The relationship between trade unions and governments depends largely on shifts in political fortunes. In Hungary in 1998, the victory of the centre-right further diminishes the political prospects for the unions in the near term. The results of the 1998 Czech elections were also disappointing for labour. It was hoped that a victory by the Social Democrats would offer labour a voice in government but the Social Democratic-led minority government is too weak.

The ability of unions to influence policy is hindered by their low levels of public confidence. The trade unions in Hungary had only a 37 per cent confidence rating in 1997 (Perczel, 1997) while those in the Czech Republic had a 34 per cent approval and a 42 per cent dis-approval rating at the end of 1996 (*Lidove Noviny*, 1996). In 1997, Solidarity enjoyed only a 42 per cent approval rating and the OPZZ a 26 per cent rating. The disapproval ratings for both unions exceeded their approval ratings: 45 per cent for Solidarity and 39 per cent for OPZZ (PAP, 1997c). Such low ratings can be attributed to a number of factors. There is a considerable lack of connection between the rank and file and the leadership. Bill Lomax argues that trade unions are 'self appointed bureaucratic fiefdoms' whose leaders 'make a living out of the pretense of representing workers' interests' (1997c: 50) rather than functioning as intermediary institutions of civil society. In each country, successor unions clash with independent unions, with neither being able to present a substantive response to the painful economic reforms. However, there are many unresolved issues, such as effective reform of the social security system and issues regarding EU accession (the impact on labour of the continued austerity measures needed to meet the criteria for accession) where unions may have a role in the policy process.

Economic transition literature, analysing the recovery of Germany and Japan after the Second World War and the transitions in Latin America and Asia, points to the existence of a solid entrepreneurial middle class as a vital prerequisite to the development of capitalism (Nonneman 1996c: 40). Do East-Central European societies exhibit patterns of an emerging middle class? Contrary to ideology, communist society did have identifiable class patterns, with manual workers and peasants forming the lower class, the intelligentsia, white collar workers and skilled labourers forming the middle class, and party officials forming the upper class (Kurczewski, 1997: 22). In East-Central Europe the nomenklatura and the former black marketeers constituted the early entrepreneurial class in the days of wild privatization, but diversification and deepening of the middle class is now critical for the consolidation of democratic capitalism. Today, higher education is even more important in determining one's membership in the middle class, at least in the private sector. Those who are educated but remain in the state sector as academics, teachers, bureaucrats or health care professionals are unable to maintain the middle class status they had in the communist era and increasingly leave the state sector for private business, often in unrelated fields.

Since class identification is a social structure, it is impossible to obtain an objective measurement of the middle class but subjective measurements are still important. Despite the fluidity of the Polish economy, a consistently high percentage of Poles identify themselves as 'middle class' – 76 per cent in 1988; 72 per cent in 1992; and 73 per cent in 1996 (Kurczewski, 1997: 22). It is important to track the changes in support for liberal democracy that occur as the middle class evolves, according to sociologist Kurczewski. There is a strong correlation between class and preference for the current system. While 85 per cent of employees with degrees and 83 per cent of the self-employed (who generally perceive themselves as middle class) expressed a preference for the current system in Poland, only 60 per cent of farmers and 59 per cent of unskilled labourers did. Both the new middle class of business people and the traditional middle class of intellectuals strongly favour participatory democracy and free enterprise, though the business class generally supports more liberal policies. A gradual shift in the attitudes of educated workers is evident in Kurczewski's surveys. While they generally share the same values as the middle class, educated workers are increasingly supportive of socially sensitive policies (Kurczewski, 1997: 25).

Participation in the electoral process in East-Central Europe is beginning to reflect the pattern of established Western democracies, with members of the middle class considerably more likely to participate not just in elections but also interest group formation and political party activities than are members of the working class. However, the emergence of a solid, stable middle class will take more than just several years of economic growth and increased enrolment in institutions of higher education. Even as the middle class expands, great polarities within these societies will remain. In the long run, it is important that the wealthy not be allowed to dominate the political process, nor that the underclasses remain neglected to the point that large numbers of people throw their support behind national/populist parties or withdraw from legitimate forms of political activity.

Lessons learned from the economic transition

The transformation of the economic system has been more drawn out and politically divisive than was anticipated. Policy makers focused primarily on macroeconomic recovery, largely ignoring the need for a well coordinated industrial policy that would include labour–employer relations and enterprise restructuring. One of the greatest policy short-falls was the *laissez-faire* approach to enterprise restructuring. Much of the transition literature contends that enterprise managers and employees were unwilling to make the changes necessary to survive the onslaught of the free market. In actuality, many enterprises were willing to build on their strengths but were simply overwhelmed by market forces in the absence of any coherent industrial policy. The neo-liberal experiment pushed upon these countries by multilateral organ-izations ignored the wisdom of government policies in such areas as technology, competition, trade and investment (Amsden et al., 1994).

Both the gradualist and shock therapy approaches had social conse-quences which necessitated policy adjustments. In Poland and Hungary, the first post-communist governments did not adequately assess the limits of the public's tolerance for dislocation. When the era of extra-ordinary politics ended, the Polish government failed to establish a credible dialogue with the people in order to 'sell' the continued reform process. The Hungarian Socialist Party, the beneficiary of the failure of the centre-right forces to generate popular support for the reforms, made the same mistake with the implementation of the Bokros Package in 1995. By the end of 1997, it appeared that the Socialists might have recovered from the post-Bokros decline in their support, but issues of crime, corruption and the uneven benefits of economic recovery proved to be their undoing in the 1998 elections. One of the issues affecting support for painful reforms has been the question of 'ownership' of the reforms, whether reforms are perceived as homegrown or designed and imposed by foreign economic experts with little understanding of local conditions. More often than not, it is the latter interpretation.

A suitable social safety net, designed to protect society's most vulnerable, is essential to maintaining political support for reforms in the long term. Interestingly, it was in Czechoslovakia where the most concerted social protection policies were enacted. Social democrats in the Ministry of Labour and Social Affairs were primarily responsible for establishing a minimum safety net, while transformation of the macro-economic system was left to the neo-liberals of the Finance Ministry, then led by Václav Klaus. A comparison of real price increases for rents, energy, education and health care in Poland and Czechoslovakia/Czech Republic from 1990 through 1993 shows that Poles had to absorb much higher increases. Even after the self-proclaimed Thatcherite Klaus became Prime Minister, increases in the cost of such services were gradual (and subject to postponement when popular support for the ODS waned). The success of these policies was largely responsible for helping sustain support for reforms in the early years (Orenstein, 1996: 16).

The transformations of East-Central Europe are far from complete. Efforts now have to be shifted from macroeconomic management and privatization to enterprise restructuring, tighter regulation of the economy, particularly taxation and financial institutions, industrial relations, employment policies, the maintenance of an adequate social safety net and ensuring fiscally and politically viable health care and pension programmes. These items are critical for cultivating social support for market democracy and developing sound, competitive economies that will allow for EU entry.

6

Interest Group Articulation in Post-Communism

The transition from communism has created both the conditions and the impetus for the development of various socioeconomic interest groups, some of which are visibly active, while others remain latent. Due to the impoverishment of the public sector, limited resources are available to address social ills, creating an environment of new social cleavages which may or may not be reflected in the current party politics of the post-communist countries. What types of interest groups have emerged, and why are some politically active while others remain unorganized? The issue of interest representation is important for the long-term sustainability of democracy for it is critical that disadvantaged groups be able to raise their concerns with their leaders, lest they turn to undemocratic methods to effect change. While the spectrum of interest groups developing in East-Central Europe is similar to that in Western democracies (labour, business, ethnic minorities, women, environmentalists, youth), the nature of interest articulation is still very much in the developmental stage. What are the chances for these groups to mobilize resources and to find representation in the new political system? Restricted media access, a shortage of financial resources and the fluid nature of party politics hinder the emergence of a stable and democratic pattern of competitive interest politics. In cases where these interest groups lack adequate resources, is the state strong enough and willing to ensure the rights of the most disadvantaged? Does the political system provide access for new issues, and can it accommodate a pluralism of competing issues with some degree of equity?

Interest groups which predated the transitions of 1989–90 had little or no authentic voice in the communist system. Grassroots environmental and anti-nuclear groups often were co-opted by the communist party in order to keep a lid on dissent. The party-sanctioned women's organizations were created to help institute policies of full employment rather than to serve the genuine interests of women. Trade unions, farm collectives and educational associations were expected dutifully to implement state directives regardless of their authentic interests. Still other potential groups, such as ethnic minorities, existed under communism but generally were not permitted even nominal self-organization.

An important body of literature exists on the integral role of interest groups in representative democracy. David Truman's classic treatment of the role of interest groups in the American political process (*The Governmental Process: Political Interests and Public Opinion*) is in many ways applicable to the situation evolving in East-Central Europe. Truman defines an interest group as 'any group that, on the basis of one or more shared attitudes, makes certain claims upon other groups in the society for the establishment, maintenance, or enhancement of forms of behaviour that are implied by the shared attitudes' (Truman, 1953: 33). The diverse economic, religious and ethnic composition of modern societies, combined with people's different perceptions and experiences, precludes the existence of a universally held public interest, though certain interests may be shared by a large portion of the population at any given time.

By definition, interest groups are not political groupings but become political when they choose to make their claims through governmental institutions (Truman, 1953: 37), though they may also employ other means of petition, such as intermediary institutions, direct appeals to the media or other interest groups, labour stoppages, or street demonstrations. The politicization of interest groups is almost inevitable, though. As one group successfully appeals to the government for intervention on a given issue, the existing equilibrium is disturbed. The newly 'disadvantaged' group is likely to appeal to the government for an adjustment favourable to its interests (Truman, 1953: 106). Issues of a redistributive nature (regarding wealth, power, access to goods and services) are the most divisive for a society.

Truman's analysis, by focusing on shared interests as the basis for interest groups, allows for the inclusion of unorganized interest groups, which is critical to post-communism. Mancur Olson referred to these as latent interest groups in his work *The Logic of Collective Action*. Interest group formation can result from increased interaction among individuals affected by 'disturbances and dislocations' associated with the establishment of a market system (Truman, 1953: 61). Despite severe economic disturbances, the metamorphosis from latent to organized interest group for members of the growing underclass in East-Central Europe has not yet occurred. The transformation of the underclass into an organized interest group is hampered by both the nature of class-based interest groups and what Olson calls the logic of collective action. C. Wright Mills identified the factors necessary for the development of class-based interests:

1 a national awareness and identification with one's own class interests;
2 an awareness of and a rejection of other class interests as illegitimate; and
3 an awareness of and a readiness to use collective political means in achieving one's interests. (1951: 325–328, cited in Olson, 1971: 104)

With the economic transitions not completely consolidated, citizens have not fully formed their subjective class identities. The logic of collective action holds that individual members of latent interest groups often will not sacrifice the time and energy necessary to organize others into political action, especially in the case of large latent groups where the potential economic reward of organization for any individual member is small (Olson, 1971: 108, 126).

Access to the institutions of government and the intermediary institutions of civil society depends on a number of factors. These include a group's strategic position within society, which depends on the status and prestige of both the group and its leader; the extent to which key government officials are members of that group; an interest group's effective organization (internal cohesion); the skills of its leader; and the group's financial resources. The structure of governmental institutions, rules governing the process of interest articulation, and the number of access points (legal and illegal) to the governmental institutions also impact on interest groups' political effectiveness (Truman, 1953: 265, 269, 319, 506). Finally, access to the institutions of government depends also on the receptivity of the parties in power to the interests of the many groups pressing them for action.

The rules of the game for interest articulation, which evolved in the West in lengthy periods of political stability, are neither clearly defined nor commonly understood in post-communist countries. Extra-constitutional institutions of interest articulation, such as the parliamentary committees and political party conventions, will undergo further evolution. While critics may argue that access by interest groups to these institutions should be restricted, thereby limiting political lobbying and allowing government to regain a greater focus on the business of law and policy making, such mechanisms serve to make these processes more transparent and democratic.

Sociological studies demonstrate a greater tendency toward membership in organized interest groups as one climbs the socioeconomic ladder, but there remains a large percentage of the population of East-Central Europe on the bottom rung of that ladder. Truman warns

> The specialization of organized interest groups along class lines and the atrophy or deficiency of such groups in the less privileged classes may be a source of political instability for at least two reasons. In the first place, organized interest groups normally provide standardized procedures for asserting group claims and for settling conflicts. . . . Segments of the population that lack such organized means of participation in the political process may none the less experience drastic changes in expected relationships, changes that may result in their making increased demands upon the political institutions. In the absence of standardized means of participation they may more readily identify with movements that poorly reflect widespread unorganized interests or that explicitly repudiate portions of them. . . . In the second place . . . specialization of organized groups in certain classes of the population may provide a pattern of governmental access in which only those groups reflecting a particular class interpretation of the broad interests can gain expression through the governmental institutions. (1953: 522)

The success of populist movements such as Tyminski's Party 'X' in the early Polish post-communist elections or Vladimír Mečiar's Movement for a Democratic Slovakia adds credence to Truman's admonition. As interest representation demands substantial financial resources, the growing underclass will likely remain outside the fold of organized interest politics unless their cause is taken up by others, such as labour unions or social democratic parties.

In the still fluid post-communist societies, people have difficulty formulating their subjective identities in light of 'overlapping memberships' in interest groups, actual or potential. In a complex society, 'no single group affiliation accounts for all of the attitudes or interests of any individuals' (Truman, 1953: 508). For example, citizens in heavily polluted regions have an interest in tighter environmental regulations but they may be dependent on the continued operation of a polluting factory as a source of employment. The struggle with overlapping interests can lead to widespread voter non-participation as well as a decline in interest group participation as people seek to overcome the conflict by withdrawing from one or both of the overlapping interest groups (Truman, 1953: 163). A widespread feeling of powerlessness to effect change has caused some interest groups in the transitional countries to disengage from the political process after the initial euphoria of democracy.

Robert Dahl characterizes a democratic state as one in which all citizens have opportunities to formulate preferences, communicate those preferences to the government (either individually or collectively) and 'have their preferences weighed equally in the conduct of government' (1971:1). In weighing the interests of citizens, the democratic state must counter groups which seek to deny other groups' legitimate rights. The exchange of information required for policy formulation depends on the existence of facilitating institutions such as unbiased media (as opposed to merely *free* media) and non-governmental organizations. Post-communist governments often seek to manipulate the media in an effort to distort their role in interest articulation. While non-governmental organizations generally have not come under direct attack by East-Central European governments, their effectiveness is limited by organizational, managerial and financial constraints.

Policy makers are still confronting the legacies of four decades of communism in the form of conflicting demands from interest groups. The year 1989 represented a clean break from past political and economic systems but not the disappearance of the social legacies of those systems. James R. Millar and Sharon L. Wolchik see these legacies falling into three categories:

1   Those which flow from the tacit social contract between the population and the state.
2   Those which represent values, attitudes and behaviour that the state attempted either to instill in or extirpate from the population.
3   The unintended consequences of communist rule. (1994: 4)

The first two legacies, when combined with the socioeconomic consequences of the transition to a market economy, form the basis of many interest groups in the post-communist era. The tacit social contract during communism, most notably in Hungary after the crushing of the 1956 uprising and in Poland after the bloody put-down of the Gdańsk strikes in 1970, was that the state would guarantee a steady increase in the standard of living in exchange for the people's acceptance of the communist party's dominant role in both the state apparatus and society. This implicit social contract did not end with the demise of communism. Post-communist politics is marked by an extant socialist value culture with high expectations of socioeconomic equity. This underlies the rejection of the neo-liberal experiment. Many people believe that the democratically elected governments have the obligation to create the conditions for the kind of steady economic growth which will allow the standard of living of East Europeans to catch up with that of West Europeans. Popular support of post-communist governments depends on their ability to deliver a new social contract based on joining the West and ensuring a stable market economy, where the systems of Germany, Sweden and Austria serve as popular (albeit unrealistic) models.

With their newly gained rights to free speech and free media, East-Central Europeans are beginning to articulate their interests, but there remains a legacy of passivity and powerlessness from the time when the state provided citizens' basic needs in exchange for silence and obedience. What kind of balance must the post-communist governments strike in order that their citizens perceive not only an equal opportunity at interest articulation, but more importantly that the government is responsive to those interests? Without this confidence on the part of the electorate, democracies could be threatened in their long-term effectiveness, if not also in their survival, by populist/nationalist parties able to mobilize the vulnerable and frustrated.

An effective system of interest articulation remains to be developed over the longer-term, as people become aware of their objective socio-economic situation and as the rules and norms of interest articulation become clearer. This chapter will focus on the generational issues of the post-communist societies and the social interest groups of women, minorities, environmentalists and the new poverty class.

The elderly: difficult times with limited prospects

Under state socialism, elderly citizens were ensured a minimally sufficient level of financial security. Since work was mandatory for all able-bodied adults, and maternity leave counted toward years of service, nearly everyone was entitled to an adequate pension. In addition, the elderly benefited from free health care and the high subsidization of rent, food and utilities. The fact that many pensioners lived with their offspring also eased their financial concerns. The Eastern household is more likely to be multigenerational than its Western counterpart, partly as a consequence of the chronic housing shortage but also due to the rural tradition of family farming, with the multigenerational family structure often maintained as people migrated to urban areas (Łobodzińska, 1995a: 271). On the other hand, the shortage economy created additional burdens for the elderly, for it was pensioners who often stood in lines to obtain scarce consumer goods and foodstuffs. A significant part of the child rearing fell to grandmothers because of inadequate day care facilities and the need for mothers to work outside the home. As state day care facilities close due to budgetary constraints, grandparents are taking on an even greater role in raising their grandchildren.

The economic transition has affected older workers in some unique ways. Since the new economy demands entirely new skill sets and frequent upgrading of skills, the young and better educated can more easily adjust. Older workers often were not even given opportunities to learn new skills but were forced/induced into early retirement, reducing their income at a time when the cost of living was increasing. The psychological adjustment to a new and very disorienting system is particularly difficult for those with decades of experiences in the old system. Depression can set in for those who feel that they are too old to benefit from the reforms or who are overwhelmed by the reversal of a lifetime of assumptions about economic security.

The plight of pensioners has drawn much attention, but contrary to popular belief, pensioners in East-Central Europe have not suffered the greatest dislocation in the transition period. A UNICEF survey from 1995 covering eighteen post-communist countries concluded that average pensions had outpaced average wages in ten countries and had fallen only slightly behind in another four. In Poland, pensions in 1989 equalled 45 per cent of the average wage, while in 1994 they had increased to 73 per cent of the average wage (*Economist*, 1995). The ratio in the West is closer to 30 per cent (McKinsey, 1997). Between 1990 and 1994, the percentage of Polish pensioners receiving incomes above the national average almost quadrupled (Leven, 1996: 128). There was little evidence that pensioners were unduly victimized by marketization, as their consumption patterns were on par with or even 'more robust' than those of the average Pole (Leven, 1996: 132).

Statistics from Poland, the country probably best studied, reveal that poverty among pensioners is less widespread than for most other social groups. The poverty rate for pensioners was 10.9 per cent compared with 14.4 per cent for the total population, 11.0 per cent for workers and 23.2 per cent for farmers (World Bank, 1995: 172). When one uses the subjective poverty line, though, the poverty rate for pensioners greatly increases over the rate derived from the objective poverty line. Factors other than income and expenses, such as loneliness, deteriorating health and a nostalgia for the security of the past, influence pensioners' perception of their socioeconomic status (*Zycie Gospodarcze*, 1996).

How does one account for the portrayal in the popular media that the elderly were the big losers in the economic transition? First, pensions were not immediately indexed to either inflation or wages, leading to rapid impoverishment when prices were liberalized. The extremely high inflation levels in some countries meant the complete loss of a lifetime of personal savings, without the ability to recoup their savings through work. Although comparisons of pensions to average wages are favourable, statistics on average wages cannot take into account the extensive grey economy, the domain primarily of the young and middle aged. Were it possible to measure the income generated from the grey economy in addition to official wages, the economic position of the elderly would compare less favourably to that of younger generations.

Because of a lower retirement age and the fact that older workers were often moved on to pension rolls, the ratio of workers to retirees is lower than in the West, resulting in a high tax burden on workers and the fledgling middle class. In Poland, there is one pensioner for every person employed in the non-agricultural sector (McKinsey, 1997). The cost of providing old-age pensions accounts for more than 10 per cent of

GDP in Hungary. The average for the G7 countries is 8 per cent of GDP, while that for Argentina, with a standard of living similar to Hungary, is 6 per cent (*Economist*, 1995). The retirement age will have to be raised to reflect present life expectancies, but this will have to be implemented gradually to minimize political fallout. In addition to raising the minimum retirement age, the funding of the pension systems has had to be restructured, moving away from the pay-as-you-go state system to one requiring individuals to take greater responsibility for their own retirement through investments in private pension funds. Chile's highly touted pension reform is often cited as a model for East-Central Europe to imitate. This system involves worker investments in private retirement funds which are regulated by the government. Such measures are being introduced in East-Central Europe as part of the reform of the social services sector but legal issues and concerns about the health of the financial markets have led to considerable opposition.

There are clearly distinguishable patterns of political support correlating to generational divisions. During communism, support for the communist parties was highest among the older generations, for they were able to compare the positive effects of the modernization and limited liberalization programmes with the more repressive era. In the post-communist era, support for the successor parties is highest among older people. These parties promised an easing of the economic transition and symbolized a time of certainty and security. While the younger generations can believe that their economic situations will improve in several years, for the elderly the longer-term perspective is relatively unimportant. In addition to supporting the successor parties, older voters are more likely to support peasant and other populist parties, and less likely to support the overall economic liberalization.

The most noteworthy attempts at political organization of the older generations in transitional countries have been the Czech Republic's Pensioners for Secure Life and Poland's National Party of Senior Citizens and Pensioners (KPEiR). Formed in 1994, the KPEiR initially was open only to senior citizens, pensioners and those who would retire in three years' time but in 1996, membership was opened to younger people with the slogan, 'You will be a senior citizen one day as well'. Half of the 23,000 members are very close to retirement (Staszewski and Wronski, 1997). The party's main platform calls for growth in pensioners' incomes proportionate to the rate of economic development in Poland. The requisite funds would come from collecting taxes in the grey economy and forcing delinquent enterprises to pay their back social security taxes, but the party offered no clear policies for achieving this. A CBOS poll in March of 1997 revealed that KPEiR's support base was fairly evenly divided between people in their forties and their sixties, across the rural/urban divide and along the educational spectrum. Ten per cent admitted to holding leftist or left-of-centre views and 12 per cent to holding rightist and right-of-centre views (Staszewski and

Wronski, 1997). Such a varied support base is highly subject to capture by other parties.

In the run-up to the 1997 parliamentary election, other parties began to fear measurable voter defection to this upstart party. KPEiR and the Union of Labour prepared a preliminary agreement on joint candidacy lists but the deal fell through. Three months prior to the elections, Chair Zenon Ruminski spoke of winning 12–15 per cent of the vote (*Polityka*, 1997) but his party eventually failed to win any parliamentary seats. It failed even to gain the support of Poland's main senior citizen organization, the Polish Union of Senior Citizens (PZEiR). The PZEiR chose instead to back the Democratic Left Alliance, underlining the difficulties that new political parties and interest groups face in breaking up alliances held over from communist times. After fifty years of receiving direct subsidies from the state, the PZEiR still benefited from the policies of SLD-controlled ministries. Ruminski cites as one example the policy authorizing the PZEiR to distribute vouchers for free rail travel to senior citizens, for which the PZEiR received a direct state subsidy (*Polityka*, 1997). The Czech pensioners' party also failed to enter parliament after the 1998 elections though in campaign polls it had elicited support above the 5 per cent threshold needed to enter parliament.

The middle generations: opportunities for the skilled and the well connected

The new cadre of economic and political elites in East-Central Europe comes primarily from the middle generations, though there remains considerable variation within this group. People in their thirties who had already finished school and had begun to establish themselves in a profession prior to the collapse of communism generally have profited the most in the new economy. More recent school leavers are at a noticeable disadvantage when compared with people in their thirties and the older members of the middle generations often have had great difficulty adjusting.

On the political front, the initial opposition governments were formed by intellectuals and former dissidents. Squarely rooted in the middle generations, these new governments were on average far younger than the outgoing communist regimes. The exchange of power from the neo-liberal camp to the successor parties which occurred in Poland in 1993 and in Hungary the following year did not bring back the geriatric leaders of the communist period. Rather, younger party functionaries and technocrats who were less committed to the communist ideology and had constituted the reform wing now came to power in their own right. An analysis of leadership elites in Hungary verifies a rejuvenation of the middle and higher levels of leadership (*Nepszava*, 1997c). Some politicians have reached high positions well before 'middle age': Waldemar Pawlak served as Poland's Prime Minister at the age of 34; Aleksander Kwaśniewski was elected president of Poland at the age of 41 and Viktor Orban became Hungary's Prime Minister at the age of 35.

In the economic sphere, the middle generation has both winners and losers. What differentiates one from another is a combination of skills/ education and positioning at the time the command economy collapsed. The older members of this segment face the prospects of no longer being able to contribute actively to the economy. While some have taken early retirement, this was a situation more or less forced upon them. Although the level of pensions now keeps ahead of inflation in the first tier countries, early retirement means an earlier than anticipated decline in income from the level as wage earner, with savings not always an adequate supplement. Those in their late forties and early fifties are too young to retire on state pensions but are less likely to possess the job skills necessary to remain fully employed until the normal retirement age.

The initial winners in the new economy were members of the nomenklatura. In the unregulated early days of capitalism, managers of state enterprises were able to arrange joint ventures or privatization packages which often enabled them to remain in managerial positions. It is widely accepted that the various agreements by which communist parties relinquished power contained 'gentlemen's agreements' which ensured enterprise managers a prominent role in the new economy. The nomenklatura fell squarely within the middle generation, having worked their way up the ranks of the communist party. These nomenklatura capitalists form a large part of the fledgling middle class and are strong supporters of the continuation of economic reforms.

A comprehensive sociological survey of Hungary's economic elite, conducted by the Budapest University of Economic Sciences, reveals high continuity of enterprise elites from the communist period into the transition years, although there are signs of rejuvenation under way. Sixty-three per cent of enterprise managers in the early 1990s were holdovers in their positions while 29 per cent of those surveyed came to managerial positions as a direct result of the transition. While 88 per cent of enterprise managers between the ages of 51 and 60 are holdovers from the communist era, 70 per cent of those between the ages of 31 and 40 are 'system changers', those who achieved their current roles as a result of the political change (Bartha and Martin, 1995). Rejuvenation of the economic elite will continue with the increased demand for better educated managers and those with international experience.

Prospects for workers differ from those of the managerial ranks. Low-skilled workers will be the biggest losers as the economies of East-Central Europe diversify into higher tech industries and services, with significant retraining prospects for such workers unlikely. Unskilled workers accounted for 28.5 per cent of active wage earners in the 1980s in Hungary but by 1993 that figure was down to 17.8 per cent (*Nepszava*, 1997c). The availability and quality of worker retraining programmes varies greatly and the ultimate success of any programme depends on the ability of the local economy to reabsorb workers. A study of retraining programmes in different regions of Poland shows that the prospects for reemployment range from negligible to over 50 per cent compared with rates in Western countries in the order of 70–80 per cent (World Bank, 1995: 71). The percentage of the Polish labour force starting retraining programmes each year is equal to that in Australia (0.4 per cent) but below the rate in the United Kingdom (1.4 per cent), Germany (1.5 per cent), France (2.3 per cent) or Norway (2.7 per cent) (World Bank, 1995: 72).

The success of the middle generations depends in part on the psychological factor of 'overcoming the past'. The state is no longer the provider of universal jobs and welfare, nor can it act as the guarantor of such. President Havel, when asked about the psychological mood in the Czech Republic, stated: 'If they are nostalgically longing for something, it may be a longing for the paternalistic state that solved everything for the people, that made no great demands on the people's responsibility for their own lives, that took care of the population from cradle to grave. Those people that found [all that] convenient may feel a certain nostalgia at the present' (Havel, 1997). On a personal level, it is necessary to overcome this psychological dependence on the state in order to seek out one's own economic opportunities; politically, it is important in order to gain widespread support for parties that will complete the economic reform process.

Studies from the West of middle generation unemployed provide some useful insights, though, admittedly the problem in the West has been far less dramatic. The chance for members of the middle generations to return to work depends largely on the relevance of their skills in the new job market and is negatively correlated with the length of time out of work. One mitigating factor aiding the unemployed in the West is that a spouse often remains employed, bringing partial income and perhaps social benefits to the household. With widespread unemployment in East-Central Europe, often both spouses are out of work for long periods of time.

In addition to the provision of wages, work serves a number of important functions in one's life, providing a sense of purpose, contact with other members of society and contributing to one's identity (Furnham, 1994: 207–208). The political socialization process in communist countries taught people that work was their central function in society. Thus, unemployment for Easterners is perhaps more damaging to one's feelings of self-worth than for Westerners. Unemployment often places a unique psychological burden on people of the middle generations. While there is not much of a stigma for older, displaced workers who have 'earned' the right to retire, those responsible for maintaining a household and raising children can become severely depressed and anxious if no longer able to fulfil these roles. Furthermore, since middle aged people have most of their social contacts at the workplace, long periods of unemployment can lead to greater isolation than among young people, who carry with them a circle of contacts from their schooling (Furnham, 1994: 205). The unemployed begin to develop a network of associates who are likewise out of work. As their contacts with employed people diminish, so do their opportunities for finding employment through networking connections.

Unemployment has a deeper psychological impact on middle generation workers than younger workers, affecting their self-confidence and resolve to continue in their efforts to return to work. Cognizant of the psychological effects on the long-term unemployed, employers in the East will tend to favour younger workers, of which there is no shortage of skilled applicants. Reemployment after a prolonged period of time does not necessarily reverse the psychological effect, leading to a reduction in a worker's productivity on the new job. Studies from the Netherlands indicate that workers who find new jobs within a year are more satisfied than those for whom it took longer (Henkens et al., 1996: 569–570). Those still out of work may be forced by economic circumstances to take any job available, regardless of whether or not it provides equivalent income or gratification.

For those who view themselves largely as victims of the new economic policies, affective attachment to democratic principles may be in doubt. They may easily blame external forces for their economic plight or find scapegoats among ethnic minorities. Due to the varied impact of the economic transition on members of the middle generations, their political affiliations cannot be neatly classified. Support for the neo-liberal parties is greater among members of the middle generations than among the elderly, but this support comes almost exclusively from those who have benefited from the switch to market capitalism. The losers of the transition are becoming more reluctant to continue the sacrifices in the medium-term in exchange for promises of future prosperity. It is this latter group which demonstrates greater allegiance to successor and populist parties. Democratic resocialization of the middle generations will depend on the government's ability to address the economic and social consequences of the transition.

Youth: the early optimism has not been fully realized

It was expected that the young people of East-Central Europe would gain the most from the economic transformation because they were largely unencumbered by the mindsets of the previous era and would be the first generation with the freedom not only to choose their professions but also to take full advantage of other newly won freedoms. In reality, this generation has suffered considerable dislocation and exhibits considerable political apathy in the new system. This apathy, if not reversed, could have far-reaching consequences for the consolidation of democracy.

The disillusionment of the younger generation is not unique to post-communism, for youth had become increasingly disenchanted with the communist system. With the economic stagnation of the late 1970s and 1980s, it became increasingly clear to young people that communism could not provide them with increased well-being over the previous generation, as had happened for their parents' generation. Better educated and unencumbered by the fear of authorities, youth increasingly came to question the merits of the communist system and the dominant role of the state. As a result of the 1975 Helsinki Accords, youth had more exposure to the West through media, culture and even limited exchange programmes; they could see for themselves that the communist system was falling farther and farther behind the capitalist model. They came to compare their lives and opportunities not with those of the previous generations, but rather with their counterparts in Western Europe (Garton Ash, 1990: 259).

Polish authorities began to track the problem of youth apathy in the 1980s. A government survey on youth in 1985 'found, surprisingly, that only three percent were "very keen" about "sociopolitical activity" and concluded that the chief characteristics of youth were passivity and apathy. . . . Official publications complained that young people "distance themselves verbally from the socialist system and question its many achievements." They bemoaned the lack of commitment from young people given the resources spent on their political education' (Mason et al., 1991: 210).

The disillusionment of youth was manifested in different ways. Some young people became outwardly conformist without really accepting the system, while others retreated from society and politics. Some turned to alternative politics and culture, much as the youth in Western Europe at the time. Still others were galvanized into action by single issue politics, notably the environment or social causes (Brown, 1991: 39–40; Wallace and Kovacheva, 1996: 203). By the end of the 1970s, and especially in the 1980s, religion was attracting large numbers of youthful adherents in search of the meaning that was absent in the ideology of communism. The mix of Polish Catholicism and Polish nationalism, strengthened after the elevation of Karol Wotyła to the papacy in 1978, drew many young people to political awareness, particularly surrounding his visits to Poland. An ecumenical religious revival was evident in Hungary and Czechoslovakia (Brown, 1991: 41). Some young people channelled their disillusionment into anti-social behaviour such as petty crime, drug abuse and the skinhead movement. The communist regimes largely denied the existence of these anti-establishment subcultures, as they were considered antithetical to socialism. However, they were evident even to the casual Western visitor to the communist East (Agócs and Agócs, 1994; Hockenos, 1993).

Lacking official political outlets, many young people vented their frustration with the communist regime through rock music. An illegal or semi-legal alternative music movement emerged to challenge the system for its unfulfilled promises and cultural stagnation, drawing 'from the social malaise and contradictions, from the family and the political system' for its inspiration (Kürti, 1991: 489). By the middle of the 1980s the alternative music had grown increasingly anarchic, racist and xenophobic (cf. Hockenos, 1993: Ch. 6; Kürti, 1991). Concerts by alternative bands began to serve as rallying places for skinhead groups from the East and the West.

Drug abuse was quite prevalent among the youth of communist Europe, with causes similar to those in the West (low self-esteem, peer pressure, an unstable home life) combined with factors peculiar to the communist system (repression and the bleakness of life) (Kramer, 1993: 162–163). Despite restrictions on international travel, drugs made their way into the Eastern bloc, in increasing quantities after the easing of some travel restrictions in the 1980s; other drugs were locally produced. Poland was the first communist country to confront the drug problem both at the official and civil society levels. In 1981, the Young People's Movement to Combat Drug Abuse (MONAR) was formed to educate youth about the dangers of drug use. A few years later, both MONAR and the Catholic Church began operating treatment facilities for drug addicts. Comprehensive anti-drug legislation which included provisions for mandatory treatment was passed in 1985 (Kramer, 1993: 168).

The economic dislocation of the transition period has led to a sharp increase in drug abuse, especially among teenagers. Efforts to stem drug abuse are complicated by the positive aspects of freedom: open borders, convertible currency and freedom of movement. Since drug abuse is just one of many social ills competing for scarce fiscal resources, educational programmes and treatment facilities are woefully inadequate to confront this upsurge. In the Czech Republic, most teenagers who use drugs begin at the age of thirteen or fourteen, and teenage drug use now rivals the rate in the United States. One study from Poland reports that over 25 per cent of Polish teenagers are using drugs, a rate that again far exceeds that in America. In contrast to Poland and the Czech Republic, Hungary apparently has not seen a significant increase in drug use since the collapse of communism (Kramer, 1997: 37–38), although many young people there face a similarly bleak economic future.

Some young people in communist Europe turned their disillusionment with the system into political activism. Polish youth were involved in the underground Solidarity movement after the declaration of martial law in December of 1981, producing and distributing opposition literature. Young people, in conjunction with intellectuals, played an active role in the transitions in Czechoslovakia, Hungary and East Germany (Brown, 1991; Garton Ash, 1990), though the middle generations played the dominant role. Of all the generations, youth were perhaps most inspired by Mikhail Gorbachev's programmes of perestroika and glasnost, seeing in them the hope that the communist stagnation could be reversed. The younger generations were less willing to accept the self-compromising of their parents' generation (Garton Ash, 1990: 237) and in some ways were less afraid to take part in anti-regime demonstrations, since they had not lived through the Stalinist terror, the violent crackdowns in 1956 and 1968, or the repression that followed. The young people who participated in anti-regime activities were by and large students and white collar workers, while the working class youth were generally left out of the revolution (Hockenos, 1993: 212). With economic prospects of these young people bleaker than those of their white collar counterparts, they remain outside of mainstream politics and form the base of support for the skinhead movement.

Many youth in East-Central Europe had developed a rose-coloured picture of the West as a result of their exposure to Western popular culture and contacts with Western youth in the 1980s. With the establishment of market capitalism, they expected their standard of living to quickly match that of their Western counterparts but they soon became frustrated with the lack of resources available to attain this lifestyle (Jung, 1995: 300). Frustration over their economic situation did not result in significant political participation though, as the new consumerism was accompanied by a politically inactive mentality, especially among better educated youth (cf. Mason et al., 1991).

Some young people have sought economic opportunity in the West, though this does not necessarily constitute an abandonment of their home countries. Already in the 1980s, educated youth from Hungary and Poland worked in the West, sending back hard currency to their families. Fears of an incipient 'brain drain' did not materialize, as many of them returned home, bringing with them much needed skills (Krajewska, 1995: 45) and start-up capital. The brain drain does represent a serious problem for countries with more unstable economies, such as Bulgaria, Albania and particularly Russia.

The root of many youth problems is the entrenched high youth unemployment rate, running about twice the level of that of the middle generations (cf. Mroziewicz, 1996). In Poland, a full two-thirds of those under 34 years of age are unemployed (Swiecka, 1996). As in Western countries, youth are particularly vulnerable to unemployment because upon leaving school they usually lack work experience. Many young people obtain some or all of their income from casual jobs, no matter what their level of education or place of residence. In fact, the easy opportunities and quick reward for casual work may actually delay some young people's entrance into the official job market (Jung, 1995: 302) and skew the unemployment statistics. The high unemployment rate results in part from a demographic shift. A mini-baby boom occurred in all countries of East-Central Europe in the mid-1970s (Sipos, 1991: 29) as a result of the financial incentives of pro-natalist policies, and in Hungary and Poland in response to the new prosperity brought on by the partial reforms of Kádár and Gierek. These baby boomers reached working age just in time for the economic downturn caused by the collapse of communism.

Work is important for young people to feel that they play a meaningful societal role and have a stake in the success of the market economy. In the absence of paid employment, volunteer work can give young people a sense of contributing to society, particularly if they were to fill a social need left by the bankrupting of state social programmes. Volunteer work would also provide opportunities to develop job skills. Without the daily connection to society provided by work, young people come to feel marginalized. Studies from the West point to a number of social consequences of the marginalization of youth: increases in crime (particularly in the economic hinterlands), drug abuse, out-of-wedlock births, homicide and suicide, as well as low voter participation (Hess et al., 1994: 13). While many young people turn to outwardly destructive behaviour, others turn inward, withdrawing from family and society and in the process destroying their own ability to take the initiative to find work.

Youth are spared some of the problems faced by older unemployed. Since most young people still live with their parents, they do not have the financial responsibilities of a household and therefore do not experience the same sense of failure for not being able to care for one's family which can have serious psychological consequences for the middle generation unemployed. There is also not a high stigma attached to youth unemployment since many are in the same situation as they pass from school to the working world (Furnham, 1994: 205). Nevertheless, long periods of unemployment can lower one's self-esteem, making it more difficult to integrate into the job market.

Significant changes are needed in the educational system in East-Central Europe in order better to prepare youth for the demands of the market economy. However, with the state's fiscal constraints comes the fear that higher education increasingly will become the realm of the wealthy, particularly with the establishment of private schools, but also with proposals to charge tuition for tertiary education. The low pay for professors and lecturers has forced many to leave academia altogether for the private sector, sometimes in completely unrelated fields, or has forced them to supplement their income through side jobs.

The funding of higher education has been a hotly debated topic. Proposals by the Hungarian government in 1995 to charge tuition fees had to be postponed after student protests. In Poland, the Democratic

Left Alliance wanted a guarantee of free and equal access to education placed in the new constitution approved in 1997. But Marcin Krol, dean of history at Warsaw University, argues that free education would only intensify the cleavages between rich and poor, urban and rural. He suggests that talented students from poor families should be assisted with living and tuition stipends, with the wealthy paying the full cost of their education (Krol, 1997: 82). Stipends for the disadvantaged students would add no additional burden to the state budget if fees were instituted or increased for those able to pay.

At a time when youth are in need of greater direction, many traditional authority figures have been discredited. This goes far beyond the lost authority of communist party leaders and police after the collapse of communism. Teachers have been discredited since they were considered indoctrinators of the old ideology. In many countries, youth are turning away from organized religion after the upswing in the waning years of communism. Unemployed parents are reduced in stature, seen as inadequate to meet the needs of their families. Additionally, parents are overwhelmed by the full responsibilities of child rearing after relying so heavily on the state and party to socialize their children (Drozdiak, 1998). The communist youth organizations provided valuable social activities in addition to party indoctrination. Now, afterschool activities are available primarily to those with money. With the collapse of communist youth organs, the socialization of youth is now even more a peer- and self-socialization process, with youth gangs a sign of an extreme 'political socialization through peer group interaction' (Nagle, 1997b: 19, 23). For other young people, the *nouveau riche* in the East or sports and entertainment figures from the West serve as role models, representing the success which the young people hope to achieve themselves, however unrealistic these aspirations.

With the end of communism came the end of affirmative action programmes which offered children of workers and peasants increased opportunities to enter the leadership ranks. Today the leading elite is comprised increasingly of children in the middle class, a trend which began in the late communist period in Hungary and Poland. In Hungary in the 1970s, 34 per cent of children of manual workers in agriculture reached the leadership circles but today only 21 per cent do. In the late 1970s, 9 per cent of leaders came from intellectual families but today that figure is up to 14 per cent (*Nepszava*, 1997c). Young people from rural communities are at the greatest disadvantage. With higher levels of unemployment, local governments have to spend a greater percentage of their budget on social support programmes, leaving less money available to fund schools and training facilities. Young people from rural areas who cannot afford to pay for a place to live while studying at university have less access to higher education than their urban counterparts. Recently, the enrolment of students from small towns and villages dropped to an unprecedented 2 per cent in Poland (Krol, 1997: 82). These narrowing educational opportunities will further reduce the chance for rural youth to attain leadership positions in the long run.

In spite of the gloomy picture presented here, more young people than middle aged or elderly have embraced the new economic system with its promises of greater opportunity, a more comfortable standard of living and more material possessions. Overall, young people can most readily adjust to the new conditions, as their ideas and work habits are not yet entrenched. They can take advantage of educational opportunities that lead to more lucrative and challenging work than was available to their parents. Already, the percentage of young people among the intellectual class has dropped sharply as these careers become less remunerative. Young university graduates and skilled workers are increasingly attracted to positions that allow them greater independence, such as self-employed businessmen and traders (*Nepszava*, 1997c). The youth of East-Central Europe form part of the budding entrepreneurial class. There is also a class of young people with Western language and business skills who have found employment with international companies, donor agencies and export-oriented local companies. They have been able to achieve the high standard of living missing for most youth.

Between the newly emerging yuppies and the disaffected skinheads lies a vast middle ground whose political socialization is critical to the consolidation of democracy but which may hinge on steady economic growth (Nagle, 1997b). With few exceptions, the region's youth are largely indifferent to politics though still subject to mobilization around issues of critical importance to them. Political apathy is in part a latent reaction to the forced political socialization of the communist youth organs but also an expression of the lack of hope that one's vote can have an impact. A sense of complacency has set in as well, since many young people take for granted the freedoms gained since 1989. They do not remember the reversal of early political liberalizations, as do their parents and grandparents. As democracy becomes consolidated, and with the main political parties exhibiting a commitment to parliamentary democracy, there is no fear of turning back, at least not in the first tier countries. The sense of urgency to participate in the political process in order to maintain democracy does not exist for today's youth. Many are instead preoccupied with the pursuit of a good career and material wealth in this era of new opportunities.

Right-wing parties in East-Central Europe openly court skinheads. The Republican Party in the Czech Republic found its initial support almost exclusively with skinheads and their sympathizers (Hockenos, 1993: 224), attracting them with a platform of law and order and anti-minority scapegoating. In Hungary, the right-wing youth movement 'National Youth' has received political and financial support from the national-populist Independent Smallholders Party (Agócs and Agócs, 1994: 79).

Largely, the youth vote is overlooked by the major parties in East-Central Europe and there are few youth-based political movements. The Federation of Young Democrats (Fidesz) in Hungary represented an early hope as a force to mobilize young people. The party is comprised mostly of the younger neo-liberals from the opposition movement in the 1980s, the so-called 'generation of the change'. In the intervening years, it has not reached out to the first 'post-communist generation', those who came of age after 1990. Furthermore, with its strong adherence to the neo-liberal message, Fidesz has little appeal to unemployed young people alienated by the new system. In 1994, half of Fidesz's voters were under the age of 30 but by the 1998 elections, the extreme right-wing Hungarian Justice and Life Party enjoyed greater support from young people than did Fidesz (Hann, 1998).

The Hungarian Left-Wing Youth Association (BIE), with its socialist/social democratic bearing, stands in contrast to the neo-liberal Fidesz. Most of BIE's early members were the disappointed members of the communist youth movement 'who wanted a modern interest association keeping the social and financial situation of youth in view' (MTI, 1994). In the 1994 parliamentary elections BIE won 31 parliamentary mandates within the Socialist Party delegation, one and a half times the number of seats for Fidesz. BIE is led by engineers, public officials, economists and professionals around the age of 30, with equal membership of second-ary students under 18 years of age, students, professionals and skilled workers. The Left-Wing Association played an important role in post-poning for one year the introduction of tuition fees at Hungarian universities and colleges. Specific policies espoused by BIE include state-guaranteed first jobs for young people; tax breaks for firms hiring the young; and the use of some privatization revenue for youth job training. As with Fidesz, its membership is primarily from the educated, white collar segments of the population.

In Poland, almost 3 million more people reached voting age between the 1993 and 1997 parliamentary elections. This new generation of voters was largely conditioned by the events of the transition period: political scandals, an inefficient plurality of parties in parliament, limitations of the neo-liberal experiment, and debates over the proper role of the Catholic Church in modern society. They are disinterested in political battles over the past but look more to issues affecting their own future – jobs, the cost of education, environmental protection, and economic freedom. Where do Polish youth stand on the left–right spectrum? Surveys of 18–20-year-olds conducted in 1995 reveal that 44 per cent are left leaning; 21 per cent are rightist-liberal; 13 per cent 'rightist-Solidarity' and 6 per cent expressed support for both the SLD and the Freedom Union. Among youth, support is high for 'soft capitalism', whereby the state safeguards economic freedoms but at the same time subsidizes enterprises that otherwise would have a hard time dealing with the rigours of the market system (Padorska and Janicki, 1997).

Young people view politics as a highly suspect and compromised arena, dominated by careerists and the morally corrupt. In a 1995 sociological survey of secondary school students, only 5 per cent of respondents rejected the statement 'politics is a dirty business' and just 3 per cent expressed an interest in politics. Young people may not be fully cognizant of the connection between democracy and a market economy. Only 24 per cent agreed that 'democracy is superior to all other forms of government' while 22 per cent agreed with the statement 'sometimes a non-democratic government can be more desirable than a democratic one' (Padorska and Janicki, 1997). With such low levels of faith in democracy, today's youth might be willing to support a non-democratic regime if it could provide greater job opportunities and economic efficiency, though the preference still would be for honest, effective democratic leadership.

The ineffective political socialization of youth could be problematic if their disappointment with the new economic system is sufficient to allow populist parties to establish a strong support base. Even though they have perhaps the greatest stake in the success of the market economy, many are indifferent to the political process, especially since changes in government have brought little variance in economic performance. This serves to solidify their contention that the individual act of voting has little impact on the policy making process. Political apathy among young people is not surprising, especially in the face of acute economic conditions which cause them to focus on developing career opportunities. Western Europe experienced a similar phenomenon in the 1980s, when young people were no longer galvanized by the peace movement, nor for that matter, any other sociopolitical issues. Economic concerns and career development became more pressing as the economy began to stagnate (*US News and World Report*, 1986). In Western Europe, this withdrawal had no significant impact on long term political stability, in contrast with East-Central Europe, where youth are expected to provide the support necessary for democratic consolidation, given the low levels of civic faith among older generations.

Women: limited resources for real political activism

Marxist-Leninist ideology had a unique interpretation of the emancipation of women, claiming that the abolition of private property, the socialization of domestic work and child care, and the participation of women in the productive sphere would end their exploitation and enable them to achieve 'self realization in public life' (Heitlinger, 1995: 88). After the Second World War, the communist countries were faced with huge reconstruction tasks, unaided by the resources of the

Marshall Plan. In order to induce women to enter the workforce, the communist governments offered generous maternity leave and an extensive system of socialized day care. These benefits served primarily to enable women to serve the common good as directed by the state, rather than allow them to fulfil their own self-interested career ambitions (Graham and Regulska, 1997: 67). The misperception among Western feminists was that women in the East had it all – career, secure employment, family, low-cost child care, guaranteed health care and adequate retirement benefits. The reality was far less attractive. Women bore most of the responsibilities for domestic work and child rearing, while also working full time. This double burden was intensified by the shortage economy, in which many of the time-saving appliances utilized in Western households were unavailable. It was women (and pensioners) who stood in line to obtain scarce consumer and food items. As birthrates declined in East-Central Europe in the 1960s and 1970s governments instituted pro-natalist policies, offering extra subsidies for bearing more children or extending maternity leave. Traditional gender roles remain more deeply entrenched in the East than the West, as the large-scale employment of women was not accompanied by the kind of dialogue on gender roles which took place in the West.

At first appearance, it seemed that women in the communist countries had achieved greater advances on the political front than their Western counterparts. Although women's representation in the communist parliaments was far higher than in most liberal democracies, this was accomplished through a quota system established by the communist parties. It did not reflect greater political advancement on the part of Eastern women, but rather the manipulation of the political system for ideological reasons. Women rarely achieved positions of influence in the communist parties, not only limiting their impact on policy but also denying them opportunities to acquire political skills (Graham and Regulska, 1997: 67). With the rapid transition from communist to democratic party politics, women did not have the time to acquire the requisite skills and contacts before critical decisions on economic and social policies were made.

An early phenomenon of the post-communist era was the sharp drop in the number of women parliamentarians after free elections. Between 1987 and 1994, the percentage of women in parliament in Hungary decreased from 21 per cent to 11 per cent, in Czechoslovakia from 30 per cent to 9 per cent, and in the NIS from 33 per cent (in the Soviet Union) to less than 3 per cent in many of the successor states (Hunt, 1997: 4; Kligman, 1994: 257). However, since these political positions were largely symbolic due to the quota system, the declining numbers of women office holders does not necessarily mean a drop in their political influence (Gigli, 1995: 18). In fact, women today arguably have more real political influence than they did under communism (cf. Iankova, 1996). Still, the political rhetoric demonstrates that women are not viewed as equal political partners. Czech Prime Minister Milos Zeman explained the absence of women in his Social Democratic government by saying that government work was too difficult for them (RFE/RL Newsline, 12 August 1998).

On an organizational level, women generally had little spare time for party or trade union activities under communism. Some even took refuge in the domestic sphere, gladly avoiding the activities demanded by the party which amounted to a triple burden of household work, full time employment and political participation (Einhorn, 1994: 58). Women who participated in Charter 77 and Solidarity were not on equal terms with men, more often doing the grunt work and typing or translating documents rather than drafting them (Bystydzienski, 1995: 195; Regulska, 1992; Siklova, 1998a). Women in communist Europe traditionally participated in movements that reflected their motherly role of protector, such as peace, disarmament and environmental movements. Even in these movements, women were not viewed as major players. Furthermore, such activism served to reinforce stereotypes of traditional gender roles.

While women's rights improved in the West in the 1970s, women's rights in the communist countries remained subordinated to the advancement of the socialist state (Wolchik, 1994b: 50). An easing of the double/triple burden through the development of part time employment opportunities would not have served the economic interests of the state. The only large-scale women's organizations allowed to exist were communist party organs. In the post-communist era, 'feminism' is viewed with suspicion as a legacy of the co-opting of women's emancipation by the communist party. The women's rights movement is sometimes dismissed as male-hating, or rejected as another ideology being imposed upon the people. Eastern women perceive Western-style feminism as focusing primarily on full employment for women but they know from experience that this did not liberate them. The Western feminist movement sought to liberate women from the home but in communist Europe, the household often served as a welcome place of refuge. Czech philosopher Jirina Siklova comments, 'Under socialism the family was not a place of oppression; on the contrary, it was a place of relative freedom, a place of privacy, a place to assert identity . . .' (Kaufman, 1998). Following the backlash in the West against feminism, the focus has shifted to the role of gender in the division of power and economic resources but this concept is not readily transferable to the East, for women do not perceive gender to be the root cause of their social problems (Siklova, 1998b).

The successor organizations to the official women's organizations still represent the largest organized women's groups in these countries but they have largely been discredited. They enjoy an organizational capacity which perhaps could be used to mobilize large numbers of women to political action but they have not undergone the type of internal rehabilitation and transformation that many former ruling parties and official labour unions underwent in their effort to remain relevant in the new political culture. The absence of such a reworking indicates perhaps that there is not the perceived need for national institutions devoted primarily to women's issues.

The communist educational system was gender-tracked, with men pursuing technical training that prepared them for well-paying industrial jobs and women being trained for light industry. Certain professions became feminized, among them business, economics, medicine and teaching, leading to their decreased status and lower levels of remuneration (Łobodzińska, 1995c: 37). Even in feminized professions, women did not generally achieve positions of authority. In Hungary, for example, women comprised one-third of university lecturers but held only 4 per cent of full professorships (Einhorn, 1994: 53); they held 88 per cent of elementary school teaching positions but fewer than 15 per cent of the positions as principal (Weil, 1994: 286).

The changing economic situation has created a mixed picture of the situation of women. Women have faced discriminatory layoffs, a greater decline in the feminized industries than in the masculinized ones, and greater hardships in returning to the workforce. With firms having to take on all operational costs, women are deemed too expensive because of the cost of maternity benefits, and are among the first let go (Fong and Paull, 1994: 232) and the last to be reemployed. The lighter industries, such as textiles and food processing, which employed more women then men, were hit particularly hard in the new economic environment as export markets disappeared. For political reasons, heavy industry and mining (which employ proportionately more men than women) were not subject to immediate restructuring which would have resulted in large-scale layoffs. There is some indication that in industrial sectors, initial staff reductions were aimed at the administrative support staff, where women dominated, rather than the more masculinized production staff (Fong and Paull, 1994: 231; Kostova, 1994: 102). Female school leavers find it more difficult to obtain their first job than do male school leavers, particularly for those just with vocational training. Enterprises prefer to hire young men because family obligations will likely disrupt a woman's term of employment later on. The situation improves somewhat for women with a university education (World Bank, 1995: 120–121). Since men are still considered the primary breadwinners, a man's unemployment is thought to be a greater social hardship than a woman's (cf. Hunt, 1997; World Bank, 1995). Another factor working against women is the fact that they were traditionally underrepresented in trade unions and positions of power (Zajicek and Calasanti, 1995: 183), weakening their bargaining positions in the downsizing process. Despite these problems, unemployment statistics do not illustrate a dire situation for women. In Poland and the Czech Republic, the women's unemployment rate is only slightly higher than the men's but in Hungary, it is actually lower, perhaps a legacy of the New Economic Mechanism, which created a more extensive service sector than existed in other countries.

One must look beyond employment to get a more complete picture. Women in the East remain concentrated in low paying professions to a greater extent than women in the West, though there have been improvements. In 1984, Czech women earned on average 68.4 per cent of men's wages, but by 1993, the figure had increased to 74.8 per cent (Stastna, 1995: 26). In Poland, the wage gap has declined in the post-communist period, particularly in the private sector (World Bank, 1995: 124). Furthermore, the social safety net (though not as sturdy as it was under communism) has played a major role in equalizing the incidence and depth of poverty between male-headed and female-headed households in Poland (World Bank, 1995: 117). In Hungary, women's incomes were 35.2 per cent lower than men's in 1986, but by 1994 they were 'only' 20.1 per cent lower. A more careful analysis reveals some problems, though. There is evidence that the tightening of the wage gap in Hungary has resulted because men's incomes have 'caught down' with women's in certain sectors, such as farming, construction and railways. In contrast, in fields requiring higher education, the men's advantage has increased as they begin to enter fields such as information technology and economics, and assume the leadership positions (Abraham, 1996).

Women face a number of obstacles in returning to the workforce after being unemployed and thus comprise a much higher percentage of the long-term unemployed. For women with children, the return to the workplace is complicated by the increasing shortage of affordable day care facilities. The number of places in public nursery/child care facilities (factory plus municipal) in Poland fell by about 50 per cent between 1989 and 1992 (World Bank, 1995: 125). Job vacancies are often specified by gender, with men especially preferred by international companies and for managerial positions (Fong and Paull, 1994: 233; Zajicek and Calasanti, 1995: 183). Employment ads in East-Central Europe even go so far as to call for 'attractive female receptionist' (Hunt, 1996: 2), discriminating heavily against older women. Such issues are just beginning to be tackled by the post-communist governments. In 1997, a commission was established to guarantee equal opportunities for women in Hungary, where two-thirds of women still work in the so-called 'female positions' (RFE/RL Newsline, 23 July 1997). While some women are pleased to stay home, relieved of the double burden, polls demonstrate that the majority of them prefer to work outside the home (Fong and Paull, 1994: 240; Łobodzińska, 1995b; Kostova, 1994: 104). They choose careers not just for fulfilment, but out of economic necessity.

Possibilities for career advancement for women have also changed. The need to undergo continual training in a climate of rapidly changing skills requirements places another burden on the working mother. A survey conducted by the Central Statistical Office of Poland shows that in 1991, 8.2 per cent of women saw their household responsibilities as an obstacle to career advancement, compared with 5.9 per cent in 1987. The situation is more acute for single mothers. Fifteen per cent of single mothers surveyed in 1991 cited exhaustion as preventing them from achieving promotions, compared with 6.1 per cent in 1987 (GUS, cited in World Bank, 1995: 124–125). Some Western style business schools which have sprung up restrict entrance to managers of state enterprises, who are overwhelmingly men (Białecki and Heyns, 1994: 130). Such positions were generally rewards for political participation, which was lower for women than men.

Western companies have been attracted to East-Central Europe due to low wages and the relatively high skill level of the workforce, perhaps favouring women, who earn lower wages on average than men. This is not necessarily an encouraging sign, as it will further the exploitative nature of the increasingly globalized economy. Women enjoy some advantages in the new economy due to the past gender-typing of employment. With the adoption of Western style business practices and increased international trade, professions such as accounting, economics and those requiring foreign language skills have expanded. While these traditionally 'women's fields' gave women a competitive advantage (Fong and Paull, 1994: 230) in the short term, women are starting to lose their competitive edge as men recognize the rewards for pursuing such careers. Women will also face competition for jobs in light industry as men displaced from heavy industry take employment in light industry (Kostova, 1994: 102). On a positive note, the private sector offers greater career development, as the traditional gender segregation of employment is less pronounced than in the state sector (cf. Stastna, 1995).

In addition to the economic dislocation, women face a number of unique social problems. Incidents of rape and domestic abuse have increased in the economically difficult times, a sociological phenomenon not unique to these countries, as men lose their self-esteem along with their jobs. Domestic violence is exacerbated by alcohol consumption, which has increased in response to the economic hardship. Patriarchy, still very common in East-Central Europe, is a major culprit in domestic violence. Wife beating is often considered a private matter, even a man's right or duty in such societies (Bystydzienski, 1995: 198; Corrin, 1994: 208), inhibiting public discourse on domestic violence. In a region with acute housing shortages and economic hardships, women do not have the same ability to escape abuse as Western women. Such institutions as hotlines, support groups and safe houses for victims of domestic violence and rape were virtually non-existent in the communist era. In post-communism, such networks have been established but exist mainly in larger cities, compete with other social issues for funding and struggle to overcome the backlash against feminism (Corrin, 1994: 208).

Even in very large cities, women's shelters are a rare occurrence (cf. Perlez, 1998).

In Poland, women's groups are working to sensitize the police and prosecutors to the issue of domestic violence. Still, they face an uphill battle in keeping the issue on the political agenda. The Minister of Family Affairs in the AWS–UW government, Kazimierz Kapera, argues that the state's limited resources should be devoted to keeping families together, not spent on assisting abused women. In 1998 he suspended a UN programme to train lawyers and psychologists to treat victims of domestic violence (Perlez, 1998).

Exploitation of women has also increased with the newly gained freedom. Media freedom has led to the explosion of pornographic magazines and videos, much of it hard core even by Western standards. Out of economic desperation, some women have turned to prostitution or pornography to support their families, with immigrant women particularly vulnerable. Women are lured to the West for work in prostitution rings run by organized crime groups which run ads promoting high paying jobs in Western Europe. It is estimated that 15,000 women from the former Soviet bloc work in Germany's red light districts alone (Caldwell, 1998: 71). The spread of AIDS and other sexually transmitted diseases is an acute danger as these women tend to be very naive about the risk.

The post-communist political parties have been slow to address women's issues, claiming that there are more pressing concerns. Women's socioeconomic issues are not viewed as an important component to economic development. As in the communist era, women's rights are subordinated to the perceived greater needs of the country as defined by the male-dominated political elite. The reality is that many people in East-Central Europe do not perceive women's rights to be distinct from those of men (Einhorn, 1994: 57). A consciousness-raising effort is needed to overcome this perception. Women's publications in the East at first covered more the beauty and fashion trends than socioeconomic issues (cf. Harsanyi, 1993), but more recently they have begun to challenge gender stereotypes and serve as a forum for critical dialogue on women's issues (Regulska and Roseman, 1998: 29).

Western literature has focused much attention on the abortion issue in its analysis of women's issues in East-Central Europe. Abortion laws under the communists were very liberal, with the exception of Romania, where most abortions were banned under Ceauşescu's pronatalist policies. The first post-communist regimes of heavily Catholic Poland and Croatia enacted strict anti-abortion laws, while Romania liberalized its policy considerably. In Poland, abortion was restricted to cases of incest, rape, risk to the mother's health or life, or irreparable damage to the fetus. In October 1996, the left-liberal majority of the Sejm passed a law allowing abortion until the 12th week for women with personal or financial problems. The following May, the Constitutional

TABLE 6.1   Political participation, 1995[a]

Country	All men	All women	Men with higher education	Women with higher education
Poland	28	24	42	39
Czech Republic	48	38	68	60
Slovakia	41	36	56	62
Romania	30	26	39	42
Bulgaria	34	30	52	54

[a] Figures represent an average of the percentage of respondents who had voted in the last election, had ever signed a petition, had participated in a political protest or had joined a political party.

Source: Gigli, 1995: 20. Reprinted with permission of the publishers.

Tribunal ruled that the abortion law would have to be re-examined by the Sejm because it lacked clarity regarding the economic and social hardships under which abortion would be allowed. In December 1997, the newly elected and more conservative Sejm restored the stricter law. President Kwaśniewski declared that any new abortion initiative would have to come from the Sejm. The abortion issue has served as a mobilizing force for Polish women, with their political activism now expanding into other issues. Still, polls indicate that in Poland women and young people are less likely to support the legalization of abortion than are men and older people (Karpinski, 1997c).

The symbols, language and ideology of the post-communist political culture remain largely determined by men (Graham and Regulska, 1997: 66). Women tend to avoid the hierarchical forms of political organization (Wolchik, 1994b: 36) and the often confrontational and abusive nature of the new politics (Corrin, 1993: 197). The Open Media Research Institute conducted a survey to measure political interest and political involvement in 1995 in eleven transitional countries. Across the regions, roughly twice as many men as women classified themselves as 'very interested' in politics (Gigli, 1995: 18). The survey also revealed that women became less active in politics as the demands of participation increased, a result of the continuing double burden. However, women with higher education were more politically active than their less educated counterparts and sometimes more politically active than men with higher education (see Table 6.1). The mobilization of women in the post-communist era likely will continue to centre on issues related to family (Wolchik, 1994b: 43) and the quality of life, such as the environment, health care and access to decent housing.

What mechanisms currently exist for women to articulate their socioeconomic interests on a broad scale? Currently, non-governmental organizations are the locus of activity for most women involved in the political process in East-Central Europe (Graham and Regulska, 1997: 73). It is impossible to get an accurate picture of the number of non-governmental organizations (NGOs) which have formed to address women's issues because many of these are small and operate at the local level. In the Czech Republic, 84 per cent of the NGOs are headed by women (though they do not all concentrate on women's issues) (Hunt, 1997: 6). In the United States, the non-profit sector provided the political training ground for women in the 1960s and 1970s (Hunt, 1996: 7) and can serve a similar purpose in East-Central Europe. An analysis of tripartite mechanisms in Poland and Bulgaria reveals that women generally are underrepresented in these social partnership forums, particularly at the national level. They are more likely to serve on forums as experts or in administrative positions, rather than as elected officials (Iankova, 1996: 148–149). Iankova questions whether quotas should be established to effect higher women's participation rates but ultimately rejects them as undemocratic and of questionable effectiveness in addressing the myriad women's interests. Better, perhaps, would be 'gender equality committees' in the different branches of tripartism (labour, management, government), whose purpose would be to discuss the impact of reforms on gender issues (1996: 152). It is perhaps at the local level where women can be most influential, especially as local governments become increasingly responsible for the provision of social services. Their effectiveness will depend largely on whether the localized political culture values women's voices (Graham and Regulska, 1997).

Women still face many obstacles to effective political participation. The extant patriarchal and religious rhetoric which calls on women to resume their 'proper' role has led to a backlash against women's political participation. Women will continue to face the double burden, depriving them of the time and energy needed for active participation. It remains unclear whether women become significantly more active in the political sphere in direct response to the hardships of the market economy (Gigli, 1995: 21). Because women themselves do not discern that the economic transition affects them in unique ways, much work has to be done to change the perceptions of both genders.

Minorities: ethnos, demos and democratization

The problem of ethnic minorities had been a poison pill for the interwar democracies in East-Central Europe. Internally, ethnic nationalist sentiment had offered multiple opportunities for the enemies of democracy to mobilize popular support for anti-democratic politics. Externally, the Versailles settlement had created new grievances generating cross-border conflict over lost territories and disconnected ethnic brethren which strengthened the hands of nationalist and militarist forces.

Would the post-communist democracies be able to transcend this past, offering decent treatment for minority communities, and cooperative relations with neighbouring states, which the postwar Western democracies had achieved?

In the immediate postwar years, communist elites appealed successfully to nationalist aspirations in order to gain support and legitimacy. Tito and Ceauşescu were the most successful practitioners of national communism, presenting Yugoslav and Romanian brands of communism to their own people and breaking with Moscow. In Czechoslovakia, Gustav Husák chose to retain the 1968 federalization of the Czechoslovak state after the crushing of the Prague Spring, for he remained committed to his goal of Slovak political rights. 'Husák's nationalism, like most East European nationalism, was superbly adaptable' (Glenny, 1990: 206). The same can be said of Mečiar's and Milošević's nationalism today.

The manipulation of nationalism by communist leaders for political ends evidenced the fact that ethnic self-identity was still very important to the people. Official claims of equality for all members of society in the pursuit of the international brotherhood of man served only to mask the deep-seated ethnic tensions in many communist societies. Long dormant nationalism was unleashed again with the collapse of authoritarian rule, as people struggled to conceptualize their identities in a post-communist world. Still, this intolerance is not as virulent as that of the interwar period. The modernization policies of the communist governments had led to a rapid urbanization of many regions. Since ethnic minorities generally had lived in rural areas, many were assimilated into society in the process. Policies of assimilation did not, however, eliminate prejudice toward minorities because the policies were not accompanied by an open dialogue on ethnic issues. Factors not to be overlooked in the reduction of ethnic tension from the interwar years are the large-scale genocide of the Second World War and the emigration or expulsion of ethnic minorities from many countries in the aftermath of the war. Consequently, most of the countries are more ethnically homogeneous than in the interwar period.

In the early 1990s, as the countries of Western Europe were deepening decades of integrative policies, it appeared that the countries of Eastern Europe might regress to the interwar conditions of strident nationalism and ethnic hatred. The depth of ethnic tensions in the region after the collapse of communism was largely unanticipated by many analysts. Disregard for the rights of minorities seemed incompatible with the values embodied in the long struggle for human rights and liberation from the Soviet hegemony. It was reasonable to hope that these countries would develop a more rational way of dealing with the historical ethnic disputes (Glenny, 1990: 205).

The redrawing of political boundaries in Eastern Europe left large national minority communities 'stranded' outside the borders of their respective nation states. The Trianon Treaty in 1920 reduced the size of Hungary by two-thirds, turning over control of Transylvania to Romania and the Uplands to Slovakia. Today, ethnic Hungarians form the largest group in the region residing outside the borders of its nation state. They comprise 10.7 per cent of Slovakia's population and 7.1 per cent of Romania's (OMRI, 1996: 25, 161), with smaller populations also present in parts of the former Yugoslavia.

Tension between ethnic Hungarians and Slovaks has risen since the breakup of the Czechoslovak Federation. Though ethnic Hungarian and Slovak parties operated in a spirit of cooperation immediately after the collapse of communism, the growth of nationalism in Slovakia has made it very difficult to maintain such cooperation (Fisher, 1995: 58–59). Independent for the first time since the Nazi puppet state during the Second World War, Slovakia today struggles to define its national identity. Many Slovaks believe that the demands of ethnic Hungarians for protection of minority rights undermine the construction of the Slovak nation-state.

In March 1995, the Hungarian-Slovak Basic Treaty was signed; it was quickly ratified by the Hungarian Parliament but the Slovak parliament delayed ratification until the following March. The United States and the European Union had warned Slovakia that ratification would be an essential prerequisite to EU and NATO membership but the treaty was only ratified after the Slovak Parliament added two clauses stipulating that the treaty cannot be interpreted as granting minorities collective rights or the right to autonomy. In November 1995, the Slovak parliament passed the State Language Law limiting the rights of minorities to use their native language in official functions. Hungary, the European Union, the Organization for Security and Cooperation in Europe and other international organizations have urged Slovakia to pass a minority languages law but a draft law was rejected in November 1996 by the Nationalities Council (Fisher, 1996). In September 1997, the Hungarian minority won a partial victory when the Slovak Constitutional Court ruled that ethnic minorities could use their native language when writing to state bodies. Ten other complaints regarding minority rights were dismissed at the time because it was ruled that they had been improperly filed (RFE/RL Newsline, 10 September 1997).

In August 1997, Vladimír Mečiar suggested to Hungarian Prime Minister Gyula Horn a voluntary exchange of Hungarians who were unhappy in Slovakia with Slovaks living in Hungary (Spolar, 1997c). Public opinion polls reveal that there is considerable tension at the local level, as well. Forty-two per cent of Slovaks polled in late 1994 believed that Hungarians wish to annex the southern regions of Slovakia to Hungary (29 per cent did not believe this and 30 per cent were uncertain). Eighty per cent of Hungarian minorities polled denied such plans. Tensions between the groups could be eased by bringing them together on the numerous issues of common interest. In public opinion polls from 1993 and 1994, people of both nationalities gave the same hierarchy of pressing social issues: health care, unemployment, criminality, education, the strength of the currency, social security and old age pensions (Butorova and Butora, 1995b).

A state treaty between Hungary and Romania was signed in September 1996 after five years of difficult negotiations and was ratified by both countries later that year. This agreement demonstrated the countries' willingness to put aside ethnic tensions in their pursuit of entry into the European Union and NATO. However, it failed to satisfy completely the Hungarian minority in Romania, who wanted stronger calls for autonomy. One of the most contentious issues between the two countries is the issue of a Hungarian language university in Cluj to replace one shut down by the communists. Romanian political leaders generally opposed a Hungarian-only university, arguing that the current university, with its bilingual programme, or a unified university for all minority languages would be better. After years of rancorous debate, the Romanian government announced in September 1998 that it would set up a tuition funded multi-cultural university offering instruction in Hungarian as well as German. The Hungarian government under Orban had also expressed a willingness to help finance the new university. Despite a relatively open political dialogue between Hungary and Romania on the issue of minority rights, more than 100,000 Hungarians have left Romania since the collapse of communism (RFE/RL Newsline, 6 May 1998).

The defence of Hungarian minorities living abroad is recognized as an obligation of the government under Article 6 of the Hungarian constitution. The Antall government placed a greater emphasis on this issue than did the subsequent Horn government, mostly for domestic political reasons. Immediately after Fidesz's election victory, Viktor Orbán pledged that his government would serve the Hungarian nation, which he emphasized encompassed also Hungarians not living within the boundaries of the nation state. Such sentiments 'threaten to derail Horn's meticulous efforts to ease the tension' between Hungary and Romania (Haraszti, 1998: 52). Furthermore, the practice of a state stridently defending the rights of its minorities abroad against abuse, real or alleged, may actually increase the minority's isolation and hinder reconciliation efforts (cf. Balogh, 1994).

Poland has been devoid of the severe ethnic tensions plaguing other countries, for it is the most ethnically homogeneous state in the region. Post-communist Poland has not witnessed an irredentist movement, as have many of the countries to the south, though it should be noted that a sizable number of Poles still view Vilnius as a Polish city. Perhaps because of Poland's painful history of division and redrawing of borders, its political culture is less prone to irredentism and its elites more willing to seek a satisfactory compromise from the start. The shifting of the country's borders after the Second World War was accompanied by the expulsion of most of the Germans from Poland. Only a small German minority, approximately 1.3 per cent of the country's population, remains (OMRI, 1996: 44) but is largely assimilated into Polish culture. After the collapse of the Berlin Wall and before the first all-German parliamentary elections, German Chancellor Helmut Kohl displayed great reluctance in recognizing the Oder–Neisse line as the official Polish-German border. This campaign tactic, intended to win the support of conservative Germans, briefly raised the spectre of German irredentism and damaged German-Polish relations in the short term. Kohl officially recognized the border in a treaty signed in November 1990. As part of the reconciliation process, he agreed to write off some of the Polish debt to the Federal Republic of Germany in exchange for the promised protection of the cultural rights of ethnic Germans in Poland.

Despite an early solidarity for the Lithuanian freedom movement by Poles, Poland and Lithuania struggled over their mutual relations after Lithuania gained independence from the Soviet Union. The Polish minority, which comprises 7 per cent of Lithuania's population (OMRI, 1996: 56), consists mostly of peasants and workers who are poorly assimilated into Lithuanian culture and society. The Polish intelligentsia was virtually eliminated through a combination of death during the Second World War, exile to Siberia or emigration to Poland. When Lithuania declared independence in March 1990, Poland immediately renounced any claim to Lithuanian territory and Foreign Minister Krzysztof Skubiszewski pointedly declared that Vilnius was a Lithuanian city. When Soviet tanks attacked the television station in Vilnius in January 1991, thousands of Poles took to the streets of Warsaw in protest and Solidarity sent medical supplies, food, and clothing (Snyder, 1995: 318–319). However, during Lithuania's drive for independence, the Polish minority worked for an autonomous status within the Lithuanian Soviet Socialist Republic (Snyder, 1995: 321), making the Lithuanian government suspicious of their loyalty. The Lithuanian government has restricted the Polish minority's self-governance and there has been additional tension regarding the rights of Polish language schools and possible language requirements for citizenship.

A treaty regulating Polish-Lithuanian relations was not signed until April 1994, after Lithuania backed down on demands that the 1920 seizure of Vilnius be renounced. Changing international political realities compelled Lithuania to reach agreement with Poland, the last of Poland's seven neighbours to sign such a treaty. The strong showing of Vladimir Zhirinovsky's Liberal Democrats in the 1993 Russian parliamentary elections, the fear of being left behind when Poland joined NATO, and the realization that European integration led through Poland all factored into the equation (Snyder, 1995: 331–332). The two states have maintained a fruitful dialogue through the several changes of government in each.

After the collapse of communism, tension between Czechoslovakia and Germany arose over the issue of coming to terms with the Nazi treatment of Czechoslovakia and the expulsion of the Sudeten Germans after the Second World War. The Sudeten Germans are a powerful political force in Germany's Christian Social Union, a member of Kohl's coalition government. The Czech and German governments wrangled for some two years over the precise wording of a joint declaration of mutual grievances, finally signing the document in January 1997. In the declaration, the Germans 'recognize their responsibility and express sorrow for' the Nazi occupation of 1938–45, while the Czechs 'express regret' over the 'suffering and injustices' caused to innocent people during the expulsion of the roughly 3 million Sudeten Germans (Pehe, 1997a). A formal apology by the Czech Republic was supported by only 7 per cent of Czechs (Pehe, 1996b), though 55 per cent were willing to accept a declaration that the expulsion of the Sudeten Germans was morally incorrect (Pehe 1996a). The declaration was opposed by the extreme right in both countries and the extreme left in the Czech Republic. Prime Minister Václav Klaus opposed a return to the Czech lands by Sudeten Germans or the restitution of their property but Sudeten Germans will likely continue to press restitution claims since the declaration cannot prevent individual claims against the Czech government.

The Slovak minority in the Czech Republic accounts for only 3 per cent of the population (OMRI, 1996: 16), despite several waves of migration in search of economic opportunity (after the collapse of the Habsburg Empire, after the communist takeover in 1948, and after 1968 in an effort to balance jobs between the two groups) (Spolar, 1997d). Despite the considerable economic equalization during the communist era, Slovaks still perceived a lack of parity but were unable to organize politically in order to articulate their economic interests. In the post-communist era, this interest articulation took on a nationalist tone, due largely to the mobilization of the Slovak minority around ethnic issues by its political elite (Wolchik, 1994a: 163–164), helping bring about the dissolution of the Czechoslovak Federation.

Given the cultural and linguistic similarities and historical ties between Czechs and Slovaks, the Slovak minority is more likely to assimilate with the Czechs than are other ethnic minority groups in East-Central Europe. Other factors contributing to assimilation include a rejection of the nationalist politics of Slovak Premier Vladimír Mečiar by Slovaks living in the Czech Republic, and a desire to fit in as the Czech Republic joins the West. Though the Czech Republic funded education and cultural programmes for the Slovak minority after the Velvet Divorce, these programmes later fell victim to financial cuts and, surprisingly, to disinterest among Slovaks. For example, an attempt to found a Slovak language secondary school in Prague failed to find even thirty interested students, among a Slovak population of 30,000 (Spolar, 1997d).

The post-communist governments have been eager to reach accords on minority rights within their countries and with neighbouring countries, as these are preconditions for joining NATO and the European Union. But the act of signing treaties and the formal protection of minority rights are not enough to erase centuries of grievances, real or perceived. An essential component of the diminution of ethnic tension is increased economic development of regions with concentrations of minorities, for economic decline is often a cause of increased strain between ethnic groups (cf. Balogh, 1994; Glenny, 1990; Karkoszka, 1993). Ethnic minorities face greater discrimination in a tight job market. Members of the majority populations disadvantaged by the economic downturn will become resentful of minorities and may resort to violence it they perceive that the protection of ethnic minorities has turned the tables against them, threatening their economic well-being.

A necessary corollary to economic development is the increased self-confidence on the part of members of both minority and majority groupings (cf. Fisher, 1995; Karkoszka, 1993), though this may appear at first to be a prescription for continued divergence. The peoples of East-Central Europe are in the process of defining their national identity in an environment of political pluralism. Some groups are experiencing their first opportunity to do this in an environment of freedom and true independence while others are redefining that identity and learning that they cannot revert to the self-identities of the interwar period. Only when they become confident in their ethnic identities and, more importantly, perceive that these identities are no longer threatened by international politics, can they begin to overcome their distrust of ethnic minorities. This will be an essential step toward defining a national identity based on concepts of inclusive citizenship and shared civic/political (demos) values, rather than culture and ethnicity. The minorities, for their part, cannot rely entirely on legislated protection of their cultural identity but must move to promote their culture in such a way as to foster understanding between themselves and members of the ethnic majorities without appearing as a threat.

The Roma comprise the largest ethnic group in Eastern Europe with no nation-state to defend their interests, nor do they enjoy sponsorship by any sizable political parties or the intellectual community. The Romani population is small, economically isolated, culturally diverse and poorly organized. They account for 4 per cent of the population of Hungary, 2.4 per cent in the Czech Republic and 1.6 per cent in Slovakia (OMRI, 1996: 36, 16, 25), though compiling accurate data is difficult because Roma often fall through the bureaucratic cracks and many prefer not to identify themselves as Roma (Druker, 1997).

Racially motivated violence, aimed primarily at Roma but also foreigners, has been particularly widespread in the Czech Republic, perpetrated predominantly by skinheads and claiming about thirty lives since the Velvet Revolution. Government officials in the Czech and Slovak Republics have appeared largely indifferent to this violence. The intensity of the anti-Romani violence in the Czech Republic is particularly out of step with the country's supposed Western-oriented political culture and the relative absence of economic hardship, which often leads to patterns of scapegoating against minorities. In a 1996 public opinion poll, 87 per cent of respondents said that they would mind having Romani live in their neighbourhoods (Kratochvilova and Gallo, 1996). However, polls conducted by the Public Opinion Research Institute in 1997 indicated that racial intolerance was lower than it had been in seven years (RFE/RL Newsline, 13 February 1998).

It is not just skinhead violence, but also official policies and neglect that indicate the breadth of anti-Romani sympathies in the Czech political culture. The Czech citizenship law passed in 1993 effectively deemed some 100,000 Roma stateless due to the retroactive residency and clean criminal record requirements (Lyman, 1994). Postal delivery and utility services at times have been suspended to Romani housing complexes. In 1998, the town of Usti nad Labem announced plans to build a wall around a Romani housing complex. The mayor argued that the plan was not racially motivated but simply meant to 'separate the decent people from those who are not' (RFE/RL Newsline, 3 June 1998).

After Canada lifted visa requirements for citizens of the Czech Republic in 1996, disaffected Roma began to arrive by the hundreds, seeking political asylum but also that country's generous social welfare benefits (Schneider and Spolar, 1997). In the first nine months of 1997, 1,285 Roma arrived in Canada, compared with only twenty-nine the previous year (Schneider, 1997). In order to stem the tide, Canada reintroduced visa requirements for Czech citizens in October 1997. Shortly thereafter, Britain announced that it was considering similar measures after some 800 Roma had arrived there seeking asylum. Both Canada and Great Britain granted asylum to a small number of Roma in 1998 on the basis of racial discrimination. This was a great embarrassment for the Czech Republic, which prides itself on its legacy of inter-war democracy and its post-communist economic growth.

Such embarrassment helped launch the first real public debates in the Czech Republic on the plight of the Roma. Roma have also been induced into political action as a result, launching new educational and social initiatives (Penc and Urban, 1998: 40). Václav Havel pardoned two Romani who beat the Republican Party leader Miroslav Sládek (though the pardon was in part because Sladek had maligned Havel and his wife). Havel has warned, 'If this portion of the Czech society which shows racial tendencies and xenophobia keeps on behaving in the same way as they have been so far, it should not come as a surprise to us that our admission to the EU may be postponed' (Sierszula, 1998). After years of silence on the courts' practice of handing down light sentences for racial crimes, Havel began in early 1998 calling for tougher penalties for racially motivated crimes. Czech intellectuals who, like the country's political leaders had remained largely silent, also began advocating greater racial tolerance by 1998. Shortly after taking office,

Prime Minister Zeman also pledged that his government would take a much tougher stance against skinheads than did the Klaus government.

On average, Roma are worse off economically now than they were prior to the collapse of communism (Bollag, 1996). Official statistics record much higher levels of unemployment for Roma than for other groups, although the statistics may not present an accurate picture. First, the definition of Roma for statistical purposes depends on how researchers define 'Roma'. Researchers often overlook more affluent, assimilated Roma, even those who might consider themselves part of this group. Furthermore, since many Roma have been forced to seek unofficial employment due to widespread discrimination in the labour market, they do not become part of the official statistics (Lemon, 1996c: 28). In the Czech Republic, Roma are more adversely affected by sectoral unemployment than the Czech majority. Large numbers of Roma who relocated to the mining areas of Bohemia and Moravia after the expulsion of the Sudeten Germans are now being laid off as the mines and industries close down. Lax enforcement of anti-discrimination labour laws means that Roma are excluded from jobs for which they are qualified. When given employment, it is usually in the least prestigious occupations, often as heavy labourers for very low wages. They are virtually non-existent in the service sector, for the majority populations would prefer not to come into contact with them.

Hungary has gone farthest in making the plight of the Roma a national concern, but the efforts have had limited success. The law on minorities passed in 1993 set up a system of minority self government at the local and national levels. By 1997, some 400 Romani councils had been established but inadequate funding and lack of cooperation from local and national governments have diminished their effectiveness. Critics have argued that the law was never really intended to address discrimination at home, but rather to try to influence Slovakia and Romania in their treatment of the Hungarian minority (Roe, 1997). A parliamentary resolution passed in December 1995 prioritized improved living standards and increased economic opportunities for the Romani community. But debates have arisen regarding the prioritization of funding of employment programmes for adults versus focusing on education and health programmes for children. Romani children in Hungary (and the Czech Republic) are overrepresented in schools for the mentally retarded out of pure discrimination, hindering chances for the next generation to rise out of the current abject poverty.

While small Romani political parties exist, they have little voice in the new political systems and face considerable obstacles in effecting change. 'The idea that Romani would want to organize themselves politically has . . . been resisted; it presumably gives lie to non-Gypsy perceptions of the Gypsy as a happy-go-lucky wanderer' (Hancock, 1991: 138). In fact, Roma were organized politically throughout Eastern Europe in the interwar period and in the post-communist era have developed hundreds of political, cultural and self-help organizations. The considerable linguistic and cultural diversity of the Roma hinders the formation of large, more effective political parties and merely splinters the vote. Some interest groups formed in their name are run by non-Romani who, while finding more receptivity from the political mainstream, fail to represent Roma's true interests. It was hoped that the International Romani Union, founded by a small group of Romani intellectuals in the 1970s, would effectively take up the cause of East-Central European Roma. According to Rudko Kawczynski, Director of the Regional Roma Participation Programme in Budapest, the IRU remains a loose association lacking regular democratic procedures and a clear strategy. Furthermore, it places greater emphasis on gaining acceptance from non-Romani institutions than the Romani themselves. At this point, the most effective supporters of Romani rights may well be non-Roma international organizations, such as the OSCE, which has established a unit to monitor human rights violations and a coordinating body to facilitate communication within the Romani movement, and the Soros Foundation, which sponsors Romani schools, media and independent associations (Kawczynski, 1997: 28–29).

In contrast to the interwar period, the new democracies of East-Central Europe have been born into a much friendlier climate, among an enlarged group of well-established democracies. There is no threat from the classic anti-democratic forces, either the Leninist left or the fascist right. Poland, the Czech Republic and Hungary are also more ethnically homogeneous than in the interwar period. The extreme and brutal ethnic nationalism, seen now in the Balkans, has not returned to East-Central Europe.

And yet, the politics of ethnic nationalism have re-emerged as significant forces in the region. Anti-Semitism, even without a local Jewish minority ('anti-Semitism without Jews'), has been used by national-populist parties and leaders on the right in Poland and Hungary, by Wałęsa's personal priest, Father Henrik Jankowski, and by Radio Maria under Father Rydzyk's direction. The Church in Poland and Hungary (and even more in Croatia and Slovakia) has permitted this anti-liberal nationalism within its institutional boundaries because the Church is deeply divided in its attitudes to Western social pluralism (including liberal democracy), especially as it affects traditional Catholic culture.

The concept of nation as ethnos, an ethnic community, defined by blood ties (*ius sanguinis*) has reappeared and is now firmly rooted in the new democracies as a new ethnos-politics of the political right, which has blocked the development of a more modern and unambiguously democratic conservatism in Poland and Hungary. In the Czech Republic, Czech ethnos-politics has been part of Václav Klaus' success formula. Despite some early hopes (Goldfarb, 1992; Hoffman, 1993) that this would be a childhood disease of the new democracies which would be outgrown quickly, a new ethnos-politics has become one major pattern of political behaviour in East-Central Europe. Political liberalism alone has been unable to contain the challenge of the new ethnos-politics, and only a combination of liberal and democratic socialist parties has so far held it in check. It remains to be seen whether the conservative right will continue to rely on ethnic nationalist themes and issues for its political success, or whether, under challenge from a left-liberal demos-politics, a new and modernized conservative politics will gradually abandon ethnic scapegoating and conspiracy theories. The painful post-communist transition and the growing influence of Western finance and political influence, however, continue to give new life to national-patriotic ideals based on ethnic rather than civic solidarity.

Struggling to keep the environment on the political agenda

The collapse of the old political and economic order has led to a greater awareness of the environmental degradation wrought by a system that stressed economic advance through industrialization with little regard for the ensuing pollution and health problems. Pricing of inputs into the production process did not reflect their level of scarcity, as the prices were set by the state. Utilities for homes were generally provided free of charge, giving no cost incentive to the consumer to conserve energy. Cheap and abundant energy from the Soviet Union meant that the Eastern bloc countries did not experience the same urgency of energy conservation as did Western countries in the aftermath of the oil crisis in the 1970s. Although environmental laws were passed by the communist regimes they were often ignored and loosely enforced (Černá and Tošovská, 1995; Manser, 1993). Environmental regulations followed the polluter pays principle, but in reality, there was little substance to the measures. Fines imposed on polluters were so low that they were simply budgeted into the cost of production. Since the managers of state enterprises were part of the nomenklatura, they exploited party ties to avoid paying fines. This network continued to stymie environmental restructuring in the post-communist era, as members of the nomenklatura in environmental ministries continued to look out for their friends in the industrial sector (Manser, 1993: 34–35).

While the nuclear accident at Chernobyl in 1986 helped focus attention on the international dimensions of environmental destruction, each country had its own share of problems. Chief among them was the use of indigenous brown coal as the prime energy source in Poland and Czechoslovakia. It is characterized by low efficiency and large byproducts of sulphur dioxide, the main factor in acid rain. In the early 1990s, it was estimated that 30 per cent of Czechoslovakia's forests were irreparably damaged, with another 50 per cent partially damaged from acid rain (Glenny, 1990: 33). Environmental damage in Czechoslovakia was estimated at 5–7 per cent of GDP in 1990 (Černá and Tošovská, 1995: 6). In Poland, it is estimated that environmental degradation caused material losses amounting to 5–10 per cent of the national income due to such factors as accelerated corrosion, decreased harvests, lost work time due to illness and damage to the forests (Ministry of Environmental Protection, Natural Resources and Forestry, 1991, cited in Nowicki, 1993: 27–28). The industrial triangle of southeast East Germany, southern Poland and northern Czechoslovakia was an environmental nightmare, with disproportionately high rates of respiratory diseases and declining life expectancies. Non-industrial areas were not immune to the problem, as airborne and water-borne toxins spread to other regions, including agricultural areas.

While the communist governments chose largely to ignore environmental issues, the environment served as a mobilizer of civil society in the 1980s. Ecologically minded groups formed primarily in East Germany, Hungary, Poland and Bulgaria. The most significant movement developed in Hungary in opposition to the proposed construction of the Gabcikovo-Nagymaros hydroelectric power system along the Danube River. The dam was to be a joint effort by Hungary and Czechoslovakia, but mass popular mobilization led Hungary to pull out of the agreement in 1989. Slovakia's decision to continue the project led Hungary to take the case to the International Court of Justice, arguing that the environmental costs were too severe. In September 1997, the Court ruled that Hungary had violated international law by unilaterally abandoning the 1977 agreement to build the dam and ordered both countries to resolve the issue within six months. The Horn government pledged in early 1998 to build a dam but in July 1998, Viktor Orban's cabinet annulled the decision, asserting (correctly) that the International Court had not ordered Hungary to construct a dam and pledging to work to reach a new agreement with Slovakia only after further environmental impact studies. Public opinion polls at the time of the Horn agreement to proceed with construction showed that more than 60 per cent opposed the project (RFE/RL Newsline, 5 March 1998). The stalling on the part of the Hungarian government prompted Slovakia in September 1998 to appeal again to the International Court to intervene.

Though Poland lacked a single, significant and mobilizing environmental issue, its environmental movement had something of a head start on other communist countries since environmental issues were openly debated in the press during 1980–81. The Polish Ecological Club (PKE) was formed in 1981 to focus on environmental protection, education and scientific cooperation. Other movements included the youth movement Wolę Być ('I prefer to be'), founded in 1984, which waged campaigns around localized issues; the Ecological Movement of St Francis of Assisi, founded in 1985, which concentrated on one's moral responsibility to nature; and 'Freedom and Peace', which mainly protested against military service but also nuclear power and environmental degradation (Hicks, 1996: 78–81). The Catholic Church sanctioned the environmental movement, sponsoring seminars and special masses for the environment.

The Polish government attempted to co-opt the environmental movement by forming the Social Ecological Movement in 1986 as part of the post-martial law normalization policy to deactivate society (Hicks, 1996: 160). By making the environment an official topic for public discussion, the government only brought more attention to the issue and, through its own press coverage, provided the movement with more information than otherwise would have been available (Hicks, 1996: 86).

Having served to raise public consciousness, it was expected that nascent Green parties would find broad political support in the post-communist era. Instead, the Green movement has been disappointing as a political force. In Hungary, its failure is attributable primarily to factionalism but overall, the various Green parties faltered because they were unable to develop comprehensive economic plans (Glenny, 1990: 203). In the heady days just after the transition, environmentalists sought to avoid the pitfalls of traditional economic development in favour of integrated, sustainable development. Instead, economic restructuring is following the liberal economic model, which fails to account for the full cost of natural resource use. Were the transitional countries to adopt such measures as internalizing the externalities of the production process, their industry would remain non-competitive with Western industry. In 1990, the environment was high on the political agenda (Csagoly, 1998: 75; Manser, 1993: 12–14) but in the struggle for economic subsistence, the environment became a luxury. Public opinion surveys show that people are willing to make some sacrifices for the environment but remain torn between the need to create jobs and to save the environment (see Table 6.2). As characterized by Václav Klaus, 'The environment and the economy are like whipped cream and cake; whipped cream can be used to decorate the cake, once the cake is ready' (cited in Bisschop, 1996: 43).

Given the difficulties of implementing sustainable development policies, the transitional countries are turning more frequently to market mechanisms, as well as fines and taxes to combat environmental degradation, but these are often applied on an ad hoc basis and are subject to manipulation and evasion since they are often viewed as barriers to economic growth (Bisschop, 1996: 45). Increasing energy prices to international market levels was supposed to decrease energy consumption, thereby reducing pollution. While this has worked in the industrial sector, energy demand in the household sector is relatively inelastic. Still, the economic restructuring alone has led to a partial reduction in pollution through the closing of many state industrial enterprises.

TABLE 6.2   *Environmental concerns in comparison, 1997*

'Environmental protection should take priority, even at the risk of slowing down economic growth'

Hungary	39%
Poland	32%
Britain	69%
Germany	71%
United States	69%

'I would give part of my income if I were certain that the money would be used to prevent environmental pollution'

	Strongly agree	Somewhat agree
Hungary	18%	19%
Poland	13%	42%
Britain	16%	48%
Germany	33%	41%
United States	23%	50%

Source: *Environmental Monitor* by Environics International of Toronto, cited in *The Washington Post*, 22 November 1997, A15

Privatization provided an incentive for Eastern enterprises to reduce emissions, as managers needed to demonstrate familiarity with and commitment to Western standards. There have been some innovative market approaches to pollution reduction, including the use of pollution rights, with some Western firms paying for pollution abatement mechanisms in the East in exchange for the right to continue the level of particulate emissions at their home plants. An Ecofund has been established in Poland using funds from debt-for-nature agreements with Western countries for ecological investments.

Poland has made some of the greatest strides in pollution reduction. Efforts were focused first on industrial centres with severe health problems. Fines have been used to support the National Fund for Environmental Protection, which helps finance cleaner technology. Poland has realized dramatic decreases in the levels of airborne particulates in its industrial regions (cf. Spolar, 1997a). Blessed with substantial natural gas and geothermal reserves, Poland has taken the lead in the development of cleaner energy sources. Currently, this production is funded primarily with grants, but it is hoped that it will become economically sustainable in the long run without the infusion of outside funds.

Substantial levels of Western aid were expected to be directed at the environmental devastation in the East; like most Western aid, this has been disappointingly meagre and largely self-interested. Western countries often finance efforts to reduce pollution in areas bordering on their own countries, ignoring the interior of transitional countries. Western credits and grants are used to transfer pollution abatement technology to the East rather than to develop indigenous technology (Manser, 1993: 91).

Progress in some areas has been offset by problems caused by Western-style consumerism. In Hungary, the number of automobiles in use has doubled in ten years, with the average automobile being more than ten years old (Bisschop, 1996: 45). Many of the heavily polluting East European automobiles remain in use and affordable second-hand Western automobiles generally lack catalytic converters. The increased consumption of heavily packaged consumer goods is straining current waste management capacities. Most of the waste sites in the region are unregulated and lack effective emission reduction mechanisms, and recycling of plastics and cardboard is years behind the rate in the West.

Countries seeking to join the European Union will need to demonstrate a commitment to enforcement of EU environmental codes in order to gain membership. One of the scenarios for the early entry of East-Central European countries provides a longer time frame for these countries to bring their environmental standards in line with those of the Western members (Coleman, 1997: 24). It is important to remember that beyond aligning environmental regulations, the EU will need to work with its prospective members to clean up existing environmental degradation. The World Bank estimates that Poland will need to spend 3.3–4.6 per cent of its GDP on clean-up if it is to catch up with EU standards, but it presently spends only 1.5 per cent (Forowicz, 1988b).

The newly poor – an underclass in post-communism?

The communist system served as a great social equalizer by eliminating class divisions which had developed over the centuries. Although the privileged nomenklatura enjoyed luxuries denied the average citizen, great disparities in income and wealth were eliminated. The transition to a market economy has seen a rapid increase in the number of people living below the poverty level throughout East-Central Europe but indications are that an entrenched underclass has not yet formed. At this stage, poverty in the first tier countries is starting to resemble more the structure in Western industrialized countries than in Latin America or the developing world.

Despite the fiscal constraints of the post-communist states, there may be room for effective anti-poverty policies. A World Bank study of Poland concluded that a large percentage of the poor live just below the poverty line. Continued economic growth combined with sound, targeted policies aimed at the most disadvantaged should be able to lift many of these people above the poverty line. Steady annual GDP growth of 5 per cent in and of itself could reduce poverty to less than 5 per cent by the year 2000, down from the 14 per cent at the time of the World Bank Study in late 1993 (World Bank, 1995: XV). Furthermore, since it is estimated that up to three-quarters of social spending in Poland goes to recipients who are not poor (World Bank, 1995: XXIV), the neediest can be targeted by redirecting funds, rather than increasing overall social funding, which would be out of line with IMF guidelines. Social conditions have also deteriorated since the start of the transitions, but some of this is a latent result of conditions during the communist era. In the period 1965 to 1989, male mortality rates of Warsaw Pact countries increased, while those in Western Europe decreased, despite comparable increases in per capita GDP in both blocs (Eberstadt, 1994: 218–219). The dietary, smoking and drinking habits of Easterners contributed greatly to this decline but the medical profession focused more on combating infectious diseases than on poor lifestyle habits. Recent statistics show that countries where the transition has been most complete (the Czech Republic, Poland, Hungary and Slovenia) have experienced the biggest drops in infant mortality rates in the 1990s (*Economist*, 1996a: 46). The health care delivery system in these countries is also generally in better shape than in other transitional countries (Sebastian, 1995: 50), though it still struggles with low remuneration for medical professionals and outmoded technology. It will take a combination of steady economic growth, effective policies and lifestyle changes over the long run to raise the standard of living in transitional countries to that of Western Europe.

Interest representation

The hard-won freedoms of speech and the press allow interest groups to express their demands in the political arena, though they often lack the requisite resources. It is feared that interest politics will be dominated by those with money to influence the political system, with the party system offering little substantive representation to the disadvantaged. Critical to the long-term stability of democracy is whether these interest groups will perceive that their demands are being addressed within the political system. Experience has shown that most single interest parties, with the exception of those with a large electoral base, such as the agrarian parties in Poland and Hungary, do not stand much chance, especially when their issues are deemed of lesser importance than the macroeconomic problems associated with the transition. In order to survive in the post-communist political landscape, interest groups will either have to align themselves with larger groups or develop comprehensive political platforms in order to appeal to a wider base and gain entry into the legislative process. This pattern is only slowly evolving. One remnant of the 'us versus them' mentality of the communist era is a deep-seated distrust of one group for another, making it difficult for narrow interest groups to find common ground on which to work together.

The effective articulation of group interests will continue to be constrained over the medium term since these societies are in continual flux. Western concepts of interest articulation may be quite irrelevant in a fluid political environment. The incomplete break with the past, coupled with the enormous stress of the newly evolving economic system, has left many people clinging to past values. Insufficient time has elapsed for the development of systems, roles and rules of interest articulation (Bunce and Csanádi, 1993: 262). The conflict between the remaining institutions of the old system (such as state owned enterprises) and those of the evolving system complicates interest articulation. In the first place, institutions serve to define interests, shape perceptions and structure behaviour. The weakness of new institutions, and the fact that the elite-centred political parties of the region do not value policy input by non-governmental organizations, result in weak interest articulation. The communist legacy, which denied and to a large degree eliminated class interests, poses another obstacle. It is difficult for political actors to move from the politics of values characteristic of the old system to the more divisive politics of interests associated with market economics (Bunce and Csanádi, 1993: 265).

The post-communist societies are experiencing a degree of socio-economic uncertainty unknown in the communist era. The strategic response one makes to such uncertainty is not predictable using traditional Western concepts of the rational actor. East-Central Europeans, overwhelmed by the new choices, responsibilities and demands thrust upon them by the market economy, are not necessarily able to act strategically in pursuit of their own interests. In order to do so, they must first define their interests, then assess the interests of other political players and finally weigh the possible outcomes of alternate choices. With societies in flux, so too are people's subjective identities. Lacking clearly defined self-interests, and given the weakness of interest-based parties, the electorate in the medium term remains subject to mobilization by the politics of ethnicity and religion and by populist politicians promising quick fixes to economic and social problems.

7

Political Party Formation and Electoral Competition

Party formation: early expectations and new realities

After the great regime-change breakthroughs of 1989–91, and with the first round of free and fair elections, one of the central issues for the newborn democracies of the region was the formation of a party system suitable to sustain democracy. In the first months of post-communist politics, it was assumed by many observers that the new party systems would gravitate towards recognizable Western models; as with so many other things, the goal was to become a 'normal' political system, which was another shorthand expression for 'joining the West'. In this area as in many others, it seemed to many that the Western success formula of the Cold War era, exemplified by some of the most admired Western nations like the United States, Great Britain, Germany or Sweden, would now provide the new goals for political parties and the party system. The 'Eastern European syllogism', as Adam Przeworski has termed it, argued that 'If not for communism, we would have been like the West. The minor premise asserts, "now communism is gone". The conclusion not only asserts that Eastern Europe should and will embrace the Western model, but also promises that this model will generate the glitter of developed capitalism' (Przeworski et al., 1995: 3).

Western party systems, which had promoted stable and strong democracies in the fortunate half of Europe during the Cold War, were certainly seen as the appropriate models to emulate. Lipset and Rokkan (1967) had described, in an early comparative political sociology, the typical political cleavages and voter alignments of Western party systems, which followed from the historic projects of nation-building and industrialization; major party formations had emerged from centre–periphery, Church–state, agriculture–industry and worker–owner cleavages. Could East-Central Europe now consciously replicate, if belatedly, this pattern? Two lessons seemed to predominate in the earliest conceptualizations: parties in the new post-communism should be very different from the ideological and tightly disciplined Leninist parties; and the new party system should offer pragmatic and limited choices to voters in order to avoid weak and splintered democracy.

Some intellectuals in the Solidarity leadership wanted to avoid parties in the European sense, and set up instead a more American-type system of 'non-ideological' catch-all parties. 'The most influential Solidarity politicians propagated the theory of an end to parties as such, and they planned for the creation of two electoral machines (like early US parties) that would be called into being by Solidarity and that would compete against each other in the next parliamentary elections' (Gebethner, 1996: 63). Some of this feeling was a reflection, at the end of the communist era, of popular sentiment against 'the party' or 'political parties' in general. Surveys done by Stanislaw Gebethner in Poland, before, during and after the 1990 presidential elections, confirmed widespread indifference or antipathy towards parties. Jan Gross was one of those advocate-observers who foresaw an American two-party system emerging in 1989–90 Poland, with both parties coming out of the Solidarity movement, one championed by the Wałęsa wing and the other by the liberal intellectuals. For Gross, 'The 1989 revolution in East Central Europe was driven by the idea of empowering society rather than of national liberation. "Citizen", "civic", "society" – rather than "Pole," "Czech," "Hungarian," or "nation" – were the key labels for what was going on' (Gross, 1992: 59–60). And with this civic society now seemingly empowered, the next natural step was the formation of a political society, most likely based on the American two-party model.

A populist party – Porozumienie Centrum (Centre Alliance) – emerged to champion his [Wałęsa's] candidacy for the Polish Presidency. Now that the liberal-democratic ROAD (Civic Movement for Democratic Action) has emerged in response to Porozumienie Centrum – a two-party system has begun to take shape in Poland. Somewhat paradoxically the American paradigm of two large nonideological parties may have been actualized by

Wałęsa, indeed by his refusal to go along with the attempt to transform the Citizens' Committees in the fall after the elections into a political movement. Despite his evident taste for personalized power he may have effectively pre-empted the possibility of Peronist- or Mexican-style presidential politics in Poland by forcing a split in Solidarity. (Gross, 1992: 71)

This was a mistaken judgement, as was evident within a few months with the extreme splintering of Solidarity into a dozen personality-parties, and within a few years by the resurgence of the ex-communist successor parties in the 1993 elections. But at the time, these sentiments and predictions were so often repeated that they reinforced themselves as the 'normal' thinking of the new era. Doubters or critics were often suspected of less-than-appropriate enthusiasm for the collapse of communism, and antipathy to the restoration of capitalism, and their opinions carried little weight in those first years.

In retrospect, these early expectations neglected deeply rooted realities, which made it unlikely that the post-communist party systems would adopt the US or European models from the Cold War era.

1   Western party systems were the political end-product of a long process of social conflict over the political economy of industrialization led primarily by a capitalist business class and contested by an urban working class. This is not anything like the social or economic situation which faces the new democracies of East-Central Europe, and it is misleading to expect that parties there will mirror the earlier Western experience.

2   At the end of the Cold War, the Western party systems, which had served so well during the best years of the Keynesian welfare state, were themselves under growing pressure to change, and the party landscape was beginning a new though gradual transition to a yet unclear type of political contestation over the political economy of a globalizing capitalism. The original goal of 'joining the West' through adoption of Cold War–Keynesian party systems was illusory from the beginning.

The political economy of early post-communism is historically *sui generis*, an original formation of new openness and volatility. The communist period produced its own form of statist industrialization and modernization, now privatizing and marketizing into a globalizing capitalist order. The formation of new political parties, and their style of electoral competition, matches the struggle over this new political economy. Although there are growing ties of the new political economy to Western Europe and to the European Union, which certainly act as normative guides for the new political class, the domestic forces which seek representation are more important for the actual shaping of party competition.

Exit from communism, entry into uncharted territory

There have now been several rounds of national elections in Poland, Hungary and the Czech Republic. In the first round of free multi-party voting for a new regime, the main theme was to oust the communist party (or its newly formed successor) from office. For this purpose, the parties born out of Solidarity in Poland, the parties born out of the Civic Forum in Czechoslovakia, and the parties born out of the 'negotiated revolution' in Hungary did not need much clarity in programme and their lack of experience in government was a badge of honour. The first free elections in two generations required a clear break with the ruling Leninist parties, and this was the great achievement of that first round. The importance of this first-round clean break should not be under-estimated, since it was not universal throughout post-communist East Europe. In some parts of Eastern Europe, particularly Bulgaria, Romania and Albania, this was not achieved in the first multi-party elections, where renamed successor parties won control of the new parliaments and formed post-communist regimes but with ex-communist parties in control. In each of these nations it took a longer period of struggle, hardship and disappointment to produce the first anti-communist regime shift. In Albania this occurred in 1992, after a round of mob rioting and looting of public facilities, with the election of Sali Berisha's Democratic Party (which led to a new authoritarianism and to national disaster). In Bulgaria, it took six more years to oust the successor Bulgarian Socialist Party from the national government, and to achieve the first solid anti-communist regime shift through massive public demonstrations in early 1997. In Romania, only the third round of elections in the autumn of 1996 produced victories by an anti-communist coalition of parties, ousting Ion Iliescu as President and his semi-successor Party of Social Democracy in Romania from office.

The victory of the anti-communist opposition led almost immedi-ately to its political splintering into feuding factions and personal animosity among allies from the days of dissident anti-regime struggle. For Jacques Rupnik, the disintegration of the broad anti-communist Civic Forum was actually a sign of its triumph: 'the real victory of the Forum as the movement guaranteeing the revival of Czechoslovak democracy will come only with its extinction. The groups born from it will form the basis of a new political pluralism' (cited in Blahoz, 1994: 244). This was not the original intent of Civic Forum, which foresaw in its founding statutes that it would become a policy making body to fill the void left by the communist party, but clearly this goal was a fleeting one which was undone by the rapid proliferation of parties of all types.

Adam Michnik argues that this rude awakening was the inevitable opening to a free political competition which is the real trademark of a

TABLE 7.1   *Parliamentary election results in Poland, 1991–1997*

Party	Percentage of popular vote for the Sejm		
	1991	1993	1997
Democratic Left Alliance	12.0	20.4	27.1
Polish Peasant Party	8.7	15.4	7.3
Democratic Union/Freedom Union	12.3	10.6	13.3
Union of Labour	2.1	7.3	4.7
Confederation for an Independent Poland	7.5	5.8	—
Non-party Bloc to Support Reform	—	5.4	—
Fatherland Catholic Election Committee	9.8	6.4	—
Solidarity	5.1	4.9	33.8[a]
Centre Alliance	8.7	4.4	—
Liberal Democratic Congress	7.5	4.0	—[b]
Real Politics Union	2.3	3.2	—
Party X	0.5	2.7	—
Coalition for the Republic	—	2.7	—
Polish Peasant Party — Peasant Alliance	5.5	2.4	—
Movement for Poland's Reconstruction	—	—	5.5
German ethnic minority	1.7	0.7	—

[a]   Solidarity Electoral Action.
[b]   Merged with Freedom Union.

Sources: Rzeczpospolita, 27 September 1993; Karpinski, 1997a

functioning democracy, neither black nor red, but grey; it was a loss of innocence for the dissidents, and yet a necessary precondition for the development of a party politics which, unpretty though it often seems, is the real stuff of a free society. And yet Michnik adds a warning note as well:

So, we rejected communism for reasons equally dear to a conservative, a socialist, and a liberal. In this way, a peculiar coalition of ideas emerged, which Leszek Kołakowski noted in his well-known essay, 'How to be a Conservative-Liberal Socialist?' This coalition collapsed along with communism. But before it collapsed, the coalition had marked public debate with a specific tone of moral absolutism.

The moral absolutism of the anti-communist opposition required us to believe that communism is inherently evil, the devil of our times, and that resistance to communism is something naturally good, noble, and beautiful. The democratic opposition demonized communists and angelicized itself. I know because this moral absolutism was also my experience to a certain degree. I don't regret this experience, nor do I think I need to be ashamed of it. . . . The most outstanding witnesses of resistance in those years – Aleksandr Solzhenitsyn, Havel, Zbigniew Herbert – defended absolute values. . . . And in the end it was we who won. But, woe to those moral absolutists who emerge victorious in political struggles – even if only for a while. (Michnik, 1997: 16–17)

TABLE 7.2   *Parliamentary election results in Hungary, 1990–1998*

Party	Percentage vote for the parliament (first-round)		
	1990	**1994**	**1998**
Hungarian Democratic Forum	24.7	11.7	3.4
Free Democrats	21.4	19.7	7.9
Independent Smallholders	11.7	8.8	13.8
Socialists	10.9	33.0	32.3
Young Democrats (Fidesz)	8.9	7.0	28.2
Christian Democrats	6.5	7.0	2.1
Workers Party	3.7	3.2	4.1

Sources: *Magyar Hirlap*, 10 April 1990; *Economist*, 16 May 1998

Michnik, one of the most imaginative thinkers in the Polish opposition and later a major commentator on the post-communist democratization process, now sees this moral absolutism as a hindrance to the messy give-and-take, the unpretty compromise and the crass political deal making of real existing democracy.

If the first round of elections were successful in Poland, Czechoslovakia and Hungary in turning the communists out of power, they only opened the door for the more vexing problem of building a new system in which social interests could be represented in the new parliamentary democracy. The skills and talents which had been appropriate for leading broad popular coalitions to achieve the first breakthrough to democracy were now suddenly put to very different tasks. Michael Roskin, in his analysis of the early emergence of party systems in the region, has pointed to the difficulties facing the new democracies in building party systems for democratic competition and representation of social interests:

> Eastern Europe does not have the time to gradually develop parties and party systems; with the collapse of Communist regimes in 1989, competitive elections were thrust on most countries of the region in 1990. Instead of patiently building party strength and gradually obtaining electoral success and parliamentary seats, East European parties had to suddenly contest elections with little practice, organisation, or political skill. (1997: 48)

Without much idea of potential constituency, or accurate guidelines of electoral viability, and with a general overestimation of each leader's call to office, the number of parties rapidly proliferated: about sixty-five parties registered in Hungary and a further thirty-two political associations could be identified; ninety parties campaigned for parliament in Poland in 1991 (Hill, 1994: 272). These festivals of democracy included, in both Poland and the Czech Republic, Beer Lovers parties, a sign of whimsy and also perhaps disillusionment with conventional party politics at the very outset of building a new party system. These parties actually secured some minor electoral support, with the Polish Beer Lovers getting over 3 per cent of the vote and sixteen seats in the Sejm. Many other tiny 'sofa parties,' whose members could be seated on one sofa, could be seen as both new beginnings of political entrepreneurship and as an early illness which if not treated could present problems for democratic stability, that classic worry derived from the interwar period of weak and paralysed democracies.

The big conceptual question was whether the process of splintering and then reconfiguring of parties would end up with the kind of 'moderate polarization' which Seymour Martin Lipset (1959a) found desirable for stable democracy, or the 'polarized pluralism' of five or more relevant parties which Sartori (1976) warns against as a potential threat to democracy.

With the death of the old regime, individuals were set free to find their own way into or out of political life; the competition for political support among the atomized population had just begun. Czech scholar Erazim Kohak, in his description of the difficulties facing the Czech democracy, has argued that one major barrier has been the breakdown of civil society, a legacy of the communist period which has continued on into post-communism:

> The results were felt long before the fall of the old regime. As the command economy destroyed all economic initiative, so the command society destroyed all social initiative. Then, when the command structure collapsed, what was left resembled Machiavelli's Italy or the modern state as Hegel imagined it: a mass of atomized individuals ruled by a central government. That is the basis on which Central Europe's leaders are seeking to build democracy. (Kohak, 1997: 23)

This is an important point, and well taken, because, in contrast to other democratizations in other regions, the citizen's new class position, subjective or objective, is relatively more volatile in post-communism, making interest articulation and interest aggregation through party politics more difficult. And yet aggregate judgement does not recognize the important differences among individuals in their paths towards new political self-identification, and their judgements as to which party, if any, might be able to further their interests. Kohak's blanket judgement of the legacy of communism makes its seem like everyone is starting from ground zero, and everyone is more or less facing the same quandary. Some groups clearly had more stable economic interests than others to defend, and some groups had more resources in finances, organization and political skills.

TABLE 7.3 *Parliamentary election results in the Czech Republic, 1992–1998*

| | Percentage popular vote for the National Council[a] | | |
Party	1992	1996	1998
Civic Democratic Party	33.9	29.6	27.7
Communists	14.3	10.3	11.0
Social Democrats	7.7	26.4	32.3
Republicans	6.5	8.0	3.9
Christian Democrats	6.0	8.0	9.0
Liberal Social Union	5.8	–	–
Civic Democratic Alliance	–	6.3	–
Freedom Union	–	–	8.6
Pensioners Party	–	–	3.0

[a] The Czechoslovak lower house of parliament was called the House of the People in 1992; after the 1993 split, the Czech lower house became the National Council.

Sources: CSTK, 8 and 10 June 1992; OMRI Daily Digest II, 3 June 1996; RFE/RL Newsline, 22 June 1998

In the subsequent rounds of elections, the shape of the new party systems became somewhat clarified by the emergence of parties able to credibly present themselves as the political representatives of an increasingly class-differentiated society. Even then, Michael Bernhard speaks of a 'dual society' still in the midst of a great remaking of social classes and interests, corresponding to the prolonged processes of privatization and marketization: '. . . mobilization of groups in pursuit of market-based economic interests becomes more difficult because the basis of those interests is in flux. The entire class structure is being remade and it is unclear which effects of reform are temporary and which represent permanent losses in status, power, or welfare. Because of this there is a time-lag before new cleavages acquire political force' (1996: 322).

An additional signal from the first rounds of elections is that post-materialist parties like the Greens have been unable to find a place for themselves in the emerging party landscape, except as a minor fixture in a larger electoral coalition with other parties. This is despite some early signals, in pre-election polls, that the environmentalists might do quite well (as high perhaps as 12–18 per cent in Czechoslovakia for example, cf. Frankland, 1995; Waller, 1995). Yet the elections gave the Greens less than 5 per cent of the vote, and their fortunes never recovered. While a general recognition of environmentalism has been pinned to virtually every party platform, the Greens as the special representative of post-materialist quality of life politics 'are out of phase with the dominant demands of the post-communist period' (Waller, 1995: 236). Frankland agrees that 'East European publics may not have been ready for participatory focus and democratic organization of the Green parties' (1995: 339). The politics of post-communism are certainly not centred around quality of life issues that have gained attention in the West.

Agrarian parties: Hungary and Poland

Which groups would be able to identify their interests with a specific party and which parties would be able to mobilize a popular base of interest group support in the period after the first elections? In Hungary and Poland, one group which found its way to a political party was the small farmers or peasants; in fact, in many post-communist political systems (including Russia and Moldova), an agrarian or peasant party has emerged as representative of the interests of farmers, whether former collective and state farm workers or small private farm owners. As part of the Hungarian 'goulash communism' after 1968, farm families were able to rent or lease land for essentially private agriculture, and over two decades this had developed as part of the Hungarian gradual path to commercialization and privatization. In Hungary, the Smallholder Party, which had been the largest party in the first postwar years before consolidation of the communist monopoly, reappeared as the most important political vehicle for rural and traditional farm interests; the new Smallholder Party also carried with it some of the less attractive ideological baggage of its former incarnation, such as ethnic chauvinism, territorial revanchism and anti-Semitism. Smallholder Party leaders have distinguished themselves by vilifying both liberals and socialists as foreign elements in Hungary, as traitors to Hungary, who are responsible for all that has gone wrong and who must be eliminated so that real patriots can defend true Hungarian interests. Roskin (1997: 56) in particular views the back-from-the-past Smallholder Party (the 'Rip Van Winkle' effect) as a dangerous contender in the bidding for nationalist sentiment, especially if there should be mistreatment of Hungarian minorities living in Romania, Slovakia, or northern Serbia.

In Poland, one might have expected Rural Solidarity to establish its hold over the peasantry after the collapse of communism. Yet the former communist-allied United Peasant Party (UPP), which switched sides in 1989 to give Solidarity a majority in the Sejm and to force acceptance of a Solidarity-led government, was able to outmanoeuvre Rural Solidarity, which had split into several factions. The UPP leadership was able to merge with one of the Rural Solidarity factions and reappear as the historic Polish Peasant Party (PSL). By 1992, under the leadership of a young engineer Waldemar Pawlak, the new successor party to the communist-allied UPP was able to claim the leading role for political representation of Polish farmers (Dziewanowski, 1996: 190–193). The party programme of the PSL does not reject market economics, but emphasizes a gradual evolution very much at odds with the 'shock therapy' of the Balcerowicz reform project, and argues for 'long-term strategic planning of socio-economic changes that would respect Christian ethics and social justice' (p. 191). In this respect the PSL mirrored the programmes of other agrarian parties of post-communism, which have been able to rather quickly mobilize a popular base of support in the still-sizable rural population. With its moderate emphasis on Catholic values but support for a secular state, the PSL has made itself into a party of balance and moderation, able to form coalitions with either the left-successor Democratic Left Alliance or with the centre-right parties of the former Solidarity. In the 1993 elections, the PSL was able to garner fully 46 per cent of the peasant vote (up from 34 per cent in 1991, Millard, 1994a: 308).

The weakness of a specifically peasant or agrarian party in the Czech Republic is another sign of its earlier and more complete industrialization; indeed, it is one more piece of evidence that the Czech Republic is indeed more of a 'bourgeois democracy' than the other Visegrad nations. Many observers have noted this attitude among the new political class in Prague, and it is a pervasive if elusive presence in the Czech political culture which reminds them of a return to the prewar era. 'Evidently, there is some truth in that: one cannot help being struck by a demeanor in the Czech Republic that recalls its pre-war, bourgeois past' (Nowotny, 1997: 70). One element of this is an absence of an agrarian or peasant party from the post-communist spectrum. Yet this is at least somewhat surprising, since in the interwar First Republic the Agrarian Party (officially the Republican Party of Agricultural People and Small Farmers after 1922) was a mainstay of the party system, generally getting 13–15 per cent of the vote in a fairly fractured multi-party system. Most of the prime ministers were members of this party, and its leaders maintained a good working relationship with Masaryk (Krejci, 1995: 187). In the short-lived Third Republic (1945–8), the ban on all parties outside the National Front applied to the Agrarians, who were accused of collaboration with the Nazis. Whatever the truth of these allegations, popular sentiment at that time probably precluded the revival of that party in its interwar form. In the post-communist evolution of new parties in the Czech Republic, the Liberal Democratic Union (a coalition movement of the Agricultural Party, the Greens, the Czechoslovak Socialist Party, and the Peasants' Movement), did capture about 6 per cent of the vote for the lower house (Chamber of People) in the June 1992 elections, but there has been no important role for any agrarian party in the new Czech democracy (Krejci, 1995: 325). As Waller (1996: 37) argues, this was a mixed case of revival and of remarkable change in the policies of the agrarians, who went from ardent supporters of family farms to defenders of co-ops against privatization. The larger point is the relative weakness of a specifically agrarian or peasant politics in the Czech Republic, as compared with the Polish and Hungarian cases.

Revival of the left successor parties

There were initial predictions that the left, both communist and social democratic, had been thoroughly and forever discredited by the experience of the Leninist party-state: 'Why, in the immediate post-tyranny period, there is only a weak left in Eastern Europe is clear: the Communists defined themselves as the left and coerced or coopted other parties or groups into uniting under this banner, often bearing the misleading name "workers" or "socialist". Now, any party with socialist, social democrat, or even "left" in its name tends to repel voters' (Roskin, 1997: 54). Many thought that the former ruling parties could never make a comeback, that they were all 'living fossils' or 'dinosaurs' of a previous era, now drawing their last breaths. Yet the pain and injustices of both shock therapy (Poland) and gradualist approaches (Hungary) produced preconditions for a revival of a left politics. Geoffrey Pridham and Paul Lewis would later term the revival of the successor (ex-communist) left parties as 'one pillar of the new party systems' (1996: 15). Yet there was also economic hardship in Czechoslovakia (and after 1 January 1993 in the Czech and Slovak republics), but no electoral resurgence of the left successor parties, the Communist Party of Bohemia and Moravia in the Czech Republic and the Party of the Democratic Left in the Slovak Republic. One might better say that given the hardship and disappointment of marketization and privatization, the growth of crime and corruption, there was a window of opportunity for some party to mobilize the early 'losers' of post-communism, but there was no inevitability that it would be the left successor party that would in fact have the winning formula. Why would the political backlash against the liberalization policies not have come from the nationalist right, since they too were present and attempting to harness popular and populist discontent in virtually all cases (cf. Mahr and Nagle, 1995)?

There were three basic alternatives for a new left politics in the first wave of disillusionment in East-Central Europe:

1   an unreformed Leninist politics;
2   a Western-sponsored or imported social democracy;
3   a reformed but authentically domestic democratic left.

The Czech case shows the dead-end of an unreformed Leninism; despite retaining a significant membership and political experience from the communist period, the Communist Party of Bohemia and Moravia (significantly retaining its 'communist' label) could not expand its vote beyond the 13–14 per cent it received in the first round of elections. Its leadership was old and unreformed, its obstructionist anti-market and anti-privatization policies were completely unrealistic to all but its small but loyal following: in short, this was the real 'dinosaur' of Leninism which had no future, but rather had relegated itself to the left ghetto of the new party system in the Czech Republic. According to survey data, the CPBM draws a relatively consistent 60–70 per cent of its support from former CP members (Toka, 1996: 115), but has failed to widen this appeal. Clearly, even in the midst of great social dislocation and disappointment, an unreformed Leninism was a losing proposition. Oskar Krejci argues that 'The Communist Party of Bohemia and Moravia is the only party in any post-socialist countries which did not experience a radical transformation that would make it a credible representative of the ideas of democratic socialism. By this it lost the opportunity to help the leftist intelligentsia and cleared room at the left side of the political spectrum for Social Democracy' (1995: 381–382). The Leninist formula as a losing strategy is confirmed by the minimal showing of the hardline Leninist splinter parties in Hungary and Poland.

Another strategy for a new left (or at least centre-left) politics in post-communism was complete imitation of Western-style social democracy built on an entirely new and uncompromised organizational and perhaps Western-sponsored basis. Indeed, in the earliest months of the 1989 collapse of communism, there were widespread predictions of Western-style social democracy as a major pole of voter attraction in the region. After all, in terms of value systems, new opinion polls showed strong majorities or pluralities in favour of full employment, egalitarian income structures and comprehensive social services; the continuation of this socialist value culture might well be represented by untainted new social democratic parties.

> In 1989 social democracy could be expected to attract many workers, as it could not be blamed for Stalinist repression. Furthermore, the economic reform policies, as proposed by reform communists in eastern Europe had provided in the past a new legitimation for social democracy. Contrary to other socialist formations, both reform communists and social democrats had defended market principles as an economic prerequisite to the implementation of welfare state policies. Liberals, on the contrary, could not count on so much support. It was thought that the lack of a strong upper and middle class would result in their failing to acquire a backing similar to that afforded their Western counterparts. And there was no reason to believe in 1989 that the workers would ever think that it could be in their interest to vote for a liberal programme. (Waller et al., 1994: 6)

Yet Western-style social democratic parties have done poorly, with the exception of the Czech Republic. The failure of the historic Polish Socialist

Party (PPS) for example, with a century of working class tradition behind it, to emerge as a viable political force in the post-communist party landscape (Gortat, 1994), demonstrates the inadequacy of predictions based on historical assumptions from the prewar era of industrializing capitalism, and the failure of predictions based on nominal or presumptive social class affiliation (worker, middle class, business owner) in a qualitatively new political economy still taking shape. The PPS could only find a place in the post-communist party system as a small element of the Democratic Left Alliance (SLD) led by the communist successor party, the Social Democracy of the Republic of Poland. In Poland and Hungary, most clearly, an anti-communist social democracy had failed to find firm footing, and instead it was the reforming ex-communist successor parties which could, despite all the presumed burdens of their communist past, mobilize the still-strong socialist value culture (cf. Millard, 1994a). In Czechoslovakia, the Slovak Communist Party was reformed under Peter Weiss' leadership into a social-democratic format as the Party of the Democratic Left (PDL); this Western-style radical remake lost out in the electoral competition to Vladimír Mečiar's left-leaning national populist Movement for a Democratic Slovakia (MDS), which effectively spoke to both Slovak nationalism and economic insecurities (cf. Mahr and Nagle, 1995: 405; Waller, 1996: 35).

The exception which proves the rule is the Czech case; here, where the communist party refused to break with Leninism, the political space was left open for a social democratic offering in the new party landscape. Although the Czech Social-Democratic Party (CSSD) fared poorly in the 1990 elections and failed to achieve any seats in parliament, it did better in 1992, winning 6–7 per cent of the vote, and made its real breakthrough in the May/June 1996 Czech national elections, getting 26.4 per cent of the vote and for the first time surpassing the left-ghetto CPBM to become the major political force on the centre-left of the Czech party spectrum (Václav Klaus' ruling Civic Democratic Party got 29.6 per cent). In the June 1998 elections, the CSSD improved its support to 32.2 per cent, becoming the single largest vote-getter in the Czech Republic. After failed negotiations with several minor parties, CSSD leader Milos Zeman concluded an unusual pact with Václav Klaus, providing for a minority CSSD government with Zeman as Prime Minister, but with Klaus' Civic Democratic Party holding key parliamentary posts. Zeman's government provides an important test for the viability of non-successor social democratic politics in the region.

Even where social democratic politics has made some impact, however, it cannot follow the Western model, now in retreat and lacking a future-oriented strategy. Social democracy in the West grew out of the long democratic struggle between capital and labour; this is not the situation in the new marketizing and privatizing transformations in the East, which are guided not by a strong capitalist class but by a dependent liberal state. The post-communist liberalizing state, weak in resources of all types, is closely monitored by Western finance and government advisers, who give their approval or disapproval for loans, credits and new investment. 'Solutions proposed by international funding bodies are seen by the political elite in eastern Europe as the only ones appropriate in the circumstances, and those funding bodies are in turn able to make their grants and loans dependent upon certain conditions being met. The economic policies applied in east-central Europe are part of a dependent modernization process, in which the relatively backward social, political and economic structures of eastern Europe are dominated by the Western model of reference' (Waller et al., 1994: 190–191).

The revival of the successor parties in Poland and Hungary illustrates the desire for a locally authentic democratic left, neither a continuation of Leninist politics nor just another Western import. This element of 'authenticity' (Mahr and Nagle, 1995: 405), while surprising to many Western observers who could not imagine any political comeback for the ex-communist parties, also shows that there was, within the former ruling party, some experienced political talent with reform ideas, who were able, during the Gorbachev years, to carry out their plans for a break with Leninism and a radical reformulation of a democratic socialist politics.

Jerzy Wiatr, a leading Polish political sociologist at Warsaw University with longtime ties to the communist Polish United Workers Party (PUWP) and a leading role in the birth of the successor party, the Social Democracy of the Polish Republic (SdRP) in January 1990, describes the new SdRP as the final result of a long factional conflict between democratic socialists and Leninist hardliners within the old PUWP, going back to the very founding of the PUWP as the forced unification of communists and socialists after the Second World War (Wiatr, 1994). The factional struggle, made possible first by Khrushchev's destalinization policies after 1956, was over the eventual 'decommunization' of the left, which intensified under the period of martial law and suppression of Solidarity in the 1980s, ending finally with the agreement of the majority of delegates to the last PUWP Party Congress in January of 1990 to terminate the PUWP and at the same time to found the new social democratic successor party. The SdRP, which later became the core element of the Democratic Left Alliance (SLD), represented both an authentic continuity with the past, and a decisive breakthrough for the reformist faction of the old PUWP. The SdRP proclaimed its loyalty to parliamentary democracy, its support for a mixed economy and its rejection of communism and Leninism. The first party elections of a new leadership produced a youthful core group including Aleksander Kwaśniewski (then only age 35) from the more intellectual wing, and Leszek Miller (then age 44) from the previous party apparatus. Overall, the average age of the 97 members of the new Supreme Council of the SdRP was only 41 years; a plurality (forty-two) were from professional party functionary backgrounds, another large group (thirty-three) were from education backgrounds, and a further fourteen were journalists. There were eleven workers and two farmers, but this was hardly a working class stronghold (Wiatr, 1994: 259–260). Wiatr predicts that 'the role these parties play in the future may have more than a marginal impact on the type of democracy that emerges and consolidates in East Central Europe' (p. 261).

With a diminished but still considerable membership (60,000), a rejuvenated leadership team, a renewed tie to the non-Solidarity and former official OPZZ trade union and organizational and property inheritance from the communist period, these successor parties were able to defeat, in the second round of elections, social democratic and national populist challengers for mobilization of specific discontented and angry 'losers' of marketization/privatization. In 1993 the Democratic Left Alliance (SLD) in Poland got 20.4 per cent of the vote, and its rural ally, the Polish Peasant Party (PSL), got an additional 15.4 per cent; because of an electoral law passed by the Solidarity-controlled Sejm to magnify the weight of the top vote-getting parties, the SLD won over 37 per cent of the seats and the PSL won an additional 29 per cent. The splintering of the political right added to the resurgence of the successor left: 'It is as accurate to say that the fragmented right lost the election as to say that the left won' (Bivand, 1994: 65; Millard, 1994a: 295). The elements which the SLD was able to mobilize, according to exit polls, were the retired (22 per cent of all pensioners voted for the SLD) and white collar workers (24 per cent), also good though not overrepresented proportions of blue collar workers (19 per cent), self-employed (17 per cent) and students (15 per cent). Likewise, the SLD's showing was stronger among those 36–60 years of age (23 per cent) than among 18–25 or 26–35 age cohorts (both 16 per cent); yet here too the SLD showed its ability to attract voters from a wider popular base than its competitors of the liberal centre or religious and nationalist right; it garnered more votes by both men and women, in large and medium sized cities, and in all age groups, than any other party (Millard, 1994a: 307–308). The voter turnout rose from 43 per cent in 1991 to 52 per cent in 1993, so the SLD victory was not due to greater voter abstention; the SLD did well (22 per cent) among those who had not voted in 1991, but were motivated to come out for the 1993 elections. Gabor Toka also shows that the SLD, like the post-communist successor parties in other countries, was largely built on the framework of the social composition of the previous ruling party: the SLD, at its low point in 1991, had 50 per cent of its support coming from former CP members, although by May 1994 this had dropped to 26 per cent as the SLD succeeded in reaching out to a broader electorate. Conversely, in these years, the percentage of former CP members who supported the SLD ranged generally between 25 and 40 per cent (Toka, 1996: 113–115). Toka's conclusion is that 'it is enough to note that the social composition

of the post-communist vote reflects hardly more than the social composition of the ruling parties in the last forty years. After controlling for
former party membership in a multivariate design, not a single socio-
demographic variable appeared to have a consistent impact on post-
communist party preference . . .' (p. 114). In the 1997 elections, the SLD
actually increased its support to reach 27 per cent, even though it trailed
the AWS coalition. The SLD retained over 80 per cent of its 1993 supporters, and attracted significant numbers of Peasant Party and minor
party voters. The SLD is still more attractive to 60-year-olds (30 per
cent) than 20-year-olds (21 per cent), to pensioners (over 25 per cent
better than its average support), and increasingly to the better educated
(*Gazeta Wyborcza*, 1997b).

One should note here the failure of the left-socialist Union of Labour
(UP), a Solidarity remnant led by respected activists Ryszard Bugaj and
Zbigniew Bujak (Hockenos, 1995: 82). By 1997 the UP had lost all its
parliamentary seats; in the end, Polish Solidarity had little inspiration
for a new democratic left.

In the 1995 presidential elections, the SLD candidate Aleksander
Kwaśniewski, despite a well-funded smear campaign directed against
him by the Catholic hierarchy, most of the media and Wałęsa's allies,
was able to get 34 per cent of the vote in the first round, and was able to
defeat Wałęsa with 52 per cent of the total vote in the run-off election
(cf. Nagle, 1997a: 48–50). This was a critical test of the successor party to
consolidate its voter base in the face of the new hard-fisted national
chauvinist politics of the Polish centre and right-wing parties and their
institutional allies. In the November run-off, Kwaśniewski won in the
more highly developed areas, bested Wałęsa among voters aged 18–50,
drew 50 per cent of former Mazowiecki (democratic centre) voters from
1990, and 42 per cent of Jacek Kuroń's (democratic centre-left) first-
round voters from 1995.

The successor Hungarian Socialist Party (MSZP) fashioned its resurrection in similar style. The communist party in Hungary had managed a
very smooth democratic transition, and its democratic credentials were
pretty strong for the second round of elections. In September 1992 the
Socialist International meeting in Berlin gave the Hungarian Socialists
observer status by a 42 to 4 vote, expressing confidence in its new
democratic commitment. The Socialist leadership was strongly reformist,
pragmatic and technocratic (though there was also a significant tradi-
tionalist wing among the party membership), the party had retained the
support of the main trade unions, and the socialist National Confederation of Hungarian Trade Unions (NCHTU) had defeated rival trade
union groups in the May 1993 elections to enterprise works councils with
71.7 per cent of all votes. In 1994, the Socialists ran an intelligent campaign, with a non-controversial programme, with candidates without
tainted histories who could present an image of professionalism and
expertise (Deak, 1994: 37).

The MSZP, after receiving only 10.9 per cent of the vote in the 1990 elections, rebounded in the May 1994 elections to about 33 per cent of the first-round vote. Neither the Leninist Socialist Workers Party (MSZMP) nor the Western-style Social Democratic Party (MSZDP) received enough votes to break the 4 per cent exclusionary barrier, and did not get into the 1994 parliament. The Socialists had consolidated their voter base on the left, while the conservative Hungarian Democratic Forum (MDF) and its allies were in disarray. More importantly, while the MDF tried to regain its popular support with a shift to more nationalist right-wing rhetoric, the Socialists stuck to bread and butter issues of unemployment, taxes, inflation, funding of health care and education, and the general decline in the standard of living for most Hungarians. The MSZP did well among the middle (30–49) and older (over 50) generations (33 and 30 per cent respectively), although its 21 per cent showing among the 18–29 age cohort was also a relative success, up from only 10 per cent of votes among the 18–33 age group in 1990 (Mahr and Nagle, 1995; Racz, 1993). The MSZP, as with the Polish SLD, regrouped a voter core of former CP members (55 per cent of MSZP support in 1991, 28 per cent by May of 1994), on which it steadily built its adaptation to electoral political competition and the circumstances of the economic hardships of the transition (Toka, 1996: 115). Again, the percentage of former CP members supporting the MSZP ranged from 30 to 60 per cent during this period.

The general lesson is that with the hardships of economic and social transition, and the continuation of a popular socialist value culture, there would be a new political space for a left politics in post-communism. Paul Hockenos characterizes this as electoral opportunism rather than socialist principle, with little impact on actual economic and social policy orientation:

> Opportunism more than anything else has guided these parties' transformations. In opposition, they effectively portray themselves as the principled voice of protest against the most painful, unpopular consequences of the market reforms. Though their demands for the maintenance of jobs, pensions, child care, industrial subsidies and so forth are legitimate, without concrete programs to back them up they smack of empty, apolitical populism, not all so different from the demagoguery of the nationalist right, or the tirades of their predecessors against Western capitalism. Like the right, when they come to power, their promises dissipate and, as in Poland and Hungary, they adopt a little changed version of their predecessors' economic course. (1995: 80–81)

In Hockenos' view, the successor party victories are neither a sign of a new socialist vision for the future, nor a strengthening of civic democracy, but rather an electoral victory for a contending party elite.

In neither Poland nor Hungary are the successor parties working class parties in the classic Leninist or Western social democratic senses.

They are the 'vanguard' of a socialist politics of transition to capitalism, for which there is no precedent. As such, their new electoralism and their past experience form a mixture of continuity and change which sets them off from other parties. In Poland and Hungary, the successor parties now seem to be one anchor on the moderate left of the new party system.

Liberalism: weaknesses and strengths

The relatively weak mass base for political liberalism may seem surprising, given the ideological hegemony of liberal ideas in the first years of post-communism. To espouse anti-liberal values has been 'politically incorrect' in the first stages of democratization, and both domestic and Western media have been quick to punish those who express any doubts about Western values, including markets, liberal democracy, civil society and private property. Yet from the Western European perspective, liberal parties as such have been for most of the Cold War minor parties, although often important coalition-makers of the centre-right or centre-left. In Germany especially, the liberal Free Democrats have generally won between 5 and 10 per cent of the vote, but were almost always a necessary coalition partner for either the Christian Democrats or the Social Democrats. Post-war European political liberalism has carried much greater weight than its vote totals due to its attraction of solid middle class, financial and professional support. The larger conservative as well as social democratic parties have often sought coalitions with the liberals as a means of building a government with solid economic credentials among powerful business and financial interests. So in the European context, one might more reasonably have expected post-communist liberal parties to develop a modest electoral base, but with an important legitimizing role with domestic and international business and financial interests. This is close to the actual case, but with important variations.

In Poland, the clearest party vehicle for political liberalism has come out of the intellectual (Warsaw) Solidarity faction first called the Democratic Union and in recent years the Freedom Union. Under this banner can be found the liberal intelligentsia of Solidarity (Mazowiecki, Kuroń, Geremek, Balcerowicz, Michnik), which broke from the nationalist populist (Gdańsk) faction under Wałęsa in 1990 (Hoffman, 1993). The liberals were also split within their own camp for the 1993 elections, with the Liberal Democratic Congress (KLD) led by Donald Tusk and former prime minister Jan Bielecki challenging the UD leadership. In the 1993 elections, Polish liberals suffered the brunt of the backlash against the hardships of the privatization policies, for which they were (rightly) held most responsible. Additionally, the Catholic press and radio station were clearly hostile not only to the ex-communist left but to the Democratic Union and the Liberals (Millard, 1994a: 305). The vote for the UD, the major branch of Polish liberalism, fell from 13 per cent in 1991 to 10.8 per cent in 1993 (due to the new electoral law which rewarded the larger parties it actually rose in parliamentary seats from 62 to 74, however). The KLD did not make the 5 per cent cut-off and lost all of its previous 37 seats in the Sejm.

Polish liberalism has been marked by its strong anti-communism. After the 1993 elections, the victorious SLD suggested a coalition with the liberals, who refused. In 1995, despite the Democratic Union's deep differences with Wałęsa and his Church-backed national-patriotic politics, the UD leaders backed Wałęsa's presidential campaign after the first round of voting (Nagle, 1997a). The liberals were, along with the Church, the big losers in Wałęsa's failed re-election campaign (Dobrosielski, 1996), since they had betrayed their liberal principles due to their hostility to the successor SLD and the Kwaśniewski candidacy. Polish liberalism has proven too weak to act as a counter-balance to the politics of Polish Catholic nationalism, yet it has cut itself off from possible alliance with the modern centre-left politics of the successor SLD. Polish liberalism in these circumstances can play only a minority role in shaping the politics of the country, although it is privileged by extensive Western support for its free market policies.

In Hungary, in the first elections in 1990 there appeared to be two liberal parties, the Alliance of Free Democrats (SZDSZ) and the Alliance of Young Democrats (Fidesz). The Free Democrats were popularly seen as a party of the urban intelligentsia, with several of its founders coming from the Budapest community and including several Jewish leaders. The Young Democrats initially took in only members under age 35, and became quickly associated with a strong support of capitalist entrepreneurship and free market libertarianism (Waller, 1996: 39–40). Although these differences seemed to revolve in part around personality differences arising out of the 1989 roundtable negotiations for the first free elections, over time they have become more clearly associated with real policy differences. The Young Democrats have since 1990 moved to the right, espousing an odd mixture of libertarian and national-populist slogans.

The Free Democrats, on the other hand, have maintained their liberalism, and have represented the values of both market principles and social tolerance in their party platform and their governmental coalition after 1994 with the victorious Socialists. The Socialist leadership of Gyula Horn, despite its absolute majority in parliament, wanted badly to build a left–liberal coalition with the Free Democrats, who had received 19.7 per cent of the first-round vote in the May elections. Together the Socialists and Free Democrats would represent a clear majority of Hungarian voters; after some hesitation, the Free

Democrats agreed to a coalition. They played an important role in continuing the privatization process, in restoring confidence in the radio and television broadcasting, in the restitution of Jewish properties and reconciliation with the Hungarian Jewish community, and in supporting the state treaty with Romania, which improved state relations and stabilized the status of the Hungarian minority there (but which was denounced by the right as treasonous). In Hungary, the Free Democrats and Socialists have repudiated the anti-Semitic and ethnic nationalist rhetoric of the Smallholders, the Democratic Forum, Christian Democrats and the Young Democrats, not to mention István Csurka's extreme right Hungarian Truth and Life movement.

The Civic Democratic Party of Václav Klaus, although often pictured as a conservative party of the right, is more accurately seen as a centre-right form of liberal-conservatism (Jan Pauer, 1995), combining a good measure of Czech nationalism into a national-liberal politics. Jan Pauer provides an insightful analysis of the success of Klaus' political synthesis, which includes elements of Friedmanite monetarism and Thatcherite economic libertarianism, a specifically Czech national conservatism, and leadership pragmatism. Klaus himself in 1994 described this synthesis: 'If we understand liberalism as the opposite of socialism, conservatism as the opposite of radicalism, and pragmatism as the opposite of funda-mentalism, then I would see myself simultaneously as a liberal, a con-servative, and a pragmatist, without the slightest contradiction' (from the German, cited in Pauer, 1995: 23–24). In his defeat of the human rights dissidents (the anti-politics utopians) and his disdain for the intellectuals generally, his free-market economic commitments, his pragmatic dealing with the communist past and his decisive handling of the Czech national interest in the split with Slovakia, Václav Klaus may be regarded as the great political innovator of post-communist politics, especially in com-parison to the sudden weakness and splintering of other conservative, nationalist, religious and christian democratic political forces on the centre-right in Hungary, Poland, Slovakia and elsewhere. This synthesis included elements of tradition: in combining a pre-existing Czech ethnic identity with support for economic reform and economic success, at the price of a 'Velvet Divorce' with Slovakia; and in including a tradition of Czech egalitarianism in his coupon-privatization plan. But Klaus' liberal-conservatism also included some major breaks with the past: his ele-vation of status for 'economic man' versus the 'intellectual man'; and his turn away from European corporatism towards the Anglo-Saxon free-market model.

Peter Rutland regards Klaus' Civic Democratic Party as 'the only liberal party with any substantial presence' (1997: 54) in post-communist politics generally. For Rutland, the success formula for Klaus has been his synthesis of Czech nationalism with economic liberalism, which has given his party its mass base far beyond what political liberalism alone could provide. Klaus and his CDP first gained recognition for their strict economic liberalism (for which Klaus became known as a Thatcherite, a not entirely accurate label); but his politics also gained support (among Czechs only) for his Czech nationalism, which was an apparent factor in his overwhelming victory in Bohemia and Moravia in the June 1992 elections. He appealed to the sentiment that the Czech lands could do better economically if they were emancipated from their poorer Slovak cousins. The Klaus regime has been able to reinforce its nationalist credentials through its new anti-Romani (anti-Gypsy) citizenship law of 1993, and its tough talk in negotiations with Germany over the misnamed 'reconciliation' agreement over the postwar Czechoslovak expulsion of Sudeten Germans. And Jan Pauer, writing at the height of Klaus' political success, still left room for doubt about the longer-term viability of his politics: 'It remains to be seen, if the rise of Czech liberal-conservatism is only a swing of the pendulum in a particular phase of the transformation process or if it has laid the cornerstones for a lasting political tradition' (1995: 68, authors' translation). None the less, Klaus' Civic Democratic Party was a political achievement unmatched in post-communism on the centre-right of the new political landscape, in sharp contrast to the lack of innovation within political conservatism generally. The banking and campaign finance scandals and the downturn of the Czech economy finally forced the resignation of Klaus in December 1997. Yet Klaus and his CDP defied predictions of political demise and came back to get 27 per cent of the June 1998 national vote, despite the split-off of the new Freedom Union under Jan Ruml.

Jerzy Szacki (1995; see also Cain, 1998) has argued that in many ways political liberalism remains still a Western import, a foreign element whose local roots are weak compared with other doctrines. Political liberalism is struggling to build up its own authentic local tradition, and the economic liberal transformation has not automatically translated into support for liberal politics.

Disorder on the right

The relative disorder, feuding and splintering on the right side of the post-communist party spectrum can in part be attributed to a historic misunderstanding, which Michael Waller (1996: 38–40) calls the 'liberation myth' of 1989. Key elements of this myth were its anti-communism and often anti-Russian sentiment, which rejected the past in its entirety and had a vision of a reborn society which would reclaim its Western heritage.

> The liberation myth therefore came to unite in a common purpose a community of people whose policy preferences would turn out to be at variance with one another when forward-looking strategies replaced the attitude to be

taken to Communism as the determinant of party identity after 1989. At that point differing national cultures and historical experiences led to differing outcomes . . . the preparatory phase of the transition created a powerful myth of liberation – but it was not one that could in the long term provide differentiated identities for the new parties that came into being after 1989. (1996: 38–40)

In a certain paradoxical way, the myth of some commonality among those groups that had self-identified as part of the broad anti-communist popular movement created a false expectation of cooperation which then turned into politically harmful behaviour for the centre-right pre-party factions and new party formations which emerged from Solidarity, Civic Forum and the Hungarian roundtable. The leaders of the emerging parties on the centre-right therefore often viewed each other as 'betrayers' of the liberation myth, as personal enemies, as those who were destroying the historic mission. The formation of new party identities which were separate from the original anti-communist movement, and the painful learning of new patterns of inter-party cooperation and compromise, were in some ways more difficult for these parties than for the successor parties of the left, or for the most group-specific agrarian parties in Poland and Hungary. The sad parting from the illusory liberation myth of 1989 was summed up by Zbigniew Bujak, leader of one of nine ex-Solidarity parties represented in the 1991 Sejm, when he said simply: 'Sorry about Solidarity' (quoted in Waller, 1996: 39). While the splits on the Polish right were often seen as situational personality conflicts (Bivand, 1994; Millard, 1994b) which could rather quickly be overcome through new coalition-building, especially given the lessons of the 1993 and 1995 elections debacles, it appears that the cleavage lines on the right reflect some deeper ambiguities about a conservative politics in Poland. Questions about the direct role of the Church in political life have not been settled; the right's preference for a stronger presidential form of governance has bordered on an authoritarian attitude which is at best semi-democratic; the right's protectionist and cultural nationalism has been at odds with its protestations about Poland's place in Western Europe's historic integration project.

On the other hand, after several election defeats, the right has mounted two efforts at reintegration, one the Solidarity Electoral Action (AWS) which has brokered an alliance among more than three dozen parties and associations of the right, and the Movement for Poland's Reconstruction (ROP) led by former prime minister Jan Olszewski. The AWS combines the core of Solidarity trade union, which is the main component of the alliance, with the right-wing nationalist Confederation for an Independent Poland, the Christian National Union and the new Conservative-Peasant Party. The AWS is internally split over major policy lines, with some elements pro-market and others state-interventionist, including the core Solidarity union. Solidarity's own policy orientation can be called neo-corporatist or neo-syndicalist (Szczerbiak, 1997: 45). The most common tie among the coalition members is traditional conservative social values of nation, family and the Catholic faith. There is still little evidence of rethinking of major issues which have divided the right, nor is there any sign of the emergence of a modern democratic conservatism which characterized the postwar Western democracies. The Polish right does not yet represent a modern conservative politics but rather a volatile mixture of conflicting and contradictory elements. The victory of the AWS in the September 1997 parliamentary elections, with 33 per cent of the vote as opposed to the 27 per cent showing for the ruling SLD, has demonstrated the strength of traditional Catholic nationalism. The opinions of the AWS electorate match the national populist rhetoric of its leaders. In a poll taken by the Public Opinion Research Centre (OBOP) just at the time of the Polish elections in 1997, the supporters of AWS were far more likely to favour strongman rule over a democratic system than supporters of any other party. Nationwide, 56 per cent favoured a democratic system, and 37 per cent favoured autocratic rule. Broken down by party, 72 per cent of Freedom Union followers, 69 per cent of Democratic Left Alliance followers and 54 per cent of Movement for the Reconstruction of Poland followers wanted democratic government, but among AWS followers, only 47 per cent chose democracy, versus 45 per cent who chose strongman rule (PAP, 1997d). AWS leader Marian Krzaklewski, an ardent Catholic nationalist from Southern Poland who played no role in the Solidarity of the 1980s, represents a politics of the past, perhaps even the distant past.

> . . . Krzaklewski talks more about the past than the present, and his account is radically revisionist. In his speeches and interviews, he lambastes the 1989 accord that ended communism and the free market reforms that followed, implying that a 'pink' opposition elite sold out the Polish people to the communist 'reds'. The new Solidarity, he suggests, will finally carry out a real revolution against communism in Poland. Krzaklewski has declared that Jesus Christ should be 'crowned king' of Poland, and implied that Christian scripture, as interpreted by the Pope, should supersede Polish law. Just behind some of his language is the suggestion – easily decoded by Poles – that Jews among the old Solidarity leadership somehow betrayed the cause. (Diehl, 1997)

It may well be that the realities of governing Poland and the popular desire to 'join the West' will moderate the populist rhetoric and anti-liberal politics of Krzaklewski and the AWS. Yet the victory of the AWS coalition in 1997 demonstrated the political strength of an unreformed Catholic nationalism, which is ambiguous about modernity in culture and economics.

In Hungary, the right has also been divided, though not as badly as in Poland, yet some of the symptoms are similar. In the first free elections, the Hungarian Democratic Forum (MDF) led by József Antall was able to garner a plurality of votes, and to combine under its umbrella moderate nationalists, traditional conservatives and some centre-right economic liberals as well. In the view of Istvan Deak, Antall's Conservatives had a good chance to build a broad-based moderate conservatism. They represented in 1990 for many Hungarians (even progressives) the best choice for government; their leaders, neither former communists nor active dissidents, promised gradual change through 'hard work, cautious economic reforms, a concern for moral standards, support for religious activity, modest restitution of property to the victims of communism, and at least some punishment for Communist crimes, especially those connected with the suppression of the revolution of 1956. The Conservatives were also committed to a vigorous defence of the three million ethnic Hungarians who live in neighbouring countries' (1994: 34). Instead of consolidating this broad base of support and initial goodwill, however, the MDF squandered its political capital over the following four years through internal fighting with the more nationalist elements of the party, led by István Csurka. Csurka and his allies in the MDF articulated a much more right-wing ethnic-chauvinist politics, and the Antall leadership was hesitant to either expel him or to distance itself from his more extreme rhetoric. 'By his reluctance to take a firm position against the far right in his party, Prime Minister József Antall did a disservice to himself and his cause. As the recent elections have shown, the Hungarian public has little patience for any kind of extremism. Many people also became irritated by the Conservatives' tendency to call their opposition "enemies of the people" and "traitors", a practice the party inherited from its totalitarian predecessor' (Deak, 1994: 34).

In general, after the breakup of the original anti-communist movements, the right-wing parties have been slower to adapt to the new electoral competition, and this is epitomized by their inability to invent a broad-based and modern political vehicle for conservative politics. Istvan Deak's analysis focuses on the weakest element in Hungary's party system, namely the lack of a moderate democratic conservative party which could, together with the Liberals and the Socialists, dominate the party competition and marginalize the extremists for a stable democratic order (1994: 38).

In the aftermath of the 1994 victory for the Socialists and Free Democrats, the Hungarian right has undergone a new round of mutations. The Democratic Forum, weakened by Antall's death and loss of government power, has further declined to minor party status. The Christian Democrats moved far to the nationalist right, splintered and were kicked out of the European Union of Christian Democrats (EUCD). The Smallholders Party, under the demagogic leadership of József Torgyan, has become a major outlet for Hungarian nationalism, ethnic chauvinism, sporadic anti-Semitism and rabid anti-liberal, anti-left sentiment. The Young Democrats (Fidesz), led by Viktor Orbán, reworked their politics to occupy the political space left by the declining Democratic Forum; in the 1998 elections, the Young Democrats (now officially the Civic Party) appeared as a defender of small business, honesty in government and Hungarian nationalism in international affairs; with this unstable mixture, Fidesz gained 28 per cent of the first-round vote in May 1998 (the Socialists got 32 per cent), but in the second run-off round (through favourable pre-election agreements with other right-wing parties), it gained 148 seats in parliament to the Socialists' 134 seats. Together with the Smallholder Party (which gained 48 seats), and the Democratic Forum (17 seats) Orbán and Fidesz agreed to form a right-of-centre coalition government. The far-right Hungarian Justice and Life Party of István Csurka (17 seats) was not included. Thus, although still splintered, the Hungarian right (as with the Polish right) has regained power, but with severe internal divisions and many uncertainties, especially about the role that Torgyan and his Small-holder Party will play in negotiations for EU admission, which began in early 1998. While Fidesz has an opportunity to create a modern Hun-garian conservatism, its dramatic shift to the right has raised questions about its reliability and stability. As Prime Minister, Orbán faces tests both within his coalition and within his party over many issues.

The Czech case is again an exception; between the national-liberalism of Václav Klaus' Civic Democratic Party on the centre-right (along with its coalition partner the Civic Democratic Alliance), and the minor but still electorally viable extreme-right Republican Party of Miroslav Sládek, there has been less political space for a conservative politics of the democratic right to develop. In the 1996 elections, the Christian Demo-cratic Union was able to collect only 8 per cent of the vote, compared to 29.6 per cent for Klaus' national-liberal CDP (and an additional 6.3 per cent for the CDA) and 8 per cent for Sládek's Republicans (Pehe, 1996c). In the Czech case, the relative weakness of the Catholic Church, and the more secular history of Czech political development, have contributed to the relative weakness of christian democratic politics in the Czech regions; in Slovakia, on the other hand, one might well expect more from Jan Čarnogurský's Christian Democrats, except that the Slovak Catholic Church, as in Poland and Hungary, has renewed its ties with Slovak nationalism rather than move towards a modern, democratic conserva-tive relationship of religion and politics.

What's missing? Christian democracy – a modernized conservatism

Finally, some attention is needed for what we don't see in the emerging party systems in East-Central Europe:

1   classic Western-style social democracy, that broadly working class
    party which reaches out to the white collar middle class and which
    represents the peaceful evolution of the democratic class struggle
    within the legal confines of democratic politics;
2   classic postwar christian democracy, a broad middle class party
    based on modernist religious concepts accepting of economic and
    political liberalism.

The reasons for the absence of Western-style social democracy in
Poland and Hungary have been discussed already, and with the rise of
a successor left party as a fairly solid anchor on the democratic left of
the party spectrum, this does not seem overly problematic. The electoral
revival of the Czech Social Democrats seems to confirm the proposition
that, given time and the continued irrelevance of the Czech Communists, social democratic politics could fill the political vacuum on the
centre-left. Even though these centre-left parties do not fulfil the same
historic role of Western social democratic parties in their championing
of the Keynesian class compromise, they do represent a politics of social
concern for the 'losers' in the politics of marketization and privatization,
and may over the longer term, once neo-liberal policies have worked
their will, come to represent more broadly the economic interests of
ordinary citizens, workers and employees not closely tied to business
class interests.

More interesting and more worrisome for democratization in the
region is the absence of a modern conservative politics, a politics based
on core conservative beliefs such as tradition, faith and love of country,
but also committed to democratic politics for better or worse, tolerant of
the Other, and open to cooperation across strict doctrinal or confessional
lines. In Poland and Hungary, especially, this has produced a divided
and 'cranky' array of right-wing parties, where overheated rhetoric has
called into question their commitment to liberal democracy. This may
well be mostly political blabber, but if the economic transformation
project should sour, or if ethnic Hungarian minorities are mistreated in
neighbouring states, or if the dominance of Western capital and culture
should prove too unbearable, a nationalist leader of anti-democratic
bearing could sweep away the insubstantial disorder on the right to
lead a new national mission: Neal Ascherson predicted as much in the
first years of post-communist optimism: 'It is unreasonable to expect a
future of calm, stable parliamentarism in this part of Europe. Politics
will be turbulent, and at times authoritarian, and the Man on the White
Horse will probably ride again' (1992: 237). Ascherson hoped for a
better outcome, one in which 'a quarrelsome and unreliable parliamentary surface conceals a hard-working citizenry. They seldom pay
taxes or obey a law unquestioningly, but they are constructing a general
prosperity without reference to politicians. They are both democrats and
patriots, but they have no illusions about prime ministers or fellow

countrymen' (1992: 237). Yet this hope for an enterprising but politically uninvolved and cynical public certainly contains a dangerous potential, especially if the economy goes bad and if individual hard work is not fairly rewarded. The danger is one of a future authoritarian backlash against corruption, political ineffectiveness and messy party politics, to which the disorder on the right contributes.

In Poland, especially, the absence of any significant christian democratic project is noteworthy. Instead, Christian political forces have vied for favour with the anti-modernist Catholic hierarchy and the community of the faithful on the basis of a more traditional and nationalist conception of Polish religious values. Wlodzimierz Wesolowski, in spelling out the possible political identities which might emerge as characteristic or defining of Polish democracy, ties the Christian and national elements together, since 'it is much easier to develop "in oneself" and "for oneself" a Christian or national identity. Patterns of "silent heroism" displayed by the ordinary person, heroism based on religious faith or faith in one's nation, are ubiquitous in Polish art and literature. These patterns of silent heroism are passed down from generation to generation within the family. People are familiar with definite incarnations of national or national-Christian leaders, and contemporary politicians can easily refer to them' (1996: 251). This is in sharp contrast to both liberal and socialist identities, which are much more difficult to construct. Wesolowski concludes by holding out a hope for a future development of Christian democracy as a vehicle for modernizing religious connections to political life, away from the ethnic nationalist pole and towards a more modern secular pluralist pole.

> There may emerge a new trend towards 'modern Christian' political identity-building. This type could deliberately combine the acceptance of most tenets of liberalism with adherence to core values of the Christian religion. Such an identity could overcome the traditionalism of Polish Catholicism, as well as its strong nationalistic and confessional tendencies. The idea of having in Poland a party which will be similar – at least in crucial dimensions – to the German CDU has attracted some circles of intellectuals and politicians from time to time. (pp. 251–252)

Yet what Wesolowski is telling us, without speaking too bluntly, is that the modernization of Polish Catholicism in political life has not occurred, rather it is only a future hope. For now the connection of the Church hierarchy is with traditional Polish nationalism, which is anti-modernist and leans heavily towards social and political authoritarianism. The watershed point has not arrived, and even those parties which call themselves Christian democratic have not yet made the break, but have redefined Christian democracy in an entirely 'eastern' way (cf. Kohn 1945), on the basis of ethnic nationalism and exclusively Catholic religious faith. This watershed point at the end of the Second World

War made possible the foundation of German Christian democracy in the postwar era, the building of an anti-nationalist, pro-democratic, confessionally pluralist party which could attract believers yet was not subordinate to Church doctrine or the Church hierarchy (Kalyvas, 1996; van Kersbergen, 1994).

For its part, the Catholic Church in East-Central Europe has chosen to reinforce ethnic nationalist politics in Poland, Hungary, Slovakia and Croatia (even going so far as to honour the Ustasha fascists of the Second World War as true sons of Croatian nationhood, cf. Hedges, 1997). The Polish Church, in its support for Lech Wałęsa's presidential re-election campaign in 1995, confirmed its intention to combine religious faith with national patriotic politics in a feverish effort to discredit liberal and left secular parties and candidates; the intemperate, demonizing language of Radio Maria in attacking Aleksander Kwaśniewski in the campaign preceding the second round of voting gave evidence of the Church hierarchy's political fundamentalism.

In short, it seems that the Catholic Church in East-Central Europe has chosen a political path which would run counter to a modernist Christian democracy similar to that of postwar Germany, Austria, Holland, or Italy. Historian J.G.A. Pocock has characterized the regions of Germany and East-Central Europe, east of the Rhine and north of the Danube, as outside the Western area of Christianity modernized by the Enlightenment thought. In these regions of Catholic Church influence, Central and Eastern Europe developed a very different philosophy, stressing 'authoritarian, hierarchical monarchism of the old regime but strengthened by a populist nationalism, which sought legitimacy in communal values based on concepts of historic group-personalities and ethnic solidarity, and which disdained as alien the egalitarianism, individualism and trivial materialism which it identified in "Western values"' (Pocock, 1997: 32–33). Post-communist political practice suggests that the eastern Catholic churches have still not accepted the modernization path which made Christian democracy possible, and which renewed political conservatism in the postwar era as a dependable support for liberal democracy. It seems doubtful that without some serious rethinking on the part of the Church leaders, and the Pope, on the wisdom of associating Catholic faith with ethnic nationalist politics, that a Western-style Christian democracy would be possible as a major anchor of the party system in this region.

In Western Europe after the end of the Second World War, the Church was forced to moderate its previous antipathy to liberal democracy, since it had collaborated too closely with German and Italian fascism, and had remained silent during the Holocaust, failing its greatest moral test of modern times. The birth of a modern Christian democracy came from this background of the Church's moral failure, which forced a break with the past. In Eastern Europe, the Church in 1989 stood tall as one of the stalwart opponents of communism, and felt vindicated in its historical role as a major force behind the defeat of the old regime. These circumstances strengthened Church leaders' confidence in making a direct entry into post-communist politics and insisting on imposition of Church doctrine through law. The Church had some early victories, but was later rebuffed in Poland and elsewhere, and these defeats have seemed primarily to increase the bitterness of its political line. Election victories of the AWS coalition in Poland in 1997 and the Hungarian right parties in 1998 have reaffirmed the strength of a traditional Catholic nationalism. The absence of a modern (moderate, pluralist, 'catch-all') conservatism is one of the peculiarities of the new party systems of the region, reflected in the continuing party divisions and redivisions on the right.

Party system development for what kind of democracy?

The historic transformations shaping the new party systems of East-Central Europe are not those which Lipset and Rokkan (1967) described for the Western democracies. Nation-building is still on the political agenda for the Czech Republic and even more for Slovakia, and has latent potential for the politics of Poland and Hungary. But in this era of globalizing capitalism, these nations and their politics must react to strong international economic forces and cultural questions about joining the West; political parties must address issues about their nation's place in an integrated economic order which reduces national economic sovereignty. Political cleavages of nationalism versus internationalism typify party systems in post-communism, most clearly evident in the right-wing populist parties and the ambiguous position of the Catholic Church. Likewise, parties are emerging in response to dramatic capitalist de-industrialization rather than classic industrialization; new class formations of business owners and workers are under way, but without the historic projects of either the pioneering captains of industry or the socialist labour movement. Parties are forming in a social order with much greater uncertainty. Agrarian parties and old-style labour parties attest to some revival of traditional Western cleavages, but they also symbolize the hybrid mixture arising from simultaneous economic, social and political transitions in a post-Cold War and post-industrial era. The new party systems are responses to qualitatively new environments; progress in party system-building should be measured accordingly, not by comparison to any typical Western pattern.

The evidence above on party and party system development may be interpreted in various ways. For many (Ágh, 1996), the progress to date has been disappointing, and shows signs of weakening popular support for parliament and political parties as major elements in a democratic political system. For others, the limited learning experience of post-communist party formation has been on the whole what one could have expected (Toka, 1996) and is not so different in terms of interest representation than in some Western democracies; in fact, one might well argue that interest articulation and aggregation has progressed rather well. Voters may understandably be disappointed with specific policies and outcomes, and they may be disillusioned with parliament's inability to foster greater job growth, social security and funding for health and education; but voters are not about to give up on democracy as the best political system, and they show an ability to vote out governing parties, in favour not of radical anti-system parties, but of other pro-system alternatives. These new party systems are also sym-ptomatic of the weak democratic state in post-communist East-Central Europe. The party systems are unsatisfactory, and the parties are not much liked, but there is no real danger of anti-system parties taking over, and so, in contrast to the interwar period, a weak and unconsoli-dated democracy can survive. Speaking of the Polish case, Wesolowski concludes that:

> Much of Poland's political elite and most of society are aspiring to develop a consolidated, liberal, representative democracy. But inherent in the notion of a 'consolidated democracy' is the assumption that there are also less consolidated democracies. Indeed, the emergence of an unconsolidated but lasting democracy seems to be a real threat in Poland and, while the transition to democracy may be judged to have finished, the political order established may be a tentative and potentially unstable one. In the country's new geopolitical setting such an unconsolidated democracy could even prove to be viable. Immature political parties would be one charac-teristic feature of such a deficient democracy. (Wesolowski, 1996: 230–231)

Peter Rutland (1997: 55) makes the point that party systems are, at least for now and perhaps for the longer-term, not very identifiable in Western terms, but they are still important in terms of electoral compe-tition among political elites. But in fact post-communist democratic socialist and liberal parties are based on identifiable political philo-sophies common to Western political understandings, and agrarian parties, while peculiar to Europe in the 1990s, are easy for both leaders and voters to identify on interest politics grounds. Overall, the party landscape in East-Central Europe is moderately identifiable on a left–right scale; it is neither a blank slate nor a close copy of a Western European party landscape (Markowski, 1997). Rutland argues that while the party systems in East-Central Europe are murky, they are still qualitatively different from the party-destroying political process of Russia, where presidential power has made parliament ineffective or dependent on executive will. In East-Central Europe, on the other hand, parliamentary power matters, and therefore the party system, with all its murkiness and elitist characteristics, still makes a critical difference.

The party systems of East-Central Europe have their own distinctive characteristics, among them the presence of specifically agrarian parties, the absence of major Christian democratic parties, and the revival of ex-communist successor parties. None of the parties of the new democracies seems at this point to represent particularly innovative political vehicles, although the national-liberalism of Václav Klaus's Civic Democratic Party did seem to capture the Czech spirit of the times from 1992 through 1996. It is on the right that more creative thought and political modernization is needed, and is so far apparently lacking.

Whatever its failings, the emerging party system in East-Central Europe has offered citizens a wider choice than the centre-right half-spectrum of parties in many of the new Latin American and East Asian democracies. In those regions, democratization was purposely limited to anti-socialist parties, and various means, from formal banning to informal death squads, were employed to keep left parties out of 'normal' political life. In post-communist East-Central Europe, however, the revival of the left, not part of the original scripting, has given these new democracies a full spectrum party landscape, and has given disillusioned voters more opportunities to express their grievances through the ballot. This is a valuable gain, one which has eluded democratization in most other regions. A viable democratic left is one element of a fully democratic politics and offers the best hope for avoiding the triumph of right-wing nationalism as the response to the hardships of this era (Mahr and Nagle, 1995; Ost, 1995)

Already, in Poland, Hungary and the Czech Republic, there have been peaceful and orderly changes of government, as the result of free and fair elections. Voter dissatisfaction has been able to express itself through the democratic process; extremist parties of left and right have done poorly, and despite their nasty rhetoric do not seem capable of mounting a serious challenge to the democratic system. These are all significant achievements, and speak well for the current maintenance of the formal institutions of parliamentary democracy.

Interestingly, in Poland, Hungary, and the Czech Republic, after several rounds of elections, a centre-left party (successor ex-communist or social democratic) has emerged as the single largest vote-getter (28–33 per cent), while severely divided right and centre-right parties garner a majority of the vote; if solidified, this pattern may represent a problem for stable and effective government, able to take clearcut decisions without losing coherence.

The longer-term question is whether political parties and the party system can overcome the dissatisfaction of large portions of the population, and build greater trust in the ability of an elected parliament to deliver on its promises of economic prosperity before public patience runs out. Even the leading parties are (in contrast to the

Christian Democrats in Germany after the Second World War) not compelling as subjects of in-depth treatment, although in the West effective political parties have been the basis for a vital parliamentary politics and parliamentary democracy.

8

Elites and Citizens: Elite Democracy and Citizen Participation

Postwar debates on elites, masses and stable democracies

The demise of many Central and East European new democracies in the interwar period characterized a period which Huntington calls a 'reverse wave' against democratization but which revealed, as it was seen at the time, a crucial weakness of liberal democracy in the face of thoroughly modern crises of capitalism, massive economic dislocations and depression. In these circumstances, the institutions of liberal democracy broke down, popular support for democratic politics sagged and anti-democratic elites and mass movements combined to paralyse and then destroy these weak democracies. Elite theories put forward by Gaetano Mosca, Vilfredo Pareto and Robert Michels argued against citizen participation in political life, and glorified the roles of elites in any political regime (Nagle, 1992). This was a low point in the confidence of liberal thinkers in the durability of democratic institutions, and the chances for the spread of liberal democracy throughout Europe, not to mention the rest of the world.

Many theorists who supported democratic politics saw the need to rethink the roles of those who were the leaders in politics, business, the military, labour and religion, as well as the reliability of the masses in their affection for parliamentary democracy. Chastened by the interwar catastrophe, and clearly influenced by the early postwar threat to democracy from Soviet communism they lowered their aspirations to conform, as they saw it, to a new hard-headed realism. And in East-Central Europe, the tragic extinguishing of democratic hopes for Hungary, Poland, and especially the more viable Czechoslovak Third Republic (1945–8) added further impetus for a 'revised democratic theory'. Joseph Schumpeter (1942), Carl Friedrich (1950), Giovanni Sartori (1962) and even the early Robert Dahl (1956) were among the protagonists of a more limited, more elite-oriented theory of democracy, which combined the insights of elite theories with minimalist requirements for a democratic political order.

Now, in the new era of post-communist democratization, the debate over proper roles for elites and citizens has been renewed. Who are the new elites? What commitments do elites and citizens have towards the democratization project? How can we characterize relationships between elites and citizens in these new democracies?

Continuity of elites from communism to post-communism

One of the remarkable features of the collapse of communism in Europe was the consensus among political elites, both in the ruling parties and in the opposition, that a regime change was necessary. The break with communism came with the support of a large portion of the old nomenklatura, and the grudging acceptance by the rest. If the 1989 'refolutions' (Garton Ash's term) were a victory for the people, they were also not very threatening to the old communist elites. The peaceful 'roundtables' of 1989 brokered in quick fashion the dismantling of the communist political monopoly and rapid transition to a democratically elected government. Those who still considered these regimes as 'totalitarian' held to the view that 'History has shown that no regime – and certainly no totalitarian regime – gives up without a struggle, so long as it possesses the means to defend itself, and there is no question that the Czechoslovak totalitarian regime possessed such means' (Blahoz, 1994: 229). But then, they had no way of explaining the peaceful and orderly transfer of power, and could only conclude that despite its historical impossibility, 'Nevertheless, the revolution did succeed' (Blahoz, 1994: 229).

The acceptance of the end of the communist regime by such large portions of the old elite, the lack of panic among these powerholders from the former regime, and their willingness to adapt to the new environment of democracy, privatization and marketization, tells a lot about the generally positive balance between hope and anxiety within the nomenklatura. As many studies have now confirmed, there has been in fact a high degree of continuity between the 'winners' of the old order, and the 'winners' of the new. Higley, Kullberg and Pakulski conclude that elite turnover was distinctly evolutionary: '. . . nothing approaching a "revolutionary" circulation of elites occurred; in this key respect, at least, there were no Central and East European revolutions in 1989–91' (1996: 139). Adam Michnik would later speak of the 'velvet restoration' of old elites, who had re-established themselves in the new system (cited in Mommsen, 1997: 267).

Data collected by sociologist Jacek Wasilewski indicated that in Poland and Hungary about one-third of the 1988 elite office-holders were still in roughly the same positions in 1993, with higher levels of continuity among the economic elite at 50.7 per cent (cited in Higley et al., 1996: 135–136). Moreover, substantial additional numbers of the new elites (as of 1993) had been at somewhat more modest ranks just below the top nomenklatura elites of 1988; these were the elite 'apprentices' of the old order, whose upward mobility had continued into the post-communist era. In Poland, these apprentice-elites of 1988 accounted for an additional 26 per cent of the 1993 elite, and in Hungary an additional 37.4 per cent. The ratio of 'winners' to 'losers' from the 1988 nomenklatura elites and apprentice-elites was extraordinarily positive for a period of presumed political and economic upheaval, nearly 23:10 in Poland, and 22:10 in Hungary.

In Czechoslovakia, the electoral victories of the Civic Forum and Public against Violence in 1990 led to some larger-scale discontinuities, as for a short time significant numbers of human rights dissidents achieved high office, bringing with them a circle of advisers and ministerial appointees from non-communist backgrounds. But by the 1992 elections the issue was no longer ousting the communist regime, but rather the division in economic priorities between Czech and Slovak parties, eventually dividing the nation into Czech and Slovak republics; here the technocratic and managerial sub-elites from the old regime made their comeback within Václav Klaus' Civic Democratic Party and Vladimír Mečiar's Slovak Democratic Movement. After the 1992 elections, about half of parliamentary and government ministerial elites in the Czech and Slovak republics came from sub-elite technocratic positions in the former communist regime (Higley et al., 1996: 136).

An excellent in-depth study of managerial elites in the Czech Republic by Ed Clark and Anna Soulsby (1996) confirmed these general propositions from interviews with 53 managers at four large privatized enterprises. Overall, 56 per cent of managerial elites were from Communist Party backgrounds, and the proportion increased at each higher rank, from 40 per cent of department managers to 74 per cent of directors to 100 per cent of general directors (1996: 288). Many more from the previous nomenklatura elite had experienced upward mobility, especially from the apprentice-elite stratum (what Clark and Soulsby call the recruitment stratum). They describe in detail the machinations and manoeuvres and group solidarity which allowed the pre-1989 managerial elite to retain their elite status and even improve upon it, despite the post-1989 electoral failures of the Communist Party and the most strict lustration laws in the region. 'Our findings confirm the continuity of the post-communist senior managerial group with its state socialist predecessor, and the ways in which it has sustained its internal integrity, external apartness and access to privilege are compatible with the concept of a social elite' (1996: 300). Of course, this social elite will continue to evolve with time, but for now, it appears to have stabilized its elite status and improved its privileges with economic marketization.

For comparison, Wasilewski's figures for Russia were even more positive for the old nomenklatura elite, with 48 per cent of the political elite of 1993 coming from the 1988 ranks; the biggest winners in Russia were the apprentice-elites of 1988, who accounted for fully 49 per cent of the elite office holders of 1993. In Russia, the ratio of winners to losers from the 1988 ranks was 86:10. Olga Kryshtanovskaya (1994; cf. also Lane and Ross, 1995) has also shown that in Russia in 1994, the elites came overwhelmingly in every category from the old elite ranks (from 60 to 80 per cent in Yeltsin's presidential council, the party leaderships and the regional, administrative and business elites).

The broad majority of communist-era elites and apprentice-elites correctly assessed their chances for career security and even promotion in a post-communist regime. Higley, Kullberg and Pakulski conclude that

Through fancy footwork, in short, the elites who operated the communist regimes largely survived those regimes' collapse. Their survival was greater in the economic and administrative than in the political realms, and it was more pronounced among 'deputies' than among top leaders. This helps to account for the generally peaceful nature of the transitions from communist to postcommunist regimes. If one asks why the elites associated with communist rule did not go down fighting against the inroads of democratic and capitalist forces, much of the answer is that they had little need to; their survival was more likely if they did not fight. (1996: 137)

If one takes the more elite-oriented view of requirements for democratic consolidation, one condition is that politics is 'tamed' to the extent of no longer being like warfare with deadly consequences. The post-1989 turnover has restored more normal evolutionary trends in elite recruitment and rejuvenation. With many of the oldest generation of communist leaders now removed, those apprentice-elites at middle levels have been able to move up, despite their past histories with the old regime, because they in fact do represent the skills and experience of the scientific and technological revolution which had developed but was blocked from reaching higher ranks during the period of late communism. Jerzy Wiatr's analysis (1994: 259–260) of the new top leadership of the successor party, the Social Democracy of the Polish Republic, shows a rejuvenated leadership (average age of 41 years for the 97 members of the party's executive council), composed mostly of the better-educated and middle class party functionaries (42 out of the 97), educators (33) and journalists (14). Only a few were categorized as workers (11) or farmers (2). The protracted internal struggle over the 'decommunization' of the former ruling party had ended with the victory of the younger middle-level and apprentice-elites. This continuity of elites gave some evidence therefore of having further 'tamed' political life among the elites, completing or at least further advancing a process which had been ongoing since the death of Stalin. This is in some respects the long-awaited generational breakthrough in normal elite advancement (cf. Hough, 1977; Nagle, 1975).

One should note here that in contrast to Poland, Hungary and the Czech Republic, political life has not remained 'tamed' in Russia, Ukraine, Belarus or Bulgaria in the first years of post-communism. In Russia, President Yeltsin resorted to deadly force against the elected parliament in October 1993, and against Chechen separatists in 1995. There have been numerous political assassinations of bankers, parliamentary deputies and political journalists in Russia, indicating the frailty of elite consensus on the rules of the game, and a new post-communist willingness to use deadly violence against political enemies. In this sense Yeltsin's regime represents a retreat from the Gorbachev reform process; Higley and Pakulski in fact postulate, in their consideration of the Russian case, that 'Had Gorbachev's reforms continued, they might have led to a negotiated settlement. But because of the Soviet Union's imperial history and multinational makeup, his liberalization unleashed powerful centrifugal forces that provoked an elite backlash culminating in the August 1991 coup attempt. This enabled Yeltsin and the main Russian elites, in what resembled a pre-emptive coup, to destroy remaining Soviet power and consolidate their own power in Russia' (1995: 430). Higley and Pakulski do not conclude from this that Russian democracy is doomed, only that it operates with a very divided elite from whose conflicts an authoritarian regime could emerge. In Ukraine and Bulgaria as well, political murders have become a new part of post-communist political life. While it may be too soon to judge whether this is a temporary phenomenon or has already become a 'normal' part of the new politics of these nations, it is surely a bad sign for any kind of democratization. The continuation of peaceful and cooperative relations across the party landscape in Poland, Hungary and the Czech Republic would constitute another important sign of elite consensus on the new democratic rules.

The willingness, despite the past, of opposition leaders to accept the continued presence in important posts of communist-era elites and apprentice-elites, is seen as a pre-condition, on the elite level, for a secure democratization in the region (Higley et al., 1996: 138). In Hungary, after the 1994 elections, the Free Democrats accepted a junior partner role in the government led by the successor Socialist Party; in Poland, the liberal Freedom Union has joined with the successor Democratic Left Alliance to support the new constitution, despite the fierce opposition of its former Solidarity allies led by Lech Wałęsa. Newly elected President Václav Havel in 1990 appointed the popular Slovak communist Marian Calfa as interim Prime Minister in an early symbolic sign of inter-elite reconciliation and cooperation. Here the lesson of the interwar period, that deadly inter-elite conflict or system-paralysing animosity among elites should be avoided, seems to have been learned. This is especially important in that the 1989 revolutions had a broad but weakly articulated (Solidarity in Poland is a partial exception) popular base, and the regime change was an inter-elite negotiated pact, not an armed overthrow, or popular storming of the gates. Massive street demonstrations, given the clear signal from Gorbachev that the Soviet Union would not intervene to prop up communist rule in the region, were carried out in relative safety and with virtually no violence (Ceauşescu's regime in Romania was a clear exception).

Of course it is not just the continuity of elites which has facilitated democratization in East-Central Europe, but the continuity within the framework of an emerging democratic system of peaceful and non-zero-sum inter-elite competition, in which all major elite groupings retain (or improve) their general status even while risking setbacks on specific issues or election results. The relative cooperation and tolerance among elites in Poland, Hungary and the Czech Republic must be contrasted with the new intra-elite feuding, including assassination, within the new Russian regime under President Boris Yeltsin. According to Schumpeterian views of a broad elite consensus on rules of the game, and willingness to accept the outcomes of periodic election competition among contending elite coalitions, the elite transition pacts of 1989 in Poland, Hungary and the Czech republic were a good beginning for democratic consolidation, but note, consolidation of the type of democracy which is elite-centred, not resting upon the more participatory or democratic cultural supports.

An elite-centred analysis of democratic development in Central and Eastern Europe leads to conclusions that clash with assumptions about communism's demise widely current among both the public at large and the academic world. First, change in elite relations and behaviour was the critical determinant of regime change. Second, continuity of elites from the communist to the postcommunist period has not meant, prima facie, an absence of democratic change, but rather a relatively high degree of security that has been conducive to democratic competition in several of these countries. Third, in countries where democracy has taken root, ex-communist elites have on balance contributed to, not undermined, the establishment and strengthening of democratic institutions. (Higley et al., 1996: 145)

For others, however, the significant continuity of elites illustrates the incomplete nature of these post-communist transitions (Cebulak, 1997).

Presidentialism and democratization

One legacy from the communist era was the concentration of power in a top party leader, and the subordination of all government institutions to that leader. Democratization in post-communism has produced many struggles over the restructuring of government institutions, including the courts, the military, the police and internal security forces, and publicly controlled television and press. But no conflict has been as decisive, in the short term at least, for addressing the issue of concentration of power as the battle between parliaments and presidents. The fate of democratization, and the quality of citizen representation and participation in politics, may be reflected in good measure in the outcome of this contest.

Post-communism provides a good test of the proposition, derived mainly from Latin American experience, that presidentialism (the concentration of power in the hands of the president, even a democratically elected one) is dangerous for democratization and democracy. Although there is no patented formula which works in every case, in general those nations where democratization has failed, or where it never really got started, are the same nations where the president has gained dominance over the parliament. This is most obvious in the Central Asian and Caucasus republics of the former Soviet Union. Otto Luchterhand (1996), in his study of executive power in the Commonwealth of Independent States (CIS), has classified the Central Asian republics of the former Soviet Union as early democratization failures, leading to dictatorial and authoritarian presidentialism.

In Russia, Ukraine, Belarus and Armenia, where the president has gained the upper hand, democratization has been at best unsteady, and each new presidential decree (not to mention the blasting of parliament out of existence as in Moscow in October 1993) strengthens the long tradition of executive authoritarianism. Fraudulent national elections in Armenia in 1996 were another sign of authoritarian tendencies in president-dominant systems. Western leaders in government and business applaud Yeltsin in Russia as a reformer despite his presidential authoritarianism, and denounce Lukashenka in Belarus as an anti-reform dictator, yet both have built up presidentialist regimes at the expense of all other institutions. Where the power of the presidency is largely unchecked, democratization has been short-circuited if not yet undone. Luchterhand has classified these systems as democratic presidentialism with strong tendencies and some realized transitions to authoritarian presidentialism. He relates the rising power of the presidential office to the general degree of political, national and economic crisis, which leads to calls, at both elite and mass levels, for stronger and more authoritarian leadership; in particular, Luchterhand singles out:

1   the background factor of a non-homogeneous society, divided by great cultural, ethnic, or even clan/tribal cleavages;
2   a highly unstable economy with deep and broad poverty, or at least economic insecurity;
3   a splintering and partial marginalization, also polarization of political parties, combined with widespread clientelism;
4   a specific or marked political stance of the military, a constant challenge of the military to civilian politics;
5   high levels of corruption and low levels of professionalism in the state apparatus, including administrative incompetence;
6   a failing rule of law through weak control over police and over civilian criminal behaviour;
7   deep-seated traditions of 'caudillismo' or the historical concept that a 'strong man' is needed to provide for social peace and order (1996: 225–226).

On the other hand, parliament has established its leading role in Hungary and the Czech Republic (and also in Estonia, Latvia and Lithuania). The presidency is more symbolic and ceremonial, though still important; the general division of power and of roles between the democratic parliament and the president follows Western European models (the Gaullist French model is an exception here). In these nations, conflicts over policy and performance have been voiced without threatening the constitutional roles or political viability of either side. Czech President Václav Havel criticized Prime Minister Václav Klaus (as well as other figures both in government and opposition) without any danger to either office; despite their mutual animosity, this was not an institutional power struggle. Hungarian President Arpad Gőncz at various times clashed with the former prime ministers Jószef Antall and Gyula Horn, and has tried to act as an active mediator of conflicting interests, as in the treaty process with Slovakia and Romania, or on media policies. Yet here too, these differences and disagreements posed no threat to democratization.

The cases in Poland and Slovakia are different again, and fall somewhere between the Russian-Ukrainian-Belarus and Czech-Hungarian-Baltic experiences. Lech Wałęsa, President of Poland from 1990 to 1995, used his office to undermine first the Solidarity-led governments and then, after the 1993 elections, the successor communist SLD–PSL coalition government. Through constant scheming and manoeuvring, which eventually cost Wałęsa much of his popularity, he attempted to aggrandize power in his hands, aided by an interim constitution (the 'Little Constitution' of 1992) which granted the president a key role in appointments to several 'power' ministries, and which did not clearly spell out methods for resolving disputes between the parliament-based government and the president. After the 1993 elections, which brought a successor left (SLD and PSL) coalition to power in Poland, the acrimony between Wałęsa's office and the government escalated, and in October 1994 the Sejm majority passed a resolution condemning President Wałęsa's scheming and calling upon him to respect the constitution. This resolution did not bring formal charges against Wałęsa, but this was explained in part by the desire of parliament not to alarm the international community with the possibility of a dangerous internal situation like the one in Moscow the year before. Klaus Ziemer (1996: 172) sees this early feuding between president and parliament in Poland as one of the continuing problem areas for Polish democratization, especially in times when the president represents a different political standpoint from that of the parliamentary majority. Paul Latawski, in a defence of Wałęsa's presidentialism, argues that his feuding with the SLD-led parliament and his fiddling with the constitution has been exaggerated: 'paradoxically, the political quarrel between Wałęsa and the coalition government tempered rather than undermined the post-communist agreement on Poland's national security policy' (1995: 43). Margareta Mommsen, however, details the many ways in which Wałęsa's erratic authoritarianism (reviving Piłsudski-era notions) damaged Polish democracy in its formative years (1997: 257–260).

Juan Linz and Alfred Stepan, in their tri-regional comparison of the problems of democratic transition and consolidation, focus on the semi-presidential system of Poland as a troubling factor, given a past history of authoritarian presidentialism and notably higher levels of Polish popular ambivalence about democracy in general. They cite two of Wałęsa's own former aides, one of whom, Jadwiga Staniszkis, in 1992 viewed Poland's young democracy as moving into dangerous waters: 'Poland does not yet see the breakdown of democracy, but it may be on the brink of it. . . . There is mounting evidence of a coming executive coup . . .' (cited in Linz and Stepan, 1996: 281). Another aide, Jaroslaw Kaczynski, agreed that when Wałęsa sent his draft constitution to the Sejm, with much-expanded power for his office, 'the president showed his hand. He wanted all power for himself' (1996: 282). They further cite polls in 1992 which showed considerable support for the 'law of the strong hand' and a ban on democracy, favoured by 30 per cent of Poles (with a further 14 per cent unsure or wavering); polls comparing Polish, Hungarian, Slovakian, Czech and Austrian public opinion show significantly higher support in Poland for authoritarian, anti-democratic

TABLE 8.1   *Attitudes toward authoritarian and anti-political options in East-Central Europe, 1991–1993*

| Country | Percentage of respondents supporting: | | |
	Dissolution of parties and parliament (1992)	One-party system (1992)	Rule by a strong man (1993)
Poland	40	31	39
Hungary	24	22	26
Slovakia	20	14	19
Czech Republic	19	8	22
Austria	8	–	22

Source: Fritz Plasser and Peter Ulram 'Zum Stand der Demokratisierung in Ost-Mitteleuropa' in Plasser and Ulram (eds), *Transformation oder Stagnation? Akuelle Trends in Osteuropa*. Vienna: Zentrum für angewandte Politikforschung, vol. 2: 46–47, cited in Linz and Stepan, 1996: 285

and anti-political options. Fully 39 per cent of Poles expressed support for rule by a 'strong man' (see Table 8.1). Still other cross-national surveys showed lower levels of Polish support for democracy as preferable to any other form of government than was the case in five Latin American and Southern European democracies. For Linz and Stepan, these data, combined with semi-presidentialism in Poland, make democratic consolidation more difficult than in Hungary and the Czech Republic, although they conclude that other factors still make democratic consolidation likely.

Robert Furtak (1996), in a comparison of presidentialism in post-communist Russia, Poland and Croatia, concludes that the attempts to concentrate power by Yeltsin, Wałęsa and Tudjman were all harmful for democratization; the Polish case is clearly different in this respect from the Czech and Hungarian cases. To some degree this is a continuation of the power shifts from the last years of the communist regime, when the 1989 roundtable compromise equipped President Jaruzelski with far-reaching formal powers relative to a semi-freely elected parliament, before the sudden collapse of communism drove him from office. There is also the continuity in the Polish case with the interwar presidentialist regime of General Piłsudski, now again revered as a model by many in post-communist politics. Whatever the historical connections, however, Furtak argues that in the Wałęsa presidency, 'the situation was characterized by a permanent power struggle between Wałęsa, the government, and the Sejm, which discredited that democracy' (1996: 149 authors' translation from the German).

Under President Aleksander Kwaśniewski, relations between the president and the Sejm between 1995 and 1997 were much calmer and less provocative, but that was in part because Kwaśniewski and the leading parliamentary majority were from the successor party, the Democratic

Left Alliance (SLD). After the 1997 parliamentary elections, which returned a Solidarity-led centre-right government to power, Poland again faced a difficult test of cohabitation of a moderate left president and a conservative government and parliamentary majority.

In Slovakia, likewise, the power struggle between President Michal Kovac and Prime Minister Vladimír Mečiar often threatened to get out of hand, and bitter feuding between president and prime minister became one of the regular features of Slovakian politics. However, Kovac left office in 1997, and after the defeat of Mečiar's government in the September 1998 elections, a new right-left coalition of parties formed a new government under Prime Minister Mikula Dzurinda of the Slovak Democratic Coalition. The personalized Mečiar-Kovac conflict which brought on the institutional feud has been ended.

Otto Luchterhand sees presidentialism in post-communism as qualitatively different from the United States case, where the powers of the president have been, from the outset of independence, circumscribed by extensive checks and balances from a fully empowered Congress, a Supreme Court, the individual states, and the free press (1996: 224–225). In post-communism, as in Latin American presidentialismo, the question is one of traditionally asymmetric power concentrated in the hands of a president in a longer tradition of authoritarian rule. Luchterhand (1996: 273) concludes that the rise of presidential power, especially in the nations of the former Soviet Union, represents a form of continuity with the communist system, which also concentrated authoritarian power in the hands of a single person at the top, even in the final Gorbachev reform years. From Khrushchev through Brezhnev to Gorbachev, a single party leader clearly stood above the prime minister, his cabinet, the rubber-stamp parliament and the courts. The president now strives for a democratic legitimation, although some recent presidential elections (Russia, Armenia, Croatia), while competitive, cannot be judged as fair. Additionally, Luchterhand sees the rise of presidential power as a popular symbolic hope, or wish, that a strong leader might bring social stability and economic security to a society 'characterized today by existential desperation and anxiety, by shameless egoism of groups and individuals, by economic exploitation, sharpening social conflicts, loss of values and spiritual loss of orientation. . . . A strong president is the dialectical answer to this condition and simultaneously an expression of the hope of overcoming this condition' (1996: 274 authors' translation from the German).

Any concentration of state power is a danger for democratization, and the rise of post-communist presidentialism is the institutional expression of that danger. In some post-communist states, presidentialism has put an end to democratization. For Hungary and the Czech Republic, this issue seems not to be problematic; for Poland, on the other hand, it has been and could again arise as a temptation, bolstered by tradition, by significant popular support and by ambitious populist leaders.

Elite consensus on democracy: possible ambiguities of commitment

Inter-elite relations are an important element of democratic politics and democratic stability. In modern societies, with highly differentiated economic and social structures, elites become more function-specific, less ideological, more autonomous and yet inter-related with other functionally necessary elites (Keller, 1963; Lenski, 1966). The overarching consensus among these elites on the rules of the democratic process allows for open and free competition without domination by any one elite group. The scientific and technological revolutions gave rise to modern functional elites even in communist systems (Fischer, 1968), leading to a less ideological and more managerial-technocratic politics. The collapse of communism in 1989–91 provided a further breakthrough for these functional elites. The question is whether the transition to post-communist politics was accompanied by a new elite consensus on democratic politics, or whether these new elites, now freed from the antiquated and artificially imposed Leninist unity, are unable to agree on the basic ground rules. John Higley and Jan Pakulski have applied this framework to East-Central Europe, categorizing eight nations (Bulgaria, Czech Republic, Hungary, Poland, Romania, Russia, Slovakia and Ukraine) on the degree of elite consensus in an era of increasing elite differentiation (see Figure 8.1). The changes in elite configurations in East-Central Europe have been in two principal directions: first, greater elite differentiation after the breakup of the communist system; and secondly new conflicts among elites that are, with significant variation, 'restrained by agreement about democratic procedures and norms of elite interaction' (1995: 415). They place Hungary, Poland and the Czech Republic most clearly in the category of consensual elites, with increasing elite differentiation, making them the best candidates for stable democracy (pp. 419–423). In their view, the break with communism, and the first rounds of elections have proved the durability of the new elite consensus on democratic politics. For Hungary,

> The first fully competitive elections, in spring 1990, were won by a centre-right coalition consisting of Democratic Forum, the Smallholders Party, and the Christian Democrats. High policy consensus characterized the campaign, and nearly all competing parties had significant numbers of ex-communists in their ranks. The Socialist victory in the May 1994 elections did nothing to weaken this unified configuration. In those elections, small and disaffected left- and right-wing elite groups gained no significant support. (p. 420)

Likewise for Poland, Higley and Pakulski view the new elite configuration as consensual and unified:

		Elite unity	
		Strong	Weak
	Wide	consensual elite	fragmented elite
		(stable democracy)	(unstable democracy)
Elite differentiation			
	Narrow	ideological elite	divided elite
		(partocratic regime)	(authoritarian regime)

FIGURE 8.1 Configuration of national elites (and associated regime types) (Higley and Pakulsi, 1995: 418)

Neither fragmenting tendencies nor the ex-communists electoral success appears to threaten the consensual unity of Polish elites. Unlike in neighbouring Ukraine, Polish debates have centred on the pace of marketizing reforms and the shape of democratic institutions, not their desirability. The main issues have been the scope of presidential power, the extent of 'welfare rights', and church–state relations, especially as regards policy toward abortion. No important elite group, including the comparatively radical Labour Union party on the left and the Christian National Union on the right, questions the democratic order. Political fireworks result from the idiosyncratic, often bumbling interventions of top politicians, especially Wałęsa, rather than fundamental ideological divisions and unrestrained power struggles. (p. 421)

In the Czechoslovakian case, post-communist elites did have a fundamental division over pace and direction of economic policy, which in 1992 combined with the division between Czechs and Slovaks to force a national division, which was peacefully effected. For the Czech Republic, the Velvet Divorce simplified the competition over basic policy within a consensual elite; for Slovakia, the split consolidated the power of Mečiar's Movement for a Democratic Slovakia, but has left a much more divided elite with serious disagreements over the rules of the game. However, the various anti-Mečiar parties (from the left, the right, and the Hungarian minority) won the September 1998 elections, which were judged to be free and fair, and there was a peaceful transfer of power to the new government led by Prime Minister Dzurinda; it remains to be seen whether in this new post-Mečiar era a greater elite consensus on the rules for a democratic politics will develop.

Higley and Pakulski conclude that 'all significant elite groups, including the military, share a commitment to democratic processes and appear disposed to pull their punches well short of the point at which democratic breakdown would loom' (p. 431). However, there are signs that this elite consensus has been strained, especially since the parliamentary election victories of the successor ex-communist parties in 1993 in Poland, 1994 in Hungary, and the defeat of Lech Wałęsa by

Aleksander Kwaśniewski for President in 1995. In Poland, both the Catholic Church and the political right reacted with bitterness and anger to their political defeats; in public statements they do not recognize the legitimacy of the SLD-led regime. Especially in the 1995 presidential campaign, the Catholic hierarchy and its affiliated Radio Maria employed intemperate language which demonized opponents as traitors, liars and evil people who were not good Poles. Likewise, in the debate over the new Constitution in 1996–7, both the Church and the Solidarity Electoral Alliance (AWS) took fundamentalist stances rather than bargaining or compromising to find a middle ground. As a result the 1997 draft Constitution was supported by the Democratic Left Alliance, the Peasant Party and the liberal Freedom Union, but was opposed by Wałęsa, the AWS and the Church hierarchy.

In the interwar period, key elites in the military, higher civil service, landed aristocracy, Church, industry and the political class were either clearly hostile to liberal democratic regimes, or were ambiguous about their support for democracy, and were willing to support anti-democratic nationalist regimes which ranged from fascist to semi-fascist or national-populist. Facing many centres of elite hostility, the interwar democracies were vulnerable to high-level conspiracies, and in crisis situations they were overthrown by coalitions of anti-democratic elites led by charismatic leaders with some popular base of support.

In post-communist Europe, it is important to take seriously signs of anti-democratic elite orientations or ambiguous attitudes towards democratic politics. On the Leninist left, the remnants of the old ruling parties are politically inert and have very little support in Poland and Hungary; in the Czech Republic, the unreformed Communist Party of Bohemia and Moravia sits in its own political ghetto, but seems unable to mount any kind of challenge against the Czech democracy. There have been suggestions that the Communists be banned as anti-democratic, and there seem to be no potential sources of support for this party from other elites.

On the far right of the political spectrum there are individual figures such as Albert Szabo in Hungary, who lead fascist movements with some core of activist support, but few signs of being able to mobilize a broad-based challenge. István Csurka's ultra-nationalist Hungarian Justice and Life Party can also be classified as anti-democratic, and a possible future danger in a crisis situation. More worrisome is the reluctance of the right-wing nationalist Smallholder Party, led by József Torgyan, to distance themselves from these anti-democratic groups, with whom they have mounted threatening demonstrations in Budapest against the State Treaty with Romania and against the agricultural policies of the Horn government. In Poland, the 1991 presidential elections gave a platform to Stanisław Tymiński, a mysterious businessman of Polish heritage from either Peru or Canada, who demonstrated the potential for a demagogic politics which would destabilize the new democracy. Winning nearly a quarter of the vote on a platform of secret plans for a miraculous cure for the Polish economy, Tymiński showed how political discontent and disorientation could be harnessed by a charismatic leader with a grand nationalist vision reminiscent of Piłsudski's interwar rule. In the Czech Republic, Miroslav Sládek, leader of the viciously racist Republican Party, is clearly an anti-democratic threat, but his party seems fairly isolated on the far right, and there have been no signs of support for his movement by economic, military, or church authorities. Most other conservative parties have denounced Sládek's violence-prone tactics, and there have been suggestions that his party be banned as anti-democratic.

It is obviously hard to judge whether people like Tymiński or Sládek or even Csurka are small-timers, political wild men who will self-destruct, or whether they might be able to develop some wider support, especially in a prolonged crisis situation. Hitler and his Nazis were also seen in the 1920s as marginalized extremists, and in the pre-depression 1928 German elections the Nazis got only 2.6 per cent of the vote; they seemed at that point to be on their way to political oblivion. The key to the Nazi takeover was the willingness of established elites to make an anti-democratic pact with Hitler to bring down the depression-weakened Weimar democracy only four years later. At this point, there can only be suspicions about how some business, agrarian, nationalist, or religious leaders would behave in different circumstances, when the new democracies might be seen as failures, incapable of meeting some economic crisis, or having lost their popular legitimacy. The kind of elite hostility to liberal democracy that was voiced openly in the early interwar years is absent in East-Central Europe today, and that is a good sign for the inability of extremist forces to combine with powerful interests to destroy the democratization process.

Civil society or a cynical society?

Scholars have coined new descriptions for these emerging realities of (old and new) elite controls and citizen alienation, including 'delegative', 'half' and 'nomenklatura' democracies (Mommsen, 1997). Attila Ágh, a leading scholar of the political transformation of East-Central Europe, concludes that at least for the foreseeable future, these new democracies will look like the elite-centred Schumpeterian model of formal electoralism combined with widespread public disconnection from political life:

> The new ECE democracies were born as elite democracies because the construction of a new democratic order and its institutions began in the political macro-sphere – i.e. from above. Therefore, unavoidably, political

transformation has stopped here and half-democracies have emerged. In these, the formal definition of democracy can actually be met (electoralism as a regular, free process entailing competitive elections in order to change the political elites). Yet full and real democratization has not yet begun, because there has been no substantial definition of what democracy should be. If this had happened organized interests and big social organizations, as well as civil society associations, would have had a better chance of being organically connected with macro-politics through different levels of interest articulation and mediation. In this elite democracy, however, no other actors have been admitted and the process of elite integration or incorporation has been blocked by those in power. (1996: 54).

Ágh's view is bolstered by 1997 opinion polls in Hungary which show that a clear majority (60 per cent) of the public still do not believe that a real 'regime change' has yet taken place. Rather a picture emerges of a more organized minority (of 'winners') who shape politics, and an alienated majority (of 'losers') who do not believe they will be heard. This supports a theory of an active elite minority and a passive subordinate majority (Perczel, 1997).

This realistic view poses some serious questions for the relationship between elites and citizens. Ágh is undoubtedly correct, despite the rhetoric of popular liberation movements of 1989, that the great regime change was an elite-negotiated transfer of power. As argued above, this provided for a peaceful break with communism, with a great deal of continuity for the old nomenklatura elite. The role of large-scale social organizations and interests was not entirely absent, the Church in Poland being the clearest exception to the general rule, but the Church hierarchy did not provide for grassroots input, since the Church itself is not a democratic organization. If one names the normal civic interest groups, including labour, business, professional and volunteer organizations, even military or civil service groups, none of these played notable roles in promoting a vision of democracy or defining the course of the break with communism. There were lots of bystanders in 1989, watching with great interest but with very little actual input. The largest demonstrations in the autumn of 1989 were grand symbolism, but the anti-communist liberation movements were gone within a year or two, leaving little organizational legacy. The new governing elites (who are in many cases also the old elites) are only weakly connected to the public, even to those who presumably supported them in democratic elections. Hopefully the new political elites are a 'transitional elite which should soon "wither away"' (Ágh, 1996: 56). The question is whether social organizations can fill the gap between individual citizens and governing elites in a way that both allows for the legitimate exercise of democratic leadership at the top, and a broad responsiveness to both public sentiment and active citizen involvement.

Bill Lomax has argued that in post-communism, many of the features of elite governance have been carried over from the period of late communism, both through the continuity of elites, and by learned behaviours of new elites from the previous era. Lomax does recognize that in Poland, Hungary and Czechoslovakia, the changes have been more far-reaching than in the former Soviet Union or in the Balkans, but even here, 'the changes are not as fundamental as they might first appear; the changes at the level of the elite have not been accompanied by the promised changes in the structure of society' (p. 180). In a focus on the first post-communist MDF government in Hungary, Lomax sees an elitist, even authoritarian, streak which evidences a continuity from the last communist government. The Antall MDF has 'increasingly come to regard any criticism of the "democratically elected government" as a form of anti-democratic behaviours and sees the duty of the media as being to represent the views and policies of that government' (1994: 181). Lomax concludes that the transition has been primarily an elite-centred transfer of power, with many continuities of attitude among elites towards citizens and citizen politics. Elemer Hankiss has described the 'new haute bourgeoisie' as 'arising in Hungary from old party bureaucrats and state managers who successfully converted their administrative powers under the old system into market privileges in the new one' (cited in Lomax, 1994: 184). This continuity of elites is seen as a new domestic bourgeois elite unlike that in Western democracies, but rather a marketization of the 'new class' long ago outlined by Milovan Djilas. The attitudes of these elites towards civil society are quite far from Western norms, but close to those inherited from the old communist order. In the absence of a meaningful role for citizen participation or citizen politics, the common disillusionment with the new system has become one of its early features.

Citizens in the new post-communist democracies have been, in fact, disappointed with the politics of the new governing elites, but still have some hope for the near future. In a poll taken in ten countries in 1993, citizens ranked the present government performance as worse than the previous communist regime in Hungary, Belarus and Ukraine, and only moderately better in Poland, Slovakia and Bulgaria (see Table 8.2); however, only in Belarus and Ukraine did citizens expect that in the near future things would remain worse than under communism, and generally citizens expected things to improve over the current (1993) situation. How long can the discrepancy between present discontent with governing elites and general optimism about the future persist, before a cynicism about political performance is consolidated into a more permanent attitude towards democracy itself?

Many observers have commented on the weakening of civil society after the 'first transition' from communist one-party rule to post-communist democratically elected government. Michael Bernhard talks about the demobilization of civil society after 1989–90, and the longer-term process of socioeconomic transformation, during which a 'dual society' of public sector/private sector interests offer both competing

TABLE 8.2   *Attitudes towards last communist government, current regime and future outlook*[a]

	Current regime performance v. last communist regime (B–A difference)	Future performance expectation v. last communist regime (C–A difference)
Belarus	−25	−14
Bulgaria	13	30
Croatia	29	60
Czech lands	42	57
Hungary	−25	4
Poland	14	27
Romania	33	47
Slovakia	10	31
Slovenia	31	41
Ukraine	−30	−6

[a] On a scale of 0 (worst) to 100 (best), respondents rated the performance of the pre-1989 (communist) government (A), the present government (B) and the outlook for the near future (C).

Source: Adapted and recalculated from original figures published in *Magyar Hirlap,* 7 July 1993

and complementary roles within the larger society. In this period of large-scale transformation, unique for post-communism,

> mobilization of groups in pursuit of market-based economic interests becomes more difficult because the basis of those interests is in flux. The entire class structure is being remade and it is unclear which effects of reform are temporary and which represent permanent losses in status, power, or welfare. Because of this there is a time-lag before new cleavages acquire political force. While there may be an increased potential for protest actions, the potential for building more permanent forms of organizations does not seem to be enhanced in the short-term (as seen in the proliferation and impermanence of political groupings. (Bernhard, 1996: 322)

A social decompression had started immediately after Stalin's death and had continued without major reversal under Khrushchev and Brezhnev, and had vastly accelerated under Gorbachev. This was not democratization, and communist regimes certainly did not intend to surrender their political monopoly, but it was a more relaxed era, marked not by forced mobilizations for rapid industrialization and cultural revolution, but by more evolutionary, bureaucratically pragmatic and piecemeal regime adaptation and response to problems and crises of a more settled urban industrial social order (Brown and Gray, 1977; Hough, 1977; Lodge, 1968; Skilling and Griffiths, 1971; Tatu, 1969) Post-Stalinist communism was moving into a phase of bureaucratic-managerial authoritarianism, in which elite groupings were gradually able to express differentiated policy and budgetary recommendations through party and state channels. To some degree, non-party professional associations and dissident groups were expressing their own interests more openly and more consciously, giving rise to concepts of independent and self-directed civil society. Frances Millard views the birth of Solidarity in 1980 as the turning point in the development of civil society in Poland as a result of this pluralization process:

> The concepts of 'interest groups' and 'strategic elites', of 'limited pluralism' or 'quasi-pluralism' were inadequate to describe the growing dissident movement in the late 1970s. The term 'civil society' appeared to capture certain of its elements and to reflect the theorizing behind it, especially in the writings of Adam Michnik. (1994b: 41)

This pluralization was carefully distinguished from democratic pluralism, but it was described as a systematic feature of the now more institutionalized, bureaucratically rationalist, and in some cases more decentralized patterns of politics. Some (Janos, 1976; Meyer, 1967) could interpret this as 'the transformation of a command system into a genuine social system. Alternatively, we can describe the process of pluralization as the reversal of the "massification" of society posited by Hannah Arendt and other students of totalitarianism – i.e., the transformation of the amorphous mass into a new class with vested interests which transcend commitment to the initial organizational objective' (Janos, 1976: 26–27). In short, the decompression from forced-mobilization totalitarianism to evolutionary authoritarianism also gave rise to a more pluralized set of interest groups, through which individuals and collectivities could identify longer-term material interests. Without a doubt, the seeds of a new civil society had already sprouted in post-Stalinist Eastern Europe, and would gradually grow into a nascent civil society by the late 1980s.

The fact that one could make a clear exception for Albania under Hoxha, or Romania under the Ceauşescu clan, is itself evidence of a growing quantitative, and eventually qualitative, difference between a few atavars of Stalinism, and the post-Stalinist political climate in East-Central Europe.

Thus Joseph Rothschild (1989) and Timothy Garton Ash (1989) and Vladimir Tismaneanu (1992) could note how, in the last years of communist rule, civil society had revived in East-Central Europe, and these societies were returning to a diversity of cultures and were experiencing a rapid rise in civic activity both within the political establishment and far outside official organizations. This gave an impression in 1989–90 of a strong civil society able to play an important role in the great political changeover. But, as Bernhard notes, only a few years later, 'Whereas there is general agreement that civil society played a key role in the overthrow of communist regimes in 1989 . . . and that among communist countries Poland had the most developed civil society in the region at the time of the collapse, there is now a widespread belief that civil society in post-communist countries is weak' (1996: 309). Bernhard then traces for Poland the factors which have weakened civil society there, including the demobilization after the initial regime changeover, and then the 'decapitation' through taking office of much of the leadership of civil society. But most important for the longer term has been the emergence of a kind of 'dual society' in which different forms of social organization coexist but with very different structures, rules and orientations, including those towards political life.

> What is unique about the situation in contemporary [East-Central Europe] is not that such a dual structure exists, but that it combines two forms of modernity. Specifically, institutions, social structures, and modes of behaviour derived from the old state-socialist mode of economic reproduction continue to exist alongside sectors of the economy which have adapted or are in the process of adapting to the market. Thus two mechanisms of economic and social reproduction also exist side-by-side, one created by the play of market forces and the other created by 40 years of state socialism and not yet fully subject to the new rules of economic reproduction posed by the market, because of protection by subsidies or by incomplete reform processes. (p. 317)

This situation of 'dual society' which comparativists have used for years to describe the conditions of many Third World or developing nations has important implications for both civil society and the consolidation of democracy. Some of the factors contributing to the weakness of civil society are clearly temporary, such as the relative weakness of new leadership after the 'first transition' phase advanced some earlier leaders into government office and party politics. But the still-incomplete socio-economic transition has left much of society in a mid-stream condition, in which stable interest group organization and representation is either very closely aligned with state budgets/sudsidies, and therefore still statist in orientation, or is uncertain as to where a citizen's real material interests lie: 'initial support for economic reform was based overwhelmingly on value orientations as opposed to concrete material interests' (1996: 323).

Bernhard concludes with an admonition that a weak civil society (see Figure 8.2) may present problems for the stability and consolidation of democracy in Poland, and by extension in other countries of East-Central Europe. In this conceptualization, only a strong state combined with a strong civil society is likely to produce an effective and responsive democracy. Since, for the foreseeable future, the state in East-Central Europe is most likely to be a weak state (cf. Holmes, 1995), the politics of East-Central Europe are to be located in the right-hand side

	Strong civil society	**Weak civil society**
Strong state	basis for responsive, effective democracy	strong state autonomy, danger of unresponsiveness, potential for prerogative state power
Weak state	overburdening – strain on state capacities, ineffectiveness in responding to the demands of constituencies	formless polity, ineffective and unresponsive state, high probability of regime breakdown

FIGURE 8.2 *State and civil society configurations with implications for democracy* *(Bernhard, 1996: 327)*

of Figure 8.2. However, it may well be that regime instability will not entirely overthrow the facade or procedural formalities of democracy, but may continue a mutual alienation between a weak and ineffectual state and a cynical and apolitical citizenry. Gert-Joachim Glaeßner argues that 'The existence of a "civil society" is not a precondition for the success of democracy in the transition period – rather this is first and foremost a functioning and effective institutional system and a calculable constitution – but it is a necessary condition for the lasting consolidation of democracy' (1997: 41).

Prospects for a participant civil culture

Here we come back to the question of resources, both for elites to be able to satisfy social interest group demands, and for civil society leaders to be able to aggregate and effectively articulate individual interests into group demands to which government must pay attention. The answer to this question rests primarily, though not entirely, with the nature of the emerging political economy which now produces great polarizations of opportunity, between the new bourgeoisie and the new poverty class, between pensioner and youth generations, between favoured urban sites and neglected rural and old-industry towns, and between men and women. Some newly moneyed interests are already making their influence felt, and will be able to command government attention to their needs. Those without financial resources are finding it hard to command such attention, even from party and government leaders who promised relief. Increasingly, those without socially organized access are deciding to abandon politics and depend entirely on themselves, and in any case they must devote their energies to the daily struggle to make ends meet. The new political economy may still be unclear in many details, and some may imagine themselves as occupying different positions than their current status (i.e., subjective versus objective social status), but in fact the broad outlines are already solidifying, and the new social polarizations are now more apparent than even a few years ago.

The citizens of the new democracies are not likely to accept Third World conditions and Third World polarizations between classes and regions, and will be very reluctant to lower their future expectations. Karol Modzelewski, a founding intellectual of the Solidarity movement, has stated that: 'Eastern European societies are quite different from those in the Third World. Their expectations are much higher and their patience much lower. These are societies that are fairly well educated. Not only do they have large intelligentsias, but also educated workers . . . [with] much higher aspirations' (cited in Lomax, 1994: 200). As citizens are better able to evaluate their prospects in the new political economies of post-communism, they will have some intellectual and organizational if not financial resources with which to build social organizations, to demand better results from the political class, and to fashion their own alternative visions for a better society. History has not ended, and there will very probably be additional surprises in the democratization of East-Central Europe.

Could these East-Central European democracies evolve in similar fashion as the reconstructed West German democracy did after the Second World War? After all, the newly reconstructed democracy in West Germany also faced problems of elitism and weakness of civil society in its early phase. The new Bonn democracy started out with some strongly elitist characteristics under Konrad Adenauer (the so-called Chancellor democracy) in the 1950s. The more 'subject' orientation of citizens in Germany as compared to Britain or the United States was broadly revealed in Almond and Verba's (1963) Civic Culture studies. The public at large was involved first with making ends meet, and building personal security and then prosperity for their families. These were understandably the dominant values of the immediate postwar years, and were fulfilled through the *Wirtschaftswunder* or economic miracle, which was in fact no miracle but rather the reconstruction of Germany's place as a leading economic power in an era of successful Keynesianism. This acquisitive generation was followed by a new generation, with more expressive values (Baker, 1981; Inglehart, 1977) which voiced new demands for openness of political debate, more transparency of policy making, and more avenues of participation outside established electoral formalities. The new social movements of the late 1960s and 1970s announced the arrival of a civic democratic culture by the 1980s (Honolka, 1987). Already by 1956 West Germany was a leading partner, with France, in the launching of the European Common

Market and the long-term integration project for Western Europe. Germany was recovering its role as a leading economic power.

The nations of East-Central Europe are, with the possible exception once again of the Czech Republic, trying to join for the first time the community of modern economies of the first rank. They are doing this at a time of sharpened economic competition within the global economy, which already has an expanded number of first-class manufacturing exporters. The Keynesian era is passing, and with it the concept of a national economy which could provide good jobs with good social benefits throughout the population, making strong efforts to buffer regions, classes and minorities against the 'creative destruction' of free market capitalism. East-Central Europe cannot replicate the success of the Keynesian era in the West; instead, it is building a much more polarized political economy, with high risks and high anxiety from top to bottom, lacking social solidarity and the broad political consensus of the German 'social market economy'. It is very doubtful that the West German experience can be repeated (even in former East Germany).

Ellen Comisso (1997) has argued that these states are already consolidated as 'procedural democracies', in that they fulfil very well the prescriptions of Schumpeter from the earlier debate over what should define democracy. Revisiting that debate, she concludes that the proponents of 'procedural democracy' (what we have called elitist democracy) have triumphed in post-communism, while the advocates of 'substantive democracy', whether national, liberal, or egalitarian, have been disappointed. Comisso argues that, on procedural grounds, the post-communist democracies of Eastern Europe, and especially those of Poland, the Czech Republic and Hungary, have passed the classic tests with flying colours: several rounds of free and fair elections, peaceful transfers of power in Poland and Hungary as a result of elections, growing independence of judiciary and general respect for an independent media (the Antall MDF regime made some attacks on media freedoms, but lost the battle and paid the price). But on substantive grounds, there is disappointment everywhere:

Thus, from a liberal perspective, the state is still everywhere, markets are distorted, entrepreneurship is inadequately rewarded, security of property rights is all too often a product of political connections rather than the outcome of legal entitlements, and civil liberties still uncertain as long as non-liberal parties control governments. From a national perspective, the state is in hock to international finance, the traditional middle class is being plundered, the culture is being invaded from abroad, and ethnic minorities are collaborating with foreigners to create a protected position for themselves. From an egalitarian perspective, new civil rights can hardly be utilized by a population struggling to make ends meet and what was supposed to be democracy for everyone has turned into the rule of the few who are only tenuously accountable to the many. (1997: 18)

Comisso's main point is that there has been a consolidation (especially if we restrict our view to the Polish, Czech and Hungarian cases) of elite-oriented procedural democracy, in which most citizens feel disconnected and substantively, if not formally, disenfranchised. Compared with the goal of joining the Western liberal democracies, 'The glass is thus half full – but by the same token, it is also half empty' (1997: 19).

Stephen Holmes (1995) has characterized post-communist democracy as a weak state, with little power to satisfy public demands and little power to manage public affairs. There is the clear danger that substantive democracy cannot be fulfilled; these systems may remain elite-oriented, with little basis for building the kind of broad public consensus that is required for civil society or a civic democratic culture. Holmes does not so much fear an outright overthrow of formal democracy as he does a litany of other problems which would undermine social support for democracy on grounds of non-responsiveness and substantive failure.

> In postcommunist systems, so far, parliaments remain poorly informed about decisions made within central ministries. Their ability to control or influence these decisions is vanishingly small. Similarly, the absence of party consolidation means that voters have little information about and less control over their elected representatives. Such snapped connections between assemblies and both the ministries above and the voters below mean that parliaments cannot function effectively as arenas where conflicting social interests are articulated and reconciled and where national goals are defined. (1995: 49)

However, Holmes ends on a rather hopeful note, that the formal electoral process itself may provide a learning method for more effective state-building. Referring largely to the Russian case, Holmes concludes: 'Moreover, national elections . . . provide an instrument of state building more palatable than the war making by which virtually all states in the past have been created. The slowly developing sense of a procedural community, where the millions of members of a large nation vote together, on the same day, for political representatives, gives some modest experiential legitimacy to civic-territorial definitions of citizenship' (pp. 50–51). But even here, Holmes is arguing for avoiding the worst, a return to blatantly anti-democratic regimes of whatever stripe, not providing for substantive redress of citizen and interest group needs through effective and open governance. It is quite likely that, especially in East-Central Europe, Western sponsorship for EU or NATO membership would not countenance any formal break with democracy. Thus Western dominance, in politics, finances and security, provides some political correctness guidelines against outright dictatorship.

The real question is whether the weak democratic state can be made strong in the substantive sense of working on behalf of citizen interests as expressed through a broad-based democratic pluralism. In the absence of a political economy which could more effectively require elite attention to public concerns, and a democratically elected regime with a state capacity for satisfying public needs, these regimes may for some time consolidate as Schumpeterian elite democracies, meeting formal procedural requirements but not promoting and even blocking the evolution towards a civic democratic culture.

PART THREE

REGIONAL AND INTERNATIONAL CONTEXTS OF DEMOCRATIZATION

9

Regional Comparisons of Democratization: Southern Europe – Lessons from Another European Region

CONTENTS

Comparison of regional politics has produced a growing literature since the revitalization and modernization of comparative politics in the early Cold War. After the failures of democratization in interwar Europe, Western mainstream scholarship took on the task, with formal and informal government support, of studying the development and maintenance not only of democracy but of stable (that is, consolidated) democracy. With the current 'end of history' triumphalism about democracy still strong, it is well to remember that just before the Second World War there was a quite different atmosphere.

> The pessimism about democracy and free institutions occasioned by the events of this period was inverted by the victory of the Allied powers in the Second World War. Democracy was imposed on Germany, Italy, and Japan, and surprisingly took hold and endured. Beginning with India in

1947, a host of new nations in Asia, Africa, and the Middle East that had been colonies of the Western democracies were granted independence under constitutions and following election procedures modelled on those of their former colonial rulers. The wave of excitement and optimism about the prospects for democracy and rapid development in these newly independent nations spawned a new generation of scholarly thinking and research. (Diamond et al., 1989a: xi)

This new focus of comparative scholarship on regional development and political democratization has gone through periods (cycles) of greater confidence and optimism related to new democratic breakthroughs followed by periods of critique (from both left and right) and pessimism bolstered by democratic breakdowns. In the latter 1960s and early 1970s, there was much criticism of the original Western-inspired modernization theory, from those on the right (Huntington, 1968) who were sceptical of the Western model's universalism, and those on the left, who connected Western policy toward development in various regions to Western ethnocentrism, the dependency syndrome and imperialist domination. This was probably a low point in postwar confidence in the general theoretical and empirically backed connection between economic development and political democracy, especially with numerous military takeovers of government in Latin America, Asia and Africa, and with several communist takeovers through armed struggle in Vietnam, Laos, Cambodia, Angola and Mozambique. And yet, by the late 1970s, the reappearance of political democracy in Southern Europe, in Spain, Portugal and Greece, had begun to revitalize scholarship and attention to positive democratic potentials, rather than failures. While one may anticipate future periods of renewed theoretical criticism and sagging optimism, as some of the many democratizations end in failure or are stunted, regional comparisons of democratization will remain a pillar of comparative research, and a source of lively debate with important policy consequences for the West.

Within this large and growing literature, there are also approaches which do not take regional comparisons as a main organizing principle, but rather focus more strictly on the political economy of transitions from authoritarian to democratic rule. Haggard and Kaufman (1995) develop theories of democratization through non-regional comparisons along thematic lines heavily centred around economic reforms and their relation to democratic consolidation. A purely political economy approach tends to downplay local cultural and sociopolitical legacies of nations and regions, in order to highlight economic policy issues and to develop more universal policy preferences. Regional approaches will tend to provide an analysis more attentive to cultural and historical differences. But there is no inherent need to abandon political economy issues using a regional basis for comparison of democratizations.

One of the 'grand themes' of regional comparative analysis has been the development toward democracy, and how transitions from authoritarian rule to democracy have fared in different regions in some specific period. Since the latest 'third wave' (Huntington, 1991) began in Southern Europe in the 1970s, increasing attention has been given to the modalities and patterns of democratization in successive regions where authoritarian regimes have faltered and collapsed. Democratizations in Southern Europe, Latin America and East Asia offer broad comparisons with the circumstances of democratization in post-communist Europe, and especially the East-Central European nations.

The democracy trend in Europe

The generally quite positive experiences of Greece, Spain and Portugal in their democratizations after a long period (for Spain and Portugal at least) under authoritarian dictatorships served as a clear and constant model for the anti-communist opposition in East-Central Europe. Despite all the differences among the various dissident groups, and despite the wide range of dissident political opinions, from ethnic nationalist to democratic socialist and Thatcherite *laissez-faire* capitalist, the democratizations of Southern Europe in the mid-1970s leading to European Community membership by the 1980s was a common ideal for the dissenters. As Michael Waller has said, 'even the most strenuous marketeers among them took integration into Europe, in one sense or another, as their guiding light, and that meant a commitment to democracy. The examples of Spain, Portugal and Greece were no doubt never far from their minds' (1994: 140).

Democratization in Southern Europe had already become a major object of comparative study in the mid-1970s, with the overthrow of the Greek colonels' junta, the Portuguese military revolt against the Salazar–Caetano dictatorship and the rapid phase-out of Spanish authoritarian rule after Franco's death, all within a few years of each other, and all leading to democratic breakthroughs which were able to consolidate a democratic politics. One might add to this regional grouping the contrasting and far less successful case of Turkey (cf. Liebert and Cotta, 1990) as an historically important player in European politics for many centuries, and as a nation which has been a member of NATO and an aspirant for European Community (now European Union) membership.

Southern Europe is an important region for comparison in that its democratic successes have led, rather quickly, to joining these nations with the integration project of the European Community (now the European Union), which is of course a top-priority goal for the post-communist democracies of Poland, Hungary and the Czech Republic.

The success stories of democratization in Southern Europe are important for comparisons with Eastern Europe due to some broad geo-political similarities. The regional proximity to Western Europe, the gradual expansion of economic relations with the successful European Community democracies, and the prospect for joining this success model for regional growth and democratic political stability played a strong role in strengthening the hand of pro-democratic forces in Spain, Portugal and Greece. The European Community had begun the process of widening its membership to less prosperous democratic nations (Ireland), and the prospect of EC aid for economic integration into the community was a significant selling point for continuing democratization and consolidating a democratic politics. The level of EC financial aid (structural adjustment funds) amounted to a transfer of about 5 per cent of gross domestic product for these three nations (Linz et al., 1995: 120). Geoffrey Pridham (1995: 175) argues that EC membership prospects provided a kind of democratic discipline for strengthening the transition process, since it was clear that only strong democratic credentials would facilitate EC entry and the benefits that would bring. In fact, Greece was admitted in 1981, Spain and Portugal in 1986, indicating a waiting period of five to ten years after the inception of democratization.

The supportive international context for democratization in Southern Europe in the first ten to fifteen years after the fall of the authoritarian regimes was combined with the ability of the transition governments to concentrate on political reform and political consolidation first, without having to demand wrenching social and economic transformation from citizens at the same time. These were systems with already functioning market economies, which had made some progress (much more in Spain, much less in Portugal) during the boom years of postwar Western Europe. Their authoritarian regimes had been laggards in social welfare spending, but their economic policies were largely compatible with the norms of Western commerce and finance. With additional support from the EC, these new democracies could afford to put in place social services and substantial benefits to those displaced by later restructuring.

They did not have to face the 'simultaneity problem' of economic, social and often territorial transformation at the same time that political democratization was being attempted. Linz, Stepan and Gunther consider this a major feature in the success of democratic transition and consolidation in Southern Europe: 'The Southern European countries were structurally able, and consciously chose, to concentrate first on politics, secondly on social welfare policies, and only later on structural economic reforms, except in Portugal, where the nationalizations and collectivizations of the revolutionary period made subsequent economic restructuring even more difficult. We consider this the optimal sequence if it is at all possible' (1995: 118). One major contrast between Southern Europe and East-Central Europe is therefore the ability of the first region to sequence reforms in a manner that avoided system overload on the agenda for change, versus the relative inability in post-communism to avoid pressures for simultaneous political, economic and social restructuring (cf. also Burton et al., 1992: 346).

Pessimistically, German scholar Hans-Joachim Giessmann argues that: 'Never before has any nation been trying to establish both a democratic political system and a market economy at the same time – especially as each . . . is usually taken as the foundation of the other. Neither in structural terms nor in terms of human capacity were the societies prepared sufficiently – taking into account only . . . their national resources – to manage this dilemma easily' (1996: 4–5). This alone makes the kind of Southern European outcome unlikely, and instead Gliessmann foresees 'the creation of modified or mixed forms of democracy and market economies, including a stronger role for individual politicians, at least for a long period and possibly more suitable to the challenges of simultaneousness. . . . The most impressive changes towards capitalism in this century, incidentally, began under an autocratic rule and opened only later the road to democracy' (p. 8). In other words, an authoritarian politics may arise to deal with economic restructuring, and only if this proves successful will political democratization revive (i.e. the Pinochet Chilean or perhaps East Asian model).

In Southern Europe, the new democratic regimes were able to increase government revenues and spending for social welfare and state-sponsored employment and thereby buffer the social and economic reform projects which were only launched in the mid-1980s. Total government spending (as a percentage of GDP) rose in Spain (from 26 to 42 per cent), in Portugal (37 to 44 per cent) and in Greece (21 to 51 per cent) between 1976 and 1988 (Maxwell, 1990). Linz, Stepan and Gunther contrast this with the new 1990s logic of 'state shrinking' in the new democracies of post-communist Eastern Europe (and in Latin America as well), and note that 'all three of the new Southern European democracies strengthened their states by increasing tax revenues during the transition and consolidation processes. All three Southern European states used this revenue to significantly increase social welfare expenditures and state employment' (1995: 119). They were able to do this because their transitions to democracy began at a time of still-strong Keynesian consensus politics in Western Europe, where the model of a prosperous and generous social market economy was the norm, and the challenges of Thatcherism and Reagonomics were still off-stage in preparation. The authoritarian regimes of Southern Europe were, in the 1950s and 1960s, in close contact with the vigorous economies and strong democracies of Western Europe; trade relations were expanding, large numbers of workers from Greece, Spain and Portugal were employed in the Western democratic welfare states, and brought these experiences back home with them. The demonstration effect, which was said to have played such an important role in the victory of the Western model over communism, played a strong and perhaps even more convincing role in encouraging the democratizations of Southern Europe.

José María Maravall supports the view that the successful Southern European democratizations were facilitated by strong states able to provide more, not less, social justice, along with democratic freedoms, all in contrast to the East European experience. 'In Southern Europe, the installation of democratic regimes was accompanied by a strengthening rather than a weakening of the economic capacity of the state. . . . As the states of Eastern Europe are scaled back, they also will have to perform essential new economic and social functions' (1995: 22). For Maravall, democratization does not require less social equity along with economic reform:

> Certainly no trade-off between equity and economic liberalization has been in evidence in the cases of Spain, Taiwan, South Korea, and Portugal, all of which liberalized while establishing comparative income equality. In South Korea and Taiwan, income equality both preceded and followed the turn to export-led growth. In Portugal, income distribution became more equal with democratization and has come closer to that of other advanced industrial countries. In Spain, income disparities decreased both with democratization and economic growth. (pp. 22–23)

Gosta Esping-Andersen (1994) concludes that in Spain and Portugal, democratization unleashed a policy shift toward social equity, more pronounced and permanent in Portugal, more incremental and temporary in Spain.

However, one must note again that the Spanish and Portuguese transitions came during the period of Keynesian consensus, which has now eroded and is being gradually replaced by a neo-liberal model fostering greater inequalities. Maravall's commentary amounts to a protest against the new neo-liberal model, and an implicit warning that the East European new democracies must try to provide some elements of social welfare in a new way, or risk losing their legitimacy. The building of a new 'social citizenship' as part of the legitimation of a democratic politics is not a luxury, but a necessary corollary of economic reform (1995: 23).

Who belongs to Europe?

By contrast, in the Turkish case, the undoubted attraction of joining the European Community and later the European Union has not been able to overcome the mass cultural and elite institutional blockages to a democratic breakthrough that would lead to democratic consolidation (Heper, 1991); rather, Turkish politics has remained in the hands of entrenched parties run by small cliques with weak ties to the populace, challenged now by Kurdish and Islamic movements whose leaders are also not credible supporters of democracy. Turkish 'democracy' includes systematic political interference by the military, repression of the Kurds, the savage treatment of independent labour activists, and close links between right-wing gangs and the security forces. The Human Rights Watch of the Helsinki Commission reported in 1997 that: 'While criminal suspects also face the prospect of torture and maltreatment at the hands of the regular police, Turkey's anti-terror police have become quite infamous because of their widespread use of sophisticated torture methods, which they constantly attempt to perfect to inflict pain without leaving the traces of their abuse' (CSCE, 1997: 2). Turkey remains an example of impressive economic growth combined with multi-party competition and a human rights record incompatible with political democracy.

Samuel Huntington regards Turkey as a classic 'torn country' (1996: 18), with strong internal pulls in different civilizational directions. Huntington's prediction of future civilizational clashes after the Cold War is of course controversial, since it posits an ongoing struggle between the West and the rest in terms of values and cultural traditions; he also has no analysis of the role of global capitalism in either dividing nations and regions or integrating them into a larger cooperative political and economic project like the EU. Yet he does raise the important issue of how elites and masses identify themselves, and how these cultural identities may hinder or facilitate an assimiliation into the Western community: 'First, its political and economic elite has to be generally supportive of and enthusiastic about this move. Second, its public has to be willing to acquiesce in the redefinition. Third, the dominant groups in the recipient civilization have to be willing to embrace the convert' (p. 21). Given the long history of Eastern Europe as the 'lands between', Huntington is asserting that Eastern Europe is not yet part of Western civilization, but must still prove itself an adequate convert, and must be accepted as such. The Catholic societies of Poland, Hungary and Slovakia, as well as the Catholic and Protestant Czech lands, are better suited in Huntington's view than the Eastern Orthodox societies of Romania, Bulgaria and, of course, Russia, but his point is that their civilizational conversion still remains to be completed. However, Huntington produces no empirical evidence on public or elite attitudes toward Western-style democracy and democratization.

It has often been argued that public attitudes must provide the foundation for a civic culture in which liberal democracy can operate and maintain itself (Almond and Verba, 1963). Key factors in public attitudes needed for a civic culture include trust in public institutions, a moderate willingness to participate in political activities as active citizens and, in particular, interpersonal trust, a healthy level of confidence in one's fellow citizens. Comparative empirical studies (Ester et al., 1997) of post-communist and Western societies in the early 1990s

TABLE 9.1 Confidence level in major institutions in post-communist Europe, Southern Europe and selected Western democracies, 1990–1991[a]

Country	Parliament	Unions	Press	Legal system
Czech Republic	37	24	32	44
Hungary	39	29	39	58
Poland	61	21	48	49
Slovakia	28	33	39	44
Romania	20	28	27	46
Bulgaria	48	31	35	45
Spain	43	40	51	45
Portugal	34	29	36	41
Italy	32	34	39	32
France	48	32	38	58
West Germany	51	36	34	65
Britain	46	26	14	54
United States	46	33	56	58

[a] Figures indicate percentage of respondents expressing 'a great deal' or 'quite a lot' of confidence in each institution.

Source: Adapted from Ester, Halman and Rukavishnikov, 1997: 91, 99

show some surprising variations in both East and West. With respect to public confidence in government and other major institutions (Table 9.1), the levels of confidence in parliament, in trade unions and in the press in the first years of post-communist democratization are not so different from levels existing in the Southern European nations of Spain and Portugal (or Italy), and in some cases are higher than levels in the more established democracies in West Germany, France, Britain or the United States. In the Western democracies public confidence in government institutions, unions and the media has declined in recent decades, but these admittedly broad (and therefore superficial) comparisons would still seem to indicate that the mass basis for a political culture supportive of a democratic politics existed in 1990–91 (with Slovaks and Romanians showing lesser levels, and Poles and Bulgarians showing generally higher levels of confidence among the post-communist nations). These figures may show that public attitudes are either not that determining or that there is great variation which is still compatible with democratization.

Another factor in public attitudes is willingness to engage in citizen protest, to take an active part in public affairs even in opposition to government policy. Table 9.2 shows the percentages of citizens who expressed willingness to engage in various political activities in 1990–91. Once again, nations of post-communist Eastern Europe and Russia show relatively high levels of citizen willingness to take part in political protest and citizen engagement, fairly similar in levels to the more recently democratized Spain and Portugal (and Italy in Southern Europe

TABLE 9.2 *Citizen willingness to engage in political protest in post-communist Europe, Southern Europe and selected Western democracies, 1990-1991*[a]

Country	Signing a petition	Joining in boycotts	Attending a legal demonstration	Joining an unofficial strike	Occupying a building
Czech Republic	32	30	42	32	17
Hungary	30	14	26	27	4
Poland	35	23	37	15	11
Slovakia	38	37	52	38	18
Moscow (1990)	47	41	51	31	14
Russia (1993)	60	32	37	23	8
Spain	40	25	40	18	17
Portugal	46	31	49	19	11
Italy	35	46	37	18	20
France	29	40	32	25	25
West Germany	31	37	42	19	10
Britain	17	34	35	19	10
United States	20	45	44	30	17

[a] Figures indicate percentage of respondents expressing a willingness to undertake each action.

Source: Adapted from Ester, Halman and Rukavishnikov, 1997: 67

as well), and above levels in some established democracies (Great Britain especially). Here too, it would appear that in the year of communist collapse, citizen mobilization for political participation had reached levels generally comparable to Southern European democracies. Of course, these comparisons are skewed by the proximity of the 1989–90 regime changes in Eastern Europe, and the relative lack of protest occasions in Southern Europe and the most established Western democracies; this difference-of-season was a weakness of the original Almond and Verba study, because a single snapshot comparison across many countries misses what each political culture is really capable of given the right circumstances.

The third factor, interpersonal trust, has been mentioned as a prerequisite for a civic culture able to support a stable liberal democracy going back to the original Almond and Verba studies of the late 1950s. This factor has been emphasized by scholars as different in views as conservative Edward Banfield (1958) and liberal Robert Putnam (1995a, 1995b).

Interpersonal trust creates a positive attitude towards the society one lives in and reflects a general set of shared cultural norms and values. Confidence in one's fellow-citizens is essential to the viability and effectiveness of democracy. A high level of interpersonal trust generates a high level of overall support for a representative democracy and for democratic rules and procedures, and vice versa (Huntington, 1984). Inglehart (1990) showed a

TABLE 9.3   *Popular support for greater equality, state-paternalism and personal responsibility in post-communist Europe, Southern Europe and selected Western democracies, 1990–1991*

| Country | Percentage agreeing with the statements: | | | |
	I	II	III	IV
Czech Republic	26	28	55	64
Hungary	33	58	26	57
Poland	13	45	33	81
Slovakia	28	49	36	58
Spain	44	45	33	31
Portugal	50	28	25	41
Italy	34	39	47	40
France	40	19	40	59
West Germany	27	22	52	60
Britain	22	33	58	42
United States	18	14	62	70

Statements:

I   Incomes should be made more equal.

II   The state should take more responsibility to ensure that everyone is provided for with a job and a good living.

III Individuals should take more responsibility for providing for themselves.

IV   There should be greater incentives for individual efforts.

Source: Adapted from Ester, Halman and Rukavishnikov, 1997: 84

strong correlation between personal trust and economic development and found trust levels in various European countries to be extremely stable over time. (Ester et al., 1997: 101)

Yet the findings of the European Values Systems surveys would seem to contradict some a priori expectations of lowest trust levels for post-communist Russia. Overall the level of interpersonal trust, based on affirmation of the proposition that 'most people can be trusted', shows wide variation for the Western democracies, with lowest levels of trust for France and Portugal, and high levels for the Scandinavian countries and Russia! The nations of East-Central Europe (Poland, Czech Republic, Hungary and Slovakia) are at similar levels with Spain, Portugal, Italy, France and Belgium, a pretty mixed bag of political histories; in general, however, there are some similarities between East-Central Europe and Southern Europe on this score. Ester, Halman and Rukavishnikov thus conclude that 'there is no mono-causal relationship between democratic experience and interpersonal trust as assumed by authors such as Inglehart. Short-term dramatic economic events do not seem to have affected personal trust' (p. 103). Here again it might be concluded that at least in broad outline the levels of interpersonal trust in East-Central Europe are not so different from those in Southern

Europe, and therefore would not disfavour democratization in that region. On the other hand, it is also possible that the level of inter-personal trust has been overrated as a critical variable.

There are other doubts about public and elite attitudes which pre-sumably are needed to provide consensus for democratization and marketization at the same time. Lipset (1993: 126–127) and Tamas (1993) argue that in Eastern Europe in the 1990s socialists have not yet fully accepted the free market and capitalist economics, liberal individualism is also much weaker than in all of Western Europe and the anti-communist nationalists also hate capitalism. To the extent that broad elite and public acceptance of capitalism, now in a much more global-ized stage of competition, and acceptance of free market economics generally is a prerequisite for democratic consolidation, they point to a more problematic scenario for the post-communist East and Central European nations, as compared to the earlier democratic transitions and consolidations in postwar Western and Southern Europe. Yet if we look at the general attitudes of the public toward the government role in the economy, toward levels of inequality, and toward individual respon-sibility for one's economic fortunes, once again the record is far more mixed between Eastern and Western Europe, with some broad simi-larities to Southern Europe. Results from the European Values Study show that, as might be expected, the support for free market capitalism is strongest in the United States and Britain (also Canada and the Scandinavian nations), but less pronounced in West Germany, France and Italy. The nations of East-Central Europe are quite varied, with Hungary closest to the Spanish pattern, and Poland and the Czech Republic closer to the British and United States patterns of response. Slovakia's response pattern is similar to that of Italy.

Spain as a success model

Among the successful Southern European democratizations, the Spanish case in retrospect possessed many favourable conditions for the demo-cratic transition. Yet Omar Encarnacion reminds us that, given Spain's history of social conflict and political violence, 'early assessments of the prospects for a peaceful and negotiated transition to democracy were filled with "bleak scenarios" and even "pessimism"' (1997: 389). Encar-nacion outlines the central role of the Spanish state in engineering a politics of 'social concertation' that overcame this past and shepherded the transition to a stable democracy and EU membership. This positive role for a strong state in the new democracy is at odds with the neo-liberal prescription that 'democratic politics and market principles will flourish, automatically, if intrusive states step aside and let the popular will and entrepreneurial zeal flourish' (p. 414). This positive view of state coordination, combining elite consensus, cross-class cooperation and positive-sum outcomes, is much closer to the continental European practice of democratic corporatism than to the Anglo-American model of democratic class conflict.

Richard Gunther (1992) calls the Spanish case a 'model of the modern elite settlement' for a democratic transformation; indeed, the Spanish democratization was undertaken under the most favourable of conditions, with respect to elite consensus and mass support under conditions of economic growth and social stability that must be considered unusual. Under the Franco regime, the Spanish economy grew at nearly 8 per cent per year between 1955 and 1975, benefiting from the general economic expansion in Western Europe. Leaders from various political parties, from communist and socialist left to conservative right, supported the entrance of Spain into the European Community, which would be possible only after a democratic regime had been established. The general consensus on this goal among the political elites facilitated a political pact for the transition, so that when Franco died on 20 November 1975, there was already a broad elite agreement on a smooth transition, including parts of the military. When, in 1981, Colonel Tejero and General Milans del Bosch attempted their ill-conceived putsch, they found that they were pretty much isolated from the officer corps; their arrest, trial and sentencing aroused neither military nor popular support for them. Felipe Agüero argues that NATO played a generally positive role in strengthening the democratic transition, although not in initiating it:

> Although the presence of NATO was generally beneficial for the purposes of accommodating the military during democratization, it certainly was not a panacea. It will be recalled that NATO had unquestioningly accommodated authoritarian Greece and Portugal, and the Secretary of State Alexander Haig, former NATO commander, had dismissed the 1981 coup attempt in Spain as merely 'an internal affair'. Nevertheless, in very specific ways for each of the three Southern European cases, NATO provided an opportunity for redirecting military missions to external professional concerns, and this certainly aided democratization. (1995: 161)

As a reward for its successful democratization, Spain was offered NATO membership, which it accepted in 1982 under the conservative government of Calvo Sotelo, and which was ratified, in modified form, in the 1986 referendum under the Socialist government of Felipe González.

Linz, Stepan and Gunther consider the Hungarian case to be the closest to any of the Southern European transitions, and especially close to the Spanish circumstances:

Only one of the other postcommunist transitions, Hungary's, resembled the Southern European (particularly the Spanish) patterns of regime change. While Hungary can be classified as having evolved from a posttotalitarian society, its detotalitarianization began earlier and reached a greater extent than has been the case in any of the other countries in the Soviet Union's 'outer empire'. Thus, the extent of pluralism and rule of law in Hungary came closer to Southern European levels than elsewhere in the Eastern bloc. Because of this, and because Hungary had a negotiated transition and lacked an acute stateness problem, it faced less severe obstacles on the path towards democratic consolidation than did any other Eastern bloc country. (1995: 117)

Hungary had also begun its own economic commercialization in the late 1960s, developing a growing trade between Budapest and Vienna. In terms of economic compatibility with the Western democracies, Hungary had also gone much further before 1989 than the other countries of the region. Hungary, like Spain, would seem to share a set of most favourable characteristics for democratic consolidation. However, Hungary does still have a potential 'stateness' problem in its relations with neighbouring states in which millions of Hungarians live as ethnic minorities, raising issues of mistreatment, discrimination and demands for autonomy for Hungarians within Romania and Slovakia.

Sequencing transitions

In summary, the regional experience of democratization in Southern Europe from the mid-1970s to the mid-1980s was blessed by a combination of several major factors. Internally, the old authoritarian regimes had exhausted their hold on power, and there was general consensus at both elite and mass levels on the desirability of regime change to a democratic political order. Some form of elite consensus or pact on the regime transition was possible and, especially in the Spanish case, had been carefully crafted in advance of Franco's long-expected demise. This elite consensus was made easier by the relative health of the economies of these nations, which, while much poorer than the EC nations, had experienced growth and had profited from the general economic prosperity of Western Europe.

The democratizations in Southern Europe could also concentrate, at least in the early years, on getting democratic institutions in place and establishing democratic party politics as the new norm. These nations, in general, could sequence the tasks of political, social and economic restructuring so as to not overload the new democratic regime. The more painful aspects of social and economic transformations could be spaced out in time, and buffered by a generally prospering European Community. The often-cited dilemma of simultaneity did not come into play for Southern Europe as it would in post-communism.

> Most analysts of post-Communist Europe, especially policy advocates, implicitly rejected a Spanish-like sequence as unfeasible because of their perceived need for *simultaneous* economic and political change. Indeed, despite frequent obeisance to this simultaneity imperative, domestic and foreign activists and advisors often *privileged* economic change first. (Linz and Stepan, 1996: 435)

Western advice and Western policy have given priority to economic compatibility with the West, neglecting the building of a strong democratic state. But for Linz and Stepan, it is democracy that will legitimize the market, not the other way around: 'Logic implies that a coherent regulatory environment and a rule of law is required to transform command economies into economic societies. If this is so, then a major priority must be to create democratic regulatory state power' (1996: 435).

Another factor in regional experiences of democratization has been the international environment, and especially the influence of neighbouring countries. The democratic transformations in Southern Europe could depend on external discipline from the European Community, which offered strict conditionality for the possibility of membership – only consolidated and relatively stable democracies need apply. Gunther, Puhle and Diamandouros conclude that the international environment created by the European Community played a strong though indirect role in aiding democratic transition and consolidation in Southern Europe. Eastern Europe, in this view, should also benefit from its proximity to the European Union in the 1990s.

> The strong support for democracy exhibited by such organizations as the European Community and the Council of Europe reinforced new democratic institutions and behavioural norms in each of these countries. The positive, though indirect, impact of the regional international factor on democratization in Southern Europe stands in contrast to the ambivalent and oscillating historical record of the United States with respect to democratization in Latin America. (1995: 409–410)

The Southern European experience marks the beginning of the most recent 'wave' of democratizations, and it took place under the most favourable of circumstances, which is not to say that the outcomes were inevitable or without any conflict. But this was the period of high Keynesianism, of outstanding success for the European Community as a model and as a functioning body for supporting and disciplining the democratization processes in Spain, Portugal and Greece. The European Union of the 1990s is itself now exiting, in fits and starts, that Keynesian model. At the same time that it offers a positive attraction for the nations of East-Central Europe, the EU is trying to find a new politics to deal with already high and rising unemployment. Its budgets are under great pressure; the role of Germany as the financier of expansion and deepening is much weakened (Walker, 1995), and this will mean less generous structural adjustment aid to new prospective members from East-Central Europe, who arguably need it even more than the Southern European nations. After the first years of economic contraction, observers were overjoyed with the return to growth in Poland and the Czech Republic (less clear in Hungary). And yet, with the downturn in the Czech economy in 1997, it is clear that the economic transformation, which Václav Klaus pronounced as already completed in 1995, will take much longer and will involve successive stages of painful reform effort. The chance of a 'soft landing' for the democratization process in this serial economic transformation is less likely.

Still, the democratic requirement for entry into the EU remains a strong positive factor for East-Central Europe. As long as EU membership is still held to be a top priority for the new governing elites and for a broad majority of the public, this provides clear limitations on anti-democratic practices and abuses of citizen rights.

10

Structuring Executive Power in Emerging Democracies: Warnings from Latin America

In the democratizations in Latin America and in post-communist Europe, there are two key aspects worthy of theoretical comparison. First is the marketization and privatization of statist economies under International Monetary Fund (IMF) guidance and discipline, which addresses the question of what type of political economies will emerge as correlates of the democratization. Second is the institutional question of presidential domination, which relates to the need both for effective government and for democratic checks and balances. These two key issues are linked, so that the degree of social polarization in the emerging political economy becomes a critical factor for the structuring of executive power.

The role of IMF liberalization

Perhaps the most important area of similarities between democratization in Latin America and East-Central Europe has been the IMF-guided liberalization of debt-ridden and statist economies in both regions. Both regions had experienced an earlier period of state-directed growth, followed by stagnation and inability of the state to continue its financing of growth. In both regions, many nations (Brazil, Argentina, Mexico, Poland, Hungary) had fallen into the debt trap (Payer, 1976), and had to submit their national monetary and fiscal policies to review and approval by the IMF. In order to raise new capital and avoid default, the new democratic (or not fully democratic, i.e. Mexico) governments engaged in successive rounds of economic marketization and privatization which sold off state-owned enterprises and drastically curtailed social spending (education, health care, public transport, subsidies for consumer basics). The politics of IMF liberalization have hurt the poor and working class and have helped both new foreign capital and newly enriched members of the old party-state nomenklatura. Privatization in Brazil and Mexico, carried out by reform presidents Fernando Collor de Mello and Carlos Salinas de Gortari, enabled those within the old party-state power networks to suddenly expand their considerable wealth. Privatization in post-communist Europe, carried out by both non-communist and ex-communist governments, has enabled those within the old party-state nomenklatura to acquire great private wealth for the first time.

In both regions, the IMF liberalizations are producing greater social inequalities and damaging chances for those at the bottom to develop the human capital or human skills most needed for accessing the opportunities of the newly marketized economies. This IMF economic liberalization is very different from the economic environment which accompanied democratization in southern Europe, or which accompanies the more gradual democratization in East Asia. It requires more social pain and dislocation, while at the same time benefiting those already in privileged positions within the former networks of power and influence. But in both Latin America and post-communist Eastern Europe, the debt situation and the shortfall in domestic capital has produced much higher levels of external discipline, a political course of greater social inequality and sudden new wealth for those with good political connections to the privatization processes.

In Latin America, of course, levels of inequality were already very high under the old regimes; in East-Central Europe, the new inequalities are much more of a shock to socialist value cultures, but in both cases, the new liberalized and privatized economies are characterized by great inequality and by very unequal opportunity structures. This raises questions about the long-term stability of the new democracies, since for some (Dahl), great social polarization is inimical to peaceful political competition and political consensus-building. For the moment, in both regions, the political voice of labour, of the working class, has been lost, but over the longer run extreme class polarization will produce political challenge; will that challenge be contained within the framework of democratic institutions, or will it prevent consolidation of democratic institutions (Nagle, 1997a; Ost, 1995)? In Latin America, the growth of new working class parties, the Workers Party (PT) of Ignacio da Silva ('Lula') in Brazil (Sader and Silverstein, 1991), and the Party of Democratic Revolution (PRD) of Cuauhtemoc Cardenas in Mexico, are signs of working class challenge to the great inequalities of the liberalized economy. In East-Central Europe, the ex-communist successor parties (Hungarian Socialists, Poland's Democratic Left Alliance) are just as obedient to IMF guidelines as their centre-right opponents. In fact, the most anti-IMF voices come from the far right, from the Independent Smallholders Party in Hungary, the Republicans in the Czech Republic, and the Movement for Polish Renewal and segments of the Solidarity Electoral Alliance (AWS) in Poland. It may well be that the first major anti-IMF and anti-liberalization challenges will come from the national-populist right, rather than a reconstituted left (Tamas, 1993).

Paul Cammack, a Marxist critic of the mainstream view which sees capitalist marketization and political democratization as unproblematically reinforcing, argues that this ignores the basically contingent nature of political democracy in a capitalist economic order, and in particular overlooks the great differences between democracy in the core capitalist powers, which was itself very hard to establish and still requires constant maintenance, and democratic instability in the peripheral capitalist nations, where the internal contradictions between capitalist economy and political democracy are immense, and in this view unbridgeable. Cammack uses Adam Przeworski's thesis of a rational acceptance of capitalism by workers in Europe, because democratic capitalism proved capable of providing material gains for workers. In these circumstances, European core capitalist nations did 'prove to have the material and institutional resources to move, in Gramscian terms, from domination to hegemony' (1994: 187–188).

But in Latin America, Cammack argues, peripheral capitalism does not have the resources to provide steady material gains to the great majority, cannot bring the great majority of workers into the political mainstream, and therefore is structurally stuck with a political system of either unstable democracy or stable dictatorship, as Seymour Martin Lipset (1959a) once pointed out.

> One significant conclusion to be drawn from the preceding discussion is that in Latin America democracy and citizenship have been contradictory rather than complementary categories. . . . For it is not just that democracy has functioned despite relatively low levels of participation and associational activity; rather, it has required them, and has broken down – as in Brazil in 1964 and in Chile in 1973 – whenever the assertion of citizenship has looked likely to breach imposed limits. The structural weakness of peripheral capitalism and the associated weakness of locally dominant classes have combined to produce the poor record of democratic achievement in the region. The contradiction between democracy and citizenship is a structural effect of peripheral capitalist development at a specific historical moment. (Cammack, 1994: 186)

Other scholars, from different perspectives, are also cautious about the recent democratizations in Latin America. Burton, Gunther and

Higley (1992) note that the great and growing work on political elites as central to both democratic breakdowns and democratic transitions and consolidations has not been able to develop any 'coherent theoretical model' (1992: 342). James Malloy, writing before the democratic trend had reached its highwater mark, sounded the caution that 'there are no readily identifiable structural parameters that allow us to project – let alone predict – the outcomes' of these democratization attempts (1987: 251). In fact, he adds that 'one possibility – in fact a probability – is that the basic cyclical swing between authoritarian and democratic modes will continue. Perhaps the region is trapped' (p. 256). Twenty years after the democracy trend first emerged in Latin America, Howard Wiarda and Francis Kline (1996) stress the failings and lack of consolidation of fully democratic politics ('chaos and regression' in Brazil, 'enduring authoritarian legacy' in Peru, 'precarious progress' in Paraguay, 'fragility of dependent democracy' in Ecuador, 'preserving a fragile democracy' in the Dominican Republic). In their conclusion, Wiarda and Kline express both optimism that this round of democratization is indeed stronger, and the disappointment that nothing has been consolidated, because the most basic questions are still open:

> Among the most important questions remaining to be answered are whether Latin America can succeed in consolidating and institutionalizing its democracies, whether it can combine economic growth with equity and social justice, and whether it can reconcile its new-found democratic precepts with its own history and traditions (organist, corporatist, patrimonialist). (1996: 536)

The leading Mexican scholar Jorge Castañeda has summarized the basic requirements for democracy in Latin America according to what he claims are the common-sense expectations of most people:

> electoral competition for power, with free choice, fairness, and at least a moderately level playing field. In addition, representative democracy involves the prevalence of the rule of law and relatively independent judiciary and legislative branches of government; respect for human rights by at least Latin American standards (i.e. that the central government not wantonly torture people or permit others to do so); and the upholding of basic freedoms of the press, association, demonstration, and organization, including free labor unions, collective bargaining, and the right to strike. (1994: 327)

By this standard, which goes beyond the minimalist Schumpeter definition, most of the Latin American systems fall short of full democracy. What is bothersome to many observers is that since the beginning of the latest democracy wave in Latin America in the latter 1970s, little further progress in democratization has been made. Larry Diamond notes the stagnant quality of democratization in the region: 'And since 1987, despite commonplace North American perceptions to the contrary, Latin America has not made significant net progress toward greater democracy. Rather, while the level of democracy has improved in some countries (and in some aspects in a number of countries), it has generally declined in the region' (1996: 61).

Castañeda sees an impasse for democratization created by the IMF-dictated economic reforms, which have restored growth but at the price of greater inequality in a region with already great social polarization. In his view, the further development of democracy is blocked by the lack of social equity in current economic policies, which further polarizes society and alienates the poor. While democracy itself should allow for popular demands for economic justice to be voiced, these demands must be ignored or suppressed in order to pursue growth according to liberal doctrine: '. . . a necessary condition for equity in Latin America appears to be democratic rule, but democracy seems incompatible with growth under actually existing circumstances' (1994: 398).

The new neo-liberal political economies of Latin America have not transcended their peripheral and dependent status in the global economic order, they do not provide social justice and income equity for their peoples, and the result is a blocked development of a stable elite and mass consensus on a democratic politics. This reflection on the doubtful status of democratization in Latin America provides a basis for comparison with post-communist Europe.

The question which this line of thinking raises for East-Central Europe is obvious: will that region, in its marketization and privatization, become part of the capitalist periphery, or part of the capitalist core? To the extent that the emerging political economy of Poland, the Czech Republic and Hungary can bridge the gap with other European Union nations (as Ireland has done), it may be able to offer broad material gains that would solidify a mass-based consensus on political democracy, that is, democratic consolidation and stability. However, to the extent that these nations remain, as they are at the moment, on the periphery of the capitalist core, the dilemma of achieving mass consent for a system of great inequality and scant material gains for the majority may block the democratization process, and lead to bouts of instability and retreat from democratic norms. This possibility of a 'Latin Americanization' of post-communist politics is much more visible in Russia, Ukraine or Romania, or other republics further to the east and south, where the struggle for power in an economy that does not provide even basics for large portions of the population, drives politics beyond democratic practices.

In this respect Poland, the Czech Republic and Hungary are better placed, and their economies had returned by the mid-1990s to modest (not yet 'miraculous') growth; yet the levels of inequality are rising, indicating new levels of social polarization which, if these harden into class divisions, may reproduce the basic failures of peripheral capitalism. Data from the first several years of economic marketization in Poland,

TABLE 10.1   *Some estimates of income inequality in post-communist Europe and Western democracies*

Country	Year	Gini ratio	Year	Gini ratio
Czech Republic	1992	.189	1993*	.266
Slovak Republic	1992	.208		
Hungary	1991	.289	1993*	.270
Poland	1992	.291		
Russia	1992	.437	1993*	.496
West Germany	1984	.250		
Great Britain	1986	.304		
France	1984	.296		
Sweden	1992	.229		
Spain	1990	.308		
United States	1991	.343		

Sources: Luxembourg Income Study (cited in Torrey, Smeeding, and Bailey, 1996);
* World Development Indicators 1997 (Washington, DC: World Bank, 1997)

Hungary and the Czech Republic show rising inequality in income distribution, but only to levels comparable to other nations in the European Union and lower than in the United States (Table 10.1). (The greater the Gini coefficient, which varies between zero and one according to the deviation from perfect equality, the greater the degree of inequality.)

This still-moderate inequality is apparently due to the widespread ability of families to use several legacies from the communist period in new efforts to bolster their incomes (Torrey et al., 1996). In particular, the 'second' economies which existed under communism did not disappear, but became the basis for larger and more extensive informal economies during the early marketization years; the extended familial networks of the communist era continued to function to redistribute resources to minimize economic poverty; and, importantly, in East-Central Europe, the social safety net of the former communist system did not totally collapse, but continued to provide some protection, especially for pensioners in Poland and the Czech Republic. However, certain groups in the population, especially the unemployed, those with low education and female-headed households, are most vulnerable to the new poverty (Szulc, 1996). Pension support levels, which have moderated the overall rise in inequality in East-Central Europe, may not be sustainable for much longer, yet the rise in inequality has not been nearly as marked as in Russia.

In broader regional comparison, the levels of income inequality in Eastern Europe as a whole are still well below the levels of Latin America and other regions in the developing world (Table 10.2). The very low levels of income inequality of the 1960s, 1970s and 1980s are now giving way to significant rises; the larger question is where the rise in inequality will level off. Will capitalism in East-Central Europe look like Western or Southern Europe, with moderate levels of inequality within an affluent

TABLE 10.2   *Trends in inequality by region, 1960s–1990s*

Region		Gini coefficients		
	1960s	1970s	1980s	1990s
Latin America and Caribbean	.53	.49	.50	.49
Sub-Saharan Africa	.50	.48	.43	.47
Middle East and North Africa	.41	.42	.40	.38
East Asia and Pacific	.36	.34	.35	.32
Industrial countries and high-income				
developing countries	.35	.35	.33	.34
Eastern Europe	.25	.25	.25	.29

Source: adapted from Deininger and Squire, 1996: 584

aggregate, or will it look like Latin America, with very high levels of inequality amidst a considerably less affluent aggregate?

The shape of the emerging political economy in Poland, Hungary and the Czech Republic is still at an early stage, and shows some points of comparability to the liberalization politics of Latin America in recent years, as noted above: dependence on the IMF, the debt trap, a corrupted politics of privatization and the exit from statist and protectionist economic policies to export-oriented and open economies are broad commonalities. It may well be that this classic 'Latin American condition' (Wynia, 1990) will hold important lessons for post-communist Europe. Mexican dictator Profirio Diaz once described the Mexican version of this condition as 'so far from heaven yet so close to the United States'; the frustration of failed modernization in close proximity to the strong and prosperous neighbour, whose model is appealing and yet dominating at the same time.

There are very significant differences between the two regions: the traditions of an organized working class, the re-entry of post-communist left parties, and stronger sponsorship of democratic standards by the EU, may give rise to new syntheses. Even if East-Central Europe becomes a new capitalist periphery, it may still fare better from its political geography as the European Union's 'near abroad' than Latin America as the peripheral backyard of the United States.

Presidentialism and democratization

One of the great issues of Latin American democratization has been the power of the president, including a competitively elected chief executive, relative to the other institutions of government – the legislature, the courts, and state and local authorities. Most Latin American republics, in their earliest years of independence from Spain in the 1810–1830 period (Brazil's longer period of separation from Portugal was rather different),

TABLE 10.3 *Attitudinal support for democracy in Poland compared with Latin American and Southern European nations, 1992*

	Percentage of respondents supporting:			
	Democracy is preferable to any other form	Democratic and non-democratic are the same	Non-democratic could be preferable	don't know
Poland	31	40	13	16
Brazil	42	24	22	12
Uruguay	73	8	10	9
Spain	70	9	10	11
Portugal	61	7	9	23
Greece	87	6	5	2

Source: adapted from Linz and Stepan, 1996: 286

adopted a constitutional order which closely mirrored the American Constitution. These US-patterned constitutions prescribed a federal system, an elected President, an independently elected Congress, and an independent judiciary. This early democratic federalism was testimony to the impact of liberal thinking within at least one part of the political class in Latin America, which took the United States (another new nation of the times) as a role model for a modern nation-state (Wiarda and Kline, 1996: Part I). Yet, the realities of practical politics in Latin America have been quite different from the formal constitutional principles. Most notably, the office of President has dominated the politics of most Latin American nations, regardless of whether the President came to power through free and fair elections or through force of arms. The power of the incumbent President has given even formally democratic regimes an authoritarian character, sometimes benevolent and reformist (Peron in his early years), sometimes malevolent and extraordinarily corrupt (Peron in his later years), sometimes both at the same time. In even the best of cases, effective checks and balances, from other institutions or from the general public, which is part and parcel of a stable democracy, were sorely lacking. Hernando de Soto and Deborah Orsini have argued that, 'the only element of democracy in Peru today is the electoral process, which gives Peruvians the privilege of choosing a dictator every five years' (quoted in Wiarda and Kline, 1996: 59). They could have been speaking of most Latin American countries. Even today, in this most recent of Latin America's waves of democratization, which is probably stronger than earlier ones, there are traditional methods for presidents to act as autocrats, whether through 'state of siege' or 'state of emergency' declarations, with the President dependent only on the good will of the military to back even more concentration of power.

For many years scholars have debated the role of 'presidentialismo' in the struggle for a democratic politics, and the debate is far from over

(Lijphart, 1992; Steffani, 1979). Juan Linz, a leading scholar of Latin America, for many years believed that presidential power could be democratized in a stable fashion in Latin America (to fulfil Maurice Duverger's concept of a democratic semi-presidentialism); but this notion rested on the unclear concept of 'semi-presidentialism', while the accumulation of power in the hands of even recently and democratically elected presidents has remained for Linz problematic. He has therefore abandoned this earlier standpoint, and has become a chief advocate for more radical system reform in the direction of a clear parliamentary system, such as that in Britain or newly democratic Spain, with their constitutional monarchies, or even the chancellor system found in Germany (Linz and Valenzuela, 1994; Steffani, 1996: 32).

On the other hand, there are some scholars, like Dieter Nohlen at Heidelberg University, who see the presidential tradition in the region as too strongly anchored to abandon. While supporting the goal of democratic consolidation, Nohlen suggests working within the long-established and historical tradition of presidentialism to reform the institution within its current framework (Nohlen, 1992). While Linz sees an institutional change to a more parliamentary system as plausible and necessary, Nohlen judges the chances for realistic reform to be within the boundaries of the existing presidential framework and therefore in greater historical continuity with the past. Donald Horowitz has argued that Linz's concept of presidentialism is itself flawed, that presidential systems vary and can be improved; furthermore, Horowitz argues that authoritarian outcomes can also come from Westminster parliamentary models, citing the unhappy experience of sub-Saharan Africa and especially Nigeria after independence (1992: 206). Lipset (1992) also cites the broader positive experience of presidentialism in the French Fifth Republic, pre-1970 Chile, pre-1970s Uruguay and Costa Rica. In Lipset's view, there exists a variety of cultural and developmental pre-conditions which may be supportive of democracy, and it is unwise to put too much emphasis on the independent role of political institutions. Yet precisely along these lines, Fred Riggs (1992) argues that for the Latin Catholic cultures, presidentialism cannot replicate the United States experience, and has proven itself to be part of the problem, not part of the solution. Presidentialism may be appropriate for democracy in some cultural contexts but for Latin America, it has been problematic.

Steffani sees this argument as being carried over into the new institutional conflicts in post-communist Eastern Europe, with many of the same arguments about presidential versus parliamentary power in those new democracies. In this sense especially, the Latin American experience may have some comparative relevance to the cases of post-communism generally.

Elected civilian presidents have become the norm since the early 1980s. And yet, many of the new 'reform' presidents have continued the tradition of 'presidentialismo' even while they were carrying out needed economic and financial restructuring programs. President Alberto Fujimori of Peru staged his so-called *autogolpe* (self-coup) in 1992, with the backing of the military, to break what he perceived to be the gridlock of power between himself and the Congress and courts, in order to take effective action against guerrillas and drug cartels. While mildly denounced by the Western democracies, Fujimori's coup was popular in Peru, and he was overwhelmingly re-elected to office. Other economic liberalizers, presidents Carlos Menem of Argentina and Fernando Henrique Cardoso of Brazil, have manipulated the constitutions to allow for second consecutive terms for themselves. These are all signs of a still-strong presidentialismo which is antithetical to a more balanced division of political power needed for a consolidated democratic politics.

The Peruvian case is particularly instructive, since the new 'Fuji-populism' (Kay, 1996) associates neo-liberal economic reform not with decentralization of power but with increasing presidential monopoly of power in an era of a generally weakened state authority. Bruce Kay describes this phenomenon as 'a technocratic populism centered on the Olympian presidency of Alberto Fujimori, financed by the spoils of economic liberalism' (1996: 2). Kay further concludes that in the neo-liberal age, this type of populism may be an electoral necessity for an incumbent president, who needs to have control over distribution of the benefits of growth during a period of painful economic adjustment, if he wants to survive politically. This neo-liberal populism with its presidential authoritarianism is a survival mechanism, though it comes at the expense of democratic institutions and civil society. This new breed of Latin American presidentialism cannot lead to consolidated democracy, since it destroys the essence of democratic politics, a competitive pluralism capable of constraining government power through peaceful means. The new reform-populist presidentialismo may utilize the procedures of polyarchy, but in practice it reinforces the concentration of executive power. This conception not only runs counter to liberal theory, which associates liberal economic reform with democratization and democratic consolidation, but rather uncovers a new reformist rationale for a modernized authoritarian executive. The relevance of these basic features to much of post-communist Europe is obvious; given the simultaneity of economic and political transformation, there is a new and compelling logic for presidential attempts to dominate parliament, the courts and local institutions, a logic based not on democratic norms but on political survival.

There are, however, some challenges to presidentialismo in the recent democracy wave; in a few important cases, congress and the courts have been able to remove an elected president from office for cause. In Brazil, President Fernando Collor de Mello, an economic liberalizer, was brought to the point of impeachment for financial corruption in 1992, and was forced to resign his office. This unusual display of the potential oversight of the presidency by congress, and the ability to remove a president for malfeasance, was however of limited value, since the congress itself was held in low public esteem for corruption. Although it was a victory for Brazilian democracy that a corrupt president was peacefully and constitutionally removed, Brazilians voted the following year to continue a strong presidential form of government over the parliamentary or monarchical models. In Mexico, the emergence of a real multi-party system, with the Party of Revolutionary Institutions (PRI), which has ruled since 1929, is now challenged by the conservative Party of National Action (PAN) and the left-populist Party of the Democratic Revolution (PRD). For the first time in the congressional elections of 1997, the PRI lost its majority in the lower house of Congress, the Chamber of Deputies. An unstable left–right coalition of PAN and PRD deputies has begun to challenge the power of President Ernesto Zedillo from the PRI.

One legacy of presidentialismo in Latin America has been the atrophy and corruption in the development of other government institutions. While there have been recent signs of legislatures uniting to oppose a particular president, there is still little sign of a general development of a strong and stable party system, or the emergence of an effective legislative branch. The same Brazilian Congress which ousted the corrupt liberal reformer Collor de Mello has a well-deserved terrible reputation for ineffectiveness and corruption among its members. The Brazilian party system is weak, unstable and fragmented, unable to provide strong links between the national Congress and social constituencies. More than 40 per cent of all deputies have switched their party allegiance since the last elections; many have switched party for pay-offs, as the result of personality clashes within the party leadership, or simply to take on a new and temporary image needed for re-election. Latin American specialist Riordan Roett states that 'Until Congress is able to develop a clear sense of national interest, lasting social change will be difficult to achieve' (Dyer, 1997). The atrophy or marginalization of parliaments and courts is both a result of executive concentration of power, and reinforces that concentration through the continued absence of an effective alternative institution. This debate over the power of the president is very important for post-communist political development, since in many nations of post-communist Europe the elected president has battled with the elected parliament for political dominance. The rise of presidents can also be connected to an emerging pattern of weak parties and the corruption of parliamentary behaviour. The Russian Duma, the parliaments in Ukraine and Belarus, and in the Balkans and Caucasus regions, may oppose presidential rule on given occasions, but they hardly represent credible alternatives for governing, or for legitimizing democratic rule. Party systems in those post-communist regimes with strong presidential power are still weak, amorphous and opaque, giving voters little confidence and only blurry choices. Presidents know this, and are perfectly

capable of furthering corruption and instability within parliamentary
bodies for their own ends.

The debate over presidentialism rests on a basic judgement of
whether national character or traditional attitudes toward authority,
which in the past have favoured a single top leader, be he president or
party secretary, have already changed, or at least are capable of basic
change as a result of democratization efforts. Glen Dealy has argued
that Latin American political culture is traditionally corporatist and
monist, not liberal and pluralist, and that nothing has yet happened to
change that basic popular mindset: 'In Latin American minds the vision
of freely competing factions all too often seems a choice between chaos
and privilege. Latin Americans maintain that union comes from unity,
not from diversity – *Ex unibus unum*, not *E pluribus unum*, has been and
still is their motto' (1992: 281–282). The United States cannot simply
overlay its notion of liberal, pluralist, tolerant democracy in this region,
either by forceful intervention or by financial bribery; such attempts (as
in Central America in the 1980s) do not promote democracy, but
perpetuate existing elite domination.

> While the United States attempts to foster pluralistic democracy in Central
> America, in reality it is perpetuating one faction, endorsing rigged elec-
> tions, bribing the armed forces with materiel, and tacitly favoring exile or
> elimination of the opposition. America unwittingly advances state central-
> ism. But the center can no longer hold because it excludes the interests of
> the campesinos [peasants], a majority on the move. (Dealy, 1992: 286)

Peter Smith, however, disagrees that Latin American culture contains
no support for the concept of liberal democracy: 'Some ideas, I think,
extend all the way back to the pre-Enlightenment formulations of
Francisco Suarez and other Hispanic thinkers, and it is precisely this
historical persistence of democratic thinking that sets Latin America
apart. It is the only region in the Third World where the idea of democracy has stood in permanent opposition to the doctrines of authoritarianism' (1992: 303). Interestingly, Smith connects this issue over the
concept of democracy immediately with the issue of presidentialism
versus parliamentarism – which he argues has never really been tried in
Latin America. Smith argues that the current democratization may
recreate linkages to European (parliamentary) democracy and to European democratic political currents such as Christian Democracy and the
Socialist International (p. 310); his hope is that the influence of the United
States, which Smith sees as more harmful than useful, may decline with
the current democratization, and open paths to real transformations of
political culture in the region. The examples of democratization and
democratic consolidation in Portugal and Spain are of great importance
here as new role models and new European influences. The re-
Europeanization of politics in Latin America would mean some conflict

with the United States, but that might be the only way to break the authoritarian traditions of presidentialismo and consolidate a fully democratic system.

> If Latin nations succeed in creating full-blown democracies – with competition, participation, and accountability – the long-term likelihood of conflict becomes a near-certainty, for this would entail the enfranchisement of the political Left, not just the Center and the Right. In this sense democratization, fragmentary and pragmatic, might be acceptable to the United States; democracy, inclusive and ideological, might appear dangerous to traditional interpretations of U.S. national interests. (Smith, 1992: 311)

A fully consolidated democracy in the European sense, with strong elements of christian democratic and social democratic politics, would be seen as non-threatening only if the United States would redefine its own national interests; as long as a politics of social justice and equity is seen as threatening US economic interests, the United States cannot be a good mentor for democratization in the region.

In the most recent wave of democratization in Latin America, military regimes have virtually disappeared, and nominal civilian control over the military has been re-established. Yet this return to elected civilian regimes has been incomplete in virtually every country, because in the process of handing over control to a civilian successor, exiting military elites were able to extract concessions which maintained certain privileges for the military leadership. The military has often carved out protected areas of anti-democratic military sovereignty for itself, first and foremost being immunity from prosecution for past crimes. Special control over military budget policy, control over certain regions of the country and specially reserved positions in the legislature or government have often been extorted in the transition to civilian rule. Stephen Fidler has noted the continued military interests in the economies of the military–industrial complex, which has often expanded in partnership with local or foreign capital. In Ecuador, perhaps an extreme case, after the handover of power to civilian politicians in 1979, the military has expanded its investments to include 'mining, vehicle manufacturing, a commercial airline, farming and even the luxury Marriott hotel being built in Quito' (1997).

While most military regimes retreated from power in the 1980s with less than shining reputations, the Pinochet regime in Chile withdrew from power after forcefully restructuring the Chilean economy and social welfare system to build a more competitive export-oriented future. The social cost was high, and the transformation was undemocratic, but Chile's economy experienced impressive growth, and the 'Chilean model' became a success story for free market reforms. General Augusto Pinochet, one of the last dictators to leave the presidential palaces, embodied this model in the tradition of authoritarian 'presidentialismo'.

His programme of economic restructuring for Chile, under the guidance of US economic advisers (the so-called 'Chicago boys'), has been admired by many would-be reformers in post-communist Europe, who look to a strong top leader to push through difficult changes decisively and quickly; democracy, in this view, can come later, once the free market economy has started to function effectively. However, military dictators as presidents are currently 'politically incorrect'. It seems unlikely at this point that an explicitly military model of reform from above has much prospect for realization.

Stunted democratization

The forceful introduction of neo-liberal economic reform under international discipline into debt-ridden and statist societies in Latin America bears some resemblance to the experience of post-communist Europe. The most recent Latin American experience with democratization illustrates the sad possibility that an initial electoralist democratic breakthrough may fail to advance, to deepen and to consolidate itself over a long period of time. This has raised new criticisms about the quality of democratization in that region, and this issue may well emerge in the post-communist democracies of Europe as well (cf. Bartlett and Hunter, 1997).

Tied to the new political economies has been the struggle over presidential power, over the concentration of power in one office. Will East-Central Europe, these 'lands between,' be drawn fully into the Western European pattern of parliamentary democracy, toward the more authoritarian presidentialism of Russia, Ukraine, Croatia, Armenia and Belarus, or will they evolve a unique mixed system? While the Czech and Hungarian democratizations seem clearly on a parliamentary path, the Polish transition may still be open to shifts towards a more presidentialist system.

11

Economics First, Then (Maybe) Politics: the Challenge of the East Asian Model

The East Asian experience – what basis for comparison?

On first considerations, the experiences of East and Southeast Asia might seem to have little relevance for comparison with post-communist Europe. Their cultural background, their more recent independence as nation-states, and their very different economic trajectory and current status within the global economic order would seem to be worlds away from the situation that confronts democratization efforts in post-communist Europe, and especially in East-Central Europe. Comparison, of course, also benefits from dissimilar cases, but there may also be some relevant points which do connect the two regions.

In particular, some East Asian nations experienced very thorough authoritarian dictatorships for long periods of forced industrialization heavily managed by a comprehensive state or party-state bureaucracy and enforced by a military and secret police apparatus; in some periods of this process, the ruling regimes easily approached the levels of internal control and intimidation of dissidents found in post-Stalinist communist Europe. In the case of South Korea, under the eighteen-year dictatorship of Park Chung Hee, and especially in the post-1972 Yushun period, regime terror against opponents reached startling levels, including the kidnapping in Japan of regime opponent Kim Dae Jung and his incarceration until the assassination of President Park in 1979 by the head of his secret police, the KCIA. Faced with the threat from the Stalinist regime of Kim Il Sung in North Korea, the South Korean regimes practised their own brand of Cold War paranoia against all enemies, real, imagined, or artificially constructed. The South Korean laws against subversion were (to some extent are still, as of this writing) intentionally broad enough to intimidate any substantial social, religious, or political opposition, which could immediately be charged as aiding North Korea and endangering national security.

Korean military dictatorships were tolerated and given continued support by the United States under the double standards of the Cold War. Minxin Pei (1995: 115) lists the United States support for authoritarian dictatorships as one of the reasons that democratization has lagged behind economic reform, or even failed to appear. No major power provided external pressure for democratization.

The Taiwanese Nationalist regime of President Chiang Kai-shek was also a brutal dictatorship, ruling under martial law for over forty years. Just before the arrival of the exile Nationalist elite (constituting the Republic of China) in Taiwan in 1949, Chiang's armies had carried out a horrible massacre of native Taiwanese in 1948, in which thousands of people were butchered; the details of this massacre are just now beginning to come to light, but were long hidden from international view, and though known to Western governments, also were overlooked as part of the Cold War double standard. In its origins, the Nationalist Party was semi-Leninist in its organization and discipline, and thoroughly anti-democratic in its attitude toward opponents. Chiang's son had been trained in the Soviet Union, and while Chiang came to oppose communism, he utilized Leninist forms of party organization. The Taiwan regime was thus an anti-communist party-state dictatorship, complete with its secret police informer system and extensive censorship and social controls.

Minxin Pei, a scholar at the conservative Hoover Institute in the United States, even regards communist China and Vietnam as further examples of what he calls the neo-autocracy path (which again stresses the priority of economic reform over democracy), in the same general category as the regimes of Park Chung Hee of South Korea (1961–79), Chiang Kai-shek and his successor and son Chiang Chingkuo of Taiwan (1949–88), Suharto of Indonesia (1964–98), Datuk Seri Mahathir of Malaysia (1981–), and Lee Kuan Yew of Singapore (1960–91).

In short, the transition from authoritarianism in parts of East Asia has been from draconian regimes, which at their height exhibited some features characteristic of (post-Stalinist) communist systems, in the thoroughness of suppression of personal liberty and political dissent. Only with economic modernization well under way in East Asia, did the level of repression gradually decline between 1972 and 1992 (Haggard, 1994: 102–103).

Secondly, these East Asian dictatorships pursued a forced developmentalism which, though quite different from the forced industrialization of Soviet-style central planning, was also clearly a top regime priority and a characteristic feature of these regimes. These were quite different authoritarianisms from Franco Spain, or the Salazar–Caetano regime in Portugal, or the Colonels' junta in Greece. This Asian developmentalism (Amsden, 1989) has proved to be more viable than Soviet industrialism, but it was centrally state-driven and it also enforced a coercive break with the traditional economy and lifestyles of the population. Alice Amsden has shown that South Korean developmentalism was far removed from any Adam Smith or Thatcherite free market model; the strong state inspired, managed, financed and transitioned the Korean economy into the dynamic world trading power it has become. It controlled prices and markets, repressed labour, steered scientific research and development, and targeted winners and losers among economic sectors and corporations (the giant industrial conglomerates or *chaebol* were initially put together with state guidance). There was a messianic purposefulness in these dictatorial developmentalist regimes that was generally missing in Latin America and Southern Europe.

Therefore, to a greater degree than one would expect in Southern Europe and Latin America, the transitions from authoritarian dictatorship in South Korea, Taiwan and Singapore have involved overcoming a regime type which was much more comprehensive in its goals and methods of transforming society, and which forced through an industrialization revolution from above in a historically short timespan, uprooting traditional and village life, in order to 'catch up' to modern Western industrial society. The ideologies of Asian developmentalism were certainly not Marxist–Leninist, but they were a reaction to the experiences of backwardness and weakness which had put their societies into dependent positions in the past, and which the regimes were determined to overcome.

In East Asia, and with some differences of degree in Southeast Asia, the primacy of economic development over political liberalization has been an outstanding feature of the Asian success model. Authoritarianism and the conscious delay and suppression of democratic reform were legitimized by the achievements of economic growth and the emergence of a strong and capable national business class. Although that legitimization is now fading after the financial crisis of 1997, and new democratizations are under way, ruling elites have generally been able to manage and moderate the pace of political opening, using democratization to maintain, in altered form, their dominance.

Superiority of the Asian autocratic model

Minxin Pei (1995) has spelled out the challenge that the East and Southeast Asian model (the East Asian exceptionalism) presents for theories and practices of democratization: namely, the notion that an autocratic project for economic modernization and development should come first, and democratic political reform should be delayed, and then only gradually introduced by the autocratic regime itself. To be sure, this is not strictly an Asian model, since, in Pei's reckoning, it is also found in Pinochet's Chilean dictatorship and in Franco Spain.

Distinctive features in the success of East Asian authoritarian developmentalism include:

- Growth was broad-based, with high investment in human capital, primacy given to agricultural reforms, and the forging of extensive links to the world economy via the promotion of exports and foreign direct investment.
- Reforms created beneficiaries before victimizing important social groups, and reformers avoided ideological battles and confrontations with entrenched interests in the early stages of the reform.
- There were good 'neighbourhood effects' – the East Asian region has benefited from a positive *regional* macroeconomic environment since the 1960s and from increasing regional integration through the expansion of intraregional trade and investment.
- Political stability accompanied reforms, in no small part because top leaders committed to economic restructuring remained in power for so long. . . .
- Despite the absence of democracy, economic reforms in East Asia were generally accompanied by declining levels of repression, rising levels of political institutionalization (especially in the area of movement toward the rule of law), and increasing (although limited) political participation and interest representation (mainly through semi-open local elections). (1995: 116)

Pei goes on to criticize the notion of an Asian 'autocratic superiority' in fostering first economic success, and then at some later point, a gradual and more orderly democratization than has been the case in Latin America and now post-communist Europe. He notes for example that the success level of the first generation of Asian 'tigers', Taiwan, South Korea, and Singapore, has not been reached by the second generation including Thailand, Indonesia and Malaysia, or by the communist Asia developmentalist regimes in China and Vietnam. He rightly notes that not all Asia authoritarian regimes have been successful, notably Burma, the Philippines under Marcos and communist North Korea. He also notes the high level of corruption in several reform regimes, including China, Indonesia and Vietnam (Thailand and South Korea should also be added). His general point, however, is that it has not been the regime type (Asian authoritarian) which is responsible for the economic success of East Asia; rather it has been, first, the presence of a skilled and highly networked business class of ethnic Chinese, a regionwide transnational entrepreneurial society, and secondly, the availability of tremendous amounts of investment capital, controlled not only by ethnic Chinese but also by expansionist Japanese corporations, that have driven the East Asian developmental model. These two factors, and not the special role of the authoritarian state, are responsible for the Asian success, which then leads, with some lag due to political authoritarianism, eventually to democratization. One must note, however, that this dynamic and ethnically defined entrepreneurial society has developed within the same culture which has produced on a consistent basis highly authoritarian politics; one cannot for ideological convenience just pretend that the one has nothing to do with the other. Values of discipline in work, loyalty to group, respect for hierarchy and strong traditions of corporatist, non-democratic decision making have both political and economic outlets. Chinese Confucianism gave birth to twins, even if only one is beautiful according to some Western value standards.

In the end, however, Pei is optimistic that democratization will come to China and Vietnam as well: 'Regarding the democratization of neo-autocracies, the question is not whether, but when and how' (1995: 124). Pei thus strengthens the notion that the East Asian authoritarian model (like that of Pinochet's Chile), is indeed a success model, since it achieves the twin goals of economic prosperity and democracy. Even though, in Pei's argument, the role of the authoritarian state is more negative than positive, this is the type of regime that was generated by local and external circumstances, and its reform track record of economics first, and politics later, has gained considerable credibility; Pei himself predicts democratization as the result of economic spillover effects and new pressure from below which are results (intended or not) of successful growth. In a world of nations and regions where neither prosperity nor democracy are by any means sure things, this is hardly an unattractive record, despite its obvious hardships in the early stages.

José María Maravall attacks the supposed 'authoritarian advantage' in fostering economic growth and prosperity. He cites Prime Minister Mahathir of Malaysia, one of the most vocal opponents of Western liberalism among the leaders of the newly industrialized 'tigers' of Southeast Asia, who puts forward the notion that post-communist Europe is on the wrong track, and Southeast Asia is on the right track:

In the former Soviet Union and the East European countries, democracy was introduced along with the free market. The result is chaos and increased misery. Not only have the countries broken up, mainly through bloody civil wars, but there is actual recession and more hardship for the people than when the Communists ruled. One may ask whether democracy is the means or the end. Democracy at all costs is not much different from Communist authoritarianism from the barrel of a gun . . . In a number of East Asian countries, while democracy is still eschewed, the free market has been accepted and has brought prosperity. Perhaps it is the authoritarian stability which enabled this to happen. Should we enforce democracy on people who may not be able to handle it and destroy stability? (cited in Maravall, 1995: 13–14)

Maravall argues against Mahathir's profession of superiority for Asian authoritarianism that the democratic disadvantage is not absolute nor pre-determined, and he points especially to the experiences of Southern Europe in the 1970s and early 1980s. He argues that new democratic regimes are able to take difficult decisions, and are enabled in this by their democratic legitimacy. Maravall does, however, advocate a 'capable state' which can foster a 'social citizenship' that does not marginalize and therefore alienate large groups of the population from democracy itself. In contrast to the Asia model, Maravall argues that political democratization was the necessary breakthrough to economic reform:

In Eastern Europe, prolonged and painful economic mismanagement could have persisted only under conditions of dictatorship: the social costs would not have been tolerated under democratic conditions. Authoritarian politics also made the implementation of necessary reforms impossible: modest changes were thwarted by party and state bureaucrats, and more ambitious transformations were prevented by the regimes of individual countries or by the USSR. . . . Eventually, democratic elections provided a window of opportunity: in Poland, Hungary, the Czech Republic, Slovenia, Estonia, and Latvia, elected governments turned out to have the legitimacy necessary for the launching of reforms. (1995: 16–17)

Maravall's argument is for a European 'social' path of democratic breakthrough first leading to regime legitimacy and the launching of painful but long overdue reforms. Yet he is aware that in requiring painful social and economic changes, democracies have to work hard to overcome the 'democratic disadvantage'. Maravall would like to see a higher priority in the new democracies of post-communist Europe on social safety nets and political inclusion of labour, rather than just on IMF guidelines and free market criteria, since without durable public support, and in the midst of change, the democratization process itself may be threatened. Maravall is aware that universal provision of social welfare of the previous communist era, or of the high Keynesian era in the West, is now out of reach, but that does not mean that social security is a luxury that can or must be dismissed (1995: 24–25).

In this sense, the ordering of democratization and economic reform in Eastern Europe is inherently different from either East Asia or

Southern Europe. Eastern Europe cannot avoid some burden of simultaneity of transitions. The question remains, however, if that burden proves to be too great, what is the next choice? Maravall is critical of the lack of social spending and provisions for the most severely impacted in post-communist Europe, but if he is right that this has risked alienating citizens from a democratic politics, there are certainly other alternative models for avoiding simultaneity, and the East Asian experience is one such model.

The most recent financial crisis in East and Southeast Asia has revealed new weaknesses of its authoritarian developmentalism, and it is now argued that 'crony capitalism' of Malaysia, Thailand, and even South Korea needs stronger democratic oversight to combat elite corruption and financial recklessness. Suddenly the Asian challenge to the Western model is itself vulnerable to criticism on grounds of economic performance (Lohr, 1998), yet it would be a mistake to write off the achievements of several decades of strong growth and their potential influence outside the region.

The strength of local culture – illiberal democracy

The Asian style of democratization has distinctive features often related to strong (mainly Confucian) cultures. First, the concentration of power remains in the hands of the executive, the top leader, whether president or prime minister. There is little sign in any of the East (and Southeast) Asian nations of an active and effective parliament, or an independent judiciary, as elements of the gradual democratization taking place in Taiwan, South Korea, or Thailand, much less in Singapore or Malaysia or Indonesia. In this region concentrated executive power seems to survive whether the system remains formally parliamentary with a prime minister (Singapore, Malaysia, Thailand) or presidential (South Korea, Indonesia, Taiwan); this is rather different from Latin American presidentialismo, and indicates important limits of institutional engineering in promoting democratization. Institutions do matter, but their operation varies tremendously within a given cultural context. Japanese democracy has already illustrated this strong impact of culture on formal political institutions.

Second, the Asian democratizations have been very gradual and controlled; even the Korean popular uprisings in 1987 which led to the competitive elections of 1988, brought another military man, President Roh Tae Woo, to power. The 1993 elections still involved a merger of military and civilian party organizations for the winning candidate, Kim Young Sam. Some earlier democratic openings in South Korea, in the early years of the first Republic, then briefly in 1960–61 after the student uprisings against President Syngman Rhee, and again briefly in 1979–80 after the assassination of President Park Chung Hee, were crushed by the military after it judged that democratization was getting out of hand, that is, beyond the careful control of the state. Only the most recent financial crisis of 1997 led to a decisive breakthrough, with the election of long-time dissident Kim Dae Jung as the new president.

In Taiwan likewise, the ending of martial law in 1987, and the political space opened for the opposition Democratic Progressive Party, was a gradual process, controlled each step of the way by the ruling KMT. There simply are no examples of civil society forcing the pace of democratization against the wishes of state elites, or state elites encouraging civil society to mobilize for democratic change. In a few cases (the early period of Lee Kuan Yew in Singapore, the early First Republic of Korea) where rulers temporarily accepted political pluralism and multi-party democracy in the early stages of 'nation-building', they later changed their attitudes and ended their short flirtation with Western liberal ideas (Jones, 1995: 68).

East Asian democratization has produced a recognizably more democratic politics. The political role of the military has receded. The contrived high level of popular support for the dominant party has eroded and there is growing recognition of opposition support among the citizenry (Brown, 1995: 141). The public discourse on political issues has widened, as state controls over discussion and debate have eased, though not disappeared. The political role of the business class has also increased, and its bargaining power within the state system has grown; in part the financial power of the new middle class has shifted the balance somewhat between state elites and capitalist elites. However, this class is still very closely tied to the state, and the political role of labour is still very weak, even in Korea, which has the only significant independent labour movement in East Asia. Kanishka Jayasuriya characterizes the East Asian illiberal democratization as moving from a more exclusionary to a more inclusionary corporatism, within the orbit of the state system. In East Asia, '"democratization" is not about the empowerment of civil society, but rather reflects a renegotiation of the relationship between political elites and capital' (1995: 108). While in Western Europe a main dynamic in the struggle for democratization involved the conflicts and negotiations between capital and labour, the political economy of East Asian democratization involves a new state/capital relationship, with labour still marginalized (1995: 133).

These features of East Asian democratization lead to conceptions of a non-Western form of democracy, which some have termed 'illiberal democracy' (Bell et al., 1995). In this view, Confucian culture blocks the emergence of a Western-style liberal pluralism, but does allow for a state-managed and state-centric form of democratization in terms of formal electoralism and parliamentary or presidential institutions suitable for a modernized and more differentiated economy. Bell et al. therefore 'do not now or in the foreseeable future expect a "triumph" of liberal democracy in the modernized polities of East and Southeast Asia. . . . Rather, our claim is that democratization in East and Southeast Asia can be interpreted as a grafting of democratic practices and institutions on to societies with an alternative cultural baggage, with different ways of organizing their economic life, and with distinctive answers to the questions of who counts as "we the people"' (Bell et al., 1995: 2). The East Asian democratization is based on Confucian-rooted cultural values, which Singaporean Prime Minister Lee outlined as official government norms, including communitarianism, familism, decision making by consensus, and social and religious harmony (Bell and Jayasuriya, 1995: 8). The Western historical experience which evolved positive roles for individual citizens, and an autonomous civic culture which honours and sees virtue in social and moral pluralism, simply cannot be superimposed in East Asia, although selected institutions of liberal democracy may well be adopted. 'Instead of "democratization" resulting from a demand for autonomy on the part of civil society and its individual members, political reform ought to be viewed primarily as a state strategy to maintain or increase commitment to national goals' (pp. 15–16).

The Marxist critique of the new democratizations points out the continued marginalization of labour from political power, and a continued elite coalition of state, military and middle class. This 'low intensity democracy' (Gills et al., 1993) is consistent with the needs of globalized capitalism, and its international overseers at the IMF. The political exclusion of labour is in this view the key to understanding this minimal democratization, as well as the inherent limits to the process. In Korea, where organized labour has been more challenging to the status quo than elsewhere, the recent democratization has not brought labour into the political mainstream (Gills, 1993: 253–254).

Democratization in the East Asian context may not evolve out of the (originally Western) justifications of either the principled goals of individual rights, or the instrumental goals of fostering desirable outcomes for citizens. It may, however, find a suitable justification in terms of strengthening an Asian Confucian communitarianism, and in this sense it may garner both elite and mass support so long as it serves that instrumental purpose. Daniel A. Bell argues that this instrumentalist justification for democracy is the 'most likely . . . to capture the "hearts and minds" of East Asians, namely, the idea that democracy protects and promotes communitarian ways of life, with special emphasis on the family' (1995: 36). The values of Confucianism which stress family life and family obligation, social harmony, political hierarchy, devoted service of a meritocratic bureaucracy, may arguably be strengthened by a form of Asian democracy, but only if that democracy avoids the mimicking of Western liberalism.

However, Peter Moody takes the view that political opposition in East Asia has been taking root, and that cultural change has now gone so far that a return to a traditional Confucian state and politics is virtually impossible. The social impact of the industrial revolution into these societies now requires that elites govern in a different way.

> The east Asian countries, with their lack of liberal traditions and significant subcommunities, I think, are in a condition that might be called incipient polarized pluralism. Politics in polarized pluralist societies is chaotic, but strong (or relatively strong) democratic institutions may contain this chaos, confining it to elections and parliament. (1988: 70–71)

Moody argues that much of Confucianism may be quite compatible with forms of democracy, depending on contextual interpretation:

> Confucianism taken in the abstract is probably as consistent with democracy as the mainstream of traditional western thought (although the feeder streams in the west are more numerous and the current itself more turbulent). Alternatively, Thomas Jefferson's aristocracy of talent is very Confucian in tone. Yet Jefferson's country has been democratic while Confucius's has not. . . . On the other hand, in the absence of strong democratic institutions, ideas such as Jefferson's would probably imply rule by an educated elite. The simple point is that ideas must be considered in the interaction with other conditions. (1988: 250)

Cultural traditions can assert themselves in different political environments and systems, and Confucianism has also shown its adaptability.

Shaohua Hu argues that while Confucianism has a long history of being used as a state ideology to strengthen authoritarian rule, in general Confucianism is 'neither pro-democratic nor anti-democratic but a-democratic, and that, while not an unsurmountable obstacle to democratization, it offers little help to that process' (Hu, 1997: 347). This democratic agnosticism makes Confucianism potentially compatible to values of Western democracy, but the driving forces for democratization must then come from other sources, stimulating a democratic adaptation of Confucian values, which Moody calls post-confucianism.

In this view, East Asian societies are entering a post-confucian stage, with the impact of modernization requiring successive rounds of cultural adaptation. Moody was optimistic that democratization could proceed in these post-Confucian societies, but also at a cost.

> The east Asian states have been successful partly because they have been able to keep social discipline . . . This might imply that democratization will damage that prosperity and generate social turmoil. At worst, this might provoke a new round of authoritarian repression, even less legitimate than the earlier version. If democratization does take hold, a more optimistic outcome would be chronic instability at the political level – Italy seems to remain the standard example for this sort of thing – enhancing further the influence of the bureaucracy and technocracy while detracting from their efficiency. This would hardly be a tragedy to shake

the world and may well be worth the cost – but it does imply that democracy comes with a cost. (1988: 254–255)

Moody notes that there is a mix of both intrinsic and instrumentalist grounds for legitimacy of democracy, which may serve as arguments both for the state and for its opponents, as the occasion requires; the broad legitimacy of democratic values may become a force in itself (a kind of ideological hegemony). Peculiarly, however, it is hard to identify the larger social pressures for democratization. 'A weakness of democratic development in post-Confucian society, then, is that pressure for democracy is not closely tied to specific social interests. This discourages both the cohesion of democratic pressures and the isolation of specific goals, preventing the development of democratic institutions' (Moody, 1988: 255–256).

Western liberal ideas about democracy have been and continue to be modified and selectively applied by local political, economic and social elites to the context of their own cultures. More frequently now, observers of democratization in other regions are noting the very different functioning of political processes and institutions in non-Western European settings. With so many nations undergoing some form of democratization, analysts have been confronted with a region-ally and culturally much-expanded range of phenomena to be under-stood and interpreted, and there is growing consciousness that the Western model is less useful in many cases for comprehending the changes under way. East and Southeast Asian cases are interesting precisely because they bring to the front claims of a qualitatively different modernity, combining economic prowess with an adaptable but non-liberal politics.

At some point, the variance is so great that new democracies in different regions are being recognized as qualitatively distinct, and non-liberal or illiberal in the case of East and Southeast Asia. Despite Cold War-era theories of political development which predict democratiza-tion in the Western liberal sense as a general correlate of economic modernization, and especially the growth of a modern middle class, there is now a growing body of opinion that this is neither an accurate nor insightful account for the regional realities, either in Latin America or in East and Southeast Asia. With the Cold War double standard now in disrepute, studies of democratization are more likely to delve deeper than surface electoralism (cf. Karl, 1991) or the democratic veneer of elite corporatism to raise critical issues and to question the nature of these 'democratizing' regimes. But Western governments and many Western scholars still expect that democratization must be associated with Western liberal values, which are exportable because they are indeed universal (cf. Ravich, 1996: 289). The debate over just what variation on the Western liberal model is possible under the tent of democracy is still ongoing, with massive new evidence for evaluation.

For the present, however, in the East Asia cases especially, the strong Confucian tradition and the success of local authoritarianism have blended with requirements of state modernization to produce a rather different democratization; is this new species still related to the Western liberal democratic species? Or, on the other hand, are there multiple species of democracy, which are qualitatively different, and yet still democratic (cf. Sartori, 1970)?

For post-communist Europe, the implications are clear. It may be possible that competitive (but unfair) elections will be held, it may be that many parties will exist (with very unequal resources and media access), and it may be that there will be a formally free press (with state-affiliated owners, purchased reporting and strong state discipline). The trappings of liberal democracy, however, may either not function (parliaments may be powerless) or be manipulated by the central authorities (courts, civil service, police), so as to intimidate and purposely demobilize civil society.

How strong will Polish, Czech, or Hungarian cultures be in shaping their democratizations? How different will this be from the Russian, Ukrainian, or Belarusian cases (or the Bulgarian, Romanian, Croatian and Serbian cases)? Will the variances from the Western liberal democratic model be of a quantitative or a qualitative sort?

Lessons from East and Southeast Asia

Two primary features of development in East and Southeast Asia may be relevant for democratization in post-communist Europe, and for East-Central Europe more specifically. First, economic success allowed for a strong authoritarian regime to put off and then tightly control political democratization; especially where early attempts at a more open, more liberal, democracy were associated with economic failure, authoritarian (usually military-backed) regimes were able to step in and assert the superiority of an 'economics first' strategy, arguing that the country was not ready for political democracy. Later, the performance-based legitimacy of political authoritarianism allowed the regime to control the pace and limits of democratization, without clear-cut regime change.

Second, local culture has strongly shaped the nature of politics, whether formally authoritarian or formally democratic. For this region, and especially for the most homogeneous Confucian cultures of Taiwan, South Korea and Singapore, the quality of democracy is arguably of a different order from the Western experience. Some observers say that these cultures cannot support Western liberal democracy, although they may be able to support illiberal, more authoritarian and communitarian democracy. Others, however, view liberal democratic values as gradually taking root and modifying local Confucian values, so that process still leads toward those universal values crucial to liberal democracy. Can democracy in East Asia be consolidated along non-liberal lines that never converge with Western norms, or is this just another regional variation, unique in detail and process but not in ultimate ends?

For post-communist Europe, the failure of weak democratic regimes to deliver on economic growth and the hopes for prosperity may also revive authoritarian cultural norms and create new opportunities for strongman regimes to suppress democracy or to put off democratization so that an 'economics first' strategy can be tried. The superiority of Asian authoritarianism (as well as the Latin American Pinochet model) has some currency, but much depends on the abilities or incapacities of new but weak democratic regimes in the region. The performance or instrumentalist case for regime legitimation will certainly play a role in the consolidation or lack of consolidation of new democracies in post-communism.

Cultural influences may be expected to play a lesser role in the shaping of East-Central Europe, given their new openness to the European Union nations, and their growing association with the EU. Unless elite opinion and mass public sentiment shift strongly to hostile nationalist stances *vis-à-vis* Western influences and Western discipline in East-Central Europe, it is difficult to see how local culture can avoid being more strongly drawn toward liberal political as well as economic norms. Although there are certainly signs of a nationalist-populist backlash against Western finance and investment dominance, and IMF discipline over policies, the pull to the West for the 'lands between' has probably never been stronger, especially with unified Germany now a stable and solidly liberal member of the Western European community.

Further to the East, however, in Belarus (Lukashenka), or in Yugoslavia (Milošević), anti-Western nationalism or populism have gained the upper hand for the moment. Some regimes (the Bulgarian Socialist government, Mečiar's regime in Slovakia, Iliescu's regime in Romania) played on local nationalist sentiments while trying still to obtain Western aid and IMF loans, but this strategy of 'having it both ways' proved to be unstable and capable of only short-term political ascendancy. Western capital and Western leaders were unwilling to play this game, and clearly signalled their preferences for more clearly pro-Western and liberalizing regimes. How strong will the pull of the West be, compared with the strength of local cultures and the potential for anti-Western backlash?

Another aspect of the impact of local culture, which is often overlooked, is the tradition of labour politics and class struggle. This is very different from the East Asian cultural tradition, but it is a legitimate part of the industrial history of post-communist Europe. At the moment, this tradition has been largely demobilized, and it is clear that the political voice of labour is weak in this early stage of democratization. Yet, it seems unlikely that the labour tradition can simply be stilled forever; here one might well expect the new ties to Western Europe and to the labour movement in the European Union eventually to reactivate labour politics in East-Central Europe. Of course, labour politics in the European Union is also in transition, as the politics of labour and the left are being rethought and reformed with the end of the Keynesian welfare state. Capital and business are dominant in the short-term restructuring of post-communist Europe, while labour's revival is likely to be a more long-term and ponderous affair.

Regional comparisons and what they can tell us

Each regional experience, despite significant intra-regional variation, possesses some characteristic features, which make it unlikely that this experience will be duplicated in post-communist Europe, or more specifically in Poland, Hungary, or the Czech Republic. Rather, regional patterns of democratization highlight both problem areas and advantages which hindered and helped the transition to democracy and the consolidation of democracy in each country. The growing literature on regional democratization patterns shows once again that there is no master paradigm in political development which would enable accurate prediction, especially in the short term, but rather an impressive and accumulating wealth of detailed knowledge from which general or longer-term regularities have been inductively drawn. These hypotheses then have been offered for the latest rounds of democratization, in particular those of post-communist Europe. Each regional clustering of democratization has inspired new political leaders as well as scholars to stretch their learning and imagination, and to question once more the Cold War Eurocentric assumptions of political development and modernization.

12

East-Central Europe, the EU and Globalizing Capitalism: What Kind of Democratization, What Kind of Democracy?

Democratization studies have dealt with many issues, including types of transitions, sequencing of reforms, roles of elites and civil society, and balances between institutions; these are primarily domestic factors. More than in previous regional experiences, it is recognized that powerful international forces of the European and global economic order are shaping democratizations after the Cold War (Hyde-Price, 1996; Whitehead, 1996). The impact of globalizing capitalism in an era of declining state control over national economies gives post-communist democratization a new quality for nations which are seeking to join the West as equal partners. What impact will this have on the quality of democracy in these nations?

Western finance and the European Union: economics in command

Given that 'Eastern European society's participation in the European experience was only partial' (Schöpflin, 1990: 61), and that despite protestations from East European intellectuals like Milan Kundera, great differences existed between East and West (Mason, 1996: 165), the Western powers might have undertaken a major effort to integrate these 'lands between' into the community of developed Western democracies. Yet while the influence of the West on the post-communist East has been enormous, it has been lacking in long-term vision (Karp, 1995).

The collapse of European communism, one of the most dramatic events of the twentieth century, produced no substantial response by the Western powers, including the United States and the European Union. President George Bush, a prudent man but lacking in 'the vision thing', did not even outline anything like a Wilsonian plan for the peaceful cooperation among the newborn democracies of Europe, or a Marshall Plan II to help restructure economies. President Bill Clinton concentrated his attention in the 1992 elections on domestic affairs ('It's the economy, stupid!'), and never formulated any far-reaching goals in post-communist Europe.

After the defeat of Nazi Germany in 1945, Western leaders fashioned a far-sighted plan which created a new zone of peace for Western Europe. This included an historic bipartisan commitment by the United States to engage its resources (through Marshall Plan and NATO) in Europe for the duration of the Cold War struggle. This created the basis for a new security order, a broad-based prosperity and generous social welfare unmatched in European history. It formed the basis for reconciliation between Germany and France after a century of bitter warfare (Chirot, 1995). Post-Second World War leaders broke with their own past, and embarked on a bold strategic path of international reconciliation, political rethinking and economic renewal.

In the first years after the collapse of communism, Ken Jowitt feared that a failure of Western imagination and boldness would permit the bad legacies of Leninism and the longer history of ethnic nationalism to overwhelm the emerging civil societies and to spread disorder in the entire region: his shorthand solution was 'adoption' (Jowitt, 1992: 302). No such commitment was forthcoming, except in the *adoption* of East Germany by West Germany.

Chancellor Helmut Kohl and his foreign minister Hans-Dietrich Genscher did have a wider and strategic vision of an integration project for all of Europe, with German sponsorship backed by considerable financial aid. But German leadership was predicated on consensus, so that fears of a Germanized Europe would not be revived, and on financial generosity to ease the pains of transition. On both counts, German leadership became quickly hostage to Western dissensus and crippled by the huge burdens of German unification, and thus failed to marshal Western support for any major coordinated aid project for the post-communist East. As Jürgen Habermas (1997) notes, this was the historic chance for unified Germany to prove itself a pillar of democratic culture and international cooperation. But Martin Walker (1995) is probably correct in noting that the German capacity to help expand the European Union through its traditional Geldpolitik (cheque book diplomacy) can no longer be continued. After the election defeat of Kohl's CDU in September 1998, the new SPD-Green coalition under Gerhard Schröder is less committed to pushing for EU expansion. One might argue that Western popular support was also lacking for a grand integration effort. But, in the recent financial crisis in East Asia, Western leaders quickly found $100 billion in new money to deal with economic disorder there, without any popular support or even public debate.

This failure of political will and imagination in the West is related to the current trend internationally, which has put economics (definitely liberal or free market, not social market), rather than politics in the driver's seat in shaping and reshaping national economies and international relations. 'Economics in command' is building new relationships between affluent ex-Keynesian economies in the West and poor but aspiring post-communist economies of the East. This economic primacy is a sign of the times generally, both pushing the decline of the Keynesian welfare state (Kesselman and Krieger, 1997) and empowering a socially emancipated and globally networked finance capital. More and more is left to the global financial marketplace and its disciplines in shaping the destinies of post-communist societies. Western European support for post-communist democratization has been supplied on the cheap, and financial help has been modest (Hyde-Price, 1996: 201–202). The United States' contribution in particular has been 'insubstantial' (Mason, 1996: 177). The great beneficiaries of the EU's aid programme have been Western consultants, who have pocketed two-thirds of the total PHARE budget (Echikson, 1997; Ost, 1997: 508).

Accommodation to the liberal capitalist market has been the main rule of thumb, with the tacit assumption that the politics must either fall in line or fail miserably. Thus, while national-populist leaders in post-communist politics conjure up notions of a master plan for domination hatched by secret elites (Jewish bankers or Freemasons are frequently if unoriginally cited), the pattern of 'Western' influence in post-communist Europe is part of a larger emerging pattern of a liberated and adventurous global capitalism. No master plan was necessary, and no secret elite required – the newly invigorated capitalist synthesis of global finance and new technologies acting with its own logic of accumulation has been quite sufficient.

The Western lack of political vision did not dampen the initial optimism of 1989–91, however. At the beginning of the post-communist transitions to new political systems and to new market-type economies, the goal of 'joining the West' was a source of motivation and of direction for both new governments and for citizens. This goal was predicated on the assumption that, after a short period of transition which would include some socially painful dislocations, or necessary reform shocks, these nations would approach the norms (the normality) which characterized the Western democracies during the Cold War. Janos Kornai defended this one-time sacrifice as a welcome sign of a brighter future: 'There are cyclical and market factors contributing to the decline, but their role(s) were secondary. The primary explanation is the following: (t)he severe decline of output is a painful side effect of a healthy process of the change of the system . . . (i)t is caused by the transition from socialism to capitalism' (Kornai, 1992, cited in Berend, 1995: 141).

Economic reformers, especially in Poland and the Czech Republic, were touted in the West as leaders who would in a single round of pathbreaking reforms set their economies on the right road to Europe. The Western hero of market reform, Czech Prime Minister Václav Klaus, self-declared disciple of Milton Friedman and Lady Margaret Thatcher and an Anglo-Saxon model of capitalism (Hartmann, 1998: 161), had declared in 1995 that economic restructuring was basically completed, and the Czech Republic was now entering a post-transformation period. Did not the Czech model substantiate the positive vision?

However, the decline in the political fortunes of Václav Klaus and the now-visible weaknesses of the once highly praised Czech model in 1996–7 brought this illusion to an end. By mid-1997, some public opinion polls in the Czech Republic were, for the first time since the collapse of communism, reporting that 'almost half the population thought the pre-1989 system was better than the new democratic order' (Pehe, 1997b: 27). Over half of all Czechs believed that their income had fallen in 1997 compared with 1996, and a year-end December poll found that 64 per cent estimated that their incomes were lower than under the communist regime (Shafir, 1998c).

Given the practical experience of the 1990s, it now appears that:

1   the transformations will take much longer, decades or generations rather than years;
2   there will be repeated rounds of crisis and further restructuring, each with its own shocks; and
3   the end result will not fulfill the original conception of 'joining the West'.

The Western Keynesian model of widespread prosperity and generous social security is quickly fading as the foundations of its politics are crumbling everywhere in the West itself. What the post-communist political systems are joining is something rather different. In this new era, national and international policies of the West have become much more attentive to the demands of capital interests, in an effort to stay in good favour with financial decision makers. This is the new emerging shape of Europe, its leading economics and its laggard politics.

New dependencies of 'joining the West'

Yet in this new sense, clearly, the new democracies of post-communist Europe (and especially East-Central Europe) are indeed joining the West: these nations have already been drawn into new relations of Western guidance, discipline and influence to shape their economic and political development. The *Economist*'s Edward Lucas described this relationship bluntly as a new Western 'remote-control colonialism':

> [T]he governments of the Czech Republic, Poland, Hungary, Estonia and Slovenia look and sound independent – but in reality their freedom of action will be evermore constrained by the requirements of their western neighbours. . . . So expect to see much louder and more public pressure from Western Europe on the politicians of Eastern Europe in the coming months. Expect too some rather less public intervention to raise standards: moral standards that is. Selected law-enforcement officials from Eastern Europe have already been sent for training in the West. Under the guise of 'exchanges' the next stage will be to put Western officials in place in Prague, Budapest and Warsaw – nominally to 'liaise', but in fact to monitor, encourage, scold and warn. (Lucas, 1998: 44)

Lucas asks if this sounds familiar, given the Soviet satellite status of these nations during the Cold War: Soviet domination is being replaced by Western domination, more efficient and more subtle, but domination all the same.

Given the long-term weakness of their own capital resources, the new democracies will be dependent on their Western sponsors, who in turn are demanding compliance with austerity programmes, privatization schedules, reductions in tariffs and protection of local industries, and openness to foreign investment. Ivan Berend, in a response to the optimistic scenario of Janos Kornai, foresees a different reality:

> As the prospect of a rapidly emerging and prosperous East-Central European market democracy, integrated as an equal partner in the European Community, is disappearing, the exclusiveness of the European Community is strengthening. The harsh reality of this situation for the region still involves integration with Europe – however, not as an equal partner that is gradually catching up to the West but as its periphery. This means that the countries' only comparative advantage may remain its cheap labor, and the region might find its place as a 'backyard' of the European Community (or of a strengthened Germany). (1995: 146)

As de-industrialization proceeds in the West, there will be opportunities for the post-communist nations to compete on the basis of inexpensive labour, including much reduced social benefit levels, but this will last only if the wage and benefit differential remains large. Those best-placed nations of East-Ceneral Europe, which will have the greatest degree of integration with the European Union, will additionally offer good compatibility for Western investment in terms of political stability, sanctity of private property and contracts, and fulfilment of EU standards. But lacking other components of competitiveness, such as development of new and locally controlled technologies, or a strong and innovative business class, even these best-placed nations will have to rely on significantly lower labour costs to earn their bread. The emergence of strong and efficient entrepreneurial classes, such as the ones in East Asia, is still a long-term potential. Certainly some new entrepreneurs will do very well, but the question is whether they can take the leading role in the development of higher value-added goods and services. In a much more integrated global economy, where East-Central Europe is also competing with other low-wage regions in Latin America, Southeast Asia and other poorer parts of Eastern Europe and the former Soviet Union, it will be very difficult for the *national* wage levels to close the gap with the Western nations.

It must be emphasized that this form of economic dependency, dictated by the sudden collapse of the central planning system, comes with a discipline much more severe than the economic reforms in the Southern European nations during their democratizations in the 1970s, and probably more severe than the dependency of the Latin American nations during their democratization amidst the massive debt crisis of the 1980s. In East Asia, economic success (at least up to the financial crises of 1997) and cultural and geographic distance from Europe and the United States had provided those nations with rather different opportunities to shape their own destiny. It will be interesting to see whether the new IMF austerity and reform measures attached to the recent rescue package in Thailand, South Korea, Indonesia and Malaysia, will markedly diminish the opportunities to continue a unique Asian developmentalist path. It makes little difference that Western demands for economic restructuring, based on liberal theory, are sound (Maull, 1997). Interdependence with strong power inequalities, a striking feature of the new global economy, will generate strong reactions in the periphery, especially if that subordinate periphery status is perceived as *permanent* rather than *temporary*.

This relation of teacher and pupil, officer and cadet, master and apprentice, still contains appealing aspects, especially for upwardly mobile portions of the new middle class, and for those young entrepreneurs with much expanded opportunities. For these people, the goal of joining the West is still very much alive, and its fulfilment is now within reach. Of course, in some post-communist nations (like Bulgaria for example, cf. Muntyan, 1996), large numbers of ambitious young people have joined the West in a more direct, quicker and historically more successful manner, by migrating across the now open borders. This westward migration is however not a solution for their countries' problems; as elsewhere, 'brain drain' represents a serious loss of human capital.

The post-communist nations are now joined to a Western-centred project of reclamation, in which their own voice is subsidiary, since they have few resources and they have the greatest need for outside capital and skills if they want to continue to keep alive the dreams of 1989. Poland, Hungary and the Czech Republic are strictly bound up with IMF guidelines; they have neither the size nor the domestic capital to resist IMF discipline; as such, they should be 'star pupils' for the IMF formula, and therefore will continue to be different from the richer EU nations, which have more relative independence, and whose social and political systems have greater commitments to social service systems which cannot be abandoned so quickly.

One issue of the London *Financial Times* (from 28 November 1997) featured two side-by-side stories typical of the new pattern of dependency. The first article was entitled 'Consumerism is the new invader' and reported on Western-financed mall-building projects in Hungary, seen by Budapest Mayor Gabor Demszky as taking control of city planning and development away from elected local officials.

> The malls could be a threat to Budapest. . . . They have a bad effect on trade and shops in the centre of the city. They also complicate the transport situation, taking people out of the centre to shop. We will have to build more roads to cope.' Mr Demszky worries that the western developers' financial power gives them an influence that Budapest local authorities will be unable to resist. 'They have many means to influence decision-making,' Mr. Demszky said drily. (Lieven, 1997)

The second piece reported on the reception given new Polish Prime Minister Jerzy Buzek in Brussels shortly after the victory of the conservative Solidarity Electoral Alliance (AWS) in the September parliamentary elections.

> Although he received a warm welcome on his first visit as premier to Brussels, Jerzy Buzek was presented with European Commission demands to honour a pledge by Poland's previous government to lower tariffs on steel imports and to restructure the industry. The Commission sees the steel dispute as symbolic of the difficulties Poland will have in implementing the changes necessary for accession. . . . The Commission said yesterday that a 'substantial amount of work' needed to be done on a range of issues, including steel, before the EU could admit Poland. (Smith, 1997)

Whereas Polish President Aleksander Kwaśniewski expressed hope that Poland might join the EU by the year 2000, and Prime Minister Buzek wants Poland to join by 2001, EU sources suggested that restructuring of Polish agriculture alone might take up to ten years.

The new political geography: whose lines on the map?

'Eastern Europe' of the Cold War, the Soviet-dominated sphere on the other side of the Berlin Wall, exists no longer. There is a new conflict over the geographical description for those nations lying between the West and Russia – Central Europe, East-Central Europe, East and Central Europe, Eastern Europe, or simply Europe.

What will the new political geography of Europe look like? Some may see a Europe still divided into West and East, with a highly developed West exercising dominant influence over the development of a weakly developed and dependent East. This scenario borrows from the development-dependency debate of the 1960s and 1970s in the Latin American context, and foresees a similar relationship now emerging in post-Cold War Europe. Artur Meier (1996) amends this basic thesis by differentiating among four types of societies in a multi-speed Europe, in which there will be a core of leading advanced capitalist societies (Germany, France, UK), a group of semi-dependent 'associated capitalist societies' (Greece, Portugal, Ireland), a group of dependent 'dual societies with strong capitalist tendencies' (Hungary, Poland, Czech Republic), and a group of the dependent periphery 'dual societies with weak capitalist tendencies' (Romania, Bulgaria, Serbia).

> Evidently, we have not one Europe and we are not getting the continent as a united hemisphere. Neither economically nor politically will the divisions grow smaller. Even when new social structures, finally more or less capitalist dominated, will arise everywhere, historical variations and long-lasting unequal power relations within and between the different European societies will divide the old world anew.
>
> The emerging new Europe will continue to have clear socio-economic and political demarcation lines: frontiers disintegrating East and West, North and South – between hegemonial and dependent powers. (Meier, 1996: 14)

However, Ireland has developed as a success story in the past twenty years, and is now above the EU average. This suggests that the terrain of a multi-speed Europe could shift, with some countries able to improve their position (and others fall behind). Meier's account is too static; in the present era of capitalist restructuring, in all regions, new 'winners' and 'losers' may overturn previous conceptualizations of political geography. Certainly one might expect some surprise success stories within the range of post-communism, if not for entire nations, then certainly for some cities and provinces. Nevertheless, it is difficult to foresee a more even development of economies across Europe, with poorer nations catching up to richer nations as the general trend.

Peter Gowan argues that aside from the particular foibles and inadequacies of the Jeffrey Sachs-style 'shock therapy,' the larger model has been a great success – the implantation of Western steering mechanisms for the region, especially the key nations of East-Central Europe. Gowan makes the point that whatever the particular demands of the West or the IMF of the moment, the underlying assumption is 'rather strong on the ways of using political power to engineer change in the East' (1995: 56).

The nations of East-Central Europe are those most strongly brought into the discipline of the European Union, although the small Baltic states are not far behind. Russia is too large to subordinate quickly; some states such as Belarus, Serbia and in part Slovakia have resisted Western advice and threats by moving in nationalist and authoritarian directions; other states, Ukraine, Romania and Bulgaria, continued for several years under indecisive ex-communist governments, have now come more clearly under IMF and Western discipline.

> From the EC's point of view, so far the policy has been a remarkable success. Poland, the Czech Republic and Hungary are firmly locked into EC ascendancy. The rest of the region, given Russian weakness, still have nowhere else to go. It is true that the Visegrad states are in a weaker condition for entering the EC than they were in 1989 and would have been if their region had not been shattered, but their accession to the EU is not a priority even for Germany: what counts is their being firmly within the sphere of EU dominance. The task now for the USA is to ensure that the EU's new East-Central European sphere is brought firmly under overall US leadership. This goal is to be achieved through NATO's eastward expansion. (p. 59)

This argument neglects European and especially German desires that these new democracies become good trading partners, and that does imply some degree of integration and a new level of economic, legal and financial compatibility. If that were to fail, unified Germany would remain as the easternmost part of the West, whereas the Kohl government wanted Germany to become once again the centre of Europe, with maximum opportunities for its own export-oriented economy to both East and West. Here German and American interests may diverge somewhat, but the new strategic partnership between these two powers, first voiced by President Bush during the 1989–90 drive for German unification, and since reaffirmed by President Clinton, makes it likely that the EU and the United States want to use their newly expanded economic influence in ways that bring East-Central Europe into some closer relation to the West, and that is only possible if these new political-legal systems are minimally compatible.

Moreover, there are complications to a straightforward dependency model for East-Central Europe in its relationship to the West. In the current era of decline in social justice in the West, the growing gap between winners and losers in the former Keynesian welfare states, the focus on nations alone hides some important geo-political contours and connections which are emerging (or re-emerging) in both West and East. All of the EU nations are giving up some of their sovereignty to the European Union, especially with respect to the Euro project and the new European Central Bank in Frankfurt. Even for the most stable democracies of the West, who have been participating in the European integration project since the end of the Second World War, this loss of national sovereignty is a difficult transition, and citizens of many countries, such as the United Kingdom, but also Germany and the Nordic democracies, are sceptical about this process, which has now reached a new level of consciousness with the Euro currency project.

There are also considerable differences among the European Union nations in the variety of capitalism, from the Anglo-Saxon free market model in the United Kingdom to the Rhineland social consensus model in Germany and the Benelux nations, to the Latin paternalist style in Italy and Southern Europe generally (Rhodes and van Apeldoorn, 1997). Moreover, there is the competition among European, American and Japanese varieties of capitalism in the larger global context (Garten, 1992). The ascendancy of the minimalist-state Anglo-Saxon variety is being resisted by the continental European nations, and this will in turn impact the shaping of capitalist market systems in East-Central Europe. If the German 'social market economy' maintains itself through coherent reform, this would provide some alternative model for Poland, the Czech Republic and Hungary. If however the Anglo-Saxon model becomes a more universal norm, then that would pretty much settle the question for East-Central Europe.

The differences between the loss of sovereignty to the EU in the Western democracies and the new dependency relations of the post-communist democracies are qualitative in nature. The Western democracies went into the integration project in some sense as equal partners, to participate in shaping the European Common Market, later the European Community, and now the European Union. The post-communist polities to the East have just regained their national sovereignty, and are being incorporated into an established EU governance system. Their relationship to the EU is not that of equal partner, but rather of supplicant. Václav Klaus at his peak of popularity did offer his own criticisms of the West and its failures. What many perceived as personality flaws in Klaus were however part of his brilliant understanding of the political popularity of talking back to Western elites, while simultaneously pursuing Western-required reforms. The clash between a regained sovereignty and the new loss of sovereignty to external discipline (even if more favourable and respected than Soviet hegemony) is bound to disturb many citizens, the more so as Western rule-setting becomes more visible and durable.

The East-Central European nations cannot duplicate the Keynesian pattern, with broad prosperity and generous social security networks;

but on the other hand, their dependency relationship to the European Union is rather different from the Latin American relationship to the United States (Giessmann, 1996; Ziebura, 1995).

There are numerous attempts to outline the new lines of division in the post-Cold War order. Samuel Huntington's widely promoted views (1996) stress division along civilizational lines, especially ethnic-religious divisions, according to which the new main line of cleavage in Europe will be that between Western Christianity on the one side, and both Eastern Orthodoxy and Islam on the other (1996).

But Huntington's conception distracts from economic power relations, and while his line of demarcation certainly has some validity, it neglects the many other patterns of redivision now under way in the post-Cold War political economy of Europe. Economic forces of capital tied to new technologies are reshaping the global political economy, undermining established patterns of political order, and mounting a historic challenge to local and national cultures (Barber, 1992; Wesson, 1990).

Internal differentiation is leading to a new social separatism between the rich Northern region of Italy and the poor South (the Mezzogiorno), and between the old western Germany and its new eastern states (former East Germany). The rise of new wealth in financial sectors (London, Frankfurt) is paired with the decline of older industrial cities and agricultural hinterlands to Third World status. The new variable geometry of Europe (and the world economy generally) rests upon the ascendancy of the power of capital on a transnational or non-national basis, which faces no social counter-balancing force. The shaping of the new Europe entails a new competition among social groups, cities, regions and nations (Knox and Agnew, 1993; Ross and Trachte, 1990).

Within this struggle, the position of various nations in post-communist Europe is more complex than that of either complete dependency to some unified West or successful assimilation into some unified West. At least several new lines of cleavage may be observed in formation, and some of these cleavages cross the old East–West division of Cold War Europe.

New lines of cleavage are emerging within nations, between rich or rapidly growing, and poorer or declining cities and regions. A politics of social desolidarization is in the ascendancy, given the new competitiveness of the more flexible global marketplace. In an era of increasing inequality and greater uncertainty, the new wisdom is to protect one's own island of affluence, and cut ties and responsibilities to those with poor prospects: a smaller government economic role, reduced taxes, decentralization of economic responsibility, more pressure on labour to be flexible, and above all a politics which will attract and keep capital in one's own locality. Some areas are clear winners in this process, and draw not only financial capital but human talent, leaving other areas as abandoned hinterlands which increasingly take on the characteristics of the Third World (resource drain, capital drain, brain drain, loss of technological development, debt peonage, cf. Nagle, 1998a: ch. 12).

Gilbert Ziebura argues that a continuation of the generalized neo-liberal policy model in fact accepts the notion of a 'variable-geometry Europe' with a 'core Europe' led by Germany and France, and surrounded by associated member-states with lesser pretensions. The result would be a dynamic core freed from the responsibility for trying to bring up those poorer nations, especially the new candidate-nations of post-communist Europe. The gap in wealth between West and East in Europe, which opened so wide with industrialization over two centuries, and which increased even during the Cold War, will be perpetuated. The earliest EU agreements for liberalization of exchange ballooned the West's trade surplus with the East from 1.8 billion dollars in 1991 to 6.4 billion in 1993. 'No wonder if precisely those commodities in which the Central and East Europeans have a comparative cost advantage (agrarian products, steel, textiles, leather, etc.) suffer restrictions for fear of competition' (1995: 38). This new Europe, whatever the formal slogan, will 'create strictly hierarchical power relations both politically and economically. There is a centre and several, ranked peripheries; there is a First, a Second, a Third and a Fourth Division' (p. 38).

This Europe would be divided into different circles of development; ideally the core nations would act as a magnet for the temporarily marginalized (the dynamic of marching ahead and catching up). But Ziebura warns that these means can become entrenched as long-term ends:

> Methods have the tendency to perpetuate themselves, especially when they (intend to) achieve the preservation of property relations. An all-European centre–periphery structure as the result of a Europe of concentric circles not only fits neatly into the exigencies of the world market. It thereby contributes to their consolidation. This does not exclude a selective integration of certain elements of the periphery into the centre. Beneficiaries of modernization can also be found in Prague, Warsaw, Budapest, even in Moscow. (p. 39)

The primacy of the economic over the political, in an era of unfettered capital movements, suggests that the expansion of the EU will only continue the growing inequality of our times. For any counter-trend to have a chance, it must reassert the strength of the political (of politics as active, not reactive). The reinvention of an activist politics as at least co-equal with economics is necessary for the long-term viability of the EU project.

The quality of post-communist democracy: constrained and strained

If the above analysis has merit, what are the implications of the European and international environment for the quality of democratization and democracy in post-communist Europe? The external impacts are many and conflicting, but some regular patterns of domestic political adaptation and reaction have already emerged.

'Joining the West' does not mean achieving equality with any Western model from the Cold War Keynesian era, be it the Anglo-Saxon, Rhineland, or Latin variety. There will continue to be large gaps in wealth between Western and non-Western Europe, and there will be great inequalities within the new market economies of each post-communist nation. The popular base of support for the new democracies on economic performance grounds will be more narrow, so long as the project of global economic liberalism remains dominant. These nations are developing a constrained (Schumpeterian) variety of electoral democracy, with a large segment of the citizenry alienated or passive at best. This does not necessarily mean instability, because for the time being there will be no viable alternative to challenge these elitist democracies. Those who are best off, in the capital cities and in new growth sectors, will be in a strong position to influence political choices, while those who are losers will have few practical options for materially changing their conditions. This will create tensions within the body politic, since there remains a strong collectivist (socialist or populist) value culture among perhaps one-third to two-thirds of the population, although this may shift over decades and generations. This tension will be revived periodically, since it is now clear that there is not one economic reform crisis to be mastered, but rather a succession of crises bringing demands for new rounds of restructuring; this is now a key feature of our times, in an era of transnationally flexible and politically empowered finance capital, but it is particularly strong in the capital-poor dependencies of post-communist Europe.

Successive waves of liberal restructuring will test the breaking point of the social fabric, to see just how far the 'losers' can be pushed; international finance has no social component in its agenda. Multitudes who were unclear in 1990 about what status they might have under the new market systems will eventually get the message. The new middle classes and the small elite of big winners will become socially more separated and segregated from the working classes and the marginalized poor. One can see this process in action in the new wealthier neighborhoods and commercial complexes under construction around Prague, Budapest and Krakow, already equipped with their fences and security measures, while working class districts and public housing projects decay and fall victim to every social pathology.

Daniel Nelson warns that this economics in command is a formula for future trouble:

> . . . today, 'freemarketdemocracy' is contorted into a single expression, and applied with the vigorous enforcement of the International Monetary Fund (IMF) and other multilateral instruments. The prolonged evolution of capitalism and institutions of democratic republics that the United States (and a few other countries) were able to experience is not available to postauthoritarian states at the end of the twentieth century.
>
> It is plausible that the forced march toward free market economies, notwithstanding the exports it may generate, the industrial surge it might create, or the Mercedes dealerships which it can spawn, fosters a milieu of socioeconomic insecurity. Further, such insecurity – perhaps exacerbated by cultural, ethnic, or other factors – may harm participation, commitment to tenets of tolerance, pluralism, and competition and other core elements of democratic citizenship.
>
> Indeed, mounting empirical evidence suggests that citizens' commitment to participatory democracy suffers most in conditions of insecurity. A principal source of insecurity is economic – recognizing one's precarious economic condition relative to others, particularly if changes that could make things worse are being pursued quickly. Repeated studies have identified the strongly negative effect of income inequality on democratization. (1995: 167)

New survey evidence from post-communist Europe confirms the correlation between support for democracy and optimism about one's personal finances or optimism that the system will work for them, if not yet, then in the foreseeable future. The new political economy is itself a barrier to developing a broad-based civil society necessary for a consolidated democracy.

This is all happening in a period of global growth. But the new global economy is also volatile precisely because it is not moderated or regulated. The financial crises which shook investor confidence in Mexico in 1994, Southeast and East Asia in 1997 and Russia in 1998 will be repeated elsewhere; this is one price of the newly emancipated global capitalism. Crises of this sort bring new demands for economic adjustment at high cost to average citizens, in order to restore the confidence of major investors. It must be assumed that these crises will visit post-communist Europe as well. The first phase of economic restructuring in the East brought economic downturn, pain and dislocation, but was legitimately seen as a necessary price for overcoming the communist legacy. The first capitalist depression in post-communist Europe will bring the class polarization into a new political perspective, since it will be recognized as a part of the new system, its regular and necessary 'creative destruction' feature.

With a shaky legitimacy base, the new democratic regimes and their supporters may be tempted to maintain stability through increased executive power; economic shock therapy generally has the effect of strengthening central political authority, and successive economic shocks, in an environment of great social disparities, will most probably lead to greater executive authority and less parliamentary democracy (Orenstein, 1998). Does this mean that the Chilean Pinochet model may still be applicable for a crisis-ridden nation of post-communist Europe? Is a variant of authoritarian reformism, like Fujimori populism in Peru a possibility? Will Piłsudski-style presidentialism reappear on the scene, in some new adaptation? In the less successful transitions, parliaments are being pushed aside by strong presidents. The combination of crony capitalism and authoritarian presidentialism in Russia under Yeltsin provides a hint of what combinations of executive power and market reform might emerge. The big loser in such arrangements is effective political pluralism, usually represented through a vital party system and a functioning parliament, even if the formalities of democracy are retained (free but unfair elections, a state-dominated television system and purchased political journalism, and use of state funds for maintaining the 'party of power').

Competition from new regional projects in the global economy – from East Asia, Southeast Asia, Latin America, and even Russia – will also influence the margin for local adaptation in post-communist Europe. These economies are entering the global marketplace in a period of intensified competition. For the best-placed nations of East-Central Europe (Poland, the Czech Republic and Hungary), membership in the EU is vital for gaining some edge here, since by getting inside the larger regional political economy of Europe they will presumably be most compatible for investment and trade with Western Europe. But the price will be high, namely a willingness to offer, on a stable basis, a very advantageous investment location for European capital, with compatible banking and currency, stock market, labour market and legal frameworks more attractive than other regions. Even a second-class membership within the EU would be useful, but it would have to maintain the great gap between East-Central Europe and Western Europe in order to function. Attempts to close the gap with the West, such as rising wages, public redistribution projects or substantial social benefits, undercut this comparative advantage.

Whether as full members of the European Union, or as long-term associates, East-Central Europe is likely to develop within the historical framework of 'the lands between,' as the 'near abroad' of the core powers of the West. Structural constraints will have their consequences for the quality of democracy in the region. The features of political dependence and foreign economic influence cannot fail to call forth nationalist and populist reactions. These are proud cultures, through which people have struggled mightily to maintain their identities and to build nation-states in the modern era against some long odds (cf. Giessmann, 1996: 2–3).

What are the regular features of these economically dependent new democracies within the contraints of the international economic order? From other dependency cases (cf. Nowotny, 1997, for an explicit comparison between post-communist Europe and Latin America), we have some idea. Humiliated national pride finds outlets in anti-foreigner movements and demagogues, politics of populist backlash, and conspiracy theories of how the world works. Politics becomes personalized and party systems are weak and unstable, a situation which gives repeated opportunities to charlatans and demagogues. National populism mobilizes people to search out traitors and culpable elites, often from minority groups. On the other side, elite beneficiaries of international dependency ties are insecure, and seek to keep their hold on power through strong external support. They also hedge their bets by keeping much of their capital, and some family members, out of the country. They can, in extreme cases, lose all contact with their own culture and local society, and become doubtful or ambiguous about the educability and learning capability of their own countrymen.

In the least democratic post-communist systems, national populism quickly achieved a prominent or leading place in the political competition (Mečiar in Slovakia, Tudjman in Croatia, Milošević in Serbia, Lukashenka in Belarus); but this type of politics has not been limited to these countries. The elements of national populist backlash are already quite visible in Poland and Hungary, and may increase in the newly troubled Czech political system. From Polish Catholic nationalists, including a good part of the Church itself, one hears the usual conspiracy theories about foreign domination. Radio Maria, the Movement for Reconstruction of Poland, the Confederation for an Independent Poland, and part of the Solidarity trade union itself, articulate the politics of cultural nationalist backlash. In Hungary, the Independent Smallholders Party, the right-wing Christian Democrats, and the Hungarian Democratic Forum (not to mention the neo-fascists and István Csurka) are developing a similar politics of national populism. In the Czech Republic, the Republicans under Sládek are still relatively weak, but economic downturn may still create political backlash there.

Local nationalists and populists cannot change the larger economic environment within which their economies must try to find success. They cannot abolish the International Monetary Fund, or replace its directors and policies. A common substitute for national populist anger is mistreatment of individual foreigners and defenceless minorities, or overheated and provocative diatribes against neighbouring countries. Discrimination against Roma, bombings of synagogues and Jewish businesses, skinhead attacks on dark-skinned foreigners, are now common features of an impotent new nationalism, which materially reduces the quality of these democracies, producing and reproducing attitudes of intolerance, ethnic stereotyping and suspicion of outsiders. On the political right especially, this has impeded the rethinking and modernization of political conservatism; on the resurrected political left, the fear of being labelled as traitors to the nation or disloyal to ethnic brethren (Hungarians in Romania or Slovakia for example) has limited their ability to promote ethnic tolerance and social pluralism.

Daniel Chirot regrets that the European Union will not spread its 'protective mantle very far into Eastern Europe. At most, Poland, Hungary and the Czech Republic may be accepted as associate members. The Balkan countries and those of the former Soviet Union are not wanted. That is a great pity, and it makes the peaceful resolution of political problems and nationalist conflicts in this part of the world unlikely' (1995: 64). Chirot fears that the old model of ethnic nationalism, which was invented by Western Europe and which almost destroyed it, is being resurrected in the post-communist East. The collapse of communism was popularly received as a form of national liberation, an affirmation of those dissidents who were anti-communist but also anti-liberal nationalists. Anti-liberal nationalists see the end of Soviet domination as their triumph, and they carry on in the unbroken tradition of resistance to foreign domination and opposition to any threat to national identity. In this sense, the spectre of illiberal democracy is already haunting these new democracies.

The domestic promoters of economic liberalism and maximum openness to Western influence and investment have too narrow a popular base of support to provide a confident domestic leadership on their own. In some cases, they are dependent on the revived left (as in the left–liberal Hungarian coalition from 1994 to 1998, or in the 1997 vote on the new Polish constitution) to withstand the pressures from the national-populist right.

The new liberals of post-communist Europe have tended to buy into the most doctrinaire (von Hayek, von Mises, Friedman, Thatcher) *laissez-faire* versions of market economics, which represent the most anti-social models for state policy making. Support for this economic policy line makes them even more dependent on those with economic power to bolster their positions, and in the current period of building a new domestic business class, this means greater dependence on foreign sources of capital. This vicious cycle then hinders liberal reformers from defending themselves as authentic representatives of the nation and its people. The West was not shy about urging the Solidarity Electoral Alliance (AWS), after its victory in the 1997 elections, to give key economic ministries to the much smaller but liberal Freedom Union led by Leszek Balcerowicz, as assurance to Western finance about the economic 'political correctness' of the new government.

The watchword of the day in economics is 'lean and mean'. The new democracies in East-Central Europe will be shaped according to this current wisdom, with all of its positive and negative features. 'Lean and mean' democracies will have to manage greater class and group polarization, with little incentive for winners in the new competition to be generous to the losers. The new chasm between ostentatious consumerism and humiliated poverty will generate both fear and bitterness, as well as motivation for enterprise and hard work.

For Poland, Hungary and the Czech Republic, admission or even the current associated status in the European Union will help to maintain at least minimal standards of democracy. This itself is a great gain not to be overlooked or taken lightly. But the dependency relationship between these nations and the West will be difficult to transcend, and that will diminish the quality of these democracies until and unless the larger European and international environment itself can be reformed.

A different globalization, a different quality of democracy

It would be safer to end this study without further speculation on the forces shaping the democratization process in post-communist Europe. Comparative political analysts should know their limitations in predictive capability. Yet the neo-liberal version of economic globalization is so important that its own sustainability is crucial for any theory of democracy and democratization in East-Central Europe. There are signs that the legitimacy of doctrinaire global liberalism is now being challenged, as consciousness grows among elites and citizens that successive economic shocks are straining democracies and social peace in an increasing number of nations.

After twenty years of widespread democratization, which has so far coincided with the rise of global economic liberalism, critical debate is moving beyond the dependence on market capitalism as the sole criterion for policy and practice (cf. Nagle, 1998b: esp. ch. VI). George Soros, the major financial supporter of civil society in post-communist Europe through his Open Society foundation, has now argued that 'Although I have made a fortune in the financial markets, I now fear that the untrammeled intensification of laissez-faire capitalism and the spread of market values into all areas of life is endangering our open and democratic society. The main enemy of the open society, I believe, is no longer the communist but the capitalist threat' (1997: 45). In opposing the new Social Darwinism of our times, Soros argues the necessity for a healthy and corrective competition of different values: 'in an open society it is not enough to be a democrat; one must be a liberal democrat or a social democrat or a Christian democrat or some other kind of democrat. A shared belief in the open society is a necessary but not a sufficient condition for freedom and prosperity and all the good things that the open society is supposed to bring' (p. 58).

In 1996, the World Economic Forum (WEF), a leading liberal think-tank for the promotion of globalization, held its annual high-powered conference in Davos, Switzerland, specifically focused on the 'legitimacy crisis' of economic globalization. After the conference, Klaus Schwab, founder of WEF, and Claude Smadja, its managing director, wrote an article for the *International Herald Tribune* entitled 'Start Taking the Backlash Against Globalization Seriously', in which they recognized that global liberalism was indeed generating a popular backlash, as people react against the ongoing process of destructive restructuring which creates greater anxiety.

> It becomes apparent that the lead-on mega-competition that is part and parcel of globalization leads to winner-take-all situations; those who come out on top win big, and the losers lose even bigger. The gap between those able to ride the wave of globalization, especially because they are knowledge- and communications-oriented, and those left behind is getting wider at the national, corporate, and individual levels. (1 February 1996: 8)

William Greider (1996) has argued that the global market economy is already here, and cannot be stopped, but must be made socially and democratically responsible to the broad majority of citizens. Greider, in an editorial on the IMF and Western bail-outs in the Asian finance crisis, argues that to save the global market system, it must accept a new international social contract, which raises social equity and worker security issues to prominent levels of international concern. If the new globalists (its leading investors, banks and corporations) need financial support in these crisis situations, then they must accept social controls which have the force of democratic law (Greider, 1997). Why should democratic governments use taxpayer money to bail out high-risk investments, banking cronyism and corporate mistakes, while cutting social budgets at home?

Ralf Dahrendorf, a leading German liberal intellectual, and former Director of the London School of Economics, has recently added his voice to the shifting debate over the nature of economic globalization, and its impact on democracy. Like Soros, Greider, Schwab and Smajda, Dahrendorf does not seek to turn back the clock on the internationalization of trade, finance and technology transfer, and he warns against new nationalist protectionism or isolationism. But he sees globalization in its current form as a danger to democratic politics: 'Globalization diminishes the cohesion of civil society, on which the democratic discourse rests. Globalization replaces the institutions of democracy with inconsequential communication among atomized individuals' (1997: 8, authors' translation from the German).

Dahrendorf is not trying to paint a gloom and doom picture; many aspects of globalization have positive effects. Yet he does sound an alarm: 'But one must conclude that the developments toward globalization and its social effects give more advantage to authoritarian than to democratic systems. Authoritarian systems moreover can persist;

they are not so prone to catastrophe or so precarious as totalitarian dictatorships. A century of authoritarianism is not such an improbable prognosis for the twenty-first century' (1997: 8). This is a tendency, but not predetermined. Dahrendorf sees within the processes of globalization opportunities for different varieties of market economy and varieties of democracy. The Anglo-Saxon model (growth and democracy with little solidarity) is not destined to replace the Rhineland model (solidarity and democracy with little growth) or the Asian model (growth and solidarity with little democracy). Pure capitalism exists only in textbooks of the Chicago school of economics. The task of finding a new balance of social and economic values is still a political task of the nation-state, and the concept of 'social market economy' is still a meaningful goal. But it will require a new political struggle to discover this new balance in order to avoid the authoritarian tendencies of the globalization process.

These critiques from different political standpoints do not give a clear picture of just how, and when, the currently dominant form of globalization might be challenged and reformed. But there is now under way a growing debate over just this issue, resting upon a common recognition that 'economics in command' will not be sufficient, and is destroying its own social and political legitimacy. Widespread popular support, freely given through democratic processes, must accompany economic globalization for both globalization and democracy to prosper. Otherwise either globalization will lose out to popular demands for national self-protection, or democratic processes will be progressively undermined by economic elites in favour of more authoritarian methods.

The contradictions between non-democratic economic globalization and the newborn democratization at the nation-state level requires some new thinking about forms and processes of democracy. A hollowed-out democracy at the national level will have great difficulty convincing citizens that they have a political voice, since apparently the big decisions which affect their lives are beyond their reach, and the reach of their elected representatives. Daniel Nelson has cautioned that

> Rapid, externally enforced 'marketization', accompanied by at least a temporary surge in income inequality, will heighten insecurity while *conflicting* with a preference for gradual change. This is a mix which bodes ill for protodemocracies. . . . Free market economics coupled with democratic political institutions and processes are the conditions in which postauthoritarian countries can find peace and prosperity. The population's role in such a transition is essential. A democracy cannot exist where the public political sphere is weak or collapsing, for without such a participatory ethos there is no responsiveness or accountability. Yet, it may be unavoidable that postauthoritarian publics will turn away from new demands being placed upon them if the costs are perceived to be too high – if unemployment, inflation, crime, and political turmoil are threatening. (1995: 167–168)

Nelson recommends an international regime of supports as well as demands which would allow for more gradual change, in order to maintain the necessary popular base for a democratic politics. If the global economic order fails to extend some network of social supports for the broad majority, the new democratization will fail. 'Where people are insecure, the norms of democracy are unlikely to take root' (1995: 170).

David Held has been one of the leading thinkers on a new democratization project, embedding the nation-state democracy in a network of democratic processes that goes beyond national boundaries. The irony of our century is that the victories of representative democracy which have given citizen-voters, in principle, the chance to hold public officials accountable, have culminated at a time when the new international economic order is rapidly diminishing the efficacy of nation-state politics. 'At a time when the idea of "the rule of the people" is more popular than ever, the very efficacy of democracy as a national form of political organization is open to doubt' (1995a: 99). To avoid the danger that democracy may come to be seen as too weak or ineffectual to address citizen concerns, Held has proposed the development of 'cosmopolitan democracy', emerging from a democratization process beyond national borders, which would restore accountability to citizens and nations within the global context. 'However cosmopolitan democracy is precisely envisaged, it is based upon the recognition that democracy within a particular community and democratic relations among communities are interlocked, absolutely inseparable, and that new organizational and binding mechanisms must be created if democracy is to survive and develop in the decades ahead' (1995a: 112). Held argues that this cosmopolitan democracy does not require political and cultural integration, nor would it undermine distinctive national, ethnic, cultural and social identities which are still the foundations of individual identities. Rather it would stress that peaceful problem-solving, whether for security, economics, human rights, or the environment, should be rooted in democratic processes, in the pre-commitment to the democratic idea that the political good must rest with approval of the people. A cosmopolitan democratic process, with its emphasis on tolerance and pluralism, would in fact be the best protection for distinctive national identities.

In opening up new avenues for political participation, cosmopolitan democracy would require going beyond Schumpeter's elitist concept.

> By making politics potentially coextensive with all realms of social and economic power, it opens these domains to public regulation and control. Schumpeter thought politics so conceived would offer an enormous temptation to those with resources, whether they be majorities or minorities, to control all aspects of life. Broad concepts of politics, he suggested, may become connected for many, in practice, to a diminution of freedom.

But real though this risk is, the preference for democracy contains within itself obstacles to political hierarchy and unwarranted intrusion. It does so by the insistence that decisions be debated and taken by those who are immediately affected by them, and by the insistence that this process is compatible with respect for the rights and obligations of others. Political intervention, accordingly, finds its rationale in the pursuit and maintenance of the rule of democratic law; or, to recast the point, political issues and problems ought only to be pursued within and beyond particular associations if they deepen the entrenchment of this law. (Held, 1995b: 265–266)

If democracy and democratization are to retain their current popularity, they must continue to prove their relevance for citizens, first and foremost in support of broad-based social and economic security. The necessary counter-balance to the current dominance of globalizing capital is to be found in 'cosmopolitan democratic law – enhanced through its enactment in the agencies and organizations of economic life; through democratic deliberation and coordination of public investment priorities; through the pursuit of non-market policies to aid fair outcomes in market exchange; and through experimentation with different forms of the ownership and control of capital' (1995b: 266).

Democratization applied internationally to reform economic globalization can raise the quality of democracy nationally. That would change the picture we have presented here greatly, but that is only a potential for the future, resting upon actions and interactions so complex that no prediction is possible.

Bibliography

Note: The journal *Transition* becomes *Transitions* in 1997.

Abraham, Arpad (1996) 'Winners and Losers', *Figyelö*, 6 August. Translated by the Foreign Broadcast Information Service. pp. 96–208.

Adorno, Theodor, E. Frankel-Brunswick and D. Levinson (1950) *The Authoritarian Personality*. New York: Harper & Row.

Ágh, Attila (1996) 'From Nomenklatura to Clientura: the Emergence of New Political Elites in East-Central Europe', in G. Pridham and P. Lewis (eds), *Stabilising Fragile Democracies: Comparing New Party Systems in Southern and Eastern Europe*. London: Routledge. pp. 44–68.

Ágh, Attila (1998) *The Politics of Central Europe*. London: Sage.

Agócs, Peter and Sandor Agócs (1994) 'Youth in Post-Communist Hungary', *Society*, 31 (3): 76–81.

Agüero, Felipe (1995) 'Democratic Consolidation and the Military in Southern Europe and South America', in Richard Gunther, Hans-Jürgen Puhle and Nikiforos Diamandouros (eds), *The Politics of Democratic Consolidation*. Baltimore, MD: Johns Hopkins University Press. pp. 124–165.

Albright, Madeleine (1992) 'The Glorious Revolutions of 1989', in Larry Garber and Eric Bjornlund (eds), *The New Democratic Frontier: A Country by Country Report on Elections in Central and Eastern Europe*. Washington, DC: National Democratic Institute for International Affairs. pp. 11–19.

Almond, Gabriel and Sidney Verba (1963) *The Civic Culture*. Boston, MA: Little Brown.

Amsden, Alice (1989) *Asia's Next Giant: South Korea and Late Industrialization*. New York: Oxford University Press.

Amsden, Alice H., Jacek Kochanowicz and Lance Taylor (1994) *The Market Meets its Match. Restructuring the Economies of Eastern Europe*. Cambridge, MA: Harvard University Press.

Arendt, Hannah (1960) *The Origins of Totalitarianism*. New York: Meridian Books.

Ascherson, Neal (1992) '1989 in Eastern Europe', in John Dunn (ed.), *Democracy – The Unfinished Journey*. Oxford: Oxford University Press.

Avineri, Shlomo (1968) *The Social and Political Thought of Karl Marx*. New York: Cambridge University Press.

Bachrach, Peter (1967) *The Theory of Democratic Elitism: A Critique*. Boston, MA: Little Brown.

Baczynski, Jerzy, Jacek Mojkowski, Joanna Solska, Ewa Szemplinska and Pawel Tarnowski (1997) 'Four Weddings and a Funeral: The Polish Economy under the Rule of the SLD-PSL Coalition in the Years 1993–97', *Polityka*, 6 September. Translated by the Foreign Broadcast Information Service.

Baker, Kendall (1981) *Germany Transformed*. Cambridge, MA: Harvard University Press.

Balcerowicz, Leszek (1994) 'The European Periphery: Poland', in John Williamson (ed.), *The Political Economy of Policy Reform*. Washington, DC: Institute for International Economics. pp. 153–177.

Balogh, András (1994) 'National Minorities and International Security', *Review of International Affairs*, XLIV (1023): 24–27.

Banfield, Edward (1958) *The Moral Basis of a Backward Society*. New York: Free Press.

Barany, Zoltan (1995) 'Favorable Trends for Romania's Romani', *Transition*, 1 (19), 20 October 1995: 26–31.

Barber, Benjamin (1992) 'Jihad versus McWorld', *Atlantic Monthly*, (March): 53–63.

Bartha, Attila and Jozsef Peter Martin (1995) 'Certificate of Origin', *Figyelö*, 23 November. Translated by the Foreign Broadcast Information Service.

Bartlett, David and Wendy Hunter (1997) 'Market Structures, Political Institutions, and Democratization: the Latin American and East European Experiences', *Review of International Political Economy*, 4 (1): 87–126.

Bauman, Zygmunt (1976) 'The Party in the System-Management Phase: Change and Continuity', in Andrew Janos (ed.), *Authoritarian Politics in Communist Europe*. Berkeley, CA: Institute of International Studies.

Baylis, Thomas (1973) 'Elites and the Idea of Post-Industrial Society in the Two Germanies' APSA conference paper, New Orleans, September 4–8.

Beck, Carl, Frederic Flaron and Milton Lodge (1973) *Comparative Communist Political Leadership*. New York: McKay.

Bell, Daniel A. (1995) 'Democracies in Confucian Societies', in Daniel A. Bell, David Brown, Kanishka Jayasuriya and David Jones (eds), *Towards Illiberal Democracy in Pacific Asia*. Oxford: St Martin's Press. pp. 17–40.

Bell, Daniel A. and Kanishka Jayasuriya (1995) 'Understanding Illiberal Democracy', in Daniel A. Bell, David Brown, Kanishka Jayasuriya and David Jones (eds), *Towards Illiberal Democracy in Pacific Asia*. Oxford: St Martin's Press.

Bell, Daniel A., David Brown, Kanishka Jayasuriya and David Jones (eds) (1995) *Towards Illiberal Democracy in Pacific Asia*. Oxford: St Martin's Press.

Bell, John D. (1993) 'Bulgaria', in Stephen White, Judy Batt and Paul G. Lewis (eds), *Developments in East European Politics*. Durham, NC: Duke University Press. pp. 83–97.

Berend, Ivan (1995) 'Alternatives of Transformation', in Beverly Crawford (ed.), *Markets, States, and Democracy*. Boulder, CO: Westview Press.

Berlin, Isaiah (1958) *Two Concepts of Liberty*. Oxford: Clarendon Press.

Berlin, Isaiah (1997) 'Die Zwei Gesichter der Freiheit', *Die Zeit*, 28 November: 13–14.

Bermeo, Nancy (1994) 'Comments on The European Periphery', in John Williamson (ed.), *The Political Economy of Policy Reform*. Washington, DC: Institute for International Economics. pp. 197–206.

Bernhard, Michael (1996) 'Civil Society after the First Transition', *Communist and Post-Communist Studies*, 29/3: 309–330.

Bertsch, Gary and Thomas Ganschow (eds) (1976) *Comparative Communism: The Soviet, Chinese, and Yugoslav Models*. San Fransisco: W.H. Freeman.

Białecki, Ireneusz and Barbara Heyns (1994) 'Educational Attainment, the Status of Women, and the Private School Movement in Poland', in Valentine

Moghadam (ed.), *Democratic Reform and the Position of Women in Transitional Economies*. Oxford: Clarendon Press. pp. 110–134.

Bisschop, Gita (1996) 'Optimism Wanes for a Prompt Cleanup', *Transition*, 2 (10), 17 May 1996: 42–45.

Bivand, Roger (1994) 'Return of the New: The Regional Imprint of the 1993 Parliamentary Elections in Poland', *European Urban and Regional Studies*, 1/1: 63–83.

Blahoz, Josef (1994) 'Parties in the Czech and Slovak Republics', in Kay Lawson (ed.), *How Parties Work*. Westport, CN: Praeger. pp. 229–247.

Blocker, Joel (1997a) 'Europe: Council of Europe – A Leading Gateway to Integration'. Radio Free Europe <.http://www.rferl.org/nca...1/F.RU.971111154036.html> 11 November.

Blocker, Joel (1997b) 'Europe: EU Promises Most, Delivers Least to the East'. Radio Free Europe <http://www.rferl.org/nca...1/F.RU.971111153853.html> 11 November.

Bollag, Burton (1996) 'A Museum Devoted to the Largest Minority Group in Europe – The Gypsies – Gets a Home of Its Own', *Chronicle of Higher Education*, 42 (20), 26 January: A36.

Bottomore, Tom (1966) *Elites and Society*. London: Penguin.

Bracher, Karl Dietrich (1970) *The German Dictatorship*. New York: Praeger.

Brown, Archie and Jack Gray (eds) (1977) *Political Culture and Political Change in Communist Systems*. New York: Holmes and Meier.

Brown, David (1995) 'Democratization and the Renegotiation of Ethnicity', in Daniel A. Bell, David Brown, Kanishka Jayasuriya, and David Jones (eds), *Towards Illiberal Democracy in Pacific Asia*. Oxford: St Martin's Press. pp. 134–162.

Brown, J.F. (1991) *Surge to Freedom*. Durham, NC: Duke University Press.

Brown, J.F. (1994) *Hopes and Shadows*. Durham, NC: Duke University Press.

Brown, J.F. (1997) 'Goodbye (and Good Riddance?) to De-Communization', *Transitions*, 4 (2): 28–34.

Bryant, Stephen R. (1991) 'Polish-Lithuanian Relations: Past, Present, and Future', *Problems of Communism*, 40: 67–84.

Bunce, Valerie (1995) 'Should Transitologists Be Grounded?', *Slavic Review*, 54 (1): 111–127.

Bunce, Valerie and Mária Csanádi (1993) 'Uncertainty in the Transition: Post Communism in Hungary', *East European Politics and Societies*, 7 (2): 240–275.

Burton, Michael, Richard Gunther and John Higley (1992) 'Elites and democratic consolidation in Latin America and Southern Europe: an overview', in John Higley and Richard Gunther (eds), *Elites and Democratic Consolidation in Latin America and Southern Europe*. Cambridge: Cambridge University Press. pp. 323–348.

Butorova, Zora and Martin Butora (1995a) 'Political Parties, Value Orientations, and Slovakia's Road to Independence', in Gordon Wightman (ed.), *Party Formation in East-Central Europe*. Aldershot: Edward Elgar.

Butorova, Zora and Martin Butora (1995b) 'Improving Ethnic Relationships Is Always More Difficult Than Making Them Worse', *SME*, 27 April. Translated by the Foreign Broadcast Information Service.

Bystydzienksi, Jill M. (ed.) (1992) *Women Transforming Politics: Worldwide Strategies for Empowerment*. Bloomington, IN: Indiana University Press.

Bystydzienksi, Jill M. (1995) 'Women and Families in Poland: Pressing Problems and Possible Solutions', in B. Łobodzińska (ed.), *Family, Women and Employment in Central and Eastern Europe*. Westport, CT: Greenwood Press. pp. 193–203.

Cain, Michael J.G. (1998) 'Liberalism Under the Microscope', *Transitions*, 5 (2): 49–53.

Caldwell, Gillian (1998) 'Sold Into the Sex Trade', *Transitions*, 5 (1): 70–1.

Cammack, Paul (1994) 'Democratization and Citizenship in Latin America', in Geraint Parry and Michael Moran (eds), *Democracy and Democratization*. London: Routledge. pp. 174–195.

Carey, Henry F. (1996) 'From Big Lies to Little Lies: State Mass Media Dominance in Post-Communist Romania', *East European Politics and Societies*, 10 (1): 16–45.

Castañeda, Jorge (1994) *Utopia Unarmed: The Latin American Left after the Cold War*. New York: Vintage Books.

Cebulak, Wojciech (1997) 'Social Turmoil in Post-Socialist Eastern Europe – A Revolution Gone Astray?', *East European Quarterly*, 31/1 (March): 111–119.

CEER (1997) 'Public Pulse', *Central European Economic Review*, September: 8.

Černá, Alena and Eva Tošovská in cooperation with Pavel Cetkovský (1995) 'Economic Transformation and the Environment', *Eastern European Economics*, 33 (3): 5–43.

Chilcote, Ronald (1994) *Theories of Comparative Politics: The Search for a Paradigm Reconsidered*. Boulder, CO: Westview Press.

Chirot, Daniel (1995) 'National Liberation and Nationalist Nightmares', in Beverly Crawford (ed.), *Markets, States, and Democracy*. Boulder, CO: Westview Press.

Chirot, Daniel (1996) 'Why Central Europe is Not Quite Ready for Peron, but May Be One Day', *East European Politics and Societies*, 10 (3): 536–540.

Clark, Ed and Anna Soulsby (1996) 'The Re-formation of the Managerial Elite in the Czech Republic', *Europe–Asia Studies*, 48 (2): 285–303.

Coleman, Brian (1997) 'Eastward Ho!', *Central European Economic Review*, June: 20–21, 24, 29.

Comisso, Ellen (1997) 'Is the Glass Half Full or Half Empty?', *Communist and Post-Communist Studies*, 30 (1): 1–21.

Commission on Security and Cooperation in Europe (CSCE) (1993) 'Human Rights and Democratization in Hungary'. CSCE: Washington, DC. December.

Commission on Security and Cooperation in Europe (CSCE) (1994a) 'Human Rights and Democratization in Poland'. CSCE: Washington, DC. January.

Commission on Security and Cooperation in Europe (CSCE) (1994b) 'Human Rights and Democratization in the Czech Republic'. CSCE: Washington, DC. September.

Commission on Security and Cooperation in Europe (CSCE) (1997) 'The Continued Use of Torture in Turkey'. CSCE: Washington, DC.

Cook, Linda J. (1995) 'Labor Unions in Post-Communist Countries', *Problems of Post-Communism*, 42 (2): 13–18.

Cornia, Giovanni Andrea and Sandor Sipos (eds) (1991) *Children and the Transition to the Market Economy*. Brookfield, VT: Avebury.

Corrin, Chris (1993) 'People and Politics', in Stephen White, Judy Batt and Paul G. Lewis (eds), *Developments in East European Politics*. Durham, NC: Duke University Press. pp. 186–204.

Corrin, Chris (1994) *Magyar Women*. New York: St Martin's Press.

Crane, Keith (1995) 'The Costs and Benefits of Transition', in John P. Hardt and Richard S. Kaufman (eds), *East Central European Economies in Transition*. Armonk, New York: M.E. Sharpe. pp 25–48.

Crowe, David and John Kolsti (eds) (1991) *The Gypsies of Eastern Europe*. Armonk, NY: M.E. Sharpe.

Crozier, M., S. Huntington and J. Watanuki (1975) *The Crisis of Democracy: Report on the Governability of Democracies to the Trilateral Commission*. New York: New York University Press.

Csagoly, Paul (1998) 'Green Economics', *Transitions*, 5 (6): 74–77.

Cuthbertson, Ian M. and Jane Leibowitz (eds) (1993) *Minorities: The New Europe's Old Issue*. New York and Atlanta: Institute for EastWest Studies.

Dahl, Robert (1956) *A Preface to Democratic Theory*. Chicago: University of Chicago Press.

Dahl, Robert (1971) *Polyarchy: Participation and Opposition*. New Haven, CT: Yale University Press.

Dahl, Robert (1995) 'The Newer Democracies: From the Time of Triumph to the Time of Troubles', in Daniel Nelson (ed.), *After Authoritarianism: Democracy or Disorder?* Westport, CT: Praeger.

Dahrendorf, Ralf (1997) 'An der Schwelle zum autoritären Jahrhundert', *die Zeit*, 21 November: 7–8.

Darnovsky, Marcy, Barbara Epstein and Richard Flacks (eds) (1995) *Cultural Politics and Social Movements*. Philadelphia: Temple University Press.

Dawisha, Karen and Bruce Parrot (1994) *Russia and the New States of Eurasia: The Politics of Upheaval*. Cambridge: Cambridge University Press.

Deacon, Bob (1993) 'Social Change, Social Problems and Social Policy', in Stephen White, Judy Batt and Paul G. Lewis (eds), *Developments in East European Politics*. Durham, NC: Duke University Press. pp. 225–239.

Deacon, Bob (1997) 'Social Policy in Eastern Europe and the Former USSR', in *Eastern Europe and the Commonwealth of Independent States, 1997*, 3rd edn. London: Europa Publications. pp. 76–81.

Deak, István (1994) 'Post-Post-Communist Hungary', *New York Review of Books*, LXI/14: 33–38.

Dealy, Glen (1992) 'Pipe Dreams: The Pluralistic Latins', in Howard Wiarda (ed.), *Politics and Social Change in Latin America*. Boulder, CO: Westview Press.

Deininger, Klaus and Lyn Squire (1996) 'A New Data Set Measuring Income Inequality', *World Bank Economic Review*, 10 (3): 565–591.

Denni Telegraf (1996a) 'Trust in Constitutional Institutions Moderately Declined', 6 February. Translated by the Foreign Broadcast Information Service.

Denni Telegraf (1996b) 'The President Is Trusted by the Greatest Number of Citizens in a Year', 1 October. Translated by the Foreign Broadcast Information Service.

Deschouwer, Kris and Bruno Coppieters (1994) 'A West European Model for Social Democracy in East-Central Europe', in M. Waller, B. Coppieters and K. Deschouwer (eds), *Social Democracy in a Post-Communist Europe*. London: Frank Cass. pp. 1–18.

Diamond, Larry (1996) 'Democracy in Latin America: Degrees, Illusions, and Directions for Consolidation', in Tom Farer (ed.), *Beyond Sovereignty: Collectively Defending Democracy in the Americas*. Baltimore, MD: Johns Hopkins University Press.

Diamond, Larry, Juan Linz and Seymour Martin Lipset (eds) (1989a) *Democracy in Developing Countries. Volume 3. Asia*. Boulder, CO: Lynne Rienner.

Diamond, Larry, Juan Linz and Seymour Martin Lipset (eds) (1989b) *Democracy in Developing Countries: Volume 4: Latin America*. London: Adamantine.

Diehl, Jackson (1997) 'Visit to a Strange New Poland', *Washington Post*, 5 October: C1–C2.

Dobrosielski, Marian (1996) 'Polens Säkularisierung', *Blätter für deutsche und internationale Politik*, 1: 9–12.

Dogan, Mattei and Dominique Pelassy (1990) *How to Compare Nations*, 2nd edn. Chatham, NJ: Chatham House.

Done, Kevin (1997) 'Transition still painful for those in new markets', *Financial Times*, 3 December: 2.

Drozdiak, William (1998) 'Right-Wing Violence on Rise in Eastern Germany', *Washington Post*, 5 March: A23, A27.

Druker, Jeremy (1997) 'Present but Unaccounted For', *Transitions*, 4 (4): 22.

Dusza, Erika, Zoltan Gaal and Ferenc Sengal (1997) 'The Underworld Cannot Be Eliminated – Mafia in Hungary', *Magyar Hirlap*, 29 January. Translated by the Foreign Broadcast Information Service.

Dyer, Geoff (1997) 'Brazilian MPs show a fickleness to parties', *Financial Times* (London), 11/12 October: 4.

Dziewanowski, M.K. (1996) 'Polish Populism', in Joseph Held (ed.), *Populism in Eastern Europe: Racism, Nationalism, and Society*. New York: Columbia University Press.

Eberstadt, Nicholas (1994) 'Health and Mortality in Central and Eastern Europe: Retrospect and Prospect', in James R. Millar and Sharon L. Wolchik (eds), *The Social Legacy of Communism*. Washington, DC: Woodrow Wilson Center Press. pp. 196–225.

Echikson, William (1997) 'EU Rethinks its Funding to East', RFE/RL Newsline, 9 September.

Economic Commission for Europe (1996) *Economic Survey of Europe 1995–96*. New York: United Nations.

Economist (1995) 'Eastern Europe's Hungry Children', 16 December: 50.

Economist (1996a) 'Health in Eastern Europe: Out of the Ward', 3 August: 45–46.

Economist (1996b) 'Meciar, Magyars and Maps', 10 August 1996: 38–39.

Economist (1996c) 'Free At Last, to Die', 21 September: 53–54.

Economist (1998) 'Awkward Would-be Partners', 28 February: 54–56.

Eggleton, Roland (1997) 'Europe: How the OSCE Fosters Human Rights, Security and Civil Society' Radio Free Europe <http://www.rferl.org/nca...1/F.RU.971111153755.html> 11 November.

Einhorn, Barbara (1994) 'Democratization and Women's Movements in Central and Eastern Europe', in V. Moghadam (ed.), *Democratic Reform and the Position of Women in Transitional Economies*. Oxford: Clarendon Press. pp. 48–74.

EIU (Economist Intelligence Unit) (1991) *Country Profile for Poland (1991–92)*. London: EIU.

EIU (Economist Intelligence Unit) (1992) *Country Profile for Poland (1992–93)*. London: EIU.

EIU (Economist Intelligence Unit) (1993a) *Country Profile for Poland (1993–94)*. London: EIU.

EIU (Economist Intelligence Unit) (1993b) *Country Report For Poland, 3rd Quarter 1993*. London: EIU.

EIU (Economist Intelligence Unit) (1994) *Country Report for Poland, 1st Quarter 1994*. London: EIU.

EIU (Economist Intelligence Unit) (1995a) *Country Report for Hungary, 2nd Quarter 1995*. London: EIU.

EIU (Economist Intelligence Unit) (1995b) *Country Report for Hungary, 4th Quarter 1995*. London: EIU.

EIU (Economist Intelligence Unit) (1995c) *Country Report for Poland, 1st Quarter 1995*. London: EIU.

EIU (Economist Intelligence Unit) (1995d) *Country Report for Poland, 3rd Quarter 1995*. London: EIU.

EIU (Economist Intelligence Unit) (1996a) *Country Report for Poland, 2nd Quarter 1996*. London: EIU.

EIU (Economist Intelligence Unit) (1996b) *Country Report for Hungary, 1st Quarter 1996*. London: EIU.

EIU (Economist Intelligence Unit) (1996c) *Country Report for Poland, 2nd Quarter 1996*. London: EIU.

EIU (Economist Intelligence Unit) (1997a) *Country Profile for Czech Republic (1997–98)*. London: EIU.

EIU (Economist Intelligence Unit) (1997b) *Country Profile for Hungary (1997–98)*. London: EIU.

EIU (Economist Intelligence Unit) (1997c) *Country Profile for Poland (1997–98)*. London: EIU.

EIU (Economist Intelligence Unit) (1997d) *Country Report for Czech Republic, 2nd Quarter 1997*. London: EIU.

EIU (Economist Intelligence Unit) (1998a) *Country Report for Czech Republic, 2nd Quarter 1998*. London: EIU.

EIU (Economist Intelligence Unit) (1998b) *Country Report for Hungary, 2nd Quarter 1998*. London: EIU.

EIU (Economist Intelligence Unit) (1998c) *Country Report for Poland, 2nd Quarter 1998*. London: EIU.

Ellingstad, Mark (1997) 'The Maquiladora Syndrome: Central European Prospects', *Europe–Asia Studies*, 49 (1): 7–21.

Encarnacion, Omar (1997) 'Social Concertation in Democratic and Market Transitions: Comparative Lessons from Spain', *Comparative Political Studies*, 30 (4): 387–419.

Esping-Andersen, Gosta (1994) 'Budgets and Democracy: towards a Welfare State in Spain and Portugal, 1960–1986', in Ian Budge and David McKay (eds), *Developing Democracy*. London: Sage. pp. 112–128.

Ester, Peter, Loek Halman and Vladimir Rukavishnikov (1997) *From Cold War to Cold Peace?* Tilburg, The Netherlands: Tilburg University Press.

Etzioni-Halevy, Eva (ed.) (1997) *Classes and Elites in Democracy and Democratization*. New York: Garland.

Eulau, Heinz and Moshe Czudnowski (eds) (1976) *Elite Recruitment in Democratic Politics*. New York: John Wiley.

Eyal, Jonathan (1997) 'Eastern Europe: A Critique of the Western Perspective', in *Eastern Europe and the Commonwealth of Independent States 1997*, 3rd edn. London: Europa Publications. pp. 3–12.

Fábián, Katalin (unpublished) 'Within Yet Without: Problems of Women's Powerlessness in Democratic Hungary'. Department of Political Science, Syracuse University, NY.

Fainsod, Merle (1953) *How Russia is Ruled*. Cambridge, MA: Harvard University Press.

Farrell, Barry (ed.) (1970) *Political Leadership in Eastern Europe and the Soviet Union*. Chicago: Aldine.

Fidler, Stephen (1997) 'Forces to be Reckoned With', *Financial Times* (London), 17 September: 15.

Filas, Agnieszka and Jaroslaw Knap in cooperation with Jacek Szczesny (1997) 'The Corporate Choice: Who Are Polish Entrepreneurs Going to Back?' *Wprost*, 20 April. Translated by the Foreign Broadcast Information Service. 97–176.

Fischer, George (1968) *The Soviet System and Modern Society*. New York: Atherton.

Fisher, Sharon (1995) 'Ethnic Hungarians Back Themselves Into a Corner', *Transition*, 1 (24): 58–63.

Fisher, Sharon (1996) 'Slovak Nationalities Council Rejects Minority Language Law', *OMRI Daily Digest*, 227 (II): 22 November.

Fleron, Frederic (ed.) (1969) *Communist Studies and the Social Sciences*. Chicago: Rand McNally.

Fong, Monica and Gillian Paull (1994) 'Women's Economic Status in the Restructuring of Eastern Europe', in V. Moghadam (ed.), *Democratic Reform and the Position of Women in Transitional Economies*. Oxford: Clarendon Press. pp. 217–247.

Forowicz, Krystyna (1998a) 'Advantage to the Green', *Rzeczpospolita*, 23 April. Translated by the Foreign Broadcast Information Service.

Forowicz, Krystyna (1998b) 'Farewell to Poisoners', *Rzeczpospolita*, 17 July. Translated by the Foreign Broadcast Information Service.

Frankland, Erich G. (1995) 'The Role of Green Parties in East Europe's Transition, 1989–1994', *East European Quarterly*, 29 (3): 315–345.

Freedom House (1996) *Freedom in the World: The Annual Survey of Political Rights and Civil Liberties, 1995–1996*. New York: Freedom House.

Freeman, Richard B. (1993) 'What Direction for Labor-Market Institutions in Eastern and Central Europe?', in Bertram Silverman, Robert Vogt and Murray Yanowitch (eds), *Double Shift: Transforming Work in Postsocialist Societies*. Armonk, NY: M.E. Sharpe. pp. 95–115.

Friedrich, Carl (1950) *The New Belief in the Common Man*. Boston, MA: Little Brown.

Friedrich, Carl and Zbigniew Brzezinski (1956) *Totalitarian Dictatorship and Autocracy*. Cambridge, MA: Harvard University Press.

Funk, Nanette and Magda Mueller (eds) (1993) *Gender Politics and Post Communism*. New York: Routledge.

Furnham, Adrian (1994) 'The Psychosocial Consequences of Youth Unemployment', in Anne C. Petersen and Jeylan T. Mortimer (eds) *Youth Unemployment and Society*. Cambridge: The Press Syndicate of the University of Cambridge. pp. 199–223.

Furtak, Robert (1996) 'Zum Verhältnis von Staatspräsident und Regierung in postkommunistischen Staaten', in Otto Luchterhand (ed.), *Neue Regierungssysteme in Osteuropa und der GUS*. Berlin: Arno Spitz. pp. 115–150.

Gaal, Zoltan (1996) 'The Increase in Crime is Inevitable', *Magyar Hirlap*, 29 October. Translated by the Foreign Broadcast Information Service.

Garber, Larry (1992) 'Bulgaria', in Larry Garber and Eric Bjornlund (eds), *The*

New Democratic Frontier: A Country by Country Report on Elections in Central and Eastern Europe. Washington, DC: National Democratic Institute for International Affairs. pp. 133–160.

Garber, Larry and Eric Bjornlund (eds) (1992) *The New Democratic Frontier: A Country by Country Report on Elections in Central and Eastern Europe.* Washington, DC: National Democratic Institute for International Affairs.

Garten, Jeffrey (1992) *A Cold Peace: America, Japan, Germany and the Struggle for Supremacy.* New York: Times Books.

Garton Ash, Timothy (1989) *We The People.* London: Granta Books.

Garton Ash, Timothy (1990) *The Uses of Adversity.* New York: Vintage Books.

Garton Ash, Timothy (1996) 'Neo-Pagan Poland', *New York Review of Books*, 11 January: 10–14.

Garton Ash, Timothy (1997) 'Eastern Europe No Longer Exists', RFE/RL Newsline, 9 September.

Gati, Charles (1996, 1997) 'The Mirage of Democracy', in Open Media Research Institute, *The OMRI Annual Survey of Eastern Europe and the Former Soviet Union.* Armonk, New York: M.E. Sharpe. pp. 340–354.

Gazeta Wyborcza (1997a) 'The Line for Scanning', 19 July. Translated by the Foreign Broadcast Information Service.

Gazeta Wyborcza (1997b) 'Where the Wind Blows in the Electorate', 24 September. Translated by the Foreign Broadcast Information Service.

Gazeta Wyborcza (1998) 'CBOS on Public Institutions; NBP Goes Up the Fastest', 10 March. Translated by the Foreign Broadcast Information Service.

Gebethner, Stanislaw (1996) 'Proportional Representation Versus Majoritarian Systems: Free Elections and Political Parties in Poland, 1989–1991', in Arend Lijphart and Carlos Waisman (eds), *Institutional Design in New Democracies.* Boulder, CO: Westview Press.

Gibson, David (1996) 'High Public Confidence in the Church', *Transition*, (2) 7: 29.

Giessmann, Hans-Joachim (1996) 'Democracy as a Function of Transformation in Eastern Central Europe', paper presented at the International Studies Association meeting in San Diego, CA, 16–20 April.

Gigli, Susan (1995) 'Toward Increased Participation in the Political Process', *Transition*, 1 (16): 18–21.

Gills, Barry (1993) 'Korean Capitalism and Democracy', in Barry Gills, Joel Rocamora and Richard Wilson (eds), *Low Intensity Democracy.* London: Pluto Press. pp. 226–257.

Gills, Barry, Joel Rocamora and Richard Wilson (eds) (1993) *Low Intensity Democracy.* London: Pluto Press.

Giorgi, Liana (1995) *The Post-Socialist Media: What Power the West?* Brookfield, VT: Ashgate.

Glaeßner, Gert-Joachim (1997) 'Von der Perestroika zur liberalen Demokratie', in G.J. Glaeßner and M. Reiman (eds), *Systemwechsel und Demokratisierung.* Opladen: Westdeutscher Verlag. pp. 13–44.

Glenny, Misha (1990) *The Rebirth of History: Eastern Europe in the Age of Democracy.* London: Penguin Books.

Goban-Klas, Tomasz (1994) *The Orchestration of the Media: The Politics of Mass Communication in Communist Poland and the Aftermath.* Boulder, CO: Westview Press.

Goble, Paul (1997a) 'The Security NATO Can't Provide', RFE/RL Newsline, 1: 142, Part II, 20 October.

Goble, Paul (1997b) 'Polish Parliament Supports Tough Anti-Abortion Law', RFE/RL Newsline 1:182: part II, 18 December.

Goble, Paul (1997c) 'But Restrictive Abortion Legislation Returns to Force', RFE/RL Newsline 1:186: part II, 23 December.

Goldfarb, Jeffrey (1992) After the Fall. New York: Basic Books.

Gortat, Radzisława (1993) 'The Feud Within Solidarity's Offspring', Journal of Communist Studies, 9 (4): 116–124.

Gortat, Radzisława (1994) 'The development of Social Democracy in Poland', in M. Waller, B. Coppieters and K. Deschouwer (eds), Social Democracy in a Post-Communist Europe. London: Frank Cass. pp. 136–154.

Gowan, Peter (1995) 'Neo-Liberal Theory and Practice for Eastern Europe', New Left Review, 213: 3–60.

Gowan, Peter (1996) 'Poland's Transition from State Socialism to Capitalism', in Gerd Nonneman (ed.), Political and Economic Liberalization. Boulder, CO: Lynne Rienner Publishers. pp. 65–99.

Graham, Ann and Johanna Regulska (1997) 'Expanding Political Space for Women in Poland', Communist and Post-Communist Studies, 30 (1): 65–82.

Greider, William (1996) One World, Ready or Not: The Manic Logic of Global Capitalism. New York: Simon and Schuster.

Greider, William (1997) 'Saving the Global Economy', Nation, 15 December: 11–16.

Gross, Jan (1992) 'Poland: From Civil Society to Political Nation', in Ivo Banac (ed.), Eastern Europe in Revolution. Ithaca, NY: Cornell University Press. pp. 56–71.

Gunther, Richard (1992) 'Spain: the Very Model of the Modern Elite Settlement', in John Higley and Richard Gunther (eds), Elites and Democratic Consolidation in Latin America and Southern Europe. Cambridge: Cambridge University Press. pp. 38–80.

Gunther, Richard, Hans-Jürgen Puhle and Nikiforos Diamandouros (eds) (1995) The Politics of Democratic Consolidation: Southern Europe in Comparative Perspective. Baltimore, MD: Johns Hopkins University Press.

Gyurcsik, Iván (1993) 'New Legal Ramifications of the Question of National Minorities', in Ian M. Cuthbertson and Jane Leibowitz (eds), Minorities: The New Europe's Old Issue. New York and Atlanta: Institute for EastWest Studies. pp. 19–50.

Habermas, Jürgen (1997) A Berlin Republic: Writings on Germany (translated by Steven Rendall). Omaha, NB: University of Nebraska Press.

Haggard, Stephen (1994) 'Politics and Institutions in the World Bank's East Asia', in Albert Fishlow (ed.), Miracle or Design? Lessons from the East Asian Experience. Washington, DC: Overseas Development Council.

Haggard, Stephen and Robert Kaufman (1995) The Political Economy of Democratic Transitions. Princeton, NJ: Princeton University Press.

Hancock, Ian (1991) 'Romani Nationalism', in David Crowe and John Kolsti (eds), The Gypsies of Eastern Europe. Armonk, New York: M.E. Sharpe. pp. 133–150.

Hann, Endre (1998) 'Two Elections in Hungary', Nepszava, 30 May. Translated by the Foreign Broadcast Information Service.

Haraszti, Miklos (1998) 'Young Bloods', Transitions, 5 (7): 48–53.

Hardt, John P. and Richard S. Kaufman (eds) for the Joint Economic Committee, Congress of the United States (1995) *East Central European Economies in Transition*. Armonk, New York: M.E. Sharpe.

Harsanyi, Doina Pasca (1993) 'Women in Romania', in Nanette Funk and Magda Mueller (eds), *Gender Politics and Post-Communism*. New York: Routledge. pp. 39–52.

Hartmann, Jürgen (1998) *Politik auf den Trümmern der Zweiten Welt*. Frankfurt: Campus Verlag.

Hausleitner, Mariana (1993) 'Women in Romania Before and After the Collapse', in Nanette Funk and Magda Mueller (eds), *Gender Politics and Post-Communism*. New York: Routledge. pp. 53–61.

Havel, Václav (1997) Newshour with Jim Lehrer, 16 May 1997.

Hedges, Chris (1997) 'Fascists Reborn as Croatia's Founding Fathers', *New York Times*, 12 April: 3.

Heitlinger, Alena (1995) 'Women's Equality, Work and Family in the Czech Republic', in B. Łobodzińska (ed.), *Family, Women and Employment in Central and Eastern Europe*. Westport, CT: Greenwood Press. pp. 87–99.

Held, David (1995a) 'Democracy and the New International Order', in Daniele Archibugi and David Held (eds), *Cosmopolitan Democracy*. Cambridge: Polity Press. pp. 96–120.

Held, David (1995b) *Democracy and the Global Order*. Stanford, CA: Stanford University Press.

Henkins, Kène, Maarten Sprengers and Fritz Tazelaar (1996) 'Unemployment and the Older Worker in the Netherlands', *Aging and Society*, 16 (5): 561–578.

Heper, Metin (1991) 'Transitions to Democracy Reconsidered', in Dankwart Rustow and Kenneth Erickson (eds), *Comparative Political Dynamics*. New York: HarperCollins. pp. 192–210.

Herda, Juergen (1998) 'Klaus-Zeman Pact Could End Czech Instability', RFE/RL Newsline, 2:146, Part: II, 31.

Herrmann, Peter (1993) 'Social Goals for Media Endorsed by Poles', RFE/RL Research Report, 2 (5), 10 March: 58–59.

Hess, Laura E., Anne C. Petersen and Jeylan T. Mortimer (1994) 'Youth, Unemployment and Marginality: The Problems and the Solution', in Anne C. Petersen and Jeylan T. Mortimer (eds), *Youth, Unemployment and Society*. Cambridge: The Press Syndicate of the University of Cambridge. pp. 3–33.

Hester, Al and Kristina White (eds) (1993) *Creating a Free Press in Eastern Europe*. Athens, GA: Cox Center, University of Georgia.

Heti Vilaggazdasag (1995) 'I Have My Own Internal Criteria' (Interview with MSZOSZ chairman Sandor Nagy), 18 March. Translated by the Foreign Broadcast Information Service.

Hicks, Barbara (1996) *Environmental Politics in Poland*. New York: Columbia University Press.

Higley, John, Judith Kullberg and Jan Pakulski (1996) 'The Persistence of Postcommunist Elites', *Journal of Democracy*, 7/2 (April): 133–147.

Higley, John and Jan Pakulski (1995) 'Elite Transformation in Central and Eastern Europe', *Australian Journal of Political Science*, 30: 415–435.

Hill, Ronald (1994) 'Democracy in Eastern Europe', in Ian Budge and David McKay (eds), *Developing Democracy*. London: Sage. pp. 267–283.

Hockenos, Paul (1993) *Free to Hate: The Rise of the Right in Post-Communist Eastern Europe*. New York: Routledge.

Hockenos, Paul (1995) 'Comeback of the Communists', *New Politics*, Winter: 79–82.

Hoffman, Eva (1993) *Exit into History*. New York: Penguin.

Holmes, Stephen (1993) *The Anatomy of Antiliberalism*. Cambridge, MA: Harvard University Press.

Holmes, Stephen (1995) 'Cultural Legacies or State Collapse?', paper delivered at Collegium Budapest (November).

Holt, Robert and John Richardson (1970) 'Competing Paradigms in Comparative Politics', in R. Holt and J. Turner (eds), *The Methodology of Comparative Research*. New York: Free Press.

Honolka, Harro (1987) *Schwarzrotrgrün*. Munich: Beck.

Horowitz, Donald (1992) 'Comparing Democratic Systems', in Arend Lijphart (ed.), *Parliamentary versus Presidential Democracy*. Oxford: Oxford University Press.

Hörster-Philipps, Ulrike (1983) 'Conservative Concepts of Dictatorship in the Final Phase of the Weimar Republic', in I. Wallimann and M. Dobkowski (eds), *Towards the Holocaust*. Westport, CT: Greenwood Press.

Hough, Jerry (1977) *The Soviet Union and Social Science Theory*. Cambridge, MA: Harvard University Press.

Hu, Shaohua (1997) 'Confucianism and Western Democracy', *Journal of Contemporary China*, 6 (15): 347–363.

Hunt, Swanee (1997) 'Women's Vital Voices', *Foreign Affairs*, 76 (4): 2–7.

Huntington, Samuel (1968) *Political Order in Changing Societies*. New Haven, CT: Yale University Press.

Huntington, Samuel (1984) 'Will More Countries Become Democratic?', *Political Science Quarterly*, 99: 193–218.

Huntington, Samuel (1991) *The Third Wave: Democratization in the Late Twentieth Century*. Norman, OK: University of Oklahoma Press.

Huntington, Samuel (1996) *The Clash of Civilizations?* Foreign Affairs reprint. New York: Council on Foreign Relations.

Hyde-Price, Adrian (1996) *The International Politics of East-Central Europe*. Manchester: Manchester University Press.

Iankova, Elena A. (1996) 'Women's Participation in Post-Communist Social Dialogue', in B. Wejnert, M. Spencer and S. Drakulic (eds), *Women in Post-Communism*, Volume 2. Greenwich, CT: JAI Press. pp. 141–154.

Ignatieff, Michael (1993) *Blood and Belonging: Journey into the New Nationalism*. New York: Noonday.

Íjgyártó, István (1993) 'Codification of Minority Rights', in Ian M. Cuthbertson and Jane Leibowitz (eds), *Minorities: The New Europe's Old Issue*. New York and Atlanta: Institute for EastWest Studies. pp. 273–284.

Inglehart, Ronald (1977) *The Silent Revolution in Europe: Changing Values and Political Styles among Western Publics*. Princeton, NJ: Princeton University Press.

Inglehart, Ronald (1990) *Culture Shift in Advanced Industrial Society*. Princeton, NJ: Princeton University Press.

Ionescu, Dan (1996) 'More Controversy in Romania Over Treaty with Hungary', *OMRI Daily Digest*, 179 (II): 16 September 1996.

Jaeggi, Urs (1969) *Macht und Herrschaft in der Bundesrepublik*. Frankfurt/Main: Fischer.

Janecki, Stanislaw and Ewa Ornacka (1998) 'War of Gangs', *Poznan Wprost*, 10 May. Translated by the Foreign Broadcast Information Service.

Janos, Andrew (ed.) (1976a) *Authoritarian Politics in Communist Europe*. Berkeley, CA: University of California Press.

Janos, Andrew (1976b) 'Systemic Models and the Theory of Change in the Comparative Study of Communist Societies, in A. Janos (ed.), *Authoritarian Politics in Communist Europe*. Berkeley, CA: University of California Press.

Jayasuriya, Kanishka (1995) 'The Political Economy of Democratization', in Daniel A. Bell, David Brown, Kanishka Jayasuriya and David Jones (eds), *Towards Illiberal Democracy in Pacific Asia*. Oxford: St Martin's Press. pp. 107–133.

Joas, Hans (1997) 'Der Liberalismus ist kein politisches Heilversprechen', *die Zeit*, 21 November: 13.

Johnson, Owen V. (1993) 'Whose Voice? Freedom of Speech and the Media in Central Europe', in Al Hester and Kristina White (eds), *Creating a Free Press in Eastern Europe*. Athens, GA: Cox Center for International Mass Communications Training and Research, The University of Georgia. pp. 1–51.

Jones, David Martin (1995) 'Democracy and Identity', in Daniel A. Bell, David Brown, Kanishka Jayasuriya and David Jones (eds), *Towards Illiberal Democracy in Pacific Asia*. Oxford: St Martin's Press. pp. 41–77.

Jowitt, Kenneth (1992) *The New World Disorder*. Berkeley, CA: University of California Press

Jung, Bohdan (1995) 'Young Polish Consumers', *Journal of Communist Studies and Transition Politics*, 11 (3): 286–307.

Jurrjens, Rudolf Th. (1978) *The Free Flow of People, Ideas and Information in Soviet Ideology and Politics*. Amsterdam: Vrije Universiteit Te Amsterdam.

Kádár, Béla (1993) 'External Liberalization: Gradualism or Shock Approach', in Siebert Horst (ed.), *Overcoming the Transformation Crisis*. Tübingen: J.C.B. Mohr (Paul Siebeck). pp. 173–188.

Kalyvas, Stathis (1996) *The Rise of Christian Democracy in Europe*. Ithaca, NY: Cornell University Press.

Kaminski, Matthew (1997) 'Unequal Partners: Widening Trade Deficits Could Snarl EU Accession Talks', *Central European Economic Review*, November: 9–10.

Kariel, Henry (1970) *Frontiers of Democratic Theory*. New York: Random House.

Karkoszka, Andrzej (1993) 'A Call for Confidence-Building Measures for Minorities in Eastern Europe', in Ian M. Cuthbertson and Jane Leibowitz (eds), *Minorities: The New Europe's Old Issue*. New York and Atlanta: Institute for EastWest Studies. pp. 209–225.

Karl, Terry Lynn (1991) 'Dilemmas of Democratization in Latin America', in Dankwart Rustow and Paul Erickson (eds), *Comparative Political Dynamics*. New York: HarperCollins.

Karp, Regina (1995) 'Postcommunist Europe: Back from the Abyss?', in Daniel Nelson (ed.), *After Authoritarianism: Democracy or Disorder?* Westport, CT: Praeger.

Karpinski, Jakub (1995) 'Opinion Polls Reflect Political Stability', *Transition*, 1 (20): 40–41.

Karpinski, Jakub (1996a) 'Politicians Endanger Independence of Polish Public TV', *Transition*, 2 (8): 28–30.

Karpinski, Jakub (1996b) 'Abortion Law Eased by the Polish Parliament', *OMRI Daily Digest*, 170 (II): 3 September.

Karpinski, Jakub (1996c) 'Abortion Law Liberalized in Poland', *OMRI Daily Digest*, 207 (II): 24 October.

Karpinski, Jakub (1996d) 'Poles Divided Over Church's Renewed Political Role', *Transition*, 2 (7): 11–13.

Karpinski, Jakub (1997a) 'Poland's Phoenix Rises', *Transitions*, 4 (6): 62–65.

Karpinski, Jakub (1997b) 'Lustration Law in Polish Sejm Commission', *OMRI Daily Digest*, 243 (II): 18 December.

Karpinski, Jakub (1997c) 'Abortion Law Eased by the Polish Parliament' in Open Media Research Institute, *Forging Ahead, Falling Behind*. Armonk, New York: M.E. Sharpe. pp. 47–48.

Kaufman, Michael T. (1998) 'His and Hers, Ours and Theirs', *Transitions*, 5 (1): 3.

Kawczynski, Rudko (1997) 'The Politics of Romani Politics', *Transitions*, 4 (4): 24–29.

Kay, Bruce (1996) '"Fujipopulism" and the Liberal State in Peru, 1990–1995', *Journal of InterAmerican Studies and World Affairs* (Winter).

Kayal, Michele (1993) 'The Unfinished Revolution: The Czech Republic's Press in Transition', in Al Hester and Kristina White (eds), *Creating a Free Press in Eastern Europe*. Athens, GA: Cox Center for International Mass Communications Training and Research, University of Georgia. pp. 257–280.

Keller, Suzanne (1963) *Beyond the Ruling Class*. New York: Random House.

Kennedy, Michael D. (ed.) (1994) *Envisioning Eastern Europe: Postcommunist Cultural Studies*. Ann Arbor: The University of Michigan Press.

van Kersbergen, Kees (1994) 'The Distinctiveness of Christian Democracy', in David Hanley (ed.), *Christian Democracy in Europe: a Comparative Perspective*. London: Pinter.

Kesselman, Mark and Joel Krieger (1997) *European Politics in Transition*, 3rd edn. Boston, MA: Houghton Mifflin.

Kettle, Steve (1996) 'Czech Republic', in Open Media Research Institute, *Building Democracy*. Armonk, New York: M.E. Sharpe. pp. 16–23.

Kettle, Steve, Chrystyna Lapychak, Ustina Markus and Michael Mihalka (1995) 'Specter of Racism', *Transition*, 1 (10): 18.

Klaven, Jonathan and Anthony Zamparutti (1995) *Foreign Direct Investment and Environment*. Washington, DC: World Bank.

Kligman, Gail (1994) 'Women and the Feminization of Poverty', in James R. Millar and Sharon L. Wolchik (eds), *The Social Legacy of Communism*. Washington, DC: Woodrow Wilson Center Press. pp. 252–270.

Knox, Paul and John Agnew (1993) *Geography of the World Economy*. New York: Edward Arnold.

Koff, Sondra and Stephen Koff (1997) 'Transition to Democracy: Explanatory Models', in D. Carlton and P. Ingram (eds), *The Search for Stability in Russia and the Former Soviet Bloc*. Aldershot: Ashgate.

Kohak, Erazim (1997) 'Consolidating Freedom in Central Europe', *Dissent*, Spring: 21–26.

Kohn, Hans (1945) *The Idea of Nationalism*. New York: Macmillan.

Kolakowski, Leszek (1968) *Towards a Marxist Humanism*. New York: Grove.

Kornhauser, William (1959) *Politics of Mass Society*. New York: Free Press.

Kostova, Dobrinka (1994) 'The Transition to Democracy in Bulgaria', in

Valentine Moghadam (ed.), *Democratic Reform and the Position of Women in Transitional Economies*. Oxford: Clarendon Press. pp. 92–109.

Köves, Andras and Paul Marer (eds) (1991) *Foreign Economic Liberalization: Transformations in Socialist and Market Economies*. Boulder, CO: Westview Press.

Koza, Patricia (1997) 'A Bitter Crop: Polish Farmers Face a Tough Row', *Central European Economic Review*, June: 20.

Krajewska, Anna (1995) 'Education in Poland', *Eastern European Economics*, 33 (4): 38–54.

Kramer, John M. (1994) 'Drug Abuse in Central and Eastern Europe', in James R. Millar and Sharon L. Wolchik (eds), *The Social Legacy of Communism*. New York: Woodrow Wilson Center Press. pp. 149–177.

Kramer, John M. (1997) 'Drug Abuse in East-Central Europe', *Problems of Post Communism*, 44 (3): 35–42.

Kratochvilova, Katerina and Roman Gallo (1996) 'Racism on the Increase', *Mlada Fronta Dnes*, 6 December. Translated by the Foreign Broadcast Information Service.

Krejci, Oskar (1995) *History of Elections in Bohemia and Moravia*. New York: Columbia University Press.

Krieger, Leonard (1972) *The German Idea of Freedom*. Chicago: University of Chicago Press.

Krol, Marcin (1997) 'Measuring the Costs of "Free" Education', *Transitions*, 4 (4): 82–83.

Krupa, Piotr (1995) 'Poles Arm Themselves', *Prawo I Zycie*, 25 March. Translated by the Foreign Broadcast Information Service.

Krygier, Martin (1997) 'Virtuous Circles: Antipodean Reflections on Power, Institutions, and Civil Society', *East European Politics and Societies*, 11 (4): 36–88.

Kryshtanovskaya, Olga (1994) 'Transformation of the Old Nomenklatura to New Elites', *Izvestia*, 18 May.

Kuehl, Warren (1969) *Seeking World Order*. Nashville, TN: Vanderbilt University Press.

Kumar, Krishan (1993) 'Civil society: an inquiry into the usefulness of an historical term', *British Journal of Sociology*, 44 (3): 375–395.

Kurczewski, Jacek (1997) 'Poland's Perpetually New Middle Class', *Transition*, 3 (5): 22–25.

Kürti, Lásló (1991) 'Rocking the State: Youth and Rock Music Culture in Hungary, 1976–1990', *East European Politics and Society*, 5 (3), Fall: 483–513.

Kwasniewska, Teresa (1994) 'Who Will Vote and How', *Nowa Trybuna Opolska*, 17–18 December. Translated by the Foreign Broadcast Information Service.

Lane, David and Cameron Ross (1995) 'The Changing Composition and Structure of Political Elites', in David Lane (ed.), *Russia in Transition*. London: Longman.

Lapalombara, Joseph (1968) 'Macrotheories and Microapplications in Comparative Politics: A Widening Chasm', *Comparative Politics*, 1: 1.

Latawski, Paul (1995) 'In Defense of Presidential Prerogative', *Transition*, 1 (8): 40–43.

Legutko, Ryszard (1994) 'From Three Perspectives', *Zycie Warszawy*, 17 August. Translated by the Foreign Broadcast Information Service.

Leko, Istvan (1997) 'Did the Creators of the Transformation Fail?', *Tyden*, 22 December. Translated by the Foreign Broadcast Information Service.

Lemon, Alaina (1996a) 'Amnesty International Criticizes Czech Republic', *OMRI Daily Digest*, 119 (II): 19 June.

Lemon, Alaina (1996b) 'Czech Post Denies Mail Service to Romani Housing Estate', *OMRI Daily Digest*, 109 (II): 5 June.

Lemon, Alaina (1996c) 'No Land, No Contracts for Romani Workers', *Transition*, 2 (13): 28–31.

Lenski, Gerhard (1966) *Power and Privilege*. New York: McGraw-Hill.

Lesniewski, Bartlomiej and Jacek Szczesny (1997) 'Duty-Free: What Consumers Owe to Smugglers', *Wprost*, 21 December. Translated by the Foreign Broadcast Information Service.

Leven, Bozena (1996) 'Distributional Effects of Poland's Transition: The Status of Pensioners', *Comparative Economic Studies*, 38 (4): 121–133.

Lewin, Moshe (1988) *The Gorbachev Phenomenon: A Historical Interpretation*. Berkeley, CA: University of California Press.

Lewis, Paul (1997) 'Theories of Democratization and Patterns of Regime Change in Eastern Europe', *Journal of Communist Studies and Transition Politics*, 13 (1): 4–26.

Lidove Noviny (1996) 'The Media Are Trustworthy', 6 November. Translated by the Foreign Broadcast Information Service.

Liebert, Ulrike and Maurizio Cotta (eds) (1990) *Parliament and Democratic Consolidation in Southern Europe: Greece, Italy, Portugal, Spain, and Turkey*. London: Pinter.

Lieven, Anatol (1997) 'Consumerism is the New Invader', *Financial Times*, 28 November: 2.

Lijphart, Arend (1969) 'Consociational Democracy', *World Politics*, XXI (2): 207–225.

Lijphart, Arend (1979) 'Consociation and Federation: Conceptual and Empirical Links', *Canadian Journal of Political Science*, 12 (3): 499–515.

Lijphart, Arend (ed.) (1992) *Parliamentary versus Presidential Democracy*. Oxford: Oxford University Press.

Linz, Juan and Alfred Stepan (1978) *The Breakdown of Democratic Regimes: Crisis, Breakdown, and Reequilibration*. Baltimore, MD: Johns Hopkins University Press.

Linz, Juan and Alfred Stepan (1996) *Problems of Democratic Transition and Consolidation*. Baltimore, MD: Johns Hopkins University Press.

Linz, Juan, Alfred Stepan and Richard Gunther (1995) 'Democratic Transition and Consolidation in Southern Europe, with Reflections on Latin America and Eastern Europe', in Richard Gunther, Hans-Jürgen Puhle and Nikiforos Diamandouros (eds), *The Politics of Democratic Consolidation*. Baltimore, MD: Johns Hopkins University Press. pp. 77–123.

Linz, Juan and Arturo Valenzuela (eds) (1994) *The Failure of Presidential Democracy, Volume I: Comparative Perspectives; Volume 2: The Case of Latin America*. Baltimore, MD: Johns Hopkins University Press.

Lipset, Seymour Martin (1959a) *Political Man*. Garden City, NJ: Free Press.

Lipset, Seymour Martin (1959b) 'Some Social Requisites of Democratic Economic Development and Political Legitimacy', *American Political Science Review*, 53 (March): 69–105.

Lipset, Seymour Martin (1992) 'The Centrality of Political Culture', in Arend

Lijphart (ed.), *Parliamentary versus Presidential Democracy*. Oxford: Oxford University Press.

Lipset, Seymour Martin (1993) 'Concluding Reflections', in Larry Diamond and Marc Plattner (eds), *Capitalism, Socialism, and Democracy Revisited*. Baltimore, MD: Johns Hopkins University Press. pp. 119–132.

Lipset, Seymour Martin and Stein Rokkan (1967) 'Party Systems, Social Cleavages and Voter Alignments', in S.M. Lipset and S. Rokkan (eds), *Social Cleavages and Party Systems*. New York: Free Press.

Łobodzińska, Barbara (1995a) 'Equal Opportunities', in B. Łobodzińska (ed.), *Family, Women and Employment in Central and Eastern Europe*. Westport, CT: Greenwood Press. pp. 261–274.

Łobodzińska, Barbara (ed.) (1995b) *Family, Women and Employment in Central and Eastern Europe*. Westport, CT: Greenwood Press.

Łobodzińska, Barbara (1995c) 'The Family and Working Women During and After Socialist Industrialization and Ideology', in Barbara Łobodzińska (ed.), *Family, Women and Employment in Central and Eastern Europe*. Westport, CT: Greenwood Press. pp. 3–46.

Lodge, Milton (1968) 'Groupism in the Post-Stalin Period', *Midwest Journal of Political Science*, 12 (3): 330–351.

Lohr, Steve (1998) 'Business Asian Style: A Revaluing of Values', *New York Times*, 9 February: B9–B11.

Lomax, Bill (1994) 'Impediments to Democratization in East-Central Europe', in Gordon Wightman (ed.), *Party Formation in East-Central Europe*. Aldershot: Edward Elgar. pp. 179–201.

Lomax, Bill (1997) 'The Strange Death of Civil Society in Post-communist Hungary', *Journal of Communist Studies and Transition Politics*, 13 (1): 41–63.

Lotspeich, Richard (1995) 'Crime in the Transition Economies', *Europe–Asia Studies*, 47 (4): 555–589.

Lucas, Edward (1998) 'Eastern Europe: time to smarten up', *Economist* Special Issue: *The World in 1998*. p. 44.

Luchterhand, Otto (1996) 'Präsidentialismus in den GUS-Staaten', in Otto Luchterhand (ed.), *Neue Regierungssysteme in Osteuropa und der GUS*. Berlin: Arno Spitz. pp. 223–274.

Luczak, Maciej in cooperation with Katarzyna Zielezinska (1997) 'Nationalized Freedom', *Wprost*, 15 June. Translated by the Foreign Broadcast Information Service.

Lyman, Randall (1994) 'Mixed Reviews: A Human Rights Report on the Czech Republic', *Prognosis*, 7 December. Translated by the Foreign Broadcast Information Service.

Macridis, Roy (1955) *The Study of Comparative Government*. New York: Random House.

Magyar Nemzet (1995a) 'There Are Limits Beyond Which One Cannot Retreat', 4 February. Translated by the Foreign Broadcast Information Service.

Magyar Nemzet (1995b) 'The Still-Functioning Brakes Might Begin To Slip', 27 March. Translated by the Foreign Broadcast Information Service.

Magyar Nemzet (1996) 'Subtle Means of Manipulation in Public Television', 2 November. Translated by the Foreign Broadcast Information Service

Mahr, Alison and John Nagle (1995) 'Resurrection of the Successor Parties and Democratization in East-Central Europe', *Communist and Post-Communist Studies*, 28 (4): 393–409.

Malloy, James (1987) 'The Politics of Transition in Latin America', in Harvey Kline and Howard Wiarda (eds), *Latin American Politics and Development*. Boulder, CO: Westview Press.

Manser, Roger (1993) *Failed Transitions: The Eastern European Economy and Environment Since the Fall of Communism*. New York: The New Press.

Maravall, José María (1995) 'The Myth of the Authoritarian Advantage', in Larry Diamond and Marc Plattner (eds), *Economic Reform and Democracy*. Baltimore, MD: Johns Hopkins University Press. pp. 13–27.

Marger, Michael (1987) *Elites and Masses: An Introduction to Political Sociology*. Belmont, CA: Wadsworth.

Marian, Bela (1997) 'According to the Population, Living Standards were High During Kádár Era', *Nepszava*, 10 February. Translated by the Foreign Broadcast Information Service.

Markovits, Andrei and Philip Gorsky (1993) *The German Left: Red, Green and Beyond*. New York: Oxford University Press.

Markowski, Radoslaw (1997) 'Political Parties and Ideological Spaces in East Central Europe', *Communist and Post-Communist Studies*, 30 (3): 221–254.

Mason, David (1996) *Revolution and Transition in East-Central Europe*, 2nd edn. Boulder, CO: Westview Press.

Mason, David, Daniel Nelson and Bohdan Szklarski (1991) 'Apathy and the Birth of Democracy: The Polish Struggle', *East European Politics and Societies*, 5 (2): 205–233.

Mason, David S., Antal Orkeny and Svetlana Sidorenko-Stephenson (1997) 'Increasingly Fond Memories of a Grim Past', *Transitions*, 3 (5): 15–19.

Matthews, Donald (1954) *The Social Background of Political Decision-Makers*. New York: Random House.

Maull, Hanns (1997) 'Die Kosten der Kungelei', *die Zeit*, 12 December: 6.

Maxwell, J.M. (1990) 'Economic Reforms in New Democracies: The Southern European Experience', East–South System Transformations, working paper no. 3 (October), Department of Political Science: University of Chicago.

McClune, Emma (1994) 'Czechs Fear Crime Wave That Isn't There', *Prague Post*, 13 September. Transcribed by the Foreign Broadcast Information Service.

McKinsey, Kitty (1997) 'Poland: Pension Crisis Looms'. Radio Free Europe/Radio Liberty <www.rferl.org/nca...3/F.RU.970303160644.html> 18 November.

McLellan (1970) *Marx before Marxism*. New York: Harper.

Meier, Artur (1996) 'The New European Divide', in P. Mitev and J. Riordan (eds), *Europe – The Young – The Balkans*. Sofia: International Centre for Minority Studies and Intercultural Relations.

Meyer, Alfred (1967) 'Authority in Communist Political Systems', in Lewis Edinger (ed.), *Political Leadership in Industrialized Societies*. New York: Wiley and Sons.

Michnik, Adam (1997) 'Gray is Beautiful: Thoughts on Democracy in Central Europe', *Dissent*, Spring: 14–19.

Mihalka, Michael (1997) 'Competitive Enlargement?' RFE/RL Newsline. 1: 80, Part II, 24 July.

Milić, Andjelka (1993) 'Women and Nationalism in the Former Yugoslavia', in Nanette Funk and Magda Mueller (eds), *Gender Politics and Post-Communism*. New York: Routledge. pp. 109–122.

Millar, James R. and Sharon L. Wolchik (1994) *The Social Legacy of Communism*. New York: Woodrow Wilson Center Press.

Millard, Frances (1994a) 'The Polish Parliamentary Election of September, 1993', *Communist and Post-Communist Studies*, 27 (3): 295–313.

Millard, Frances (1994b) *The Anatomy of the New Poland*. Aldershot: Edward Elgar.

Miller, William L., Stephen White and Paul Heywood (1998) *Values and Political Change in Postcommunist Europe*. New York: St Martin's Press.

Mills, C. Wright (1951) *White Collar*. New York: Oxford University Press.

Mills, C. Wright (1956) *The Power Elite*. New York: Oxford University Press.

Misztal, Bronislaw (1995) 'The Uses of Freedom', in M. Darnovsky, B. Epstein and R. Flacks (eds), *Cultural Politics and Social Movements*. Philadelphia: Temple University Press. pp. 264–286.

Moghadam, Valentin M. (ed.) (1994a) *Democratic Reform and the Position of Women in Transitional Economies*. Oxford: Clarendon Press.

Moghadam, Valentin M. (1994b) 'Introduction: Gender Dynamics of Economic and Political Change', in V. Moghadam (ed.), *Democratic Reform and the Position of Women in Transitional Economies*. Oxford: Clarendon. pp. 1–25.

Mojzes, Paul (1992) *Religious Liberty in Eastern Europe and the USSR: Before and After the Great Transformation*. Boulder, CO: East European Monographs.

Mommsen, Margareta (1997) '"Delegative", "halbierte" und "Nomenklatura" – Demokratien', in G-J. Glaeßner and M. Reiman (eds), *Systemwechsel und Demokratisierung*. Opladen: Westdeutscher Verlag. pp. 233–277.

Moody, Peter (1988) *Political Opposition in Post-Confucian Society*. New York: Praeger.

Morawski, Witold (1992) 'Economic Change and Civil Society in Poland', in Paul G. Lewis (ed.), *Democracy and Civil Society in Eastern Europe*. New York: St Martin's Press.

Mroziewicz, Dagmar (1996) 'Polish Economic Reform Marred by High Unemployment', *Transition*, 2 (13): 26–27.

MTI – Hungarian News Agency (1994) 'Left-Wing Youth Association Examined', 10 August. Transcribed by the Foreign Broadcast Information Service.

MTI – Hungarian News Agency (1997) 'Poll Shows 47 Percent Support EU Entry', 7 August. Transcribed by the Foreign Broadcast Information Service.

Muntyan, Bernard (1996) 'A reflection on the concept Europe', in P. Mitev and J. Riordan (eds), *Europe – The Young – The Balkans*. Sofia: International Centre for Minority Studies and Intercultural Relations.

Myant, Martin (1993) 'Czech and Slovak Trade Unions', *Journal of Communist Studies*, 9 (4): 59–84.

Myant, Martin and Michael Waller (1993) 'Parties and Trade Unions in Eastern Europe', *Journal of Communist Studies*, 9 (4): 161–181.

Nagle, John (1970) *The National Democratic Party: Right-Radicalism in the Federal Republic of Germany*. Berkeley, CA: University of California Press.

Nagle, John (1975) 'A New Look at the Soviet Elite: A Generational Model of the Soviet System', *Journal of Political and Military Sociology*, 3 (1): 1–13.

Nagle, John (1977) *System and Succession: The Social Basis of Political Elite Recruitment*. Austin: University of Texas Press.

Nagle, John (1992) 'Recruitment of Elites', in M. Hawksworth and M. Kogan (eds), *Encyclopedia of Government and Politics*. London: Routledge.

Nagle, John (1997a) 'Ethnos, Demos, and Democratization: A Comparison of the Czech Republic, Hungary and Poland', *Democratization*, 4 (2): 28–56.

Nagle, John (1997b) 'Youth Political Socialization in Postcommunism: Skinheads, Yuppies and a Democratic Middle Majority?', paper presented to the International Society of Political Psychology, Kraków, Poland, 21–24 June.

Nagle, John (1998a) *Introduction to Comparative Politics: Challenges of Conflict and Change in a New Era*, 5th edn. Chicago: Nelson-Hall.

Nagle, John (1998b) *Confessions from the Left: On the Pain, Necessity and Joys of Political Renewal*. New York: Peter Lang.

Nagorski, Andrew (1993) *The Birth of Freedom: Shaping Lives and Societies in the New Eastern Europe*. New York: Simon and Schuster.

Nelson, Daniel (1995) 'Conclusion: In the Pursuit of Democracy and Security', in Daniel Nelson (ed.), *After Authoritarianism: Democracy or Disorder?* Westport, CT: Praeger.

Nelson, Joan M. (1994) 'Panel Discussion', in J. Williamson (ed.), *The Political Economy of Policy Reform*. Washington, DC: Institute for International Economics. pp. 472–477.

Nepszava (1996) 'Hungary Does Not Yet Have Organized Crime', 4 October. Translated by the Foreign Broadcast Information Service.

Nepszava (1997a) 'Opinions of Ministries Worsen', 10 March. Translated by the Foreign Broadcast Information Service.

Nepszava (1997b) 'Election Alliance Only with Guarantees', 18 November. Translated by the Foreign Broadcast Information Service.

Nepszava (1997c) 'The Leader's Elite Becomes Increasingly Closed', 24 January. Translated by the Foreign Broadcast Information Service.

Nepszava (1998) 'Appreciated Government Efforts', 14 January. Translated by the Foreign Broadcast Information Service.

New York Times (1994) 'Voices of Hope and Disquiet: Bread and Butter, Armies and the Future', 30 September: A10.

Nohlen, Dieter (1992) 'Präsidentialismus versus Parlamentarismus in Lateinamerika', *Lateinamerikanische Jahrbuch*: 86–99.

Nonneman, Gerd (1996a) 'Economic Liberalization: The Debate', in Gerd Nonneman (ed.), *Political and Economic Liberalization*. Boulder, CO: Lynne Rienner Publishers. pp. 3–30.

Nonneman, Gerd (1996b) 'Linkages Between Economic and Political Liberalization', in G. Nonnemann (ed.), *Political and Economic Liberalization*. Boulder, CO: Lynne Rienner Publishers. pp. 307–313.

Nonneman, Gerd (1996c) 'Patterns of Economic Liberalization', in G. Nonnemann (ed.), *Political and Economic Liberalization*. Boulder, CO: Lynne Rienner Publishers. pp. 31–43.

Nonneman, Gerd (ed.) (1996d) *Political and Economic Liberalization*. Boulder, CO: Lynne Rienner Publishers.

Nowa Europa (1996) 'Results of a CBOS Poll; We Rate Local Authorities and the President Highest', 19 December. Translated by the Foreign Broadcast Information Service.

Nowicki, Maciej (1993) *Environment in Poland: Issues and Solutions*. Dordrecht: Kluwer.

Nowotny, Thomas (1997) 'Transition from communism and the Spectre of Latin-Americanization', *East European Quarterly*, 31 (1): 69–91.

Nye, R.A. (1977) *The Anti-Democratic Sources of Elite Theory: Pareto, Mosca, Michels*. London: Sage.

Oberman, Jan (1991) 'Czechoslovakia: Organized Labor – A New Beginning', RFE/RL Research Institute Report on Eastern Europe, 2 (13): 23–25.

O'Donnell, Guillermo and Philippe Schmitter (1986) *Transitions from Authoritarian Rule: Tentative Conclusions About Uncertain Democracies*. Baltimore, MD: Johns Hopkins University Press.

OECD (Organization for Economic Cooperation and Development) (1994) 'Market Access and FDI/Trade Linkages in Eastern Europe', Working Paper No. 43. Paris: OECD.

OECD (Organization for Economic Cooperation and Development) (1996) *Economic Surveys: Netherlands 1996*. Paris: OECD.

Ollman, Bertell (1972) *Alienation: Marx's Conception of Man in Capitalist Society*. New York; Cambridge University Press.

Olson, Mancur (1971) *The Logic of Collective Action: Public Goods and the Theory of Groups*. Cambridge, MA: Harvard University Press.

Oltay, Edith (1993) 'Hungary Attempts to Deal With its Past', RFE/RL Research Institute Report, 2 (18): 6–10.

OMRI (Open Media Research Institute) *Omri Daily Digest* (online volumes for 1993–1997, various issues).

OMRI (Open Media Research Institute) (1996) *Building Democracy*. Armonk, New York: M.E. Sharpe.

OMRI (Open Media Research Institute) (1996, 1997) *Forging Ahead, Falling Behind*. Armonk, New York: M.E. Sharpe.

Orenstein, Mitchell (1995) 'Who's Right? Who's Left', *Transition*, 1 (14): 28–31.

Orenstein, Mitchell (1996) 'The Failures of the Neo-Liberal Social Policy in Central Europe', *Transition*, 2 (13): 16–20.

Orenstein, Mitchell (1998) 'Lawlessness from Above and Below: How Economic Radicalism Shapes Political Institutions', *SAIS Review*, 18 (1): 35–49.

Orenstein, Mitchell and Raj M. Desai (1997) 'State Power and Interest Group Formation: The Business Lobby in the Czech Republic', *Problems of Post-Communism*, 44 (6): 43–52.

Ost, David (1995) 'Labor, Class and Democracy: Shaping Antagonisms in Post-Communist Society', in Beverly Crawford (ed.), *Markets, States and Democracy*. Boulder, CO: Westview Press.

Ost, David (1997) 'East-Central Europe in Transition', in M. Kesselman and J. Krieger (eds), *European Politics in Transition*, 3rd edn. Boston, MA: Houghton Miflin.

Padorska, Joanna and Mariusz Janicki (1997) 'The Debutante has Stagefright', *Polityka*, 2 August. Translated by the Foreign Broadcast Information Service.

Palmer, Alan (1970) *The Lands Between: A History of East-Central Europe since the Congress of Vienna*. New York: Macmillan.

PAP (Polska Agencja Prasowa) (1997a) 'Opinion Center Says President Still Leads Popularity List', 10 September. Transcribed by the Foreign Broadcast Information Service.

PAP (Polska Agencja Prasowa) (1997b) 'Public Opinion Research Centre Poll Shows Majority Pleased With Political System', 9 October. Transcribed by the Foreign Broadcast Information Service.

PAP (Polska Agencja Prasowa) (1997c) 'Presidency, Army Receive High Opinion Poll Ratings', 6 May. Transcribed by the Foreign Broadcast Information Service.

PAP (Polska Agencja Prasowa) (1997d) 'Poll Finds Poles Favour Democracy

Against Strongman Rule', 1 October. Transcribed by the Foreign Broadcast Information Service.

PAP (Polska Agencja Prasowa) (1998a) '42 Percent of Poles Say Poland Better Under Communism', 20 July. Transcribed by the Foreign Broadcast Information Service.

PAP (Polska Agencja Prasowa) (1998b) 'Poland Makes Pact with EU on Combating Organised Crime', 29 May. Transcribed by the Foreign Broadcast Information Service.

Pauer, Jan (1995) 'Der tschechische Liberalkonservativismus', in I. Bock, J. Pauer and S. Mihalikova (eds), *Tschechische Republik zwischen Traditionsbruch und Kontinuität*. Bremen: Edition Temmen. pp. 11–68.

Payer, Cheryl (1976) *The Debt Trap: The IMF and the Third World*. New York: Monthly Review Press.

Pehe, Jiri (1996a) 'And Czechs on Czech-German Declaration', *OMRI Daily Digest*, 99 (II): 22 May.

Pehe, Jiri (1996b) 'Czech-German Declaration Will Not Be Ready Before Elections', *OMRI Daily Digest*, 70 (II): 9 April.

Pehe, Jiri (1996c) 'Czech Elections End in Stalemate', *OMRI Daily Digest*, 107 (II): June 3.

Pehe, Jiri (1997a) 'Czech and German Premiers Sign Declaration', *OMRI Daily Digest*, 15 (II): 22 January.

Pehe, Jiri (1997b) 'Czechs Fall From Their Ivory Tower', *Transitions*, 4 (3): 22–27.

Pei, Minxin (1995) 'The Puzzle of East Asian Exceptionalism', in Larry Diamond and Marc Plattner (eds), *Economic Reform and Democracy*. Baltimore, MD: Johns Hopkins University Press. pp. 112–125.

Penc, Stanislav and Jan Urban (1998) 'Extremist Acts Galvanize Roma Population', *Transitions*, 5 (7): 39–40.

Perczel, Tamas (1997) 'What is the Deeper Meaning?', *Nepszava*, 22 November. Translated by the Foreign Broadcast Information Service.

Perlez, Jane (1998) 'Dark Underside of Polish Family Life: Violence', *New York Times*, 8 May, A-1, A-8.

Petersen, Anne C. and Jeylan T. Mortimer (1994) *Youth, Unemployment and Society*. Cambridge: The Press Syndicate of the University of Cambridge.

Pfaff, William (1992) 'Absence of Empire', *New Yorker*, 10 August.

Pfaff, William (1993) *The Wrath of Nations: Civilization and the Furies of Nationalism*. New York: Touchstone.

Ploss, Sidney (1965) *Conflict and Decision-Making in Soviet Russia: A Case Study of Agricultural Policy, 1953–1963*. Princeton, NJ: Princeton University Press.

Pocock, J.G.A. (1997) 'What Do We Mean By Europe?', *The Wilson Quarterly*, 21: 1, Winter: 12–29.

Polish News Bulletin (1997) in LEXIS NEXIS/EUROPE/PNBUL. 17 July.

Polityka (1997) 'A Pensioner Can: Interview with Zenon Ruminski, head of the Polish National Party of Senior Citizens', 14 June. Translated by the Foreign Broadcast Information Service.

Pridham, Geoffrey (1995) 'The International Context of Democratic Consolidation; Southern Europe in Comparative Perspective', in Richard Gunther, Hans-Jürgen Puhle and Nikiforos Diamandouros (eds), *The Politics of Democratic Consolidation*. Baltimore, MD: Johns Hopkins University Press. pp. 166–203.

Pridham, Geoffrey and Paul Lewis (1996) 'Introduction: Stabilising fragile democracies and party system development', in G. Pridham and P. Lewis (eds), *Stabilising Fragile Democracies: Comparing New Party Systems in Southern and Eastern Europe*. London: Routledge. pp. 1–23.

Prognosis (1994) 'Czechs Say: We Want the Death Penalty', 2 November. Transcribed by the Foreign Broadcast Information Service.

Przeworski, Adam, Pranab Bardham and Luiz Carlos Bresser Periera (1995) *Sustainable Democracy*. New York: Cambridge University Press.

Putnam, Robert (1995a) 'Making Democracy Work: Civic Traditions in Modern Italy', *Journal of Democracy*, 6: 1.

Putnam, Robert (1995b) 'Bowling Alone: America's Declining Social Capital', *Current*, 373 (June).

Racz, Barnabus (1993) 'The Socialist-left Opposition in Post-Communist Hungary', *Europe–Asia Studies*, 45 (4): 647–670.

Rau, Zbigniew (ed.) (1991a) *The Reemergence of Civil Society in Eastern Europe and the Soviet Union*. Boulder, CO: Westview Press.

Rau, Zbigniew (1991b) 'Introduction', in Zbigniew, Rau (ed.), *The Reemergence of Civil Society in Eastern Europe and the Soviet Union*. Boulder, CO, Westview Press. pp. 1–23.

Ravich, Samantha Fay (1996) *Marketization and Prosperity: Pathways to East Asian Democracy*. Santa Monica, CA: Rand.

Regulska, Johanna (1992) 'Women and Power in Poland: Hopes or Reality', in Jill M. Bystydzienksi (ed.), *Women Transforming Politics*. Bloomington, IN: Indiana University Press. pp. 175–191.

Regulska, Johanna and Mindy Jane Roseman (1998) 'What is Gender?', *Transitions*, 5 (1): 24–29.

RFE/RL (Radio Free Europe/Radio Liberty) Newsline (online volumes for 1997, 1998, various issues).

Rhodes, Martin and Bastiaan van Apeldoorn (1997) 'Capitalism versus Capitalism in Western Europe', in M. Rhodes, P. Heywood and V. Wright (eds), *Developments in West European Politics*. New York: St Martins Press.

Riggs, Fred (1992) 'Presidentialism: A Problematic Regime Type', in Arend Lijphart (ed.), *Parliamentary versus Presidential Democracy*. Oxford and New York: Oxford University Press.

Robinson, Anthony (1997) 'A tough juggling act for ministers', *Financial Times*, 19 September: 29.

Rodrik, Dani (1993) 'Comment on Béla Kádár: External Liberalization: Gradualism or Shock Approach', in Horst Siebert (ed.), *Overcoming the Transformation Crisis*. Tübingen: J.C.B. Mohr (Paul Siebeck). pp. 189–193.

Roe, Sarah (1997) 'Progressive Inaction in Hungary', *Transitions*, 4 (4): 33.

Rose, Richard (1996) 'Choosing Democracy as the Lesser Evil', *Transition*, 2 (9): 40–45.

Rose, Richard and Christian Haerpfer (1994) 'New Russia Barometer III', *Studies in Public Policy*, 228.

Rosenberg, Tina (1995) *The Haunted Land: Facing Europe's Ghosts After Communism*. New York: Random House.

Roskin, Michael (1997) 'Party Systems of Central and Eastern Europe', *East European Quarterly*, 27 (1): 47–63.

Ross, Robert and Kent Trachte (1990) *Global Capitalism: the New Leviathan*. Albany, NY: State University of New York Press.

Rothschild, Joseph (1974) *East Central Europe Between the Two World Wars*. Seattle, WA: University of Washington Press.

Rothschild, Joseph (1989) *Return to Diversity: A Political History of East Central Europe since World War II*. New York: Oxford University Press.

Rupnik, Jacques (1979) 'Dissent in Poland, 1968–78: The End of Revisionism and the Rebirth of Civil Society', in R. Tökes (ed.), *Opposition in Eastern Europe*. Baltimore and London: The Johns Hopkins Press. pp. 60–112.

Rutland, Peter (1997) 'Russia's Broken Wheel of Ideologies', *Transitions*, 4 (1): 47–53.

Rzeczpospolita (1994) 'Public Opinion Research Institute for *Rzeczpospolita*: Politicians Want Influence, Journalists Independence', 30 June. Translated by the Foreign Broadcast Information Service.

Rzeczpospolita (1995) '"Eurobarometer 1994": Moods in the New Democracies; There Are a Few More Clouds', 8 March. Translated by the Foreign Broadcast Information Service.

Rzeczpospolita (1997) 'Reforms are a Serious Commitment', 13 November. Translated by the Foreign Broadcast Information Service.

Sader, E. and Silverstein, K. (1991) *Without Fear of Being Happy: Lula, the Workers Party and Brazil*. London: Verso.

Sadurski, Wojciech (1996) 'Freedom of the Press in Postcommunist Poland', *East European Politics and Societies*, 10 (3): 439–456.

Sartori, Giovanni (1962) *Democratic Theory*. New York: Praeger.

Sartori, Giovanni (1970) 'Concept Misformation in Comparative Politics', *American Political Science Review*, 64 (4): 1033–1953.

Sartori, Giovanni (1976) *Parties and Party Systems: A Framework for Analysis*. New York: Cambridge University Press.

Schmidt, Fabian (1997) 'Prague, Bonn Launch Reconciliation Fund'. RFE/RL Newsline, 1 (187), part II (30 December).

Schmidt, Josephine (1998) '*Gazeta Wyborcza* Comes of Age', *Transitions*, 5 (2): 92–93.

Schmitter, Philippe and Terry Lynn Karl (1994) 'The Conceptual Travels of Transitologists and Consolidologists: How Far to the East Should They Attempt to Go?', *Slavic Review*, 53 (1): 173–185.

Schneider, Howard (1997) 'In Bid to Restrict Gypsies, Canada Limits Czech Visitors', *Washington Post*, 9 October, A31.

Schneider, Howard and Christine Spolar (1997) 'Czech Prejudice – and TV – Fuel Gypsy Migration to Canada', *Washington Post*, 1 September, A23.

Schöpflin, George (1990) 'The Political Traditions of Eastern Europe', *Daedalus*, Winter: 55–90.

Schöpflin, George (1993) 'Culture and Identity in Post-Communist Europe', in Stephen White, Judy Batt and Paul G. Lewis (eds), *Developments in East European Politics*. Durham, NC: Duke University Press. pp. 16–34.

Schumpeter, Joseph (1942) *Capitalism, Socialism and Democracy*. New York: Harper & Brothers.

Schumpeter, Joseph (1997) 'An Elite Theory of Democracy' in Eva Etzioni Halevy (ed.), *Classes and Elites in Democracy and Democratization*. New York: Garland.

Schweitzer, Arthur (1964) *Big Business in the Third Reich*. Bloomington, IN: Indiana University Press.

Sebastian, Byron (1995) 'Debts and Disgruntled Doctors', *Transition*, 1 (24): 46–50.

Shafir, Michael (1996) 'Romanians Protest Appointment of Ethnic Hungarian Prefects', *OMRI Daily Digest*, 244 (II): 19 December.

Shafir, Michael (1998a) 'Czech Crown Reaches Record Low', RFE/RL Newsline (January 7).

Shafir, Michael (1998b) 'Czech Supreme Court Overturns Decision on Communist Leaders', RFE/RL Newsline (22 January).

Shafir, Michael (1998c) 'Czech "Nostalgia" For Communist Regime Grows', RFE/RL Newsline (25 February).

Sheehan, Michael (1997) 'The Emerging Pattern of International Relations in Eastern Europe', in *Eastern Europe and the Commonwealth of Independent States 1997*, 3rd edn. London: Europa Publications Limited. pp. 19–22.

Shils, Edward (1982) 'The political class in the age of mass society: collectivistic liberalism and social democracy', in M. Czudnowski (ed.), *Does Who Governs Matter?* DeKalb, IL: Northern Illinois University Press.

Siebert, Horst (ed.) (1993) *Overcoming the Transformation Crisis.* Tübingen: J.C.B. Mohr (Paul Siebeck).

Sierszula, Barbara (1998) 'I Was Looked Upon As a Funny Moralist: Interview with Czech President Václav Havel', *Rzeczpospolita*, 7–8 March. Translated by Foreign Broadcast Information Service.

Siklova, Jirina (1998a) 'Men and Women United for a Higher Purpose', *Transitions*, 5 (1): 34–35.

Siklova, Jirina (1998b) 'Why We Resist Western-Style Feminism', *Transitions*, 5 (1): 30–35.

Silverman, Bertram, Robert Vogt and Murray Yanowitch (eds) (1993) *Double Shift: Transforming Work in Postsocialist Societies.* Armonk, New York: M.E. Sharpe.

Singer, Daniel (1981) *The Road to Gdansk.* New York: Monthly Review Press.

Sipos, Sandor (1991) 'Current and Structural Problems Affecting Children in Central and Eastern Europe', in Giovanni Andrea Cornia and Sandor Sipos (eds), *Children and the Transition to the Market Economy.* Brookfield, VT: Avebury. pp. 3–33.

Skilling, Gordon (1966) 'Interest Groups and Communist Politics', *World Politics*, 18 (3): 435–451.

Skilling, Gordon (1970) 'Leadership and Group Conflict in Czechoslovakia', in Barry Farrell (ed.), *Political Leadership in Eastern Europe and the Soviet Union.* Chicago: Aldine.

Skilling, Gordon and Franklyn Griffiths (eds) (1971) *Interest Groups in Soviet Politics.* Princeton, NJ: Princeton University Press.

Skolkay, Andrej (1996) 'Slovak Government Tightens Its Grip on the Airwaves', *Transition*, 2 (8): 18–21.

Smith, Michael (1997) 'Steel obstacle on Poland's road to EU', *Financial Times*, 28 November: 3.

Smith, Peter (1992) 'On Democracy and Democratization', in Howard Wiarda (ed.), *Politics and Social Change in Latin America.* Boulder, CO: Westview Press.

Snyder, Tim (1995) 'National Myths and International Relations: Poland and Lithuania 1989–1994', *East European Politics and Societies*, 9 (2): 317–343.

Soros, Georg (1997) 'The Capitalist Threat', *Atlantic Monthly*, February: 45–58.

Spolar, Christine (1997a) 'Now Polish Candidates Must Snitch on Selves', *Washington Post*, 26 August: A11.

Spolar, Christine (1997b) 'Hot Water Helps Clear the Air in Ski Resort', *Washington Post*, 28 October: A-17.

Spolar, Christine (1997c) 'Slovak Leader Fans Bias Toward Hungarian Minority', *Washington Post*, 30 November: A-23.

Spolar, Christine (1997d) 'Slovaks in Czech Republic Strive to Keep Their Ethnicity in Check', *Washington Post*, 27 April: A-24.

Spolar, Christine (1998a) 'Hungarians Chafe at Crime, Economy', *Washington Post*, 24 May: A26.

Spolar, Christine (1998b) 'Poland Forced to Face Upsurge in Crime', *Washington Post*, 7 February: A16.

Stastna, Jaroslava (1995) 'New Opportunities in the Czech-Republic', *Transition*, 1 (16): 24–28, 61.

Staszewski, Wojciech and Paweł Wronski (1997) 'Extraordinary Career of the Party of Senior Citizens', *Gazeta Wyborcza*, 28 March. Translated by the Foreign Broadcast Information Service.

Steffani, Winfried (1979) *Parlamentarische und präsidentielle Demokratie*. Cologne and Opladen: Westdeutscher Verlag.

Steffani, Winfried (1996) 'Parlamentarisch-präsidentielle "Mischsysteme"?', in Otto Luchterhand (ed.), *Neue Regierungssysteme in Osteuropa und der GUS*. Berlin: Arno Spitz. pp. 11–62.

Stokes, Gale (1993) *The Walls Came Tumbling Down: The Collapse of Communism in Eastern Europe*. New York: Oxford University Press.

Swiecka, Agnieszka (1996) 'The Fading Bloom of Youth', *Warsaw Voice*, 10 March. Transcribed by the Foreign Broadcast Information Service.

Szacki, Jerzy (1995) *Liberalism after Communism*. Budapest: Central European Press.

Szczerbiak, Aleks (1997) 'Harmonizing the Discordant Right', *Transition*, 3 (6): 44–47.

Szelenyi, Ivan (1997) '*Socialist Opposition in Eastern Europe*', in Rudolf Tokes (ed.), *Opposition in Eastern Europe*. Baltimore, MD: Johns Hopkins University Press.

Szelenyi, Ivan, Eva Fodor and Eric Hanley (1997) 'Left Turn in PostCommunist Politics: Bringing Class Back in?', *East European Politics and Societies*, 11 (1): 190–224.

Szilagyi, Zsofia (1995) 'Hungary', in Open Media Research Institute, *Building Democracy*. Armonk, New York: M.E. Sharpe. pp. 36–43.

Szilagyi, Zsofia (1996a) 'Hungarian Parliament Amends Screening Law', *OMRI Daily Digest*, 130 (II): 8 July.

Szilagyi, Zsofia (1996b) 'Hungary Has a Broadcast Media Law, at Last', *Transition*, 2 (8): 22–25.

Szilagyi, Zsofia (1996c) 'Communication Breakdown Between the Government and the Public', *Transition*, 2 (6): 41–43.

Szilagyi, Zsofia (1996d) 'Hungarian Parliament Ratifies Basic Treaty with Romania', *OMRI Daily Digest*, 238 (II): 11 December.

Szilagyi, Zsofia (1996e) 'Scenes From the Media War', *Transition*, 2 (8): 24.

Szilagyi, Zsofia (1997) 'A Year of Scandals and Resignations in Hungary', in Open Media Research Institute, *The OMRI Annual Survey of Eastern Europe and the Former Soviet Union: 1996*. Armonk, New York: M.E. Sharpe. pp. 32–36.

Szulc, Adam (1996) 'Economic Transition and Poverty: The Case of the Vysehrad Group Countries', Luxembourg Income Study Working Paper No. 138. Syracuse, NY: Syracuse University.

Tamas, G.M. (1993) 'Socialism, Capitalism, and Modernity', in Larry Diamond and Marc Plattner (eds), *Capitalism, Socialism, and Democracy Revisited*. Baltimore, MD: Johns Hopkins University Press. pp. 54–68.

Tatu, Michel (1969) *Power in the Kremlin: From Khrushchev to Kosygin*. New York: Viking.

Tismaneanu, Vladimir (1992) *Reinventing Politics*. New York: Free Press.

Tismaneanu, Vladimir (1994) 'Fantasies of Salvation: Varieties of Nationalism in Postcommunist Eastern Europe', in Michael D. Kennedy (ed.), *Envisioning Eastern Europe*. Ann Arbor, MI: The University of Michigan Press.

Tismaneanu, Vladimir (1996) 'The Leninist Debris or Waiting for Peron', *East European Politics and Society*, 10 (4): 504–535.

Toka, Gabor (1996) 'Parties and electoral choices in east-central Europe', in G. Pridham and P. Lewis (eds), *Stabilising Fragile Democracies: Comparing New Party Systems in Southern and Eastern Europe*. London: Routledge. pp. 100–125.

Torrey, Barbara, Timothy Smeeding and Debra Bailey (1996) 'Rowing Between Scylla and Charybdis: Income Transitions in Central European Households', Luxembourg Income Study Working Paper No. 132. Syracuse, NY: Syracuse University.

Tóth, András (1993) 'Great Expectations – Fading Hopes: Trade Unions and System Change in Hungary', *Journal of Communist Studies*, 9 (4): 85–97.

Truman, David (1953) *The Governmental Process: Political Interests and Public Opinion*. New York: Alfred A. Knopf.

Tygodnik Solidarnosc (1996) 'Banners and Bread: Solidarity and Politics', 10 May. Translated by the Foreign Broadcast Information Service.

UJ Magyarorszag (1995) 'What Is in the MSZOSZ's Package – The Bokros Program's Counterweight', 30 March. Translated by the Foreign Broadcast Information Service.

Ulam, Adam (1952) *Titoism and the Cominform*. Cambridge, MA: Harvard University Press.

US News and World Report (1986) 'Europe's Youth Drop in, Not Out', 26 May: 31–32.

Vinton, Louisa (1991) 'Poland: Disparate Responses to Democracy and the Market', *RFE/RL Research Institute Report on Eastern Europe*, 2 (13): 29–37.

Volgyes, Ivan (1975a) 'Hungary: From Mobilization to Depoliticization', in Ivan Volgyes (ed.), *Political Socialization in Eastern Europe*. New York: Praeger. pp. 92–131.

Volgyes, Ivan (ed.) (1975b) *Political Socialization in Eastern Europe: A Comparative Framework*. New York: Praeger.

Volgyes, Ivan (1975c) 'Political Socialization in Eastern Europe: A Conceptual Framework', in Ivan Volgyes (ed.), *Political Socialization in Eastern Europe*. New York: Praeger. pp. 1–37.

Walker, Jack (1966) 'A critique of the elitist theory of democracy', *American Political Science Review*, 60: 285–295.

Walker, Martin (1995) 'Overstretching Teutonia: Making the Best of the Fourth Reich', *World Policy Journal*, 12 (1): 1–18.

Wallace, Claire and Suka Kovacheva (1996) 'Youth Cultures and Consumption in Eastern and Western Europe', *Youth and Society*, 28 (2): 189–214.

Waller, Michael (1994) 'Voice, Choice and Loyalty: Democratization in Eastern Europe', in Geraint Parry and Michael Moran (eds), *Democracy and Democratization*. London: Routledge. pp. 129–151.

Waller, Michael (1995) 'Starting-up Problems: Communists, Social Democrats, and Greens', in Gordon Wightman (ed.), *Party Formation in East-Central Europe*. Aldershot: Edward Elgar.

Waller, Michael (1996) 'Party Inheritances and Party Identities', in G. Pridham and P. Lewis (eds), *Stabilising Fragile Democracies: Comparing New Party Systems in Southern and Eastern Europe*. London: Routledge. pp. 23–43.

Waller, Michael, Bruno Coppieters and Kris Deschouwer (eds) (1994) *Social Democracy in a Post-Communist Europe*. Portland and London: Frank Cass.

Washington Post (1997) 'Green, Greener, Greenest', 22 November: A15.

Weil, Gordon (1994) 'Economic Reform and Women' in V. Moghadam (ed.), *Democratic Reform and the Position of Women in Transitional Economies*. Oxford: Clarendon Press. pp. 280–301.

Wejnert, Barbara, Metta Spencer and Slobodan Drakulic (eds) (1996) *Women in Post-Communism*, Volume 2. Greenwich, CT: JAI Press.

Welsh, Helga A. (1996) 'Dealing with the Communist Past: Central and East European Experiences after 1990', *Europe–Asia Studies*, 48 (3): 413–428.

Wesolowski, Wlodzimierz (1996) 'The formation of political parties in post communist Poland', in G. Pridham and P. Lewis (eds), *Stabilising Fragile Democracies: Comparing New Party Systems in Southern and Eastern Europe*. London: Routledge. pp. 229–253.

Wesson, Robert (1990) *International Relations in Transition*. Englewood Cliffs, NJ: Prentice-Hall.

White, Stephen, Judy Batt and Paul G. Lewis (eds) (1993) *Developments in East European Politics*. Durham, NC: Duke University Press.

Whitehead, Laurence (ed.) (1996) *The International Dimensions of Democratization*. Oxford: Oxford University Press.

Wiarda, Howard (ed.) (1985) *New Directions in Comparative Politics*. Boulder, CO: Westview Press.

Wiarda, Howard and Harvey Kline (eds) (1996) *Latin American Politics and Development*, 4th edn. Boulder, CO: Westview Press.

Wiatr, Jerzy (1994) 'From Communist Party to "Socialist Democracy of the Polish Republic"', in Kay Lawson (ed.), *How Parties Work*. Westport, CT: Praeger. pp. 249–261.

Williamson, John (1994a) 'In Search of a Manual for Technopols', in John Williamson (ed.), *The Political Economy of Policy Reform*. Washington, DC: Institute for International Economics. pp. 9–28.

Williamson, John (ed.) (1994b) *The Political Economy of Policy Reform*. Washington, DC: Institute for International Economics.

Wolchik, Sharon L. (1994a) 'The Politics of Ethnicity in Post-Communist Czechoslovakia', *East European Politics and Societies*, 8 (1): 153–188.

Wolchik, Sharon L. (1994b) 'Women and the Politics of Transition in Central and Eastern Europe', in Valentine Moghadam (ed.), *Democratic Reform and the Position of Women in Transitional Economies*. Oxford: Clarendon Press. pp. 29–47.

World Bank (1995) *Understanding Poverty in Poland*. Washington, DC: World Bank.

Wprost (1997) 'The Czech Scenario', 29 June. Translated by the Foreign Broadcast Information Service.

Wynia, Gary (1990) *The Politics of Latin American Development*, 3rd edn. Cambridge: Cambridge University Press.

Zajicek, Anna M. and Tony M. Calasanti (1995) 'The Impact of Socioeconomic Restructuring on Polish Women', in Barbara Łobodzińska (ed.), *Family, Women and Employment in Central and Eastern Europe*. Westport, CT: Greenwood Press. pp. 179–191.

Zakaria, Fareed (1997) 'The Rise of Illiberal Democracy', *Foreign Affairs* (November-December): 22–43.

Zavecz, Tibor (1998) 'Appreciated Government Efforts', *Nepszava*, 14 January. Translated by the Foreign Broadcast Information Service.

Ziebura, Gilbert (1995) 'The Beginning of the End for the European Union?', *Debatte*, No. 1: 33–43.

Ziemer, Klaus (1996) 'Struktur- und Funktionsprobleme der Parlamente', in Otto Luchterhand (ed.), *Neue Regierungssysteme in Osteuropa und der GUS*. Berlin: Arno Spitz. pp. 151–180.

Zubek, Voytek (1994) 'The Reassertion of the Left in Post-Communist Poland', *Europe–Asia Studies*, 46 (5): 801–837.

Zycie Gospodarcze (1996) 'Poverty in Poland', 4 August. Transcribed by the Foreign Broadcast Information Service.

Index